Prostitutes and Matrons in the Roman World

Prostitutes and Matrons in the Roman World is the first substantial account of elite Roman concubines and courtesans. Exploring the blurred line between proper matron and wicked prostitute, it illuminates the lives of sexually promiscuous women like Messalina and Clodia, as well as prostitutes with hearts of gold who saved Rome and their lovers in times of crisis. It also offers insights into the multiple functions of erotic imagery and the circumstances in which prostitutes could play prominent roles in Roman public and religious life. Tracing the evolution of social stereotypes and concepts of virtue and vice in ancient Rome, this volume reveals the range of life choices and sexual activity, beyond the traditional binary depiction of wives or prostitutes, that were available to Roman women.

Anise K. Strong, winner of the Women's Classical Caucus Award for best presentation in classical gender studies, received her B.A. from Yale and her M.Phil and Ph.D from Columbia University before beginning her professional career at Northwestern, Stanford, and Western Michigan Universities. She is also a consultant for various television series in their depictions of antiquity.

Prostitutes and Matrons in the Roman World

ANISE K. STRONG
Western Michigan University

CAMBRIDGE
UNIVERSITY PRESS

CAMBRIDGE
UNIVERSITY PRESS

One Liberty Plaza, 20th Floor, New York, NY 10006, USA

Cambridge University Press is part of the University of Cambridge.

It furthers the University's mission by disseminating knowledge in the pursuit of education, learning, and research at the highest international levels of excellence.

www.cambridge.org
Information on this title: www.cambridge.org/9781107148758

First published 2016
Reprinted 2016

Printed in the United States of America by Sheridan Books, Inc.

A catalogue record for this publication is available from the British Library.

Library of Congress Cataloguing in Publication Data
Names: Strong, Anise K., 1977–
Title: Prostitutes and matrons in the Roman world /
Anise K. Strong (Western Michigan University).
Description: New York, NY: Cambridge University Press, 2016. | Includes bibliographical references.
Identifiers: LCCN 2016008236 | ISBN 9781107148758 (hardback)
Subjects: LCSH: Prostitution – Rome – History. | Concubinage – Rome – History. | Courtesans – Rome – History. | Prostitutes – Rome – History. | Wives – Rome – History. | Women – Sexual behavior – Rome – History. | Women – Rome – Social conditions. | Sex customs – Rome – History. | Sex role – Rome – History. | Rome – Social conditions.
Classification: LCC HQ113.S76 2016 | DDC 306.740937–dc23
LC record available at http://lccn.loc.gov/2016008236

ISBN 978-1-107-14875-8 Hardback

In memory of my mother,
Helene Keyssar,
who taught me how to be a feminist,
and
Natalie Boymel Kampen,
who taught me how to look beyond the surface.

Contents

Illustrations

Acknowledgements

This work would not have been possible without the invaluable criticisms and suggestions of William V. Harris, Natalie B. Kampen, and Helene P. Foley, as well as many other scholars and readers who offered advice along the way and helped polish this manuscript into its final form. Credit is also due to Ann Ellis Hanson and Robin Winks, who taught me how to write history in the first place. I would like to thank the readers and editors at Cambridge University Press, especially Joanna Breeze, Gail Welsh, and Belinda Baker, who helped guide this book out of its larval stage; you helped me understand what I wanted to say. I am also grateful to the many archaeologists and museums who have generously shared their images, maps, and data, as well as allowing me access to various archaeological sites. I give special thanks here to the Burnham-Macmillan Fund of the Department of History at Western Michigan University, the PPP&E funding available through the Office of the Vice President for Research at Western Michigan University, and the Louis A. Park Graduate Research Fellowship in Classics of Columbia University, for funding that enabled me to complete this project and to share my work with my colleagues and other scholars in my field. I am grateful to Kristina Johnson and David D. Strong Franke for taking many useful photographs for me of the Pompeii brothel under excruciating weather conditions.

On a more personal note, I want to express my gratitude to my family, for demonstrating by example how to write and teach, and to my friends, for their helpful comments and enthusiastic support. I especially thank my husband, Adam H. Morse, for his many moments of insight and helpful perspective, as well as Rebecca Slitt and Katherine Buffington, for their constant counsel and advice throughout the gestation of this manuscript.

Introduction

Two thousand years ago, an aristocratic Roman matron named Vistilia faced a trial for adultery. Vistilia was notorious for conducting multiple extramarital affairs, but her husband, Titidius Labeo, refused to divorce her. Eventually, the Emperor Tiberius himself accused her of adultery, a crime punishable by exile to a remote island. Vistilia responded to this charge by publicly registering herself as a common prostitute, since prostitutes were legally incapable of committing adultery. The Emperor then passed a new law forbidding women of the senatorial class to become prostitutes, forced Vistilia's husband to divorce her, and duly exiled her.[1]

By itself, this story is a minor anecdote in the annals of Roman history. No wars were fought; no religions were founded; no nations were conquered. Nevertheless, Vistilia's tale encapsulates a fundamental contradiction between the version of Roman society that has been generally accepted over the past two millennia – an image constructed by elite male authors, emperors, and jurists – and the everyday social realities of Roman men and women. In her landmark 1975 text, Sarah Pomeroy divided ancient women into the categories of "Goddesses, Whores, Wives, and Slaves," emphasizing in her title these prescriptive distinctions between different social and moral categories.[2] This book explores the fluidity and mutability of the roles of "whore" and "wife" in the Roman world, analyzing the tales of the women who both exemplified and defied them. It asks not only why most Roman elite males promulgated these stereotypes in a wide variety of literary and artistic genres, but also why and how other authors and women like Vistilia subverted these normative doctrines of good women and bad women. The categories and boundaries of Roman social hierarchies intertwined with the Roman sexual and gender systems. In practice, however, both such structures were less stable and coherent than they may have appeared from the surface.

In the official decrees of Tiberius and his predecessor Augustus, the divisions between different types of women were clear and absolute. There were wives – loyal, brave, hard-working matrons devoted to a single man – and there were whores – greedy, selfish, promiscuous prostitutes focused on their own self-interests. When a wife acted like a whore, the emperor's punishment was removal from Roman society itself. She no longer fitted into established moral categories and thus could not function within the elite Roman world. Tiberius' own wife and Augustus' daughter, Julia, faced disinheritance and exile, allegedly for sexual promiscuity although possibly also for rebellious and transgressive political activity.[3]

Vistilia, Tiberius' victim, had a different view of social and moral categories. In order to evade punishment, Vistilia was willing to register herself publicly as a prostitute. She announced that she was a whore and was not ashamed. The Roman biographer Suetonius claims that many other women sought a similar loophole, suggesting that this was not a unique act of rebellion.[4] Suetonius' emphasis is on the degenerate choices of these elite matrons and youths and on the state-imposed sanctions, whereas the historian Tacitus focuses on the restoration of the normal social order in a single case.[5] Suetonius may have exaggerated a general trend from reports of the single incident of Vistilia, but this may also be an accurate portrayal of a pattern of civil disobedience against Augustus' restrictive adultery laws. Since Tacitus does not contradict Suetonius' account, I suspect Vistilia was simply the most prominent example of a group of rebellious, pragmatic elite women seeking sexual autonomy.

Notably, Vistilia's husband Titidius Labeo had neither publicly objected to her activities nor attempted to divorce her. Indeed, when reminded of the clause in the *lex Iulia de adulteriis* which forced him either to divorce an adulterous wife or himself be found guilty of *lenocinium* (pimping), Titidius Labeo asked for an extra two months to consider his decision. While he eventually submitted to the Emperor's will, his reluctance suggests that Labeo tolerated a wife who did not fit the prescriptive norm of the ideal matron. For Titidius Labeo, his wife's sexual behavior was not a matter of fundamental importance in their marriage. He may have been motivated by the financial reason of not wanting to lose her dowry; the six marriages of Vistilia's sister (or possibly aunt) suggest that both women came from a prominent and wealthy family.[6] Whatever his reasons, he was willing to be married to a wife who declared herself publicly to be a whore.

Vistilia's gambit was fundamentally unsuccessful in preventing punishment for her unorthodox behavior. However, she believed that adopting a new sexual and social identity was not only possible but also a viable solution to her dilemma. For Vistilia, the worst possible outcome was not being publicly shamed as a whore but exile from her home city. Her story suggests that Roman women's views about the importance of this social division may have differed from the harsh, dichotomous categorizations of women by elite male authors like Tacitus and Cicero. For Vistilia, the value of sexual license outweighed the disadvantage of personal shame, if indeed there was any shame at all.

It is time to take a closer look at these categorical divisions that have become a cliché in the analysis of ancient women. Roman women could and did transition between these social and moral labels. In the same era that Tiberius forbade women of senatorial descent to become prostitutes, his predecessor Augustus forbade senatorial men to marry prostitutes and transform them into elite wives.[7] While "matron" and "prostitute" may have been fixed official categories in the minds of the emperors and lawmakers, "wife" and "whore" became increasingly fluid moral categories used to praise or attack women who demonstrated appropriate female virtues or vices, most particularly the virtue of loyalty towards a male partner. Furthermore, elite male anxiety focused primarily on the dangers represented by women's economic independence rather than on their sexual behaviors.

We have relied on these labels of wife and whore for so long because so much of the written evidence seeks to inscribe them as factual absolutes. Not only legal texts, but the strongly moralizing histories and declamations of Roman literature also divide women into good and bad moral archetypes. These archetypes, furthermore, are not limited to elite texts. A tourist walking through the streets of Pompeii today might indeed conclude that there were only two types of women in the Roman world – the virtuous matrons immortalized on tombstones as faithful, fertile wool-workers and the cheap prostitutes whose names and prices were scratched into tavern and brothel walls.[8] Both prostitute and "good wife" stories may also have formed part of the lost oral tradition, which would also have been accessible to a much larger audience. However, these non-elite records still primarily indicate how literate men chose to depict and memorialize women, rather than how most Roman women might have conceptualized their own identities.

In this book, I trace the stories, images, and artifacts that illuminate the lives of women who defied traditional labels, in an attempt to understand how Roman women and men themselves negotiated between and around these categories. I discuss both the historical (if probably slandered) promiscuous whore-empress Messalina and Livy's semi-fictional "good little prostitute" Hispala Faecenia, as well as the women who fell into neither category, like the elite courtesans of the late Republic and the palace concubines of the Empire. By studying examples in different literary and artistic genres of two variants of the familiar labels – the "wicked wife" and the "good whore" – I explore the underlying social definitions of Roman female virtue and vice.

The following chapters will establish that the defining characteristic of a Roman "whore" was neither her type of work nor her sexual activity but her abandonment of ties to a male partner. Conversely, women of low social status could achieve "wife-like" labels if they demonstrated generous devotion to a male partner and support of the Roman state and the established social hierarchy. While the term *meretrix* or "whore" was originally used to describe a woman who exchanged sex for money, it became a moral label used to condemn any woman who led an overly public, economically autonomous, sexually active life unrestricted by ties to a single man. Meanwhile, my analysis of women who appear not to fall into any of these categories – concubines, courtesans, the elusive *amicae* of Roman elegy, and the women in Roman erotic paintings – suggests contemporaneous challenges to this normative dichotomy of socially segregated "good" and "bad" women.

Stories about prostitutes and about women who behaved like prostitutes, as well as moral exempla that praised matrons or women who behaved like matrons, appear prominently in a variety of genres of Roman literature. Such tales appeared in texts ranging from comedy to satirical poetry to hypothetical speeches used in rhetoric classes for elite young men. These anecdotes would have been familiar to a large audience, of one primarily composed of the prosperous and literate members of society.[9] They also likely served as didactic tales for young Roman women themselves. The orator Cicero famously urged Clodia Metelli, who had allegedly been behaving like a whore, to imitate instead the example of her virtuous ancestors Claudia Quinta and the heroic Vestal Claudia.[10]

To some extent, the general Roman predilection for tales about both good and especially wicked women can be blamed on their basic entertainment value: sex sells, now and historically. Yet this discourse also betrays a more general concern about the threat to the social order posed by publicly prominent women who were not defined by a familial role and who potentially valued profit above the welfare of their male companions. This basic distrust extended beyond professional sex workers to other Roman women who exhibited familial disloyalty through their indiscriminate sexual availability. By establishing a moral category of "wicked women" that was rhetorically aligned with the disreputable social category of "prostitute," elite men could rebuke or shun women who did not follow conventional social mores and uphold the patriarchal social system.

Augustus' programmatic emphasis on political and social stability increased elite anxiety about women who appeared to threaten the fragile structure of Roman social hierarchies.[11] Such idealized and narrow categories of social status may never have accurately depicted the complex and shifting patterns of Roman society, where freedmen could rise to become imperial advisors and provincial centurions could become emperors. However, the ideal of a stable social pyramid remained essential among the elite aristocracy, who also wrote the vast majority of surviving texts.

Both Rebecca Flemming and T. A. McGinn, the most influential recent scholars of Roman prostitution, have argued that, unlike the Greek phenomenon of famous, wealthy *hetairai* or courtesans, Roman society had little place for glamorous, elegant prostitutes who slept with elite men and also influenced them politically and economically.[12] Yet if this hypothesis were true, it would be difficult to identify any possible remaining social status for the many elegant, witty, unmarried *amicae* or "girlfriends" in Augustan elegiac poetry and Imperial epigrams. Even if the women themselves in these poems are individually imaginary characters, the invention of an entire fictional category of women for poets to make socially acceptable love with seems rather implausible.[13] Because these women fall in between the normative categories, evidence concerning them has previously been dismissed or ignored.

The first-century BCE Roman poet Ovid claims, for instance, that his racy poem the *Ars Amatoria* is intended for *meretrices* rather than adventurous wives. He cannot be alleging that his audience consists of impoverished illiterate streetwalkers.[14] By examining historical and rhetorical accounts of influential concubines and courtesans, as well as their representation in poetry, we can further study Romans' own deconstructions of social norms. The *amicae* stand as a challenge to the moral and social dichotomy of the wife–whore paradigm: are they good or wicked, or both?

My focus on the concept of semantic labels as a means of defining Roman social roles is inspired by the Roman practice of identifying prostitutes by name-boards, or *tituli*, above their individual cells in brothels. These *tituli* may have announced prostitutes' prices and names to interested customers, defining them by their perceived sexual value and, by means of a "Do not Disturb" sign, symbolically establishing the periods when they belonged, however temporarily, to a specific man.[15] For Roman authors, labeling and categorizing women as whores became a means of theoretically restraining their unconventional impulses. Even women who were defined by their lack of permanent male relationships could be controlled by the terms of the discourse about them. The possibility of gaining the negative label of *meretrix* may have served as a warning to respectable matrons of potential retribution for immoral behavior.

This concept of the "whore" is key to an examination of the fluidity of Roman moral categories for women, because Roman prostitutes played an inherently unstable and transgressive role in Roman society. The Roman whore was conceptualized as a particularly selfish individual, who cared more about her own gain than supporting and nurturing male family members or contributing to the larger community. Since the Roman era, this concept has served as a general trope in the discourse about the characters and morals of prostitutes in Western society.[16] Literary and legal texts often characterize prostitutes as permanent social outcasts and exiles from the larger community.[17] Timothy Gilfoyle presents prostitutes as "one of the ultimate subaltern subjects, outcasts from not only the dominant culture but often also from those subcultures labeled 'subordinate' – women, working classes, social minorities, radicals, or religious dissidents."[18] Despite this socially marginal status as the paradigmatic Other, professional Roman prostitutes still regularly interacted with men and women from a wide variety of different social backgrounds. *Meretrices* were both theoretically ostracized outsiders and ubiqituous insiders, separated from other subordinate subcultures yet in constant contact with both the elite and lowly men of Roman society. Furthermore, they played both inherently subordinate roles as sexual objects and potentially dominant roles as economically independent agents who, in some cases, possessed sexual choice.

At the same time, we should not overstate the agency or glamorize the lifestyle of actual Roman sex workers. The vast majority of them were slaves under the control of a pimp or madam, having little if any control over their lives, customers, or profits. Their lives were probably both miserable and short. This book is concerned not so much with the lived reality of Roman prostitutes but with the discourse about the *meretrix* as a social, sexual, and moral category. Necessarily, this involves a greater focus on the relative minority of freedwomen freelance prostitutes, courtesans, and married women accused of prostitute-like behavior, even if the stories men told about such women were not representative of the lives of most actual Roman prostitutes.

Roman professional sex workers were defined by the fact that they plied their trade *palam*, or openly. Politically or economically prominent women who conducted their activities *palam*, regardless of their sexual behavior, were often accused of being *meretrices*.[19] The frequent presence of a woman in public spaces already threatens her adherence to appropriate gender and sexual norms; if she is working outside, she is necessarily not wool-working or raising children inside the house.

At the same time, one of the key differences between Roman women of the Republic and early Empire and other ancient Mediterranean women was the emphasis on the public proclamation of their virtue, as will be discussed further in Chapter 1. A good Roman woman ought to be *nota*, well known, and publicly celebrated for her loyalty and chaste behavior, her *pudicitia*. However, a bad Roman woman was *famosa*, or notorious, and she was presumed to be behaving sexually like a whore.[20] This distinction outlined an uneasy and nebulous boundary between public women and what the medieval historian Ruth Mazzo Karras has termed "common women," women equally available to all men.[21] Unlike most other ancient Mediterranean societies, the good Roman woman had a public presence and was allowed to interact regularly with men outside her family. However, that made her relationship to the figure of the public prostitute all the more ambiguous and potentially confusing. The matron could be publicly visible but not sexually available, whereas the prostitute could be either visible on the street or invisible inside her brothel *cella* or home, and yet she was defined by her sexual accessibility. Since the physical location and even the appearance of a woman was not necessarily determinative of her moral status, as demonstrated further in Chapters 1 and 5, her potentially questionable status created social anxiety in the minds of elite men. The famous statue of Eumachia, patroness of the Pompeii fullers' guild, exhibits some of this problematic issues of definition; the statue depicts a modestly dressed matron who is nonetheless prominently placed on the edge of the Pompeii Forum, in a building almost certainly dedicated to business meetings and transactions.[22] She asserts her wealth and her public economic role in society at the same time. Numerous public statues and tomb monuments of early Imperial

Roman matrons immortalized realistic aging female heads on top of idealized young, nude, Venus-type bodies. This juxtaposition further demonstrates the complex relationship between female virtue and sexual attractiveness in the Roman world.[23] By attempting to define behavior rigidly and categorize all women as either wives or whores, male authors and jurists sought to conceal this tension, despite the evidence of social and moral intermixture that would have permeated Roman daily life.

Roman jurists and educators found the concept of the prostitute "convenient to think with," as a means of categorizing and labeling socially acceptable behavior.[24] Prostitutes were convenient to think with not just for legal jurists, but also for poets, artists, and orators. The conceptual category of "bad women" or *meretrices* both reflected and helped construct the gender identity of "good" Roman women.[25] *Meretrices* served as the dangerous, exotic, foreign Other to the good matron, most vividly represented in Augustus' propagandistic contrast of his sister Octavia and her rival Cleopatra VII of Egypt. These "bad women" were not only sexually promiscuous, but figures of chaos and disorder who disrupted the social system.

Elite male Roman discourse about *meretrices* centered on their queerness and subaltern status. I here borrow Gayle Rubin's concept of queerness to analyze the rhetorical function of Roman *meretrices* as women who did not fit into the established patriarchal and sexual hierarchy.[26] The prostitute is often used as a symbol for the unchained, disloyal woman who might challenge the accepted social structure. This figure, especially in her guise of the formerly respectable "fallen woman," becomes the symbol of societal disorder and instability.[27] Like Vistilia, she theatens the dominant narrative. However, the development of *meretrices* as this threatening, queer alternative to the normative Roman female stereotype largely served to reify and support the ideal role model of the loyal *bona matrona*: Vistilia still winds up exiled rather than pursuing her liaisons in peace and quiet.

Such elite identity judgments can only be evaluated as accurate models within their specific political and social contexts.[28] The complex Roman social pyramid of elites, freeborn citizens, freedmen, and slaves rested on a parallel and linked pyramid of female social hierarchy in which position depended largely on marital status and sexual relationships, as well as familial connections and wealth.[29] In such a system, the wealthiest freedwoman courtesan still ranked beneath a prosperous matron. However, her social status in relationship to a poor rural matron, like that of an Imperial freedman to a rural male farmer, was less clear. Such ambiguity raised the question of whether social origins might be less important than economic status, an ongoing issue within the overall Roman social hierarchy.

Arlene Saxonhouse uses the common gender paradigm of public and private, dividing men and women into separate spheres, in order to address the innately transgressive nature of ancient women in the public sphere.[30] However, her theory, while relatively applicable to the Greek and Near Eastern ancient worlds, does not consider how the public nature of Roman female virtue complicates such a paradigm for the Roman world. For the Romans, overall social stability depended on a more ambiguous understanding of the duties and place of women. The Romans sought to navigate between the ideal of a good Roman public wife – one whose public activities centered on her loyalty to family and her patriotism – and the negative caricature of the Roman common whore, whose public activities focused on gaining money through men's use of her body. A good Roman woman was necessarily public in her display of her virtues; a bad Roman woman was public in the sense of lacking any owner.

The originality and influence of the Roman label of *meretrix*

The Roman association between promiscuity and unorthodox female political and economic activity is the beginning of a long history of such labels in Western society. At the 1990 World Whores' Summit in San Francisco, the prostitutes' rights activist Gail Pheterson declared, "Whore-identified women are not considered citizens, and any woman can be called a whore at any time for somehow stepping over the line."[31] One of the questions interrogated closely in this book is precisely the ambiguity of Roman *meretrices* citizenship – what is their relationship to the larger social and political community?

This heritage does not primarily stem from any of the other major roots of Western culture. The Greeks, for instance, did not strongly associate indiscriminate promiscuity with their unorthodox, publicly active elite women, with the possible exception of the fifth-century BCE Elpinice, sister of Cimon.[32] Medea and Clytemnestra, whatever their flaws, are not represented as sexually promiscuous – Clytemnestra is an adulteress with one man, but she is certainly not openly available to all comers.

While Greek *hetairai* such as Pericles' mistress Aspasia certainly had political and social influence, the strict segregation between sexually promiscuous women and respectable citizen matrons largely eliminated the subversive threat of interaction and confusion between these types.[33]

When transgression does occur, as when Neaera and her daughter alleg-edly masqueraded as Athenian matrons, it is harshly criticized and largely concerns the issue of prostitutes misrepresenting themselves as respect-able women, rather than vice versa.[34] The Hebrew and Near Eastern use of "whore" as a general moral label and its limitations for wider applica-bility, meanwhile, is further discussed in Appendix II.

Definitions and methods of identification

Precise terminology is key for comprehending Roman use of these nega-tive and positive stereotypes. I shall briefly delineate my particular trans-lation choices for the different Roman words for "prostitute" and "wife." The Romans themselves used a variety of methods to identify sex work-ers, both with regard to their names and in terms of visual symbols asso-ciated with their role in society.

As noted earlier, the Romans used the most common word for a pro-fessional prostitute, *meretrix* (lit. "female wage-earner"), to refer also to unorthodox elite women like the Republican matron Clodia Metelli and the Empress Messalina. This general label also described a variety of different types of unmarried, sexually active adult women, ranging from streetwalkers and brothel girls to elegant freelance courtesans and long-term concubines.[35] The linguistic connection between sex work and wages also highlights the anxiety about female economic autonomy that will be discussed further in later chapters.

Other terms, such as *scortum* (lit. "skin," a neuter term), *moecha* (lit. "adulteress," from the Greek), and *lupa* (lit. "wolf-bitch") have both a stronger derogatory nuance and are usually used to refer to prostitutes of lower social and financial status.[36] Meanwhile, more generic terms like *puella* (lit. "girl") and *amica* (lit. "girlfriend"), both of which frequently occur in Latin elegy, are traditionally translated by the socially ambigu-ous word "girlfriend."

Another problem lies in the issue of English translation. All English words that refer to promiscuous women have specific negative conno-tations to a modern ear: whore, slut, nymphomaniac, hooker, harlot, etc.[37] I use *meretrix* or "whore" to refer to the broad category of women identified in Roman sources by that label, precisely because I am trying to capture the sense of condemnation and insult attached to all women labeled as a *meretrix*, regardless of their profession. While "whore" is certainly not a formal or polite word, it serves as the best translation for the derogatory general label. I prefer this term to "slut" because "whore" conveys a sense of agency on the part of the woman; she is someone who whores herself out, whether sexually or in other ways. "Slut" has more passive connotations; a slut is a woman or man who allows herself to be used.

The English term "prostitute," on the other hand, will be reserved for women who exchanged sexual favors for money or gifts, whether in temporary transactions or longer relationships. I will use *scortum* to refer to cheap streetwalkers as well as women who worked in brothels or other indoor spaces. While Roman texts sometimes used *scortum* and *meretrix* interchangeably, *scortum* has a much stronger association with prostitutes of low status and will thus be reserved for that subgroup, whereas *meretrix* is a more general term.[38]

Women who fall into more ambiguous categories, such as the elegiac *amicae* or emperors' concubines, will be referred to as "courtesans" in short-term relationships and "mistresses" in more stable, long-term relationships. I will discuss in Chapter 3 how courtesans and concubines fell in between the gaps of the "wife" and "whore" labels.[39] These women were certainly subject to the same type of potential criticism and invective as other women who did not have the protection of a permanent marital bond. However, their material lives were probably more comfortable than those of brothel women or streetwalkers. I do not treat soldiers' unofficial wives or other women who functioned as common-law spouses for all intents and purposes, due to my focus on moral categories.[40] Women who ceased to work actively in the sex trade and became wives were still subject to some degree of prostitute-like associations, although they also fell under the same legal restrictions as any other Roman wife.[41]

For the more elite, freelance prostitutes who lived in their own apartments or under the protection of a patron, I have also chosen to use the term courtesan. This word accurately conveys the requirements of elegance and sophistication that distinguished the upper strata of Roman prostitutes. While the very existence of courtesans in the Roman world has been disputed, this book will establish the historical evidence for their prominence in Roman society during certain periods.[42]

The given names of Roman prostitutes also indicate their identity as *meretrices* rather than as respectable *matronae*. Prostitutes form an exception to the general Roman convention that labeled Roman women, even in their very names, as belonging to a particular man: e.g. Cornelia, whose name indicated that she was the daughter of Cornelius Scipio.[43] In Rome, where a name indicated familial and consequently social status, prostitutes chose – or were assigned by their masters – names unrelated to any familial origins. Fortunata (Lucky), Iucunda (Pleasant), and Veneria (associated with Venus) are common examples. While these women may also have had legal names indicating the *gens* of their former owner, such official titles do not tend to appear in graffiti or literary sources.[44] Roman prostitute names often evoke memories of earlier famous Greek *hetairai*, like Thais of Athens, Ptolemy I's mistress, or Lais of Corinth, suggesting an informal allusion or even an attempt to establish a professional genealogy in lieu of a familial one. They may also be similar to slave names, which were also often descriptive rather than familial in nature.

It was highly useful for a prostitute to have a use-name that conveyed her profession, since it made advertisement simpler. Names that described positive physical or mental qualities, invoked Venus, goddess of love and beauty, or recalled legends of women famed for their sexual expertise were common throughout the Empire. We have no clear records as to how these names were chosen, although in many cases the *leno* or *lena* who trained the prostitute may have simply picked an evocative word.

This book concentrates primarily on textual, archaeological, and visual evidence from the second century BCE through the third century CE, the era of greatest Roman dominance in the Mediterranean and, not incidentally, the period possessing the most reliable source material. Spatially speaking, this work is largely concentrated on sources from the Italian peninsula, since I sought to assess specifically Roman attitudes towards prostitutes rather than the fusion of ideas found in the Eastern Empire or the limited sources on the perspectives of people from the Western provinces. However, I do look at archaeological evidence throughout the Empire in order to establish general patterns.[45]

I have primarily organized this book according to the different stereotypes of Roman women examined: good wives, wicked prostitutes, good prostitutes, wicked wives, and the morally ambiguous courtesans and concubines. Each of the first few chapters addresses the representation and consistent characterization of a particular typology in a variety of distinct literary and historic genres. Later chapters focus on the depiction of "good" and "wicked" women in art and religion, and on the evidence for interaction between prostitutes and matrons in the archaeological record. The first four labels are static caricatures that the

Roman elite used to define and restrict women's roles. I do not therefore particularly focus on the evolution or change of these stereotypes over the 400-year period that I focus on (approximately 200 BCE–200 CE), although I do discuss the significance of the Augustan "family values" legislation and the literary and historical reactions to it, as in the afore-mentioned case of Vistilia.

I draw my case studies from a variety of ancient genres, each with their own unique issues of source criticism and historiography. Historians like Livy and Tacitus or authors of moral exempla like Valerius Maximus generally narrate the stories of actual historical figures, whose lives can testify to the complexities of female roles in Roman society. At the same time, these narratives are shaped and shaded by the particular agenda of each author and a general tendency to sacrifice accuracy in favor of moralizing anecdotes and dramatic incidents.[46] The Roman comedies of Plautus and Terence are valuable for their multiple disparate iterations of prostitute stereotypes, but their depictions of courtesans are also sig-nificantly influenced by earlier Greek comic *hetairai*.[47] These plays still serve to illuminate Roman prejudices and stereotypes about prostitutes as well as Greek ones; they also showcase likely elements of daily life for prosperous freelance Roman courtesans.

Wives, whores, and women of deliberately ambiguous social status also play prominent roles in both Augustan elegy and Imperial sat-ires and epigrams. In elegies, such women serve in part as a literary trope: the narrator requires a beloved object whose relationship with him is potentially temporary, allowing for the dramatic possibilities of pursuit and rejection.[48] As Chapters 3 and 4 will discuss in more detail, in some cases these women are portrayed as adulterous wives, in other cases as elite courtesans, and often without direct reference to social status.

Wife and prostitute stories were also popular in both historical and hypothetical legal speeches.[49] Several of these declamations concern questions of female social status and, in particular, whether women can freely move from the condition of wife or virgin to whore and vice versa. As with poetry, these tales bear little resemblance to the real lives of Roman women, whose danger of being kidnapped by pirates was somewhat less dire than might be suggested by its frequency in decla-mation. However, they serve as vivid exempla of the Roman elite male discourse about the intersection between absolute moral categories and consideration of the possibility that not all women might fall neatly into prescribed boxes.

General source issues

One common source issue is the sharp distinction between the fictional literary glamorization of *meretrices* and the harsher depiction in rhetorical sources and other types of representations such as Pompeian graffiti. Many of the Roman poetic and comedic sources about *meretrices* present a misleading picture of predominantly independent, freelance prostitutes, who ply their trade openly and profitably without male supervision. Such women may be immoral, but they are depicted as possessing much more agency over their lives than many Roman matrons did.

While prostitutes were not subordinate to fathers or husbands like most Roman women, it would be risky and inaccurate to use terms like "independent" or "free" to describe the lives of most historical Roman sex workers.[50] Many if not most Roman *meretrices* were slaves and most others were freedwomen with obligations to their patrons, if their former masters were still alive.[51] Unfortunately, we have very few sources of information about slave prostitutes, much less slave women who were casually used for sex by their masters without remuneration of any sort. This type of evidence is particularly unlikely to have been chronicled by elite male authors or to have survived in archaeological documentation, due to the temporary nature of their sex acts.

While the vast majority of Roman *meretrices* were slaves or under the control of a *leno* or *lena*, some freedwomen courtesans may indeed have possessed more control over their economic and political lives than most normal married women. Any discussion of both positive and negative representation of Roman prostitutes must address the issue of whether or not such women could actually have possessed legitimate agency over their lives. An apposite example suggesting a certain degree of control comes from one of the first recorded prostitutes in Roman history, Manilia, who refused to service a drunken Roman aedile, Hostilius Mancinus, in 151 BCE.[52] According to Aulus Gellius, Hostilius brought Manilia up on charges for assault after she drove him from her house by throwing stones at him from her window. The tribunes of the plebs dismissed Hostilius' suit and found Manilia's actions justified under the circumstances.

No patron or master is mentioned in this story. Manilia was probably a freedwoman given her aristocratic name, which was presumably bestowed by her former patron. She clearly exercised the right of choice of client, even to the extent of refusing a powerful official, and the tribunes upheld that privilege. In contrast, while respectable women theoretically had the right to refuse choices of husbands made for them by their fathers, one of the only recorded historical examples is the third marriage of Cicero's daughter Tullia. The evidence suggests that most elite Roman *matronae* were married without regard to personal preference.[53]

Manilia's case also directly raises the question of whether Roman *meretrices* were considered to be citizens. The inferior legal status conferred by their *infamia* and the marital restrictions placed on them by Augustus would appear to confer a second-class legal status.[54] At the same time, one of the most fundamental social rights of a Roman citizen was freedom from rape. This privilege is vividly demonstrated in the numerous popular uprisings that were legendarily sparked by Roman elite men inappropriately using their authority to rape Roman citizen women and men such as Lucretia, Verginia, and Publilius.[55] Sexual abuse of a slave was freely permitted under Roman law; sexual abuse of a freeborn woman or man was rape and punishable by severe penalties, including death. Freedwomen prostitutes thus once again fall into a nebulous category here.

Gellius' tale about Manilia strongly implies that she had legal protection from rape and the ability to exercise sexual choice. However, there are almost no other surviving legal or literary examples of prosecution for the rape of a Roman prostitute.[56] The closest incident is a late antique successful lawsuit by an Alexandrian mother whose prostitute daughter was raped and murdered by her client.[57] Even in this case, the mother merely receives monetary recompense for the loss of her daughter's earnings; the elite male client is not punished for the murder of a citizen. *Meretrices* remain liminal figures in society and the law; any support of their legal rights to sexual and personal autonomy probably depended largely on the particular judge rather than established doctrine.

General outline

Chapter 1 discusses the two most stereotypical ancient social categories of Roman women. I examine a variety of different literary and epigraphic genres to develop the paradigms of the good Roman matron and the greedy, selfish prostitute and to note their differences from other representations in the Mediterranean world.[58] Chapter 2 explores representations of virtuous prostitutes in Roman and Graeco-Roman texts, demonstrating that individual generous sex workers could be portrayed as national heroines or benevolent martyrs. Chapter 3 analyzes the portrayal of historical Roman women who reached high levels of social status and influence without ever being legally married to their lovers. These women formed a "second class" of females in Roman elite society that threatened the established social structures. Chapter 4 uses historical and literary depictions of politically active, allegedly promiscuous matrons to establish how the "whore" label became a more general term of gendered abuse. I also discuss non-elite female workers, such as innkeepers and grocers, who were assumed to be part-time prostitutes.

Chapter 5 examines the visual representation of Roman wives and whores, focusing particularly on the domestic paintings of Pompeii and Rome. Chapter 6 uses archaeological evidence to demonstrate the prominence and ubiquity of prostitutes in the Roman urban landscape through a study of Roman brothels. Chapter 7 discusses the role of Roman religion in both delineating social and moral categories for Roman women and simultaneously transgressing them. These three chapters focus in particular on the use of material culture to locate prostitutes within both public and private spaces in the community. Finally, Chapter 8 briefly analyzes the impact of the Roman "whore" label on later Western attitudes and the effect of Christianity upon this discourse. Through a close study of Procopius' portrayal of the Byzantine Empress Theodora as a debauched whore, I examine how all these stereotypes can overlap and accentuate each other.

The Roman tradition of collectively labeling as *meretrices* promiscuous matrons, Imperial concubines, and streetwalking prostitutes has influenced modern discourse about the role of women in society and the conflict between women's careers and their loyalties to their families. Prostitutes and prostitution are common symbols today in the general debate about women's public roles and the choices that women make about their lives. The traditional stereotype that a successful career woman may have "slept her way to the top" echoes ancient Roman labels.

Roman society was one of the earliest and most influential Western cultures in which women could play even indirect public roles. The anecdotes and legends told through the generations about good and bad Roman women to their daughters and granddaughters therefore form a crucial set of texts in understanding the origins of this long-running historical anxiety. In contrast to eastern Mediterranean society, the spectre of an influential, politically and economically active woman was not simply a mythic legend designed to justify continued patriarchal oppression.[59] In the Roman world, any handful of coins would remind their owner of the prominent roles played by legendary heroines and contemporaneous empresses in shaping their society. By creating the stereotype of the "whore," elite men introduced a means of punishing and repressing women who strayed too far outside the permissible boundaries of a male-centered social structure.

I

Faithful wives and greedy prostitutes

Since the funeral tribute of all good women should be simple and alike, because their natural virtues, kept safe through their own care, do not require variations in language, since it is enough that all have done the same things, each deserving of a good reputation... In this way my mother, dearest to me, won the greatest praise of all, in that in modesty, decency, chastity, obedience, wool-making, energy, and loyalty she was like and similar to other good women nor yielded to any, [having] an equal glory from her work, wisdom, and dangers.

"Laudatio Murdia," CIL VI, *10230*

They many times ask for gifts, they never give in return: you lose, and you'll get no thanks for your loss. And ten mouths with as many tongues wouldn't be enough for me to describe the scandalous tricks of prostitutes.

Ovid, Ars Amatoria *1.433–6*

When ancient texts discuss the social roles of Roman women, they usually focus on either the ideal of the *femina bona* – the wool-working, faithful, fertile, brave Roman matron defined by her duties as a wife and mother – or the selfish, greedy, promiscuous independent prostitute – the *meretrix*. Elite literary authors distinguish these two female stereotypes by their dress, behavior, and location, but most particularly by a set of virtues or vices associated with each representation.[1] Through a comparison of these tropes in different literary sources, I will briefly establish the construction of Roman concepts of female morality. While this book focuses on atypical Roman women, this chapter briefly lays out the normative stereotypes in order to establish their nature and significance for Roman gender relations.

Crucially, neither of these archetypes appears to have changed significantly over time, although their emphasis in literature and legal sources is particularly dominant during the early Empire, due perhaps to Augustus' legislation promoting traditional "family values."[2] A *femina bona* like Cornelia, Mother of the Gracchi in the late second BCE, was characterized by the same general set of virtues as Murdia a hundred years later or the Empress Plotina, wife of the Emperor Trajan, in the early second century CE.[3]

The idealized epitaph of Murdia above represents one example of the highly repetitive discourse about the character traits of "good women" in the Roman world. Epitaphs are one of the most common sources of information about historical Roman women, but they must be interpreted as idealized narratives rather than as literal descriptions of the women whom they commemorate.[4] Von Hesberg-Tonn identifies five distinct types of morally respectable women in Latin literature, ranging from the sacrificial martyr to the urban, educated, morally impeccable woman.[5] All, however, are unified by a dominant trait of loyalty to family members and, directly or indirectly, to the Roman state itself. As Chapter 2 will demonstrate, there is no standardized system for commemorating an unmarried adult woman's virtues.

In the case of Murdia, her son explicitly praises his mother's similarity to other good women; she fits the paradigm in that she is modest, decent, chaste, industrious, and loyal. All of these attributes relate to a wife's role as helpmate for her husband. Not only her sexuality but her hard work and brave deeds are restricted to actions that serve his interests. The seven most common adjectives used to describe women in Roman epigraphy are *dulcissima* (sweetest), *pia* (dutiful), *bene merens* (well deserving), *sua* (his), *carissima* (dearest), *optima* (best), and *sanctissima* (holiest).[6] While several of these are common generalizations which appear on tombs around the world today, as a group they emphasize the woman's relationship to her family members and her gods rather than her individual identity. Unlike many epigraphic representations of ancient Greek women, the good Roman woman is considered to be a valuable and worthy person in her own right, rather than simply her husband's property.[7] However, the *femina bona* demonstrates her virtue by using her skills and her economic assets solely in subordinate support of her husband or children.

While *pudicitia*, which can be best if imperfectly translated as sexual modesty, is one of the chief virtues of Roman wives, it is distinguished from Greek ideas of female modesty and segregation in that it is an explicitly public virtue.[8] A truly virtuous Roman wife is famous for her loyalty and chaste behavior, just as a greedy prostitute is infamous for her selfishness and sexual availability. Even while Murdia's son emphasizes her similarity to other good women and the unchanging universality of female virtue, he simultaneously insists on its individual commemoration in the form of his mother.[9] A wealthy Roman *femina bona* has her name and reputation celebrated with inscriptions, statues in the marketplace, public eulogies given in her honor, or even coins.

We know from ancient sources that Roman women of all social classes traveled through the marketplace, went to schools in the Forum, attended public entertainments, and worked proudly as shopkeepers and doctors.[10] Roman female virtues are analogous to Roman male virtues with regard to their use as the foundation of a "directly political public image," especially during the Republic.[11] While Augustan Age authors focused on the redomestication of the Augustan woman, even Livia and Julia's ostentatious spinning was praised and commemorated publicly. Furthermore, their household duties did not stop them from attending the theater or strolling the porticoes commissioned in their names.[12]

Such commemoration stabilizes and establishes the gendered assignments of social roles.[13] The ubiquitous images and texts describing the *femina bona* reinforced the social and moral status quo for both women and men. A young elite Roman woman would hear the stories of virtuous ancestresses and, perhaps, the cautionary tales of black-sheep relatives or friends, as well as listen to poetry and see plays in which women earned the rewards commensurate with their virtues or vices.[14] When she walked or was carried in a litter through the Roman streets, she could view the statues and paintings of other prominent women around her; the names of revered female relatives might be inscribed on the walls of her family atrium.[15]

Roman texts lack some of the Greek paranoia about what women were doing secretly in their quarters or at female religious festivals. A *femina bona*'s activities and actions were as open to the world as her family's atrium, in which she ideally sat like Lucretia, "in the middle of the house," and wove wool while her husband conducted his daily business in the same space.[16] While not an active public participant in the business and politics of the Roman world, the respectable Roman matron was also not segregated or secluded from public life. How then, can she be distinguished from the disrespectable woman who is not just publicly known but common and *palam*, publicly available?

Dress: *stolae* and togas

According to literary and legal descriptions, Roman matrons in public were distinguished physically by their *stolae*, the long second tunic,
or *longa vestis*, that reached to a woman's ankles, and their *pallae* or
mantles.[17] The Roman jurist Ulpian in the late Roman Empire tells us
that if someone sexually harassed or accosted young women who were
dressed like *ancillae*, or slave-girls, it was a lesser offense, and still less
if they were dressed like *meretrices* rather than like a *materfamilias*.[18]
Strangers cat-calling women who were dressed in *matronali habitu*, a
wife's garment, could be punished; women who were dressed inappropriately were, in modern terms, "asking for it." What then, were these
apparently reliable visual clues as to a woman's marital and moral status,
and to what extent are the legal sources reliable guides to behavior here?

By Augustan times, the *stola* or overtunic, in particular, supposedly
indicated that a woman was a respectable matron – married, widowed, or
possibly divorced.[19] Although most Roman women, particularly poorer
plebeians, likely wore simple tunics most of the time, the *stola* and *palla*
(mantle) still served as paradigmatic signals of matrons' *pudicitia* or
sexual restraint, as well as their wealth and possibly their dressmaking
abilities.[20] Kelly Olson notes that visual representations of the *stola* exist
only from the early first century BCE through the late second century
CE, and that the garment seems to have fallen out of popularity after
that date.[21] The *stola* and *palla* became social and literary signifiers of a
woman's social status and morality, rather than accurate descriptions of
Roman matrons' everyday fashion choices.[22] Nevertheless, the conceptualization of matrons as women covered by ankle-length dresses and
mantles plays an important role in Roman perceptions of female virtue.
The *stola* and *palla* were garments that emphasized the privacy of the
Roman matron when she was out in public places; they concealed the
outlines of her body to casual onlookers.[23] At the same time, the *stola*
would not be necessary if Roman women actually remained inside their
homes; its very use implies Roman matrons' regular passage through
public spaces. Furthermore, when wearing a *stola*, the matron had legal
protection from verbal and sexual harassment, suggesting that such
treatment may have otherwise been a common feature of life for Roman
women in public.[24]

Meanwhile, the visual symbols of Roman prostitutes further defined
their officially public nature. Supposedly, Roman female prostitutes and
adulteresses were required to wear the male garment of the toga, often

yellow or bright saffron in color. While we possess only six literary and no definite visual references to togate prostitutes, the image is nevertheless a persistent one across a variety of genres, especially legal texts.[25] Furthermore, it is unclear from the literary references whether the toga was specifically associated with professional sex workers or also used as a garment of punishment for adulteresses.[26] As Chapter 5 will establish, there are no surviving visual representations of togate women.

The toga was not simply a Roman male garment, but a symbolic public garment that was reserved for ceremonial, political, and formal business occasions, due to its impracticality and expense.[27] It was the Roman equivalent of the modern Western man's business suit: togas were necessary for official occasions but uncomfortable and avoided under circumstances where casual attire was appropriate. A Roman freeborn man wore a toga if he was at a religious ceremony or running for political office – explicitly public and community-oriented functions. For a woman to wear a toga, then, is also to be prominently public. Unlike other working women who wore gender-ambiguous long tunics, as discussed in Chapter 4, the prostitute wears a garment marking her publicly as Other and transgressive. In the prostitutes' own religious ceremonies of the Floralia, discussed in Chapter 7, they are said to have performed naked, an act which rendered their bodies completely open to the gaze of the community. Here they become symbolically public in the most extreme sense: their bodies are owned by all or by none.

A woman's sexual availability appears to be equivalent visually to a man running for political office. This raises the question of whether a prostitute or adulteress wearing a toga is functioning as if she were socially a male. Is the toga equivalent to wearing drag or merely a statement that the wearer is working publicly and prominently? I would argue that a toga marks a woman as queer and outside conventional gender norms.[28] Mary Beard has noted that Vestal Virgins' costumes and legal privileges blurred the lines not only between maiden and wife but also male and female, rendering them "queer."[29] Whether this rendered the Vestals gender-ambiguous or entirely outside standard gender categorizations is still very much up for debate.[30] In either case, the unique role and status of Vestals within Roman society helped to construct Roman ideas of virtuous behavior for maidens and matrons. At the same time, *meretrices* served as the wicked counterpart to the Vestals. Like them, they had masculine and feminine aspects; like them, they incorporated elements of both married and unmarried female representation into their depiction. The Vestal is queer through being sexually unavailable to all;

the *meretrix* is queer for precisely the opposite reason. While neither precisely fits within the conventional life cycle of a Roman woman, from maiden to matron, their existence helps define and strengthen these more common normative categories in opposition to the strange Other.

Wicked whores

Prejudices and invective against actual female sex workers in Western society have historically centered on three major issues: uncontrolled female sexual and reproductive activity, the exchange of money for services rather than for a specific product, and prostitutes' lack of loyalty to a family or to any permanent bond with a man.[31] Within the Roman discourse about prostitutes as the paradigmatic "wicked women," all three of these accusations played a part, although the last dominated.

When Roman authors wished to criticize *meretrices*, regardless of their social or professional status, they most frequently accused them of greed and avarice. Greed was used as a symbol of a *meretrix's* valuation of personal profit over love or loyalty to a man. Prostitutes were attacked for their willingness to sell their bodies to the highest bidder, regardless of personal preference, and their callous abandonment of poorer lovers. While wage-earning was scorned for both Roman women and men because it suggested an abandonment of the traditional agricultural economy, it was also a reality of life for most urban Romans. Although tradesmen and regular workers might be despised by the social and literary elite, they were not faced with the same disapprobation as prostitutes, who were particularly condemned for their sexual availability. Such criticism largely stems from a broader social anxiety about female financial independence, which was legally permitted but still threatened familial stability. A woman who earned wages, the literal definition of a *meretrix*, was a woman who did not have to depend on a man for food and shelter. In practice, most such women may have been under the financial control of a *leno* or pimp, but the literary discourse focuses on the problematic concept of the freelance female courtesan.

Prostitutes in the Greek world and Eastern Empire were also associated with various types of birth control. They were often explicitly contrasted with fertile wives whose lives centered on childbearing, although there is less evidence for this in the western Mediterranean.[32] We have almost no accounts of Roman prostitutes having children. One notable exception is the loving mother mentioned in Seneca's *Controversiae*, who is discussed in Chapter 2.[33] There are also few references to Roman prostitutes actively practicing birth control, although Ovid's elegiac mistress Corinna procures a dangerous abortion against the narrator's wishes.[34] Ovid leaves Corinna's social status deliberately ambiguous: she may be either an elegant courtesan or an adulterous wife. Common sense argues that *meretrices* must have become pregnant on a reasonably frequent basis, but the idea of *meretrix* as mother is largely absent from the discourse, suggesting a conceptual separation between the duties of the matron and those of the prostitute. Although fertility thus forms another distinction between *matronae* and *meretrices*, the relative lack of source material renders it dangerous to generalize about either the conceptualization of prostitutes as mothers or the outcomes of their reproductive choices.[35]

While generally critical, Roman authorial attitudes towards prostitutes changed across both different genres and different time periods. In the comedies of the middle Republic and the elegiac poetry of the Augustan Age, characters criticize their unmarried female partners for valuing ready cash above genuine emotion. These genres portray such behavior as aberrant and specifically immoral, a particular vice of the prostitute as inculcated by the wicked, crafty *lena* or madam.

The Imperial Roman satirists and epigrammists, like Martial and Juvenal, offer praise for simple streetwalkers and brothel girls, who provide a useful service of fulfilling male sexual needs without deceit or treachery. However, they sharply condemn the more ambitious, greedy courtesans who not only take a man's wealth, but also separate him from his family and friends, thus destroying general societal ties of loyalty. This change, which will be further explored in Chapter 3, illuminates a distrust of the power of influential, unorthodox *meretrices*, which could potentially overturn the traditional hierarchies of the male-dominated Roman social system. The anxiety here is more focused on class segregation than female moral behavior. It is not the prostitutes' sexuality but their economic success and their ability to choose their clients that threatens the ambiguously elite status of Silver Age authors. Unlike Juvenal or Martial, the elite courtesans are not searching desperately for any patron willing to sponsor them. While still sexual objects, they are also independent economic agents to some extent. Through an examination of these different types of texts, as well as the surviving archaeological and legal evidence for prices charged by prostitutes, we can better understand the social motivations behind this type of criticism.

The anxiety expressed in these various texts and genres does not concern the women's sexual behavior, for prostitutes are recognized as a necessary part of the entertainment sphere for Roman men, along with baths, games, and drinking.[36] Rather, it attacks *meretrices'* lack of ties to a *familia* and their valuation of currency over romance or poetry, a fundamentally unfeminine position according to Roman mores. Such a caricature of the *meretrix* stands in opposition to the ideal exempla of respectable matrons like the so-called "Turia" and Sulpicia, the wife of Lentulus Cruscellio, who sacrificed both their wealth and safety for their husbands during the late Republican civil wars.[37] Virtuous Roman women are praised especially for their generosity and industry on behalf of their families. They also exhibit bravery and cunning in their acts of loving sacrifice and risks taken for their male relatives. These women often donate their jewels and property to aid their husbands or refuse to keep their dowries separated from their husbands' lands.[38] They even commit suicide to join their husbands in death, since their lives are apparently meaningless without their beloved men at the center.[39] These acts of bravery and economic agency can be valorized and eulogized precisely because they are done to support and uphold masculine power.

Under the influence of later Christian ideas about the immorality of sexual behavior, we might tend to assume that a fear of women's aggressive, dominating sexuality lay at the heart of Roman invective against whores. Roman elite male anxiety about prostitutes however, does not focus on their uncontrollable and excessive sexual desires. Chapter 5, furthermore, provides evidence for the frequent Roman acceptance and support of married women's sexual desires, as long as they are directed towards their husbands. These texts suggest that the issue is the abandonment of loyalty and love by women, rather than the active role they might have taken in sexual interactions, which brands them as whores.[40]

Maria Wyke argues that, at least in the case of elegiac poetry, the woman, while technically labeled as a capricious *domina*, is in fact the constructed object and passive focus of the narrator's attention.[41] In this chapter I shall use Wyke's term "elegiac woman" to refer to the poetic construction of the gold-digging *amica* or girlfriend in Augustan Age poetry.[42] In many cases, the actual social status of the "elegiac woman" is extremely vague, perhaps deliberately so as a means of avoiding the official Augustan disapproval of adulterous liaisons. We do not know whether the author necessarily viewed his *amica* as an adulterous *matrona* or as a freedwoman courtesan, but in any case, the focus of anxiety and the specific avarice-related invective remains consistent regardless of social status.

Roman tradition of invective

In analyzing negative stereotypes of Roman women, particularly women who lack the inherent social protection of a family structure, we must ask whether such portraits can be used as any sort of historical evidence of actual behavior. If these representations are stock caricatures, they may illuminate a general discourse about female immorality but do not reveal the lived reality of any actual Roman sex workers. However, this does not render these works of invective useless from the perspective of cultural history.[43] The didactic nature of elite Roman literature shaped both male and female assumptions about appropriate gender roles. Women who departed from such roles were inherently rebelling against the normative paradigms established by the dominant power structure.[44] Humor and invective police both gender and class behavior; they establish the boundaries of acceptable activity even while rhetorically exaggerating the dangers of transgression.[45]

Surviving Roman invective texts are disproportionately directed by elite men against socially transgressive women and men; it seems plausible to presume that this is not simply an accidental artifact of the manuscript tradition. For these authors, humor served as a weapon to highlight and delineate impropriety.[46] It should be viewed as a tool of verbal violence akin to a slavemaster's whip – not necessarily effective in engendering loyalty, but at least useful in suppressing open defiance. By examining these specific texts, we can learn precisely what and whom these men were afraid of – the potential threats to their positions of power.

At the same time, we can also use such texts in order to amass a general base of knowledge about Roman prostitutes' and matrons' everyday lives. For instance, these works were likely reasonably accurate in their assessment of most prostitutes' economic motivations. Roman prostitutes had every reason to try to amass wealth while still young and beautiful. Their accumulation of property could only come from the donations of grateful clients. Excoriations of such women as greedy reflect historical economic necessities, even while casting a possibly inaccurate value judgment on their actions. However, the specific details presented in rhetoric and comedies do not increase the plausibility of these stories, since a more dramatic story would be valuable in heightening the audience's emotional response. We can make general assumptions about the process of prostitute–client negotiations without relying, for instance, on specific price figures quoted in Roman elegy or comedy.[47]

Greek antecedents and Roman innovations

The "greedy girl" is a stereotype more frequently present in Roman literature than in the various Greek characterizations of *hetairai, pornai,* or adulterous wives.[48] However, Roman comedies, in particular, drew frequent inspiration from the work of Menander and others. This invocation of Greek tropes does not mean that these texts cannot inform us about Republican Rome and its societal prejudices.[49] By no later than the second century BCE, the Roman world was interwoven with the Greek world and Greek values, although not identical in its attitudes. Greek concepts of *hetairai* in the comedies affected and influenced Roman representations of *meretrices* and possibly even the actual social role of prostitutes in Roman society, particularly as many Roman prostitutes were freedwomen from the Greek East.[50]

Nevertheless, there are important differences between the representations of Roman *meretrices*, whether common streetwalkers or elegant courtesans, and Greek prostitutes of whatever type, whether lowly *pornai* or prosperous *hetairai*.[51] The most common representation of the Greek *hetaira* is that of a crafty, witty creature of elegance and delicate seduction, rather than the more typical Roman representation of a selfish woman motivated solely by greed.[52] The Roman literary *meretrices* featured in this chapter are represented as reasonably prosperous independent courtesans, like the Greek *hetairai*, rather than as poor brothel girls or streetwalkers, despite their probable rarity among the overall historical Roman prostitute population.

Greek orators like Demosthenes did sometimes invoke the spectre of the dangerous gold-digging *hetaira* who might steal rightful inheritances away from respectable widows and children.[53] Demosthenes denounces the possibility of a *hetaira* inheriting improperly from a lover by misrepresenting herself as a legitimate wife. As will be discussed later in the chapter, Roman legal cases focus more on invective against prostitutes by their bitter and impoverished former clients, rather than on any potential confusion between wives and prostitutes. While Cicero expresses outrage at Cytheris' assumption of matronly privileges in her role as Marcus Antonius' mistress, this is not seen as a legal issue but rather as a subject of gossip and social embarrassment.[54]

The overall invisibility of respectable Greek women and the prevalence of endogamous, close-kin marriage made such questions about wives' actual social status reasonable. In contrast, the more public Roman wives were well known within their community and retained tight links to their exogamous natal family. They might be accused of behaving like prostitutes, but not of an actual origin as a low-status sex worker. James Davidson analyzes at length the deliberate economic ambiguity placed on *hetaira*–client relationships in ancient Greece and the emphasis on willing "gifts."[55] In contrast, the Roman vituperative texts focus much more directly on the cash payments and other economic transactions and on the elimination of any romantic veil from the process.

The following texts briefly illustrate what may well be a genuine elite male resentment against the power of socially mobile Roman freedwomen and other women without families, whose wealth helped protect them from the demands and pleas of their would-be lovers. Such bitterness mirrors the frequent denunciation of successful Roman freedmen in elite texts, which also stems from elite anxiety about upward social mobility.[56]

The comedies

Plautus' and Terence's comedies are our earliest significant source of Roman tales about both *meretrices* and *matronae*. A common symbol of comic *meretrices'* independence and agency is a house, in which the prostitutes usually live either alone or with fellow prostitutes and slaves. For convenient dramatic purposes, this home is usually located next door to the house of the respectable young male protagonist.[57] These characters' ownership of their homes indicates that they are prosperous courtesans, with some choice of clientele.

In Plautus' *Asinaria*, the *lena*, or madam, Cleaereta explains to her petulant client Argyrippus about the "wicked tricks" of her profession:[58]

Why do you blame me if I do my duty? For nowhere is it either told in a story or painted in pictures or written in poems, that a madam (*lena*), who wishes to thrive, treats any lover well ... Just like a fish, so is a lover to a madam; he's good for nothing if he isn't fresh. (Plautus, *Asinaria*, 174–87)

Plautus explicitly argues that this particular representation can be generalized as the Roman norm. This artistic, literary, and poetic stereotype of a madam or prostitute is consistently interested only in financial gain; she views lovers as resources to be sucked dry. Cleaereta compares lovers to both fish and later to birds that are caught and eaten; they are consumables, to be trapped or baited.[59] This representation also places prostitutes and their procurers in the dominant power position: men are prey, not predators.

Furthermore, Cleaereta's series of metaphors, as well as Roman representations of prostitutes in general, tends to place women in a semi-active
position, even though they receive the presents that their lovers give. Such
discourse complicates Holt Parker's "teratogenic grid" structure, which
places women, especially in sexual situations, perpetually in the passive,
objectified position.[60] Parker proposes a hierarchical system of Roman
sexual acts that gives higher status to people who take sexually active
roles as penetrators, and lower status to people who are sexually pen-
etrated.[61] Although Plautus still conceives of the prostitute as a sexual
object, he represents her as an active agent in the economic and social
hierarchy. However, Cleaereta's imagery, as well as other common comic
references to prostitutes as consumers and swallowers, still envisions
meretrices as holes to be filled up rather than as constructive or active
forces.[62] In this case the prostitutes are demanding to be satiated with
money rather than simply with sex, an unfair substitution from the perspective of the male characters and audience. Indeed, they state that they
value hard cash more than their clients' genitals.[63] This conflict between
the prostitutes' sexual objectification and their active monetary demands
is unstable and must be resolved with a return to social norms by the
end of the play, so that the male characters can retain control in all areas
of life.

While elegy often plays with ideas of male dependency, the predator–prey
metaphor suggests not male subjugation but violence against males and
consumption of them.[64] It does not define the male as socially irresponsi-
ble but instead portrays the woman as outside the *familia*, operating as a
public figure and a tradeswoman, rather than as part of a household and
as someone defined by her relationship to a specific man. While it is a *lena*
who offers up this characterization rather than a current *meretrix*, this
character represents merely one extreme of the spectrum of independent,
profit-minded Roman women. The virginal, naïve comic *puella*, discussed
in Chapter 2, marks the other end, and Plautus appears to assume that
most Roman prostitutes fall somewhere in between these two poles in
terms of personal avarice and affection for their clients.

In various comedies, Plautus also stresses the education of the *meretrix* in particular techniques of extracting money from her lovers. This
behavior is not portrayed as a natural aspect of character connected to
moral degeneracy, but rather as a learned behavior and part of the trade.
This type of education is demonstrated by the following conversation
between an elderly gentleman, Periplecomenus, and a male scheming

slave, Palaestrio, in Plautus' *Miles Gloriosus;* they are discussing their need for a prostitute to aid them in their plot:

PALAESTRIO Can you, then, find any woman who is beautiful and charming, whose mind and body are full of merriment and tricks?
PERIPLECOMENUS Free by birth, or a slave made free?
PALAESTRIO I consider that irrelevant, if you can find one who is greedy for gain (*quaestuosa*), who feeds her body with her body (*alat corpus corpore*), who has, too, her senses (*pectus*) all awake; as for her heart, that cannot be so, as none of them have one.
PERIPLECOMENUS Do you want a polished girl (*lauta*), or one still unpolished (*nondum lauta*)?
PALAESTRIO One sober but juicy (*sic consucidam*); as sparkling a one (*lepidissimam*) as ever you can find, and as young as possible.
PERIPLECOMENUS Why, I have one, a client of mine, a very young prostitute. But what do you want with her? (Plautus, *Miles Gloriosus* 785–91)

Here the two characters discuss the typical attractive prostitute in her various incarnations. Since Plautus chooses to describe her as Periplecomenus' client and emphasizes the potentially freed status of the woman, two specifically Roman social concepts, this passage is unlikely to be simply a direct translation of a Greek comic scene. Palaestrio needs his prostitute to be *quaestuosa*, someone who seeks out profit, as well as uninterested in romance. Periplecomenus distinguishes between a *lauta* meretrix and one who is not *lauta*: the word comes from *lavo* and literally means "washed" or "unwashed."[65] This suggests an implicit understanding of a relative hierarchy of Roman prostitutes: courtesans are *lauta*, while *scorta*, common whores, are *nondum lauta*.

It appears natural for a wealthy gentleman like Periplecomenus to have such a young prostitute as a client; presumably, she is meant to be one of his own freedwomen.[66] Earlier in the play, the character explains that he has not gotten married because wives demand so many expenses on behalf of their relatives and friends and servants, and he does not wish to have that burden.[67] There is a subtle but deliberate distinction drawn here between the different types of women: all women want gifts, but wives, who have multiple bonds of loyalty to other individuals, wish the money to spend on their friends and relations, whereas prostitutes desire a lesser sum of money to spend solely on nourishing their own bodies. This suggests the independence and lack of loyalty of prostitutes not just to a husband, but also to the entire normative familial structure of Roman society. Prostitutes are single women – not just in their unmarried status but in the sense of being unconnected to others.

This distinction between "polished" and "unpolished" prostitutes also appears in other comedies by Plautus, lending further credence to a system of informal hierarchy among *meretrices*. In the *Truculentus*, the prostitute Phronesium distinguishes between clever, careful prostitutes and "fools and dirty girls" (*bliteas et luteas*) who can't "keep an eye on their own interests (*ad rem suam*) at all times, even when they are drunk."[68] The gold-digging *meretrix*, stereotypically, always has her mind on a long-term plan and is never swept away by emotion or alcohol into rash behavior. The purpose of a prostitute's indiscriminate sexual behavior is explicitly described in the *Cistaria* as the only means towards the attainment of a great fortune: "That is more suitable to a married woman, my dear Silenium, to love but one, and with him to pass her life, to whom she has once been married; but, indeed, a prostitute is most like a flourishing city; she cannot alone increase her fortunes (*suam rem*) without a multitude of men."[69]

Plautus' *Bacchides* presents perhaps the most vivid representation of the scheming, greedy prostitute in the form of the twin sisters, both named Bacchis, who in the course of the play extort a large sum of money from their young, handsome lovers and then eventually placate their lovers' angry fathers by seducing the old men themselves. They thus exchange a more sexually desirable client for one who has more available wealth, in contrast to the typical comic abandonment of a rich faraway lover for the handsome young penniless hero.

Plautus uses one of his common metaphors to describe these women when he claims, "She, too, like a tide, most voraciously swallows all up, whenever she has touched any one."[70] The prostitute here is again represented as a gaping stomach, a literal empty hole, echoing ancient medical and biological depictions of women, whose desire was supposedly to swallow up all of a man's sustenance and resources.[71] While the Bacchis sisters purport to love their young men, they readily abandon them in favor of their decrepit fathers, showing that their true interest is only in the accumulation of wealth.

The close connections between successful prostitutes and economic prosperity are repeatedly emphasized in these comedies. The character of Peniculus, in the *Truculentus*, describes prostitutes teeming around bankers' shops like flies. The women both deposit their own funds and take money in return for favors from young spendthrifts who are going to the bankers for loans.[72] The key repeated emphasis in Plautus' various plays is on prostitutes' treatment of sex work as just another type of business, one where, just as in banking or fishing, the goal is to become as proficient as possible in taking resources from others for one's own benefit.

The sexual nature of their trade is mentioned only, if at all, by the besotted young lovers or in joking innuendoes; the comic prostitutes themselves are only interested in the flow of money. They are generally represented as among the most intelligent and competent of comic characters, along with the scheming slave. *Meretrices* usually get whatever they want by the end of the play, often leaving a trail of confused and bitter ex-lovers in their wake.

The most common type of *matrona* in Plautine comedy is the *uxor dotata* or *femina irata*, the independently wealthy, nagging, shrewish counterpart to the besotted elderly patriarch (*senex amator*).[73] However, Plautus does present several ideal wives and discusses the traits, in his view, of the good *matrona*. In the *Casina*, the character of Myrrhina, herself a respectable wife, declares that a modest wife (*proba*) should not have any private property unknown to her husband, and that she and all her possessions ought to belong to him.[74] In the *Stichus*, the elderly widower Antipho asks his grown daughters for advice about the most important virtues (*mores*) of *matronae*, as he is seeking a new wife. The daughters emphasize the importance of a good reputation, or rather the lack of notoriety and the absence of bad behavior (*male faciundi*) despite opportunity. Plautus describes the wisest woman (*sapientissima*) as the woman who knows herself (*se poterit noscere*) when times are prosperous and endures hardship with calm (*aequo animo*).[75] While some of these virtues closely echo Greek models, the description of the good wife hearing nothing ill about herself as she "walks through the city" evokes Roman views about the physical freedom of women.[76] While the good Greek wife must have her morals imposed and constantly protected by her husband, since her biological impulses will inevitably lead her to debauchery and laziness, the good Roman wife is here rather a strong, self-aware figure who consciously chooses moral behavior, rather than having it forced upon her.[77] Her virtue is only increased by public knowledge of her behavior.

Elegy

Ovid: Amores 1.10 and Tristia

The Augustan poet Ovid is known for his detailed portraits of women and the relatively tolerant attitude towards extramarital sexual behavior. While Ovid's mythological poems often portray virtuous romantic heroines like

Briseis or transgressive gender-switching figures like Caenis, Ovid's elegiac and didactic poetry frequently focuses on the traditional stereotype of the greedy mistress.[78] I treat all Ovid's representations of the greedy mistress as fictional caricatures rather than as any attempt to represent the personality or actions of an actual Roman woman, although he may certainly have based some details of his poems on personal experience.

The social statuses of Ovid's poetic mistresses are somewhat ambiguous. Despite his purported intent that the audience of the *Ars Amatoria* should be restricted to professional prostitutes and men, much of Ovid's advice assumes an elite context of dining rooms, good seats at the circus, and adulterous intrigue.[79] He uses the nebulous term *amica* or girlfriend more frequently than *meretrix*: *amica* appears nine times in the *Amores* and ten in the *Ars Amatoria*, whereas *meretrix* occurs three times in the *Amores* and once in the *Ars*.[80] While the precise status of these largely imaginary women is thus unclear, their role as sexually available women interested in financial gain remains quite constant. Given the elite context, these elegiac women are more likely to be elegant courtesans than lowly streetwalking *scorta*. Ovid offers an idealized version of the sexually available and highly desirable Roman woman.

Amores 1.10 offers fertile ground for an exploration of Ovid's ideas about greed, the proper relationship of women to men, and his anxiety about the valuation of money over emotion. In this poem, Ovid rejects his previous lover, precisely because of her greed: "Why have I changed, you ask? Because you demand gifts."[81] Ovid directly and unfavorably compares his *amica*'s treatment of him to the behavior of a more ordinary *meretrix*:

Even the prostitute who is buyable for money, and seeks miserable wealth with her unwilling body; she nevertheless curses a greedy pimp's orders, and is forced to do, what you do by choice. (Ovid, *Amores* 1.10.21–4)

The surrounding context makes it clear that the *amica*'s flaw in comparison to the lowly *meretrix* is not, as we might expect, that the girlfriend seeks multiple lovers whereas the prostitute is forced to have sex with multiple partners. Instead, the prostitute is forced to seek pay, whereas the girlfriend chooses to demand pay from her lover. Ovid distinguishes between the economic necessity of hardship and the greed of a disloyal woman. Unlike the naïve prostitutes seduced into corruption by wicked *lenae*, this *amica* pursues her own goals. It is ambiguous whether this woman is a courtesan or an independent promiscuous woman. It is her very agency, her ability to choose lovers, that makes this *amica* so threatening to the status quo. She thus resembles the women of Roman comedy, who gain power either through their financial power as a *femina dotata* or through their sexual power as a freelance courtesan.

This passage draws a sharp distinction between ordinary prostitutes and women like Ovid's *amica*.[82] Voluntary avarice is the mark of a truly bad woman, whereas Ovid manages to pity or at least understand the motivations of a poor prostitute, here labeled by the general term *meretrix*. This poem overflows with explicitly financial terms emphasizing the connection between the *amica* and cold hard cash: *vendit, emit, posco, pretium*, etc.[83] Ovid suggests that the woman abandon crude, inappropriate monetary transactions in return for unquantifiable loyalty and more traditional emotional bonds; he wants his *amica* to return to an appropriately feminine status of being defined by her lover.

However, Ovid, foreshadowing the later vituperation of the second-century CE poets, then goes on to condemn all women for greedy behavior with regards to sex, particularly in comparison to the generosity of female animals:[84]

Only a woman (*mulier*) delights in collecting booty (*spoliis*) from her mate, only she hires out her nights, comes for a price, and sells what this one demands, what that one seeks, or gives it as a gift, to please herself. When making love pleases both partners alike, why should she sell and the other buy? (1.10.29–34)

In this case, Ovid criticizes neither the sexual acts of women, nor the fact that they take pleasure in them, but rather that these acts are used as a source of profit for the women involved. Ovid goes on to compare the exchange of sex for *munera* as equivalent to selling testimony at a trial or serving as a lawyer for pay rather than out of friendship. This set of metaphors alludes to the deep Graeco-Roman discomfort with the notion of paying for services rather than goods, which also held true for Roman advocates in the late Republic, among other service professions.[85] It was socially acceptable to own slaves who provided a variety of services, including sexual ones, but not for a friend or lover – who should offer such a service out of benevolence – to demand a fixed price for it instead.

The main public service that a woman could provide in Rome was sexual, and Ovid makes her sexual service an equivalent corruption of the normal bonds of emotional loyalty, comparing it to lawyers demanding pay before defending their clients or friends.[86] In reality, Ovid was perfectly aware that Roman lawyers fully expected to receive valuable presents from their clients in return for their service, but the fiction of generous donation was maintained until the Imperial period.[87] There is an ironic undertone to Ovid's complaints about his mistress's greed, as he himself received largesse as a poet and was largely dependent on Imperial and noble patrons. The explicit demand for payment, however, rather than a demure acceptance of occasional gifts, marks the *amica* as an immoral and selfish proactive woman rather than as an appropriately passive sexual object.

For Ovid, the chief problem with the *amica*'s behavior is that it destroys the existing bond of loyalty between herself and her lover: "The renter (*conductor*) loosens all bonds (*solvit*): freed by payment he no longer remains a debtor in your service (*officio*)."[88] Rather than establishing a permanent relationship through gift reciprocity, as would happen in a marital ceremony where a dowry was exchanged, the greed of the *amica* reduces the relationship to a set of singular transactions. There is no bond between the couple; the *amica* is a woman without permanent ties to a man, an inherently threatening figure.

In *Amores* 1.10's last set of mythological metaphors, Ovid invokes famous negative female exempla from Roman and Greek history. He begins by discussing Tarpeia, the woman who betrayed the city of Rome and let the enemy in through the gate in return for a promised reward of golden bracelets.[89] Tarpeia was the ultimate traitorous woman: she broke the bonds of loyalty not only to her own family but also to her city, and her punishment was to be killed by the Sabines, who treated her greed with contempt.[90] Eriphyle, also invoked by Ovid, similarly betrayed her husband Amphiaraus in return for the necklace of Harmonia, another case of female greed overcoming loyalty.[91] Alcinous, in contrast, is cited not only as a wealthy king but as a ruler renowned for generosity and hospitality.[92] The threat presented by greed is that it leads to the worst of all possible female sins: betrayal.

In the *Tristia*, Ovid invokes his own wife and daughter, as well as the Empress Livia, as idealized virtuous women. He uses the unusual term for his wife of *pia coniunx* (dutiful spouse), echoing Aeneas' most famous trait of *pietas*. He describes her as one of his only remaining supporters after his condemnation and exile by Augustus.[93] His wife begs to go with him into exile and explicitly frames her relationship in terms of loyalty:

> "Together, together we will go," she said,
> "I will follow you and I will be the exile wife of an exile …
> Caesar's wrath orders you to leave your homeland;
> Loyalty (*pietas*) orders me. Loyalty will be like a Caesar to me."[94]

This language echoes the traditional if mysterious religious terminology of the Roman marriage ceremony: *Ubi tu Gaius, ego Gaia*; here Ovid's wife attempts to embrace a shared identity as exiles rather than as happy newlyweds.[95] She only reluctantly remains in Rome at Ovid's request and falls down in a grieving frenzy at his departure. He later refers to her as his principal support – the metaphorical beam holding up his ruined house – establishing her not only as a loving wife but as an important and crucial partner in their marriage.[96] Like the figure of Turia, Ovid's wife is not a passive, silent figure of virtue but an actively loyal, brave ally for her husband – a truly Roman matron.

In an attempt to curry favor, Ovid claims that his wife learned virtue from none other than Augustus' wife Livia: *te docet exemplum coniugis esse bonae*, "she taught you how to be the example of a good wife."[97] As with Murdia, the nature of such a role model is not precisely defined – all good wives remain alike – although Ovid later commends his wife specifically for her *pudicitia … probitasque, fidesque*, her modesty, honesty, and loyalty.[98] He also points out that the tragedy of his exile offers her an opportunity to demonstrate publicly her virtue and loyalty and become eternally famous for her *pietas*.[99] Even when denied the traditional wifely duties of childbearing and maintaining her husband's household, she can still aspire to be the perfect matron through her performance of appropriate public displays of conjugal devotion. Ovid self-consciously plays with these archetypes, evoking the simultaneous desire and impossibility of ever fitting real women into such perfect boxes. At the same time that he promises his wife immortality, he never chooses to tell us her name and thus give her any actual individuality.[100]

The elegiac gold-digger represents a threat to the established social order and hierarchy, through lowering the agency, finances, and sexual success of her attempted lover, potentially raising her own social status to inappropriate levels, or choosing wealthy non-elite patrons over young aristocrats as her lovers. Her focus on money rather than on familial bonds or personal talent suggests that men and women can be measured purely on the basis of their financial assets. The logical question is why a successful female worker should be valued less highly than an unsuccessful male worker. In order to reaffirm the patriarchal and anti-meritocratic aspects of Roman society, women's acquisition of money in and of itself must be viewed as shameful and problematic. A good woman may save money and resources, but she does not produce them, especially not with her body.

Epigram and satire

The late first-century CE author Martial discusses gold-diggers in several of his well-known epigrams. In 9.2, the narrator sharply criticizes "Lupus" for spending all his money on his *amicam* rather than on his friends.[101] This *amica* is explicitly a married woman rather than a professional prostitute: she is described as an *adultera* and a *moecha*, two separate terms for adulteress.[102] Lupus' desire for this greedy woman leads him to neglect his own bonds of loyalty to his dinner guests, his *sodales*, his clients, who are led off into slavery while he has sex, and his closest friends.[103]

Martial is much more specific than most of the elegiac poets about the demands of his friend's *amica*: she wants the finest food and wine, Erythrean pearls, and a litter carried by eight Syrian slaves, itself a sign of the rights of a *matrona*.[104] In this case, it is the man who abandons traditional loyalties in exchange for material goods, although the root cause, a greedy *amica*, is still the same.

Juvenal, a Roman satirist of the late first and early second centuries CE, largely focuses in his satires on the transgressions of wealthy married women, rather than on poor prostitutes trying, like the poet himself, to strike it rich. However, he does allude to an episode in Satire 10 that is reminiscent of the most common modern trope of gold-digging. In his portrait of an old man who has grown senile and forgotten his family, Juvenal conjures up the dread threat of an inappropriate inheritance: "by a cruel will he cuts off his own heirs, and leaves everything to Phiale, so potent was the breath of that painted mouth which had stood for many years in an enclosed archway (*fornicem*)."[105] Phiale is explicitly represented as a former common *meretrix*, an outdoor prostitute who fornicated against convenient archway walls. She has successfully wormed her way into the affections of a wealthy elderly man and inherited all of his money, ruining his own kin and disrupting the social order.

This fear of gold-digging prostitutes "marrying up" was a common motif in Greek legal cases.[106] Juvenal may be drawing on well-known Greek precedent here, rather than describing an actual occurrence in the Roman world. Regardless of his inspiration, Juvenal offers another variation on the stereotype of the gold-digging prostitute. In this case, the woman successfully moves from prostitution to legitimate marriage and gains wealth through a legal, if controversial, inheritance. The highly publicized American legal case in 2000 of Anna Nicole Smith, the 26-year-old exotic dancer who married an 89-year-old Texan oil tycoon and had her inheritance of 88 million dollars temporarily vacated by a federal court in favor of the man's son, has shown that this is a stereotype, or perhaps even occasionally a realistic portrayal, that persists today.[107]

Legal and epigraphic evidence

The imagery of the avaricious prostitute, whether lowly streetwalker or elegant courtesan, appears to exist mainly in the literary imagination of elite Roman male authors rather than being reflected in the historical or archaeological records. While there is no way to measure the level of actual Roman prostitutes' greed, source material about the economics of prostitution suggests that the profits of *meretrices* varied widely depending on circumstances. In most cases, however, Roman men could buy sex cheaply, if not perhaps sex with the most elite of courtesans; they had little reason to complain about price gouging. On the other hand, most prostitutes themselves probably lived lifestyles that were far removed from the glamour and decadence painted in poetry and plays.

While many surviving Pompeian graffiti list the prices of prostitutes, ranging from 1 *as* to 23 *asses*, no graffito directly criticizes an overly expensive prostitute. The closest possible comparison is to the description of the prostitute "Parte" as *sescentaria*, 600 *asses*, or ridiculously expensive, but this may be an encomium rather than a criticism; it does not imply that anyone actually paid that price.[108]

The mention of a particularly cheap price, such as *quadrantaria*, a woman who charges one-quarter *as*, may be intended as an insult, particularly as this term is used solely to describe Clodia Metelli, who was not actually a professional sex worker.[109] An average price for a single act with a *meretrix* appears to be closer to 2 *asses*, the price of a cup of cheap wine or a loaf of bread.[110]

The relative lack of anger or slander regarding any of these prices, however, suggests that the gold-digging stereotype was either a purely literary creation born from elite men's anxiety, or that, at least, it did not trickle down to encounters between non-elite men and relatively low-status common streetwalkers and brothel girls. *Scorta* may be scorned, but they are not the targets of significant elite concern. Elite male anxiety is focused on the more transgressive figures – either high-status courtesans who attempt to infiltrate elite social circles or matrons who behave like *meretrices*.

While the average *meretrix* may have earned more than many relatively unskilled workers in the Roman Empire, as shown by Egyptian tax records, few real prostitutes probably achieved significant wealth and economic independence through their work.[111] One list of tolls for Red Sea trade in Egypt charges 108 drachmae for *gunaikon pros hetairismon*, women for prostitution, in comparison to 10 drachmae for guards and 8 drachmae for artisans, and 20 drachmae each for "soldiers' women" and "sailors' women."[112] If reliable as a standard, such figures would indicate a remarkably high amount of profit for prostitutes in the region or, at least, their owners.[113] This may be an isolated instance, however, as it certainly is inconsistent with the prices inscribed on Pompeian walls or those in Latin poetry. Rather, the vast majority of prostitutes, many of whom were slaves, would have given most of their profits to their *lenones* and earned a living wage only if they were independent courtesans living in their own apartments.[114]

As noted in the discussion of Murdia, epigraphic evidence also tells us relatively little about the actual lives of respectable Roman matrons, just as obscene graffiti like "I screwed Mola" gives us little detail about the actual lives of Roman sex workers. With regard to wives, Treggiari hypothesizes that approximately one out of six senatorial and equestrian marriages ended by divorce within the first decade and another one-sixth by death of either spouse; she lacks any hard statistical evidence to support this theory, however.[115] This suggests that the majority of women were not rapidly switching marital partners and may have followed the ideal of the *univira*. Nevertheless, a substantial minority would either have remarried once or multiple times or, like Clodia Metelli, become independent widows or divorcees after a first marriage. Women's practical levels of legal and financial control are also difficult to determine; the anecdotal accounts from sources like Cicero's letters as well as Gaius' legal commentary appear to contradict the strict laws mandating a male guardian's control over all women's public affairs.[116]

From Pompeii, we do have some apparent celebrations of happy marriages and marital love. In house VII. 2. 51 in Pompeii, a partially preserved graffito reads: *Virum Vendere Nolo meom* [sic]...*quanti quantque VIR VEN...orum*. It has generally been translated "I don't want to sell my husband for any price."[117] Such a statement implies a high degree of loyalty to a spouse, if expressed in an odd and peculiarly Roman fashion. Other marriage-centered graffiti include the wish that Eulalus and his wife Vera have "good health and good sex," written in the atrium of the House of Ariadne – perhaps as a wedding toast of some sort.[118]

Above the remnants of a bed in a *cubiculum* in house IX, 3, 25, we
may read two separate inscriptions. The first, in a fluent cursive, reads
L. Clodius Varus (*CIL* IV, 2320). The second, in stilted capital letters,
reads *L. Clodius Varus Pelagia coniunx*, Lucius Clodius Varus and his
wife Pelagia (*CIL* IV, 2321.)[119] I suggest that the first skilled writer was
Varus himself, and that the second hand is that of Pelagia, laying claim
to a shared ownership of the bedroom. By itself, this is not a particularly
eloquent statement, but it both establishes the likely presence of a woman
writer and envisions her desire to create a joint living space. Notably,
she does not simply write up her own name next to her husband's; the
new graffito represents a literal union of the couple. Chapter 5 further
discusses representations of happy and loyal wives in Pompeian art and
graffiti as well as sexually desirous wives.

Certainly, the general surviving epigraphic evidence is consistent with
the ideals expressed in more elite and formal literature. For instance, *ILS*
7472 praises "a faithful wife to a faithful husband, since she never let
avarice keep her from her duty." Loyalty and greed are explicitly placed
in opposition, just as with the comedic and elegiac commentary on
wicked whores.[120] In the late fourth century CE, Paulina was praised by
her husband Praetextatus for "putting her husband before herself and
Rome before her husband;" thus patriotism is framed as an even greater
opportunity for female virtuous loyalty than familial bonds, as will be
further demonstrated in Chapters 2 and 3. Paulina is also honored for
"helping, loving, honoring, and caring" for her husband; she is depicted
as an important partner in the relationship whose virtues should be publicly commemorated.[121]

Conclusion

The comedic and elegiac construct of the gold-digging prostitute represents a woman who, according to Roman norms, explicitly betrays the
ideal of the proper Roman *femina bona*. She is not part of a *familia*, she is
not ruled by her emotions, she is not ever described as fertile, and she performs her trade openly on the street, wearing revealing clothing. While
a desire for luxury is frequently described as a common female vice, the
greedy *meretrix* as represented in Plautus or Ovid seems less interested
in fripperies and ostentatious ornamentation than in easily convertible
forms of wealth.[122]

This greed of the literary *meretrix* signified disloyalty rather than
irresponsibility or extravagance. In comedy, epigrams, and satire, the

bonds of loyalty thus broken are likely to be those of the male lover, who neglects his duties to his own *familia* and his friends in favor of his low-status prostitute lover. The *meretrix* causes social fragmentation, but she herself remains at the edges of the picture.

In elegiac poetry, however, which centers much more closely on the binary relationship between the narrator and the *docta puella*, it is the woman herself who chooses to *spernere fidem*, to destroy the loyalty which a virtuous woman would feel towards her lover in favor instead of selling her wares to the highest bidder, regardless of his social status, age, or poetic talent. The *amicae* of the poets are heartless. They do not need the narrator, for there is an infinite supply of potential lovers. Love and poetry themselves are tarnished by the *amica*'s betrayal and abandonment of the narrator.

Meanwhile, matrons are defined by the public recognition of their loyalty to their male relatives and, to a lesser extent, Rome itself. While proudly weaving in the open atrium among their husband's clients, rather than being relegated to the silent back rooms of many Mediterranean households, Roman matrons' identities and virtues are still constructed in relationship to the male center of the household. The good matron is also notable for her frugality and industry, in comparison to the extravagance of the greedy prostitute. She seeks praise and admiration, but not necessarily individuality; the good Roman woman's goal is to be known for being just as virtuous as all the other good Roman women, achieving anonymity not through silence but through similarity. While she may have economic assets, she shares them with her husband or gives him direct control of them.

Modern incarnations of the gold-digger stereotype have focused more on the concept of "marrying up;" lower-class women use the passion of wealthy older men as a means to improve their financial and social status. For Roman prostitutes, legitimate marriage was rarely an option. While the graffiti from Pompeii and Egyptian tax records indicate that some prostitutes may have earned a decent living, it is unlikely that many were able to use that profit to enter into the life of a conventional *matrona*. Indeed, the actual successful, independently wealthy courtesans were almost certainly greatly outnumbered by the desperate streetwalkers and slaves bound to harsh *lenae* and *lenones*, just as is true in the wide range of modern sex work. Nevertheless, the image of the woman who consumed men like fresh fish, without remorse or romance, remained a potent threat in the imagination of the Roman elite male, ever concerned with his role as subject and agent.

2

Good little prostitutes

Vibia Chresta erected this monument for herself and her family and for Caius Rustius Thalassus, son of Gaius, her son, and Vibia Calybenis, freed-woman of Gaia, a madam who earned her own money without cheating others.

CIL *IX*, 2029[1]

During the Imperial period, a woman named Vibia Chresta commissioned a funerary monument for herself and her family. Among her family members, she included one Vibia Calybenis, the only Roman *lena* or madam known to have her profession recorded on her tombstone. Yet even while Vibia Calybenis and her family are apparently willing to memorialize her role in sex work, they also feel the need to offer a defense of it. Vibia Calybenis made money *sine fraude*, unlike, by implication, a stereotypical Roman madam, who would be deceptive and cheat clients. This inscription demonstrates that it was possible for Roman women to conceptualize themselves and their family as "good prostitutes," or at least "good madams." However, such a narrative was inherently subversive and extraordinary. Notably, the focus in this inscription is not on the sexual nature of Calybenis' work, but on her economic autonomy: she earned *lucrum suum*, her own money. We lack any other funerary inscriptions in which women describe themselves as *meretrices*, suggesting that perhaps there was more respectability seen in managing prostitutes than in profiting from one's own body.[2]

While Vibia Calybenis is unique in offering a positive female perspective on the Roman sex trade, literary, historical, and epigraphic texts offer a variety of male-authored tales of "prostitutes with hearts-of-gold." These stories establish that the label of *meretrix* or "whore" could be

42

detached from its purely professional definition. Unmarried sex workers of lowly social status who exhibited virtues like generosity and self-sacrifice were able to transcend a general negative moral reputation associated with the label of whore; they became "wife-like." Roman tales of virtuous, self-sacrificial whores illuminate this conflict between social categories and moral labels. While the texts discussed in this chapter are predominantly literary or rhetorical, they still subvert the dominant discourse about Roman women's virtues and vices.

At the same time, the creation of this morally good prostitute archetype offers a path for freedwoman courtesans to pursue their profession without overly disturbing the male social status hierarchy. If we assume that reasonably prosperous freelance courtesans did exist in the Roman world, their role in society offered a potential threat to the status quo. These were female sexual objects who nevertheless possessed some degree of choice of clientele and economic autonomy. By establishing and exalting the trope of the loyal, devoted, generous freelance courtesan, Roman elite authors offered a means for such women to support rather than threaten the Roman social order. Professional freelance prostitutes themselves were not inherently threatening to the Roman social order, as long as they did nothing to undermine the pre-eminence of family and offered physical and emotional support to their lovers.

Elite Roman male authors simultaneously praise both the sexual attractiveness of these *bonae meretrices* and their generosity, creating a mixture between the two common stereotypes discussed in Chapter 1 of the attractive but greedy prostitute and the faithful, industrious matron. The texts discussed in this chapter are self-conscious male commentaries upon the idea of Roman female virtue and its relationship to the representations of wives and prostitutes.

I examine several representative *meretriculae*, or good little prostitutes, in order to establish a common set of traits possessed by these praiseworthy *meretrices*. I focus on five particular examples of this trope: the character of Bacchis in Terence's early Roman comedy *Hecyra*; the Augustan historian Livy's depiction of Hispala Faecenia, a prostitute witness in the Bacchanalian Conspiracy (Livy 39.9–19), two women from early Imperial rhetorical handbooks of hypothetical legal speeches (Ps.-Quintilian, *Decl. Maior.* 14–15; Seneca, *Cont.* 2.4) and the late imperial epitaph of Allia Potestas (*CIL* VI, 37965). By examining commonalities between these representations, despite their different genres and dates, I identify the moral behaviors associated with Roman female virtue regardless of social or sexual status. These texts prove that fidelity and generosity, as well as marital status or sexual behavior, were dominant components of Roman female morality.

Some Roman literary representations of good whores appear at first to be a concession to the fictional conventions of romance and comedy. Literary scenarios demanded virtuous, maidenly heroines who were nevertheless easily accessible to young male heroes. One such archetype is the virginal or monogamous prostitute, generally a victim of kidnapping or a foundling, who eventually abandons her shameful profession and marries the male hero. The maidenly prostitute of comedy and the Roman novel is neither greedy nor selfish; she is also not sexually promiscuous.[3] These accidental prostitutes have obvious antecedents in earlier Greek models.[4] However, another group of virtuous *meretrices*, whom I will focus upon in this chapter, remain prostitutes and do not necessarily gain marriage as a result of their moral behavior. Indeed, the latter type of *meretrix* often loses her lover as a result of her generous actions.

The true *meretriculae* are unabashed polyamorous sex workers who nevertheless demonstrate all of the characteristic virtues of the good Roman wife: loyalty, compassion, bravery, and industry. The common trait of these *bonae meretrices* in both historical and literary texts is loyalty both to their lover and to the dominant societal structures and power system. While the virginal prostitutes do threaten normal social divisions by daring to ensnare respectable young men in marriage, this conflict is resolved by their own restoration to elite respectability from the low-status world of freedwomen prostitutes. The *meretriculae*, who cannot be fully redeemed from their lowly status, can still demonstrate their loyalty by supporting proper families and the orderly hierarchies of Roman society. They invert normal paradigms and use sexual promiscuity ironically to support fidelity and familial harmony.

At the same time, Roman authors also use the ambiguous figures of these virtuous *meretrices* to explore social boundaries and, especially, whether moral behavior is always and necessarily associated with wealth and free birth. The "good prostitute" stands as an Other both to wicked matrons and to greedy prostitutes – the mirror of appropriate fidelity and moral behavior. While she is a stereotype, she highlights a variety of male views towards Roman gender relations.

Bacchis: marital therapist

By examining the character of Terence's Bacchis in the *Hecyra*, we can study the comparatively rare figure of a good prostitute in traditional

Roman comedy. This characterization may be significantly drawn from earlier Greek models, but it seems to reflect specifically Roman attitudes towards *meretrices* rather than Greek stereotypes about *hetairai*.[5] However, the originality of these texts is less important than their reflection of and influence upon the Roman discourse about female virtue. Regardless of the character's authorship, the audience for Terence's plays was certainly Roman and this play helped shape their attitudes and impressions. In this particular case, Bacchis is simultaneously represented as both an unrepentant, promiscuous whore and a generous and loyal lover who, by the end of the play, is socially assimilated into the company of the elite matrons.

Bacchis is portrayed at the outset as a normal, greedy prostitute in conventional rhetorical terms.[6] However, she defies this mold by becoming the heroine who selflessly solves the conflict of the play. In Terence's plot, the young man Pamphilus initially neglects his wife Philumena out of love for his former courtesan girlfriend Bacchis. Bacchis successfully convinces him to go back to his wife and thus reunites the traditional family. Bacchis can expect no reward from her actions; indeed, she is left alone at the end of the play, sadly seeking new lovers:

I am thrilled that this happiness (*gaudia*) has come to him through my agency; although other prostitutes (*meretrices*) would not have similar feelings. For it isn't good for us that any lover (*amator*) should find pleasure in marriage. But, truly, by Castor, I will never, for the sake of profit (*quaestum*), turn my mind to evil actions (*animum ad malas*). While it was permissible (*licitum*), I found him to be kind, easy-going, and pleasant. (Terence, *Hecyra* 834–42)

Terence portrays Bacchis as a deliberate anomaly; she is self-consciously aware that her behavior is not consistent with that of most prostitutes, or at least most comic prostitutes. The "heart-of-gold" prostitute is always depicted as an exception to the stereotype, just like Vibia Calybenis.

Dwora Gilula argues that Bacchis is merely a *mala meretrix* masquerading as *bona*, and that, in fact, neither Terence nor Plautus have any true good prostitute characters but only greedy women temporarily hiding behind a facade of generosity.[7] She notes the inconsistency between the slave Parmeno's claim that Bacchis continued postmarital relations with Pamphilus and Bacchis' assertion that she immediately dropped any association with him.

However, the presence of not one but two virtuous prostitutes in the *Hecyra*, as well as in other Roman comedies, discounts Gilula's thesis that Bacchis is a fraud.[8] Rather, Terence deliberately defies the standard stereotypes and offers up an untraditional problem with an untraditional solution, in the process mocking the conventions of his own genre. Rather than simply recycling the standard comedic character tropes of haughty matron and selfish whore, he shuffles personality traits and behaviors and creates Bacchis, the self-sacrificial lover. Both the plot and characters of the *Hecyra* thus suggest alternative models for Roman women and their social interactions, at least in the world of fiction.

Although Terence's Bacchis is herself a prostitute, she promotes the cause of legitimate marriage, proclaiming that her purpose is to "make his wife return home to Pamphilus; should I succeed in that, I shall not regret the report that I have been the only one to do what other prostitutes flee doing."[9] Bacchis acknowledges the established stereotype of the whore while at the same time defying it and upholding the social status quo.

Bacchis also acknowledges her lowly social status and mentions her nervousness about even meeting a legitimate matron, her rival Philumena. The character Laches suggests that Bacchis' eventual confession to Philumena may be somewhat self-interested, as "she knows that from this act both nobility (*nobilitatem*) and fame (*gloriam*) will arise for her."[10] The very notion that Bacchis cares about her public reputation associates her with virtuous matrons like Lucretia or Cornelia, Mother of the Gracchi, famously obsessed with maintaining the appearance of *pudicitia*, female modesty and morality, rather than with the common whores or whore-like wives who want only to be well known.[11] Bacchis worries not only about what the other prostitutes will think of her refusal to sleep with a client, but also about the reaction of the respectable matrons if she does not solve her ex-lover's marital problems. Laches promises that, as a result of her testimony, the good wives will become her *amicae*. She abandons her loyalty to her natural community, her fellow lowly prostitutes, in order to assist the respectable community and reunite an elite family.

Ariana Traill notes further problems with attempting to assign the origin of "heart-of-gold" prostitutes to Menander's comedies in the fourth century BCE.[12] While the second-century CE Greek author Plutarch, in his commentary on Menander, distinguishes between "audacious and bold" *hetairai* and "good and loving in return (*khreste kai anterosa*)" *hetairai*, Traill finds little evidence for such good and loving prostitutes in the surviving comedies of Menander.[13] Furthermore, Plutarch's plot resolutions for such virtuous prostitutes are either the discovery of a legitimate father, causing them to fall into the aforementioned accidental virginal prostitute category, or merely the extension of some additional time for the unorthodox relationship. The character of the prostitute who willingly gives up her lover does not appear in Menander or in Plutarch's commentary. However, the notion of the prostitute of ambiguous social and moral status is one that dates back to Menander and that reflects the practical social nuances of life in both Hellenistic Greece and the Roman world.[14]

Hispala Faecenia: the historian's brave witness

The representation of Hispala Faecenia, Livy's *meretricula* heroine of the Bacchanalian Conspiracy in 186 BCE, further complicates the accepted discourse about Roman female virtue. Livy portrays Hispala as one of a trio of female characters who represent different points along the moral spectrum of Roman feminine virtue: the corrupt and selfish mother Duronia, the upright and noble widow Sulpicia, and the sexually active yet virtuous prostitute Hispala Faecenia.[15] Despite her lowly social status and her lack of a husband, Hispala contrasts favorably with the debauched matron Duronia, although she is still depicted as undoubtedly inferior both socially and morally to the widow Sulpicia.

According to Livy, Hispala Faecenia was a freedwoman prostitute sexually involved with a young gentleman named P. Aebutius, whose stepfather and mother tried to corrupt him or possibly even kill him by means of the Bacchanalian rites.[16] When Aebutius obediently informed Hispala that he had to abstain from sexual intercourse before his Bacchanalian initiation, she tried to dissuade him by revealing the Bacchanalian cult's evil debauchery. As the story develops, Livy mentions that Hispala's previous mistress had been involved in the cult; the virtuous freedwoman had been appalled by the deeds she had witnessed there as a slave. Aebutius and Hispala ultimately turn state's evidence and the consuls and Senate unearth and destroy the entire Bacchanalian "conspiracy." A contemporaneous inscription in Calabria establishes the existence of this cult and its extermination in 186 BCE, although the inscription makes no mention of Hispala or Aebutius.[17]

For my purposes, Livy's description of Hispala Faecenia herself is more important than the overall nature of the Bacchanalian Conspiracy and his portrayal of the wider political and social issues.[18] Livy juxtaposes multiple distinct classes of women in his initial depiction of Hispala:

The noble freedwoman streetwalker Hispala Faecenia, worthier than her trade, who had been trained while still a little slave-girl. After she had been freed from slavery, she continued to practice her profession in the same fashion." (Livy 39.9)

Hispala here is described as a *scortum*, a particularly lowly and vulgar term for a prostitute, literally meaning "hide" or "skin." Although he initially resorts to vulgarity, Livy immediately proceeds to mitigate this term; Hispala is not only a well-known *scortum* but also a noble freedwoman who deserves better than the hand fate has dealt her. Trade, or *quaestus*, here has its frequent use as metonymy for income gained through prostitution.[19]

Furthermore, Hispala did not choose her disreputable profession; she was brought up to prostitute herself while still a "little slave-girl," and after her freedom, continued to practice her only skill. Hispala is a good woman forced into prostitution by circumstances; the double meaning of *nobile* as both "well-known" and "noble" is deliberate here. While Hispala can obviously not be "noble" in the aristocratic sense of a woman with consular ancestors, Livy chooses a word with positive associations rather than the equally plausible *famosa* or *publica*, used to describe more disreputable women, as demonstrated in Chapter 1. Whores are by definition public women, but Livy here allows a space for Hispala within the acceptable zones of public visibility for respectable Roman women. She is known for her virtue, not for her sexual promiscuity or for her work as a prostitute. Livy thus shoehorns Hispala into the moral space inhabited by a Lucretia or Livia, while at the same time emphasizing her social status as a common prostitute.

P. G. Walsh has recently argued that the historicity of the tale of Hispala Faecenia and Publius Aebutius is somewhat dubious.[20] He notes that the structure of the story is highly reminiscent of comic plots, including the stock characters of the wicked step-parent, the naive but well-meaning young man, and the prostitute.[21] While both Walsh and T. P. Wiseman establish that Livy's style was influenced by the comic tradition, the characters themselves in fact defy most comic stereotypes.[22] Hispala herself, most relevantly, is not a greedy, selfish prostitute but a generous *meretricula* with a heart-of-gold, a type that appears rarely in comedy, as discussed earlier. The chief villains are a wicked stepfather and a biological mother; these characters do not fit the natural comic pair of the elderly father and wicked stepmother.[23] Sulpicia, the highly respected matron, is neither shrewish nor promiscuous.

Hispala is certainly more of a fictionalized character than a historical personality, especially given the many decades between the actual events and Livy's chronicle of them. However, she is a useful representative of the brave, generous, sexually active Roman prostitute who through loyalty and service to the forces of order moves out of her lowly status and into the respectably undistinguished hordes of freeborn Roman citizen women. As a result of her virtuous behavior, she ceases to be a *meretrix* altogether and becomes both morally and socially a *matrona*. This archetype exists largely in uneasy juxtaposition to its opposites. At the same time, Livy reminds us that not all matrons are necessarily moral; Duronia and her Bacchanalian comrades are summarily executed for their crimes against the state.

One of the first and most common characteristics of the "heart-of-gold" prostitute is her financial generosity and selflessness, a trait which stands in direct opposition to the mercenary selfishness of the standard Roman whore prototype depicted in Chapter 1. Hispala Faecenia financially supports her lover Aebutius when his immoral parents refuse to give him his inheritance, and makes him her heir in her will.[24] She appears to be a prosperous freedwoman, capable of supporting herself, who never asks either Aebutius or the Roman state for financial compensation in return for the danger she runs as a state witness. Notably, she lives in the same neighborhood as the wealthy family of Aebutius, much like the comic freedwomen prostitutes who supposedly live next door to the respectable families of their lovers.[25] This tells us little about the actual residency patterns of freedwomen prostitutes, but it does suggest that the notion of a prosperous courtesan intermingling with respectable society was not alien to Roman society in Livy's own time.

When Hispala discovers the conspiracy to induct innocent Aebutius into the Bacchanalian rites, she condemns the plot but still maintains respectable social norms, declaring, "your stepfather (for perhaps it is not allowable (*fas non sit*) to censure your mother) is in haste to destroy your chastity, your character, your hopes, and your life."[26] Even when worried about her lover's life and virtue, Hispala is still concerned with *fas*, proper social and religious behavior; she is reluctant to criticize her lover's blood relative. Hispala is not a socially disruptive figure, unlike the Bacchanalians; she respects both Roman religion and her own place in society.

Livy contrasts this image of the modest, restrained prostitute with Aebutius' mother Duronia, the instigator of the plot. When Aebutius returns home and refuses to participate in the Bacchanalian rites, his perceptive mother immediately blames his decision on Hispala, placing herself in direct contrast to the virtuous whore.[27] The irony in this particular story is that Duronia, the supposedly respectable matron, is here the greedy, sexually profligate figure, whereas Hispala Faecenia is self-controlled and generous. It is Duronia who retains no *verecundia*, a typically feminine virtue of modesty, in her plot to serve as a pander for her son and expose him to the orgies of the Bacchanalians. Hispala's virtue and affection for Aebutius serve as a startling contrast to the hypocritical *materfamilias*. This behavior suggests the dangerous ability of the Bacchanalian rites to corrupt elite women and youths, as well as exploring the relationship between morality and social status in general. Duronia abandons her natural loyalty to her son, while Hispala goes far beyond the call of duty to save her customer. Ultimately, moral character trumps noble birth and marital status.

While more morally righteous than the Bacchanalian elite matrons, Hispala never attempts to transcend her lowly social status. Livy represents Hispala Faecenia as unfamiliar with the consular trappings and grandeur of Postumius' house and terrified by her invitation there.[28] Hispala does not desire to trespass into the homes of the elite or to cross out of the Aventine neighborhood of the respectable but insignificant plebeian citizens. Throughout her entire confession to the consul and his mother-in-law Sulpicia, Hispala is never described as a prostitute, but rather as a *mulier*, an *ancilla*, a *puella*, or a *libertina* – woman, maid, girl, freedwoman. The contrast is repeatedly drawn, however, with Sulpicia, who is never a *mulier* (woman) but a *gravissima femina* (very severe wife), *nobilis* (aristocrat), or even *talis femina* (a woman of such quality). At one point, Postumius rebukes Hispala, either for daring to conceal the truth in front of a respectable matron or possibly for her description of her warning to Aebutius as a *mulieris libertinae cum amatore sermonem*, a story of a freedwoman with her lover. Such a label for the story threatens to drag the narrative back into the inappropriate genre of lowbrow comedy, rather than that of serious legal proceedings.[29]

In order to protect Hispala Faecenia during the investigation, Postumius asks Sulpicia to house Hispala temporarily in Sulpicia's own home. Sulpicia is presumably a widow, as no *paterfamilias* appears in this entire sequence. Sulpicia empties out an entire part of the upper story of the building, suggesting both that Hispala's possessions and her *familia* are of significant size and that there may be some residual desire to keep the consular widow and the freedwoman's household separate. An outside staircase is closed up, and a new separate entrance is created into the building.[30] In this way, Hispala and her *familia* are both protected from the evil Bacchanalians and segregated from the consular matron. The virtuous matron and moral prostitute share a single house together in their service of the Republic, but they are still explicitly kept separate, presumably for fear of contamination by Hispala's work. Sulpicia retains the high-status ground floor, while the courtesan is relegated to the upper floor. At the same time, such a story belies any suggestion that prostitutes and matrons were segregated by district or neighborhood, as further analyzed in Chapter 7. Sulpicia and Hispala may not be dining together, but they are certainly in visual and physical proximity.

In return for her valuable information, Hispala receives a happy ending. The Senate rewards her by giving her the somewhat anachronistic status of a freeborn woman, as well as a substantial amount of money. All of the aspects of her status conferred by her profession as prostitute are nullified or revoked; Hispala Faecenia is one of the only Roman women ever to move from possessing *infamia* to respectability, according to Livy. She is explicitly allowed to marry out of her *gens* and to choose her own guardian.[31] The future designed by the Senate for Hispala Faecenia is not one of prostitution; much of the language focuses on her ability to marry and places her currently in the status of a widow. While Livy does not tell us her fate, the fairy-tale ending of a marriage between Hispala and Publius Aebutius is a tempting idea for any reader.

The well-intentioned poisoner

Roman rhetorical writers in the early Empire frequently constructed hypothetical legal speeches using fictional case scenarios as lessons for their students. These speeches cannot be taken as any indication of actual common legal dilemmas in the first century CE, but they do suggest both some of the concerns of the male elite as well as the moral values that they wished to impart to their sons.[32] Prostitutes in these speeches lack their own voices, but their imagined words are frequently invoked or defended by their advocates.

Two speeches for the prosecution and the defense from the *Declamationes Maiores* attributed to Quintilian vividly depict a *bona meretrix* and her benevolent wiles.[33] The rhetorical exercises 14 and 15 represent both sides of the following fact pattern: the prostitute lover of a poor man gives him a hate potion, which successfully causes the young man to stop loving her. In anger at thus having his emotions manipulated, he sues her for poisoning. She defends herself on the grounds both that the potion was not deadly and that she was acting in the young man's best interests.[34] This case invokes the figure of the self-sacrificial, generous prostitute, much like Bacchis, who puts the interests of her aristocratic male lover above her own financial needs. She places conventional morality and an appropriate marriage above her own interests.

The selfless poisoner is also notable for her generosity. According to her defense, she chose to give up this relationship to prevent her lover's bankruptcy, even though his gifts personally profited her. Her advocate describes her in exceedingly fulsome terms, casting a bland haze over the factual label of her as a *meretrix*:

I fear that if I start praising the character of this very straightforward girl and mention her virtue, this beggar may start loving her again! Indeed, judges, the maliciousness of people's common beliefs causes them to label a beautiful unmarried [lit. "empty"] woman a prostitute. Some lover imposed that name on an unfortunate woman to whom fortune had not provided, along with a good body, enough means for a strict and conventional marriage. Still, she struggled to protect her virtue, according to necessity. She never disrupted the harmony of any marriage; no father had cause to complain about his son; no man facing painful regret wept over a fortune that was drained off into her greedy hands. (Pseudo-Quintilian, *Declamationes Maiores* 15.2.1.[35])

This poor girl is a prostitute only because of her lack of a dowry, and, like Bacchis, she carefully avoided not only married men but young and imprudent men, according to the argument. It seems a wonder that she can support herself at all with such a restricted clientele. Her lover, in contrast, is portrayed as dissolute and lazy, a wastrel who is spending all his time and money at the brothel.[36]

Quintilian's poisoner-prostitute also seeks to preserve the social status and respectability of her client. To prevent further humiliation and fights, as well as out of selfless love, this girl decided to end her relationship with her lover, by the force of magic if necessary. This act thus demonstrated her virtue and generosity. Her advocate suggests how a typical *mala meretrix* would have been characterized in contrast:

He seeks to arouse our hostility towards the woman through his terminology: he tells us, "It's a prostitute (*meretricem*) I accuse." ... Now really, here's the situation I would expect: first of all, she would have a menacing face and a wild expression; her hair would be bristling with dirt, and a look of sadness would rigidly overlay the monstrous thought-processes lying underneath ... You see here not the horrid appearance of a poisoner but a pleasant look.[37] (Ps.-Quintilian, *Decl. Maior.* 15.5)

This comparison gives us both a stereotype of a normal streetwalking prostitute and the different portrayal of a prosperous, moral courtesan, albeit one who still works in a *lupanar.* The normal prostitute is frightening and uncivilized; this girl is courteous and generous. The association of *meretrices* with fraud and false emotions also remains constant here. Common prostitutes are represented as neither glamorous nor safe; they are not only common but dangerous and potentially criminal in their actions. As is often true in Roman oratory, the outer appearance is supposed to offer insight into a character's personality.[38]

The prostitute-nurse

In another hypothetical case, the first-century CE writer Seneca the Elder examines the rhetorical question of whether a sane man can adopt the illegitimate offspring of his own disinherited son and a prostitute (Seneca, *Cont.* 2.4). Despite the relatively abstract nature in which the case is presented, it does discuss a plausible legal issue, given the many inheritance disputes of both ancient Roman and Greek societies. Seneca defends the potential virtue and acceptability of the child by focusing on the atypical behavior of his prostitute mother, rather than the traits of the child himself. Since the woman is shown to fall into the moral category of the *matrona*, her child is thus redeemed from potential infamy. This also suggests that both moral taint and respectable virtue might be considered hereditary, regardless of social status.

Seneca's imaginary prostitute-mother is marked both by her affection and by her servile actions. In particular, she is loving and devoted to her dying lover:

What a woman I saw! She was herself attending to all that needed to be done; attentive at the sick man's bedside she ran to do every service, her hair not merely disheveled but torn out. Where then, I said, is the prostitute? (Seneca the Elder, Controversiae 2.4.1.4)

This unnamed woman is distinguished by her industriousness and her loyalty, the precise opposite of the common attributes of a *meretrix*. Her affectionate attitude towards her lover virtually removes the *infamia* of her profession. Her behavior determines her moral status: "How true it is that I saw nothing of a prostitute's way of life (*meretriciae vitae*) in that house! At the bedside sat a woman, sad faced (*mulier tristi vultu*), ailing, herself much like the patient, her eyes cast down."[39] She is sad, loyal, modest, and solely focused on her lover, even when another, healthier man is present. The opposing side in the debate criticizes the woman for her fertility, which is also represented as being uncharacteristic of *meretrices*, who were supposedly expert in the use of contraceptives and abortifacients.[40] Seneca's loyal nurse is a humble echo of the good matron; she assimilates not herself but her child into respectability through her actions.

Allia Potestas: the perfect woman

The monumental epitaph of the freedwoman Allia Potestas unites the opposed stereotypes of whore and wife in a single character. While the epitaph purports to eulogize an actual woman, it also uses innuendo and double entendre to suggest a reflection on the very nature of praise for women. The substantial marble tombstone erected by Allia's patron, Aulis Allius, immortalizes this woman from Perugia in lengthy and flowery terms (Figure 1). It was originally located in Rome's Via Pinciana, near the Horti Sallustani and is dated, controversially, somewhere between the late first century and the early fourth century CE.[41] While Allia was not a streetwalker or brothel girl, her unorthodox sexual patterns and freedwoman status would probably have led Roman authors to consider her a notorious woman of some sort, even if not a conventional prostitute who took money for individual sex acts.[42] Allia had at least two lovers with whom she lived as a concubine. She is categorized and described by adjectives highly reminiscent of prostitutes as well as those more typical of a virtuous wife, giving her a blended status both socially and morally.

Aulus created a paradoxical monument, an elegant and elaborate tomb for a *notissima* freedwoman, whose lines repeatedly pun on the parallels between the stereotypical virtues of *matrona* and *meretrix*. In the last line, Aulus describes Allia as *Haec titulo insignis*, this woman known by a label. While this may be simply a literal reference to the inscription on her gravestone and the fame that Aulus' poem would confer upon her, a *titulus* can also refer to a sign or label above a prostitute's *cella*.[43] Once again, Aulus is enjoying his *double entendre*: Allia is a labeled woman, both in life and death.

In the epitaph, Aulus initially focuses on Allia's standard set of matronly virtues before veering into lavish praise of her less respectable attributes. This is a surprising diversion from normal traditions in the genre of funerary epitaph, so much so that the entire inscription may be intended as a mildly ironic parody on standard funeral inscriptions.[44] The first line contains a pun supporting the theory that, at least, this is a highly unconventional epitaph. Allia is described as *non pretiosior ulla*, "more costly or dearer than any other woman" (*CIL* VI, 37965.1). This could be a reference to the deep affection of her patron, but it may also be an allusion to her price, suggesting that she was either a prostitute or simply a very expensive slave to buy. *Pretiosior* is rarely used of people and, when used of women, nearly always to describe *meretrices*.[45]

1. The epitaph of Allia Potestas. *CIL* VI, 37965; *CLE* 1988, Museo Nationale Romano, 0.59 by 0.66 by 0.025 meters, marble, first–fourth century CE.

Other adjectives used to describe Allia Potestas also suggest an association with the promiscuous life of a *meretrix*. Allia is *munda domi, sat munda foras, notissima uolgo,* "clean at home, clean in the forums, very well known to the crowd" (line 9). While "cleanliness" is normally a mark of a proper woman, her presence in public spaces is more startling, as is the designation of *notissima*, a word also used of both Hispala and Bacchis. Roman ambiguity regarding the public reputation of women is very much in force here; is this the kind of fame praised by the relatives of the eulogized "Murdia" or the infamous notoriety shed on prostitutes and actresses? The epitaph is unclear.

In the following lines, Allia's subordinate status is subtly emphasized. "She never thought of herself as free" (16). Allia Potestas receives extravagant praise for not violating any social divisions, even while she lived with two wealthy men as their partner for a significant period of time and thus violated conventional social structures by her very mode of life. Allia is described as having ruled (*rexit*) over her two young lovers (*iuvenes amantes*) so that they followed the example of Pylades and Orestes, with one house being sufficient for both of them: "*una domus capiebat eos unusque et spiritus illis*" (28–9). This is perhaps another instance of the author's desire to pun on Allia's sexual status. Pylades and Orestes, while famous for being close friends, were also frequently described in antiquity as same-sex lovers, suggesting a particularly close relationship among this trio. Furthermore, the idea of "one house" being sufficient for them also suggests Allia Potestas' own body as the metaphorical house. The list of praise for Allia Potestas continues, but it is constantly syncopated with sly allusions to her sexual desirability. She is both a paradigm of domesticity and an elegiac lover, simultaneously domineering mistress and obedient slave girl.

In the passage describing her physical charms, she is explicitly compared with a comic actress: "What legs! Such is the appearance of Atalanta as a comic actress" (21). This may merely reference a standard theatrical portrayal of the mythical character Atalanta in a short running tunic, which showed off the actress's legs, but it also associates Allia herself with acting and thus with the negative social reputation attached to actresses.[46]

Aulus characterizes Allia Potestas' body as *benigno*, kindly or generous, another word suggesting both virtue and promiscuity simultaneously. He emphasizes that she plucked all her body hair, which may be more associated with promiscuous women, although this is one area where we have relatively little evidence for Roman women.[47] Aulus praises her by telling us that *nosse fuit nullum studium, sibi se satis esse putabat, mansit et infamis, quia nil admiserat umquam*, "there was no passion for knowing more – she thought she knew enough, and she remained free from gossip, because she had committed no crime" 26–7.[48] Allia is not one of Juvenal's annoyingly intellectual women, certainly, but another pun can also be read here between the lines.[49] Allia has sexual knowledge of enough men; she does not think she needs more, and thus remains free of gossip by reserving herself for only her two lovers. This must be intended as self-aware irony; the neighbors undoubtedly whispered about a *ménage a trois* arrangement even if the woman was not openly sexually available to all comers. Aulus may also be contrasting their arrangement with an adulterous liaison; although Allia has multiple lovers, she has committed no crime because she is married to neither of them. She is neither a promiscuous whore nor a wicked wife. Aulus has amused himself by creating a paradoxical monument – an elegant and elaborate tomb for a *notissima* freedwoman, with lines that repeatedly pun on the similarity between *matrona* and *meretrix*. In the last line, Aulus describes Allia as "*Haec titulo insignis* (52)," this woman known by a label. While this may be simply a literal reference to the inscription on her gravestone and the fame which Aulus' poem will confer, a "*titulus*" can also refer to a sign or label above a prostitute's *cella* (e.g. Petronius, *Satyr.* 1.7).

Between Aulus' love for clever puns and his use of standard encomia, we are left with an ambiguous portrait of a virtuous yet unconventional, beautiful yet rough-handed, modest yet sexy woman. Aulus' discourse makes little attempt to represent a historical figure rather than a surprising and humorous conglomeration of character traits. We should not assume that Aulus did not truly love and wish to commemorate Allia: the size of the monument would make a very expensive joke, if that were its only motivation.

Nevertheless, Aulus' inscription, whether ironic or earnest, deliberately plays with the idea of the space between respectability and notoriety: he advances the notion that a woman could both have marvelous breasts and be a wonderful housekeeper and wool-worker. His fantasy of the perfect Roman woman challenges accepted notions of female virtue and morality; what matters is not Allia's social status but her loving and faithful relationship with her masters. Crucially, Allia "commits no crime" in this relationship; despite its basic unorthodoxy, fundamental social structures and hierarchies are all still maintained.

Conclusion

The existence of these stories about *meretriculae* in a variety of Roman genres and time periods suggest widespread cultural ambivalence about the definition of Roman women's virtue and the relationship of virtue to social status. As Seneca the Elder says, "Where is the prostitute?"[50] Whether or not a woman is a moral whore as well as a professional prostitute depends ultimately on the nature of her relationship to a man and a family.

These examples form a composite picture of the virtuous prostitute, the woman with the moral rectitude of a matron and the sexual lifestyle of the whore. To be a *bona meretrix*, one must not behave like a prostitute, according to the Roman conception of such behavior. The good little *meretricula* is defined almost entirely in opposition to the norm of Chapter 1's greedy, selfish prostitute. She is generous where the gold-digger is greedy, loyal where the *mala meretrix* is faithless, submissive rather than haughty, and even fertile where the gold-digger is either barren or deceptive.

Hispala Faecenia, for instance, financially supports her lover Aebutius when his immoral parents refuse to give him his inheritance, and makes him her heir in her will.[51] The selfless poisoner in Pseudo-Quintilian's *Declamationes Maiores* is also notable for her generosity. This new selfless prostitute also stands in opposition to the literary trope of the miserly wife. A current of anxiety about women and their control over money runs through much of Latin literature. The *uxor dotata* or dowried wife in Roman comedy, described briefly in Chapter 1, uses her financial powers to exert abnormal influence over her henpecked husband and sons; she is represented invariably as a figure deserving of both fear and mockery.[52] Despite legal restrictions requiring Roman women to have an official guardian, in practice many Roman women managed their own business affairs with little male supervision.[53] "Turia's" husband praises her explicitly for sharing her personal property with him and letting him exercise control over it; the implication is that such a decision is a comparatively rare and virtuous act.[54]

This ability of Roman wives to use economic power to gain influence within the familial hierarchy frequently bred resentment among impoverished men. For such men, both historical and fictional, the figure of the financially generous prostitute represented a counter to that of the miserly wife or greedy whore. The heart-of-gold prostitute offered both sexual and economic favors freely, out of love rather than duty. Her economic superiority did not lead to pressure on her clients, but rather, as in the case of Aebutius, relieved them from dependence on their own mothers. Thus, these characters ultimately serve to reaffirm the independence and power of the Roman male client.

Upon first glance, the heart-of-gold prostitute appears to undermine conventional social and moral categories, and, indeed, in her own transgression of boundaries she does break the normative Roman female moral hierarchy. However, while she disturbs female social distinctions, the *meretricula* simultaneously affirms and supports male hierarchies and the larger structures of Roman society. Hispala helps bring down a supposedly dangerous and foreign cult; the poisoner-prostitute ensures a conventional respectable future for her elite male lover; Allia makes a cozy home for her patrons. *Fas*, the proper way of doing things, is restored by these figures even while they themselves defy norms. The heart-of-gold prostitutes are not a societal threat but, through their virtuous behavior, a bulwark of order. They counter the Roman male anxiety about overly powerful courtesans and concubines, which will be discussed in

Chapter 3. Through their consciousness of their own place, they help to shore up the unstable position of elite male Romans within their society.

One of the other dominant characteristics of the heart-of-gold prostitute is her own acceptance of subordinate status. Male authors present the good prostitute as not only working for the restoration of the nuclear family but as acknowledging their own social inferiority. At the same time, these tales offer hope that, through virtuous and generous deeds, the prostitutes can transcend their previous lowly social positions and gain the respect of proper matrons.

The key distinction between a good prostitute and a good *matrona* is the prostitute's lack of family, which is itself related to her identification as a prostitute and usually as a slave or freedwoman. A *matrona*'s good deeds generally concern her family, and her virtue becomes a source of praise for her descendants. For instance, the "Laudatio 'Turiae'" honors "Turia" particularly for her loyalty to her murdered parents, her orphaned female relatives, and of course her husband.[55]

While Roman male authors may praise prostitutes for their generous and kindly attitudes towards their lovers, they still characterize these women as independent agents. In several cases, such as Bacchis in the *Hecyra* and Pseudo-Quintilian's potion-prostitute, their key virtuous act is their choice to sever a romantic relationship with a client. The *meretricula* is repeatedly and paradoxically defined as the prostitute who avoids sex and gives away her money. At the end of the *Hecyra*, Bacchis is once more alone; her reward is merely the cold comfort of knowing that she has acted morally and unlike a typical prostitute. Allia Potestas will not share a tomb with either of her lovers; her reward is her solitary funeral inscription and the promise that her statue will accompany Aulus into his own grave. Even if Seneca's prostitute has the chance to see her son adopted into a wealthy noble family, it seems clear that she herself will never be welcome among the respectable classes. These *bonae meretrices* act on their own initiative, without hope of reward, and without the chance to serve as moral lessons for their daughters and granddaughters.

Both morally and economically, the heart-of-gold prostitute is transgressive. She is better than she should be. However, she remains unthreatening because she accepts both her own subordination and that of all prostitutes; like Allia, she knows her place. This figure thus provides an opportunity for elite male authors to prescribe appropriate behavior for non-elite women. While they may possess "wifely" virtues, they are distinguished from true wives through their humility. The heart-of-gold prostitute is also notable for her self-awareness and truthfulness. Unlike either wicked wives or conventional whores, *meretriculae* do not pretend to be respectable matrons. They are honest and can be trusted by men to provide sex without repercussions or financial ruin.

To a certain extent, male anxiety about the subordinate behavior of prostitutes is undoubtedly correlated with the slave origins of most female sex workers. Just as freedmen were criticized for forgetting their former lowly status (cf. Petronius' *Satyricon*), we see here examples of freedwomen being praised for still conducting themselves like slaves. Once again, this particular character and type of story is used to reinforce existing social hierarchies for the benefit of the elite male. At the same time, the sexual relationships in these cases complicate the normal relationships between free and freedpeople, blurring the lines between dominant and subordinate partners. Aebutius is emotionally and financially dependent on Hispala; the man in the prostitute-poisoner case is upset precisely because his lover has freed him from his bonds of desire.

The *meretriculae* also offer an answer to the vexed question of whether freedwomen are legitimate members of the Roman state – citizens, if ones without political rights and tainted by legal *infamia*. Roman slaves are not described as patriots loyal to the state, regardless of their gender.[56] They are foreign objects within the body of the state, whose dishonesty and potential treachery is assumed, generally lacking in *fides* or *pietas*. In rare cases of crisis, Roman slaves must be bribed with offers of freedom in order to fight for the *res publica*.[57] Although stories of loyal slaves exist, their actions are described explicitly as unnatural, *hyper physin*.[58] Furthermore, the rare faithful slaves are generally those who risk their own lives on behalf of a just and kind master, not for Rome herself.[59]

In contrast, during the crisis of the Second Punic War in the late third century BCE, when Rome itself was in danger, Roman matrons offered up their jewelry in order to contribute to the war fund, "as much as they themselves chose."[60] While Roman wives are rarely threatened by external attack, they bravely defend their families and political factions in times of civil war.[61] As will be discussed in later chapters, Roman women of all backgrounds also serve the state through promoting and supporting fertility cults that enable them to produce more legionaries for the next generation.

The stories of *meretriculae* offer new *exempla* for women who are neither loyal wives nor unnaturally loyal slaves. Their demonstrations of support for the state and to the Roman social order are particularly necessary in these texts, because the stories often end with them sacrificing their ties to their male romantic partner so that he can pursue a more traditional and stable marital relationship. Hispala Faecenia risks her life and livelihood not just to save her boyfriend but to preserve the Roman state from chaos and debauchery. Bacchis and the poisoner-prostitute end their relationships so that their lovers may establish more suitable if less emotionally fulfilling ties. Such *exempla* serve to integrate the transgressive, threatening figure of the freelance freedwoman courtesan – the financially independent woman without a man, without a clear ethnic identity, and without definite ties to the Roman state – into the larger Roman community. Despite a servile and foreign origin, the good prostitute can become citizen-like in the same way that she becomes wife-like. The inherent transgressiveness and problematic category-blurring of the freelance courtesan is here blunted by this possible path in which she can serve both individual elite male needs and the Roman state and community as a whole.

There is no place for a sex worker, regardless of her virtue, kindness, or love, within the concept of the normal Roman family. If the family forms a microcosm of the larger society, there is equally little place for a prostitute, whatever her morality, within conventional social structures. The stereotype of the Whore remains the negative, feared Other in Roman gender discourse; at best, virtuous prostitutes can become almost-wives. Even Hispala Faecenia, who is given the chance to erase her *infamia* permanently by marrying a free man, has her story end with that opportunity rather than with a happy marriage itself. Livy suggests the potential for a change in status, but he is not so daring as actually to describe the way in which a woman might ever stop being a prostitute.

Nevertheless, these Roman texts choose to envision the character of a woman who merges the best aspects of prostitute and wife. Like a prostitute, she is physically beautiful and, due to her lack of natal family or dowry, always focused on the welfare and well-being of her lover. Like a good wife, she is financially generous, a good housekeeper and nurse, and brave in defending her mate. Like a good citizen, she is brave and sacrifices her own self-interest to defend Roman social hierarchies.

Perhaps these characters are simply wish-fulfillment fantasies of male authors who found the existing paradigms dissatisfying. However, by constantly contrasting the rare praiseworthy and generous prostitutes with more typical whores and wives, the authors still reinforce the general categories of Roman female virtue. Heart-of-gold prostitutes remain the exceptions to the rule, defined by their lack of typical characteristics as much as by their combination of wifely virtues and whorish submissiveness. They are a solution to the perceived problem of the ambitious whore and a reprimand to the figure of the promiscuous, assertive matron. It is no wonder that Roman male authors view them as a rare and unnatural ideal – the loving Galatea to their patron's Pygmalion.

3

Powerful concubines and influential courtesans

But business with the second class is so much safer –
I'm talking about freedwomen ...
What does it matter whether you sin with a matron or a toga-wearing maid?
Horace, Satires *1.2.47–63, trans. adapted from H. Rushton Fairclough*

On May 3, 49 BCE, the Roman Republican statesman Marcus Tullius Cicero wrote a letter to his dear friend Atticus about current gossip in Rome. "Marcus Antonius," (the famous Mark Antony), Cicero sputtered, "is carrying Cytheris about with him in an open litter, like a second wife."[1] Cytheris was a notorious actress and Antony's mistress, as well as the lover of various other prominent Roman politicians. At a dinner party two years later, Cicero was shocked to discover that Cytheris was also attending the party and reclining in a position of honor below the host, just as if she was the *materfamilias*. As soon as the party was over, Cicero immediately wrote his friend Paetus to share his titillated outrage. Having social interactions with such a courtesan, Cicero moralized, was technically acceptable, as long as it was clear that "*Habeo non habeor*," "I own her but I am not owned by her."[2]

A hundred and twenty years later, during the reign of the Emperor Vespasian in the 70s CE, Antonia Caenis, a freedwoman long-term concubine of the Emperor, had just returned to court after a trip of several months to the Balkans. She entered the imperial palace and went to the reception hall where Vespasian's two adult sons, Titus and Domitian, were holding court. "As usual (*ut assuerat*), Caenis offered a kiss, but the younger son, Domitian, held out his hand instead."[3] The nearly contemporaneous biographer Suetonius offers this anecdote as a shocking indication of Domitian's haughty and rude behavior. He cites it as an omen of Domitian's future career as an arrogant and cruel emperor. The story also offers a glimpse of some undoubtedly complex family dynamics; Domitian, an imperial prince, is expected to honor a freedwoman and his mother's unofficial replacement with respect and affection – as if she were a legitimate member of the imperial family. Of course, this may not be due to Domitian's inherent evil nature but rather more common interfamilial tensions. For the imperial family, private drama was enacted necessarily in public, much like it is for celebrity families today.

These two stories, which are representative of their time periods, reveal a stark contrast in attitudes towards ex-slave concubines. Cicero was shocked that a man of his social stature would be expected to have dinner with a woman like Cytheris, whereas Suetonius was outraged that the Emperor's son Domitian was unwilling to greet his father's mistress Caenis with a polite kiss. At the same time, both women are clearly public figures: Cicero assumes that Atticus knows Cytheris by both name and reputation, while Caenis appears openly in the imperial court (and travels on her own as well).

These two tales exemplify the general stereotypes that were used to shape narratives of historical Roman concubines in these two different eras, as well as the influence and power of such women. Relationships that caused disgrace during the late Roman Republic were subsequently valorized and praised during the high Empire. It was not the interaction between mistress and client that particularly changed, nor the nature of high-class Roman prostitution, but the political and social climate of Rome itself. In particular, the discourse about these "second-class women" in these two eras helps demonstrate that a leading criterion for female moral virtue was not just loyalty to a specific man, but support of the established patriarchal equilibrium.[4] Even women like Cytheris, who generally had only one patron at a time, could be condemned for disturbing the Roman aristocratic oligarchy. During the Principate, women like Caenis who wielded equal or greater influence were applauded because their relationships and acts upheld the Roman social pyramid, usually by indirectly denying power to more elite, well-established women.

Romans were unusual among ancient Mediterranean and Near Eastern peoples for both their monogamous marriages and their comparative levels of integration of women into the public sphere. Most ancient cultures practiced some form of resource polygyny, in which wealthy men would claim multiple women in various forms of official and unofficial relationships, while poor men often went unmarried.[5] While monogamous marriage has become normative in modern Western societies, the Greeks and Romans were highly unusual at the time in their emphasis on the importance of the tie between a single man and a single woman. Such an ideal was perhaps most famously expressed in the centrality of the Odysseus–Penelope relationship in Homer's *Odyssey*, despite Odysseus' numerous extramarital infidelities en route and Penelope's plethora of suitors.[6] The Romans and Etruscans were particularly notable for their emphasis on companionate marriage, rather than marriage purely for the purpose of procreation or economic alliance. As Foucault notes, the Roman philosopher Musonius Rufus places equal weight on the marital goals of offspring and "community" – what Homer calls "like-mindedness" – as well as praising physical desire within the context of marriage.[7]

As previously established, Roman matrons fulfilled not only the role of sexual companion but also of financial and familial partner in their husbands' lives. While respectable classical Athenian women were expected to remain inside the women's quarters of the house except for religious occasions, Roman wives sat in the open courtyard of their homes, and dined in mixed company.[8] It may seem that in such a social system, there was little room for an elite concubine or courtesan, since men could potentially find intellectual, emotional, and sexual fulfillment within marriage. At the same time, concubines did exist and often played an important role in Roman politics and society. Because of their anomalous, seemingly unnecessary position, however, such women generated much more social anxiety and tension among elite authors than they did in many other ancient societies.

While most Roman *meretrices* were poor streetwalkers and brothel girls serving undistinguished customers, a few women used their charms to gain unofficial positions of great influence, political power, and wealth within Roman society. Successful concubines and prosperous courtesans who were the long-term mistresses of powerful Roman men had potentially more indirect power than any other non-elite women in Roman society. The discourse about these women by their contemporaries and later chroniclers sheds light on the complexity of attitudes towards Roman prostitutes and on the interactions between elite, powerful men and sexually active, unmarried women. While most of these women were not paid by the act or hour, and most concubines maintained only a single sexual relationship at a time, the elite *meretrices* still occupied a liminal status that distinguished them fundamentally from the social status and roles of respectable wives.

Roman male attitudes towards high-status *meretrices* changed significantly from the Republic to the Augustan Age and High Empire. For instance, during the second century BCE, the proconsul L. Quinctius Flamininus was dismissed from the Senate on charges that his prostitute lover convinced him to gratuitously execute a Gaulish chieftain during a banquet.[9] In contrast, four hundred years later the concubine Marcia was praised for using her influence with the Emperor Commodus to spare dozens of Christian prisoners from the mines of Sardinia.[10]

In each case, a lover possessed inappropriate levels of influence over the justice system, but the Flamininus anecdote highlights the corruption and immorality associated with Republican prostitutes, whereas the later story represents Marcia as a virtuous woman sympathetic to the cause of the poor and religiously oppressed. These two tales, along with those of Cytheris and Caenis, exemplify the general stereotypes that were used to shape narratives of Roman concubines in these two different political eras. These women's stories also support the established historical pattern that autocratic monarchies in patriarchal societies tend to offer more power to women than republican or democratic governments in similar societies.[11]

From the late Republic through the high Empire, male authors accused Roman women from all backgrounds of subverting the political process and exercising undue influence over the men in their lives. The most prominent examples are probably Fulvia, wife of Marcus Antonius and Publius Clodius, Livia, wife of Augustus and mother of Tiberius, and Agrippina the Younger, wife of Claudius and mother of Nero.[12] These were all elite, wealthy women who exercised their power during times of political transition and uncertainty; they gained their power not only through their male relatives but through their own familial backgrounds and status. During the late Republic, however, male invective was particularly directed against ordinary freedwomen who wielded such power through extramarital liaisons, such as Cytheris, Praecia, and Chelidon.[13]

These accusations were all designed to tarnish the reputations of these women's lovers, powerful politicians like Marcus Antonius, C. Cethegus, and Gaius Verres, by effeminizing them and representing them as under the control of freedwomen. Lowell Edmunds refers to this inversion of the normal power dynamic as the "scale of power," in which women dominate their lovers or husbands who in turn rule Rome.[14] Power is represented according to this theory as a line – A rules B who rules C; this structure is consonant with the late Republican emphasis on the patron–client relationship. If a woman had excessive influence over a public official, she controlled Roman politics herself by proxy and thus endangered the fundamental hierarchy of government and of society itself. This reversal of the normal power structure becomes even more extreme when the women in question were themselves former slaves and publicly notorious. Social anxiety here focused on the permeability of the political hierarchy; were inappropriate people, either by class or gender, wielding influence in the waning days of an aristocratic oligarchy?

Disparaging anecdotes about the outrageous behavior of influential concubines were not used purely as a weapon to attack male political enemies. Authors like Cicero also sought to reinforce the ideal of the traditional Roman family controlled by a respectable *paterfamilias* and his devoted wife, even despite Cicero's own early financial dependence on his wife Terentia.[15] Men like Marcus Antonius, who publicly paraded the actress-prostitute Cytheris as a second wife (*altera uxor*), threatened Roman family values and the traditional social hierarchy.[16] According to an anecdote of Plutarch's, Roman elite women feared nothing so much as the potential of legalized polygyny.[17] Regardless of accuracy, such a story suggests the perceived fragility of the unusual Graeco-Roman monogamous family structure.

Tacitus and other Imperial-era authors, in contrast, living in a more cosmopolitan world than that of the late Republic, were relieved at the prospect of emperors having freedwomen mistresses, because such women did not come from dangerously ambitious elite families.[18] In eras where the imperial family itself represented a nexus of power, reducing the status of imperial women released more power for the male senatorial oligarchy. Emperors, especially those who already had heirs, could safely indulge themselves with relatively dependent, loyal freedwomen mistresses. Like the "good prostitutes" examined in Chapter 2, these women represented a combination of the faithful, devoted wife archetype and the alluring, sexually available prostitute, which contrasted with the possibility of a powerful conniving elite wife, as analyzed in Chapter 4. Nonetheless, while these imperial mistresses were lauded for their comparative harmlessness and dedication to their lover's interests, several of them still managed to achieve economic or political influence within the imperial court, suggesting another gulf between male fantasy and female reality. Unlike their Republican counterparts, however, their influence was largely ignored or even praised, rather than viewed as a sign of dangerous social upheaval.

This chapter examines Roman mistresses' social roles and influence on their elite lovers through four different lenses: women used as political bargaining chips to form alliances between two men, women who gained personal political power through manipulation of their lovers, women accused of using their influence over their powerful lovers in order to amass great personal wealth, and those concubines who achieved the unofficial but symbolically important status of an "almost-wife."

I focus on a set of eight notable courtesans and concubines who lived from the late Republic through the high Empire.[19] From the Republic, I examine Flora, best known as Pompeius the Great's mistress; Praecia, Cethegus' mistress; Chelidon, Gaius Verres' mistress; and Volumnia Cytheris, principally known as the favored courtesan of Marcus Antonius. From the Imperial period, I study the accounts of Acte, the Emperor Nero's first concubine; Antonia Caenis, Vespasian's long-time companion; Lysistrate, the primary concubine of Antoninus Pius, and Marcia, the extremely influential mistress of the Emperor Commodus.

Flora and Praecia were both prominent courtesans of the late Republic known for relationships with multiple men, who largely served as political pawns rather than having significant influence of their own. Chelidon and Volumnia Cytheris made their reputations primarily as the mistress of one prominent politician, although they likely had multiple relationships during their careers. They possessed high levels of political influence, social status, and wealth. In contrast, Acte, Caenis, and Lysistrate are praised for their faithful devotion to their emperor-lovers and their status as almost-wives, as well as noted for their financial profiteering through their relationships. Finally, Marcia was publicly married to Commodus' chamberlain while simultaneously serving as the Emperor's concubine and influential political advisor.

These particular concubines and courtesans were accused of assuming either elite male political roles, the privileges of elite wives, or both. Through analyzing the discourse about them, we can develop an overall understanding of Roman social attitudes towards women who transgressed so many distinct normative social barriers.

Source material and modern scholarship

As always, we are circumscribed by our sources and by their inherent biases. In this case, the main primary sources for the late Republican women are Cicero, a detailed if biased contemporary, and Plutarch, a Greek biographer writing three hundred years later, who may also have relied significantly on Cicero for source material. Cicero used the threatening idea of the dominant, emasculating, freedwoman courtesan in several of his rhetorical speeches.[20] Plutarch, however, tended to emphasize and glorify the role of women in politics whenever he found them.

During the Imperial period, the major sources are Tacitus, Cassius Dio, and the *Scriptores Historiae Augustae*. The *SHA* have a notable and unusual lack of sensationalist detail about most of the imperial concubines; they are described as a standard part of the imperial household. This does not necessarily render the imperial biographies more trustworthy than they usually are, but, at the least, they do not betray the traces of melodramatic exaggeration common to the descriptions of the emperors themselves, such as the caricature of young Elagabalus.

Few modern scholars have studied the influence of Roman freedwomen upon Roman politics and governmental policies; the lack of scholarship is particularly evident for the high Imperial period. While Rebecca Flemming argues that there is no evidence to support multiple social levels or classes of prostitutes, suggesting that the elite courtesan is purely a product of the Greek world, various ancient texts contradict this assertion.[21] In 9.32, Martial proclaims his desire for a cheap, streetwalking prostitute, who stands in contrast to the greedy *amica* or courtesan:

> I want an easy (*facilis*) mantle-wearing girl,
> who strolls around (*palliolata vagatur*);
> I want one who has already given herself to my slave;
> I want one who sells her whole self for a denarius or two ...
> The cock of a thick Burdigalan can have the kind of girl
> Who wants coins and talks big. (Martial 9.32)

Greedy girls and eloquent courtesans are here reserved for rich *parvenu* Gauls from Burdigala, modern Bordeaux. As Martial frequently does, he here expresses a desire for simplicity, cheapness, and nature over expensive artifice. Although our material and legal evidence for high-paid courtesans such as those who might have formed the basis for the elegiac women is highly limited, epigrammatists like Martial draw a sharp contrast between the cheap street girls and the expensive courtesans who "talk big" (*grandia verba sonantem*).[22] This suggests, at a minimum, that while the upper strata of Roman prostitutes may not have achieved the international celebrity status of some Greek *hetairai*, not all Roman prostitutes were lowly streetwalkers or brothel girls.[23] The specific case studies addressed in this chapter will further demonstrate that some Roman courtesans achieved positions of high if ambiguous social status and wealth through their liaisons with Roman noblemen.

Various scholars have recently addressed the legal aspects of Roman concubinage.[24] In the Roman Empire, concubinage generally served as a means for men of higher social status to form long-term relationships with women of lower status, especially freedwomen. Roman men could not legally have both a concubine and a wife simultaneously, although this restriction was only fully codified under Constantine.[25] According to epigraphic evidence for the early western Empire, freeborn men's non-marital relationships generally occurred with slaves and freedwomen rather than with freeborn women.[26] This is an unsurprising conclusion that also fits the surviving literary and legal sources.

Concubines were generally of lower social status than their partners, but there is much debate as to whether freeborn women ever engaged in concubinage, particularly among the poorer urban groups. In general, Treggiari's conclusion that concubinage was legal but discouraged for freeborn women is extremely plausible.[27] The possibility that freeborn women of higher social status engaged in concubinage with lower status men, particularly freedmen, is intriguing but goes beyond the scope of this chapter. Concubines were considered by the legal sources, however, to be either a subset of *meretrices* or functionally wives, and it is according to this rubric that we shall evaluate their representation as moral or immoral women.[28]

Courtesans of the Republic

Some freedwomen or slaves were used as bargaining chips between elite men to sweeten political deals or gain allies. Unlike the common exchange of respectable women in marriages to gain valuable allies, as in the case of the marriage of Julius Caesar's young daughter Julia to his senior ally Gn. Pompeius Magnus, prostitutes were not used as pawns in formal, permanent alliances.[29] In a marriage for political reasons, the woman possessed a certain level of status and insurance due to the protection of her natal family. She could potentially break the alliance if mistreated by her husband and return safely to her family. Freedwomen mistresses, in contrast, were often given as presents against their will, even if they technically had freed status, or were used as intermediaries for communication between two powerful men. Women like Pompeius' mistress Flora, Cethegus' lover Praecia, and Nero's concubine Acte were essentially the tools of elite male political leaders.[30]

The prostitute Flora was bartered for a political alliance between Pompeius Magnus and his friend Geminus during the 70s

BCE.[31] According to Plutarch, our only source on her, she was a woman of uncertain age and origin, presumably named after the goddess whose festival was publicly celebrated by prostitutes.[32] Geminus apparently fell in love with Flora but was refused by her, as she claimed a prior attachment to Pompeius. However, Geminus then appealed to Pompeius, who promptly gave his consent to the liaison and furthermore broke off his own relationship with Flora. While at first Flora appears to have the significant right of refusing lovers, suggesting a free status, the fact that her former partner Pompeius can "give" her to Geminus without her consent or desire indicates that she may have been his freedwoman or at least under significant obligation to him.

This story thus reveals the fragility of courtesans' supposed agency, at least when faced with pressure by elite and powerful men. Flora's initial right of choice is ultimately abrogated by Pompeius. Plutarch asserts that Flora "languished for some time afterwards, under a sickness brought on by grief and desire."[33] He uses the incident as a means of displaying Pompeius' attractiveness to women and ability to inspire love in them. Flora nevertheless carried a certain amount of value for these two young men; her trade between them helped cement their own relationship.

The exchange of women to form alliances is of course a long-established tradition in exogamous ancient societies. Generally, however, such exchanges involved a father bestowing his daughter on the son of another family and creating a permanent bond between two families. The trade of a prostitute here is markedly different: Flora passes from Pompeius' hands to those of Geminus, without any possible production of shared grandchildren or any permanent link between the families.

The only contemporaneous example of Roman wife-trading for political reasons is the transfer of the respectable matron Marcia, daughter of the politician L. Marcus Philippus, between the household of her former husband Marcus Porcius Cato Minor and the elderly orator Quintus Hortensius in 56 BCE.[34] This incident caused a fair degree of scandal and gossip, as the formation of a bond of *amicitia* through the sequential sharing of a wife was highly unorthodox.[35] In contrast, Flora's favors were a specific gift that Pompeius could bestow upon Geminus, rather than the initiation of a permanent bond between the two men. Alison Keith notes the formation of homosocial networks through "the display and/or exchange of slave- and freedwoman" and equates it with more conventional elite marriage alliances.[36] However, the prostitute's lack of family means that the woman functions more as a one-time gift than as an ongoing tie.

During the same period, Praecia, a woman described by Plutarch as an ordinary *hetaira*, served as a similar intermediary between the general Lucius Licinius Lucullus and the powerful politician Cornelius Cethegus. Plutarch describes her as someone who "used her associates (*entugchanousin*) and companions (*dialegomenois*) to further the political efforts of her friends (*philon*), and so added to her charms the reputation of someone who was a true comrade (*philetairos*) and a 'fixer' (*drasterios*) and had thus gained very great power."[37] Plutarch employs masculine adjectives to categorize Praecia's influence – she is described simultaneously as part of the "Old Boys' Network" and as a woman who gained power through her sexual favors. Various vocabulary choices of Plutarch in this passage, such as *entugchano*, could be interpreted both as friendly and as sexual; the innuendoes are deliberate given the subject material. *Philetairos*, for instance, is both someone who takes good care of (his) friends and someone who is very friendly. Applied to Praecia, it implies a certain degree of promiscuity.

According to Plutarch, Lucullus secured the governorship of Cilicia in 73 BCE by appealing to Praecia to use her influence with her lover Cethegus. It is not clear whether or not Lucullus and Praecia had a purely platonic relationship. Plutarch claims that her affections were won through "gifts and flattery;" he also mentions that being publicly seen with Lucullus was a *misthos* or wage for Praecia, a Greek term often used for prostitutes' fees.[38] Praecia, according to Plutarch, also desired to increase her own reputation by consorting with famous and powerful men like Lucullus. He conferred *fama* upon her; she returned his favor by introducing him to her lover Cethegus. In any case, Praecia's support was only effective because she caused Cethegus to advocate on Lucullus' behalf.[39] As soon as Lucullus had obtained Cilicia, he promptly ceased the friendship with the scandalous prostitute "fixer" and her influential lover. This was another singular deal rather than the formation of a long-term alliance.

During the 50s and 40s BCE, Publius Volumnis Eutrapelus, a wealthy Roman knight and probable freedman (given the Greek cognomen of "Trickster") used his own freedwoman, the previously mentioned Volumnia Cytheris, to gain important friends and improve his social status.[40] Cytheris was an accomplished *mima*, an actress in Roman farces. Mimes were marked by improvisation, lewd dialogue and actions, and sometimes, especially during the Floralia, by the public nudity of the actors and actresses. In any case, such a profession gave Cytheris public notoriety and *infamia*.

It is quite likely that Eutrapelus was an early lover of Cytheris himself, although he may later have found more profit in offering her services to friends and allies, or even, as Sarah Pomeroy optimistically suggests, letting her choose such liaisons herself.⁴¹ Treggiari notes that Eutrapelus, her patron, initially functioned as Cytheris' male relative in the same way that a father or brother would have, using her in order to establish valuable political alliances.⁴² However, rather than remaining as a permanent part of Eutrapelus' *familia*, Cytheris was able to use his connections as a springboard to establish far more valuable and prominent later liaisons than her relationship with him.⁴³

It was certainly disgraceful, at least according to the view of conservative orators like Cicero, to keep regular company with an actress, regardless of her legal status. Cytheris may well have been able to purchase her own freedom through her earnings as an actress or as a prostitute, or she may have been freed as a reward for prior services. In any case, freedom did not remove her from obligations to her patron, and initially she still functioned as his political pawn.

Cytheris' first appearance in the historical record is as the publicly acknowledged lover of the propraetor Marcus Antonius in May of 49 BCE, shortly after Caesar had taken over Rome and subsequently departed to wage the civil war in Spain.⁴⁴ Eutrapelus was Marcus Antonius' *praefectus fabrum*, an important and profitable managerial post, although we do not know of any direct connection between his position and Cytheris' relationship with Antonius.

Cytheris does seem to have exercised a certain degree of political influence: in January of 47 BCE, Cicero wrote his wife Terentia about a failed attempt to gain a favor from a woman named Volumnia, who is likely synonymous with Volumnia Cytheris.⁴⁵ In any case, Cicero told Terentia that "Volumnia ought to have been more attentive to you than she has been, and even what she has done she might have done with greater zeal and caution."⁴⁶ If this Volumnia was Cytheris, then even the contemptuous Cicero and haughty Terentia found it necessary to seek her support when trying to regain admittance to Italy after Pompeius' defeat.

This letter also suggests more social contact between elite wives and prominent courtesans than has previously been imagined. Cytheris is viewed as a natural contact for Terentia's female–female negotiations, despite her lower social status. The notion that elite Roman women generally sought favors from other women rather than men, when possible, is borne out by Hortensia's speech in 42 BCE, where she declares that she and other senatorial women first sought aid from Octavian's sister Octavia, Antonius' mother Julia, and Antonius' wife Fulvia when complaining about a new tax levied on them. They only took to the Roman Forum for Hortensia's speech after Fulvia threw them out of her atrium.[47] In this case, however, Cytheris functions as Antonius' female point of contact, perhaps because he was temporarily unmarried, having divorced his wife Antonia Hybrida and not yet married Fulvia.

The next documented appearance of Cytheris is at the dinner party of Eutrapelus in 46 BCE, attended and chronicled by Cicero, and discussed briefly at the beginning of this chapter.[48] Cicero was a friend of Eutrapelus, with whom he apparently shared a passion for literature.[49] While this incident does not depict any particular political role or influence displayed by either Cytheris or Eutrapelus, it does suggest that Eutrapelus continued to exhibit Cytheris in semi-public settings as a means of impressing his companions.

Cicero himself was apparently somewhat shocked by the presence of a prostitute at a respectable Roman dinner party, claiming to Atticus that "he had no suspicion she would be there," but he also emphasized that concubines were tolerable fellow guests, even to philosophers like himself, as long as they "are not the master."[50] For Cicero, concubines are socially acceptable, if risqué, but they must be aware of the "scale of power." This story also implies that, even after her relationship with Antonius had begun, Cytheris remained in a close patron–client relationship with Eutrapelus. Appearing at elite dinner-parties may have been part of Cytheris' duties to her former master. Such displays served as a mark of Eutrapelus' pride in his patronage of a famous and attractive actress, despite her unorthodox social status.

Cytheris was one of the first Roman courtesans to be treated with a high degree of respect. Social conservatives like Cicero, however, reacted to such pandering with outrage and indignation. When Antonius was carrying Cytheris around in his litter "like a second wife" in 47 BCE, Antonius was already married at that time to his cousin Antonia Hybrida. His display of Cytheris was scandalous because it forced a public recognition of the relationship between the most powerful man present in Rome and a notorious *meretrix*. The *Boni* conservative political faction could do little to stop Antonius' blatant parade of his mistress. Furthermore, this parade blends the traditional triumphal procession, which emphasized male political and military dominance, with the raucous prostitutes' parade during the Floralia, as discussed later in Chapter 7. Cytheris' presence at Antonius' side implicitly crosses both social and religious boundaries.

Antonius may have displayed Cytheris deliberately to annoy men like Cicero and in order to demonstrate his own disregard for contemporary mores. Cicero repeatedly mentions this public parade of Cytheris and Antonius, emphasizing the presence of Antonius' lictors, which appeared to give official governmental sanction to the excursions.[51] Cytheris' presence in Antonius' litter was particularly scandalous because Roman matrons cherished their privilege of riding in litters or carriages, as known from the historical dispute over the *lex Oppia*.[52] Roman prostitutes typically walked on the street. Therefore, the means of transportation became a method of defining social status for women, implying that Cytheris here flouted social convention at multiple levels.

The "parade of prostitutes" is mentioned by a variety of later sources, including Plutarch and Pliny the Elder, who are all likely referencing either Cicero's original indignant comments to Atticus or his later denunciation of Antonius in the *Philippics*. By the time of Cicero's formal speeches attacking Antonius in the fall of 43 BCE, he had significantly elaborated on the original tale of Cytheris and the litter:

> The tribune [Antonius] was carried in a chariot, lictors crowned with laurel preceded him; among whom, on an open litter, was carried an actress; whom honorable men [greeted] not by the name by which she was well known on the stage, but by that of Volumnia. A carriage followed full of pimps (*lenonibus*); then a lot of debauched (*nequissimi*) companions; and then his mother, utterly neglected, followed the mistress (*amicam*) of her profligate son, as if [Cytheris] had been her daughter-in-law ... If you had no shame before the municipal towns, had you none even before your veteran army? For what soldier was there who did not see her at Brundisium? (Cicero, *Philippics* 2.58–61)

It is difficult to tell whether the addition of the pimps and debauched companions is factual or merely one of Cicero's stylistic embellishments to emphasize his invective, several years after the events in question. Certainly, the latter hypothesis seems rather more plausible. In any case, regardless of the facts, the additions to the account emphasize Cytheris' misrepresentation as a respectable matron – she is addressed as Volumnia, a citizen woman's name, by local magistrates, and given the status of a daughter-in-law, preceding Antonius' mother Julia in the procession. Cytheris claimed a status to which she had no right, and Cicero retroactively claims to have been horrified at both her transgression and Antonius' outrages.

Cicero also jokingly refers to Antonius as *noster Cytherius*, our Cytherian, suggesting that Antonius had taken his female lover's name, rather than Cytheris marrying into his family.[53] In the *Philippics*, Cicero also calls Antonius himself a *meretrix* and claims that he practiced the trade of a *volgare scortum*, a public streetwalker. Furthermore, Cicero accuses Antonius of wearing a *muliebrem togam*, a woman's toga, referring to the togas worn by female prostitutes, and jokes that he was "rescued" from his profession by his supposed male lover, C. Scribonius Curio.[54] In Cicero's rhetoric, Antonius loses his privileged status as an elite senator and even as a proper man, because he behaved like a *meretrix* himself and treated a prostitute like a wife. Antony, despite his considerable actual power, is represented as under the sexual subjugation of someone else.[55] Cicero repeatedly focuses on this issue of violated normative social boundaries and transgressive behavior, as will be seen again in Chapter 4 with regard to his attack on Clodia Metelli. This may be due to Cicero's own politically ambiguous status as a *novus homo* or simply because of its effectiveness as political rhetoric aimed at traditional Roman noblemen.

Cytheris' extreme public visibility defines her as an especially notorious and immoral woman. Every soldier in Brundisium is expected to have seen her, and perhaps even to have known her sexually. Cicero redefines Cytheris as notorious rather than notable; her public presence is a matter for shame rather than pride. Furthermore, her presence in the army camp discredits Antonius himself, who is again diminished to the status of an effeminate man dependent on women, rather than being portrayed as a brave Roman warrior.

Plutarch's account of the aforementioned parade is even more sensational, although of dubious accuracy given its late authorship:

When [Antonius] went on his progress, [Cytheris] accompanied him in a litter ... and common women and singing girls were quartered upon the houses of serious fathers and mothers of families. (Plutarch, *Antonius* 9.4)

Cytheris is specifically characterized as a professional actress, one of a group of entertainers, and Antonius is accused of forcing *patres* and *matresfamilias* to accept prostitutes and entertainers into their homes. Antonius' imposition doubly erases social divisions: Cytheris plays the role of a matron while the true matrons are forced to house prostitutes. This inversion of appropriate social standards reflects the later attempts to portray Antonius as the opposite of Octavian and the enemy of all traditional Roman values. It presages his later alleged subjugation to the foreign queen Cleopatra, herself reviled as a *meretrix*.[56]

Caesar, upon his return from Spain and Gaul, sternly rebuked Antonius for his luxurious and decadent behavior; Antonius either chose or was forced to sever his ties with Cytheris. In the *Philippics*, Cicero describes this breakup in terms of a divorce:

> He desired that mistress of his (*illam suam*) to take possession of whatever belonged to her, according to the laws of the Twelve Tables [concerning traditional *usucapio* divorce]. He has taken his keys from her, and turned her out (*clavis ademit exegit* ... Nothing is more honest in his life than when he made a divorce with an actress (*quod cum mima divortium*). (Cicero, *Philippics* 2.69)

Cicero deliberately chooses the formal language of divorce, including the repossession of the household keys, in a rhetorical device intended to emphasize both the importance and the inappropriate nature of Antonius' relationship with Cytheris: he has treated her like a wife in metaphorically giving her the keys to his house and chests. Furthermore, Cicero suggests that Antonius only "divorced" Cytheris for financial reasons, not out of a desire to return to sober propriety.[57] Even the end of this affair does not return Antonius to moral sanctity, as it is caused by greed.

Cytheris' other purported relationships, with Cornelius Gallus the poet and, more dubiously, with Marcus Brutus the assassin of Caesar, do not seem to have been motivated by political connections or arranged by Eutrapelus.[58] Eutrapelus, in his capacity as a literary patron, might have introduced Gallus to Cytheris, but we have no actual evidence for this hypothesis. It is possible that Cytheris, under Eutrapelus' guidance, pursued a consistent series of lovers who were members of Antonius' political faction. According to Vergil's *Eclogues*, Cytheris or at least her poetic persona, Lycoris, eventually deserted Gallus in favor of a new lover, a soldier en route to the Alps.[59] In the tense conflicts of the late 40s and early 30s between the Antonian, Octavian, and "Republican" factions, Cytheris may well have simply sympathized with her original lover and felt loyalty towards the Antonian factions, whereas Gallus supported Octavian.

Cicero accused Antonius of settling some of the legionary veterans' retirement land in Campania on *mimos et mimas*; Traina suggests that Cytheris herself may have profited from this generosity.[60] However, there is no direct evidence of such a gift. Cytheris certainly received many gifts from her lovers, but we cannot prove that she illegally received soldiers' lands. We do not know Cytheris' eventual fate. Augustan Rome may have been a less tolerant environment for proud, aging actress-prostitutes who had tried to claim the status and respect reserved for elite matrons. Alternatively, she may have simply retired into Eutrapelus' household. Either way, she departed the stage at the dawn of the Roman Principate.

While Flora and Cytheris served largely as the sexual objects of powerful Roman senators, valuable only because of their attractiveness, other courtesans and concubines managed to affect governmental policies during the Republic and were accused of virtually taking over official male roles in government. I do not wish to overestimate the power of these women. Stories of their influence were often intended to degrade their lovers rather than to glorify the mistresses themselves. The change towards a more positive attitude regarding such figures in Imperial times will become particularly evident as we examine the representation of these women as political agents.

During the same period in the late Republic when Flora and Praecia were prominent, the freedwoman Chelidon exercised power over much of Rome through her influence over Gaius Verres, urban praetor during the year 74 BCE. Our only source for Chelidon's life and role in Roman politics are Cicero's speeches *Against Verres*.[61] These orations are primarily directed against Verres' abuses in Sicily while governor there, but they also detail other instances of corruption during Verres' lengthy career.

As such, Cicero's testimony is highly biased and designed to tar Verres with the traditional charge of domination by a woman, made more spectacular by the idea of subordination to a *meretrix*.[62] While this may cause us to doubt the historicity of his account, the anecdotes that Cicero chronicles in his speeches are intended to portray a woman of almost unparalleled direct political power:

They resolve that the best thing they could do, which indeed might have occurred to any one, was to beg Chelidon for her aid. She, while Verres was praetor, was not only the real judge in all civil law, and in the disputes of all private individuals, but was also supreme in this affair of the repairs of the public buildings. Gaius Mustius, a Roman knight and tax-farmer (*publicanus*), a most honorable man, came to Chelidon … With what shame, with what suffering, do you think that such men as these went to the house of a prostitute? These are men who would have encountered such disgrace on no account, unless the urgency of their duty and of their relationship to the injured youth had compelled them to do so. (Cicero, *In Verrem* 1.136–7)[63]

Chelidon, despite her lowly and female status, is uniquely described as "the real judge in all civil law," the arbiter of private disputes, and the commissioner of public buildings. In other words, according to Cicero, she is in charge of all the internal judicial affairs of the city of Rome itself. It is precisely Chelidon's status as a *meretrix* that renders her influence over Verres so damning: she taints the praetor with her own *infamia*.[64] Indeed, Cicero claims that Chelidon's notorious reputation stains all those with whom she comes in contact: even sober gentlemen were forced to face the *turpitudinem* of association with a prostitute.

The specific nature of Cicero's example and the legal setting suggests that this particular political intercession by Chelidon may in fact have occurred. However, Cicero provides only two such concrete examples of Chelidon's influence. His generalizations concerning Chelidon's ubiquitous control of Roman affairs and her usurpation of the role of praetor are almost certainly rhetorical exaggerations. On the other hand, there were more than sufficient criticisms of Verres' character available. Cicero's emphasis on Chelidon suggests both the height of her authority and the degree to which such power infuriated his sensibilities and those of the jury.

Chelidon is not only accused of assuming the duties of a public official but also of usurping the role of a formal patron; such an act mocked the structure of the patron–client system that informally governed elite Roman society in the late Republic. She threatened the social order not just by influencing Verres but by directly exercising political power. Cicero added a lengthy description of Junius' and Titus' visits to her house, paralleling it to the traditional morning calls paid on important political patrons by their clients:

> They came, as I say, to Chelidon. The house was full; new laws, new decrees, new decisions were being solicited … Some were paying money; some were signing documents. The house was full, not with a prostitute's train, but rather with a crowd seeking audience of the praetor… (Cicero, *In Verrem* 1.137–8)

Chelidon's house, and, metaphorically, her genitalia, were stuffed full of men. While normally the Roman elite would consult renowned advocates such as Cicero himself, in this year they sought the expensive advice of the courtesan Chelidon. Furthermore, Chelidon's position made a mockery of any attempt to exercise proper justice, as Verres was willing to listen to her regardless of the merits of the case. The parallels between prostitute and politician could hardly be more explicit: rather than a train of clients for sex, Chelidon has a gathering of men seeking political favor. She wears the toga of a *meretrix*, not a praetor.

Furthermore, Cicero claims that Chelidon drove Verres' own political ambitions, claiming, "when he was made praetor, leaving the house of Chelidon after having taken the auspices, he drew the lot of the city province, more in accordance with his own inclination and that of Chelidon, than with the wish of the Roman people."[65] Chelidon may even have focused particularly on the inheritance rights of women; Cicero refers

to a case where Verres denied an inheritance to an orphan heiress after a
bribe by her distant male relative and remarks:

> Who would ever believe that Verres would be an adversary of women? Or did he
> do something contrary to the interests of women, in order that the whole edict
> might not appear to have been drawn up at the will of Chelidon? (Cicero, *In
> Verrem* 1.105)

This claim suggests that Chelidon might generally have influenced Verres
to give favorable decisions to women, although it may well be simply
another smear on Verres' supposed domination by a lowly female. Cicero
views women as natural allies with each other, despite the lack of any
known social relationship between this respectable orphaned maiden and
the notorious prostitute.

    Chelidon died shortly after 74 BCE. Cicero mentions that Verres had
received an inheritance from the deceased Chelidon sometime between 73
and 71 BCE; he specifically refers to valuable accoutrements (*ornamenta*)
as a part of this inheritance.[66] This may imply that Chelidon was Verres'
own freedwoman, as he would then be her patron and traditionally enti-
tled to some sort of inheritance. However, she may have simply bequeathed
her fortune out of affection to her lover. In any case, it suggests strongly
that Chelidon profited financially either from her activities as a prostitute
or from her peddling of access to the urban praetor, as she had substantial money to bequeath. Since the inheritance included ornaments, at least
some of her wealth was probably in the form of jewelry and items of clothing. As we know from the first-century BCE elegies, such baubles were
traditional gifts to prostitutes in return for their services.[67]

    Chelidon was replaced in Verres' embraces by two other influential
prostitutes, Tertia and Pippa, who were of even lower original social status but also apparently affected the path of politics during Verres' Sicilian
praetorship.[68] We have no other references to Tertia or Pippa, but Tertia
was definitely an infamous woman of lowly social status, since she was
the daughter of an actor and the former mistress of a flute-player. Even
after the death of the "praetor" Chelidon, new lovers supposedly drove
Verres to greater depths of excess and greed. While we should be rightly
suspicious as to the actual crimes of these women or the extent of their
power, their historical existence and status as Verres' prostitute mistresses
is highly likely, as this sort of information would have been readily available to both Cicero and the defense counsel, Hortensius. Verres may well
have been motivated more by his own greed and lust than by the blan-
dishments of his concubines. However, the Verrine orations relate a story

of almost unparalleled direct power for a freedwoman *meretrix* in Roman Republican politics. While the speeches' purpose is to attack Verres, they reveal elite male anxiety about the intrusion of freedwomen prostitutes into the masculine world of politics, echoing a similar although distinct anxiety about male freedmen.[69]

Concubines of the Principate

Acte was a freedwoman from Asia Province who became the mistress of the Emperor Nero in the mid-first century CE. She apparently remained devoted to him for his entire life. While Acte was not a professional prostitute, her informal, ambiguous status as one of many imperial concubines gives her the same sort of liminal social status as Cytheris or Praecia.

Acte, unlike the Republican courtesans, was praised for her loyalty and devotion to Nero. At the same time, her presence and influence in the imperial palace became yet another component of the general representation of the Emperor's corruption and debauchery. The first mention of Acte in Tacitus' *Annales*, our major source about her, occurs shortly after Nero's accession to the throne at the age of 17 in 54 CE. The couple remained romantically involved at least until the year 58, when Nero married Poppaea Sabina.[70] Nero was already married in 54 to his cousin Octavia. However, this marital tie proved no barrier to the liaison with Acte:

Meanwhile his mother's [Agrippina Minor's] influence was gradually weakened, as Nero fell in love with a freedwoman named Acte … and even the prince's older friends did not thwart him, for here was a girl who without harm to any one fulfilled his desires, since he loathed his wife Octavia, high born as she was, and of well-known (*nobili*) virtue. (Tacitus, *Annales* 13.12)

This relationship was actively sponsored, if not created, by Nero's friends and, in particular, by the political faction opposed to Agrippina. From the beginning, Tacitus represents Agrippina, the most important woman in this section of the *Annales*, as highly antagonistic towards Acte. Either due to Agrippina's power or some sense of propriety, Acte was initially passed off as the mistress of Nero's friends Otho, Senecio, and Serenus, while Nero himself saw her secretly.[71] She is described as a *muliercula nulla cuiusquam iniuria*, a harmless little woman. In Tacitus' narrative, Acte is a counterpart and foil to Agrippina – the submissive, obedient, loving woman as opposed to the controlling, domineering, aggressive figure of Nero's mother.

Since Nero hated his wife, his advisors reasoned, it was better for him to have a harmless sexual outlet than to pursue debauchery with respectable women, who might either be insulted or use the affair to gain power. Acte's lowly social status made her unthreatening, precisely because she was not an elite woman from a powerful family. The mention of "older friends" in these passages probably refers particularly to Nero's tutor and advisor, Seneca the Younger:

> Agrippina, however, raved with a woman's scorn about having a freedwoman for a rival and a slave-girl for a daughter-in-law … Nor would she wait till her son repented or tired of his passion. The fouler her reproaches, the more powerfully did they inflame Nero, until, completely mastered by the strength of his desire, he threw off all respect for his mother, and put himself under the guidance of Seneca.[72]

In this passage, the primary target of Tacitus' invective is of course Agrippina herself. Having initially emphasized Agrippina's power and influence, he now represents her as possessing the typical feminine vices of excessive emotion and a lack of self-control. She is angry *in modum muliebriter*, in a woman's manner. Furthermore, her particular rage is focused on issues of the household – she is unwilling to accept such a lowly freedwoman as a putative daughter-in-law (and empress, who would outrank her). Although Tacitus elsewhere represents Agrippina as having an unfeminine concern with politics and government, he here emphasizes her gender by suggesting that Agrippina has a typical motherly concern about status and familial issues. Agrippina is not afraid that Nero is hurting the state of Rome by consorting with Acte; she rather complains that he diminishes the nobility and social status of their family.

Acte herself is a mere object for their rivalry; her actual personality and motives disappear entirely from the text. However, Tacitus portrays Nero's relationship with Acte as the spark for a major power shift within the imperial household. In the early years of his reign, Agrippina served as Nero's regent and held great power. However, as a result of her contempt for the slave-girl Acte, Seneca gained Nero's ear and seized control of the malleable young ruler. Indeed, Seneca apparently actively sponsored and promoted this relationship through his friend Serenus. The entire affair might thus have been one part of larger political machinations to remove Agrippina from her position of power, at least according to Tacitus' account.

Acte appears in the accounts of Nero's life on two more occasions. Agrippina, desperate to regain power, eventually allegedly tried to seduce her own son. Seneca responded by bringing in Acte as an intermediary in order to broach the difficult subject with Nero and warn him of his danger: "Seneca sought a female's (*femina*) aid against a woman's fascinations, and hurried in Acte, the freedwoman, who alarmed at her own peril and at Nero's disgrace, told him that the incest was notorious, as his mother boasted of it, and that the soldiers would never endure the rule of an impious sovereign."[73] Acte is here again used as a pawn by Seneca to undermine Agrippina's influence. It is unclear how Acte supposedly knows the soldiers' opinion on the matter; presumably Seneca had coached her. In any case, whether represented as a pawn or a political figure in her own right, Acte again makes a move against Agrippina's power and successfully encourages Nero to further repudiate his mother's influence. Since she is allied with the largely positive figure of Seneca in the *Annales*, Acte is represented as a rare virtuous woman in the *Annales*, along with the doomed and generally ignored Octavia.

Epigraphic and papyrological evidence suggest that Acte possessed considerable property and wealth, presumably as a result of gifts from her lover. She had considerable lands in North Africa, for instance, as well as being able to spend the extravagant sum of 200,000 *sestertii* on Nero's funeral and burial.[74] Tacitus seems to praise Acte for this supposed act of generosity, rather than criticizing her for her wealth or ostentation, and the public commemoration of her property also suggests that her economic success was neither hidden nor viewed as shameful.

Suetonius and Cassius Dio further emphasize the importance of the relationship, implying that Nero treated Acte as his primary romantic partner, despite his simultaneous marriage to Octavia. Suetonius claims, "he all but made the freedwoman Acte his lawful wife (*quin iusto sibi matrimonio coniungeret*), after bribing some ex-consuls to perjure themselves by swearing that she was of royal birth."[75]

Cassius Dio adds to this account by suggesting that Nero tried to have Acte adopted into the Attalids, the royal family of Pergamum; there is no indication that Acte's original slave background was at all lofty.[76] However, this act does suggest the magnitude of Nero's passion and Acte's own position of influence. Dio argues that Agrippina's anger came specifically from being displaced as the most powerful woman in the palace by Acte.[77] The attempted royal adoption and marriage never came to fruition, probably because of the entry in 58 CE of Nero's new love interest, the elite, wealthy, and married Poppaea Sabina.

According to Tacitus, Poppaea goaded Nero into marriage by claiming that she did not wish to risk an illegitimate liaison with him when she had a respectable and lofty marriage already, whereas he was "tied down to a concubine housemaid through his attachment to Acte, and that he had derived nothing from his slavish associations but what was low and degrading."[78] For Poppaea, her rival Acte was not the innocent, harmless object of Nero's passion; rather, Poppaea refigures Acte as a negative influence who degraded the social status of the Emperor and taints him with *infamia*. Tacitus uses *paelice*, a Latin transliteration of the Greek *pallake*, here, both hinting at Acte's Greek foreigner status and invoking the Greek concept of the *pallake* as a long-term, live-in concubine or mistress of lowly social status.

Tacitus, who was sympathetic to neither Nero nor Poppaea Sabina, also explores issues of comparative social status and morality in this passage. While Acte was a freedwoman, she did not goad Nero into further excesses or crimes; indeed, most of Nero's policies during his early reign were relatively benign. In contrast, in order for Poppaea to marry Nero, Octavia had to be removed from the equation, and that meant a variety of preliminary murders and other foul crimes, including Nero's infamous extensive attempts at matricide. Tacitus' description of Poppaea is far more negative than his picture of Acte; the matron is more immoral than the slave-girl and a far more malign influence upon Nero. In particular, Poppaea's political influence over Nero and her advancement of her natal family is a threat to the power of the male politicians and philosophers like Seneca who had previously held sway.

Acte's last appearance emphasizes her devotion and loyalty to her emperor and former lover; she is portrayed as highly virtuous and characterized in the same terms as the *bonae meretrices* of Chapter 2. After the disgraced Nero's suicide, at a time when the entire city of Rome was in uproar and chaos, Suetonius tells us that his old nurses and Acte quietly took his body and buried him with appropriate rites.[79] The burial was paid out of Acte's own purse, and they deposited his ashes in the family tomb of the Domitii.[80]

Like a loyal freedwoman and a devoted lover, Acte paid her respects to Nero's grave, even after losing her own status as his dominant concubine and witnessing Nero kill his mother and both of his legitimate wives. In the *Annales*, a set of stories that feature many dangerous and highly ambitious women, Acte is represented as the ideal loyal servant, a woman who loved Nero the man rather than the emperor. Although she is described as "all but a wife," Tacitus largely uses her as a foil to compare favorably with the other powerful women in Nero's life, Agrippina and Poppaea Sabina. Acte was focused on Nero's own interests, just as a proper Roman *matrona* should be, whereas Agrippina and Poppaea were both greedy and personally ambitious. Just as Livy used Hispala Faecenia to emphasize the wickedness and impropriety of the Bacchanalian matrons, here Acte becomes a useful foil not to denigrate Nero but to attack elite women who ought to know better and behave better. As the harmless, good little concubine, she is preferable to the ambitious and intellectual empresses.

Caenis, the official concubine of the Emperor Vespasian, also gained significant influence and wealth as a result of her relationship with the Emperor. We do not know Caenis' precise social origins, but we can date her lifespan from roughly 11 CE or earlier to 75 CE.[81] Cassius Dio tells us that she was already the private secretary of the Julio-Claudian matron Antonia the Younger, in 31 CE; in that year she wrote a letter for Antonia denouncing Sejanus to the Emperor Tiberius.[82] Caenis was involved with Vespasian romantically both during the 30s and again in the 50s and 60s CE after the death of Vespasian's wife.[83]

Cassius Dio claims a high degree of influence and power for Caenis in the general realm of the imperial court:

And not only for this reason does she seem to me to have been a remarkable woman, but also because Vespasian took such excessive delight in her. This gave her the greatest influence and she gained incredible wealth, so that it was even thought that he made money through Caenis herself as his intermediary. For she received vast sums from many sources, sometimes selling governorships, some-times procuratorships, generalships and priesthoods, and in some instance even imperial decisions. For although Vespasian killed no one on account of his money, he did spare the lives of many who gave it. While it was Caenis who received the money, people assumed that Vespasian willingly allowed her to do as she did. (Cassius Dio 64.14)

Caenis fits readily into the Chelidon mold of the greedy, politically active concubine; she perverted the normal Roman administrative sys-tem in order to serve her own needs. However, in Caenis' case this is not depicted as a dire offense against appropriate roles for women or even as a sin against Rome itself. Rather, the assumption is that Caenis served as an intermediary for Vespasian, and that he allowed her to take lobbying fees. Furthermore, she is represented as merciful; she took bribes to spare lives, not ruin them, in contrast to the alleged callousness of Chelidon, who sold her influence to the highest bidder.

Vespasian and Caenis had a relationship both before and after Vespasian's official marriage to Flavia Domitilla; however, they appar-ently did not maintain their romance while he was married. This implies that Caenis had a semi-formal status that was incompatible with

Vespasian's simultaneous marriage to another woman.[84] According to Suetonius, after the resumption of their relationship Caenis possessed a very lofty if still unofficial status:

> After the death of his wife he resumed his relations with Caenis, freedwoman and amanuensis of Antonia, who was formerly his chosen companion; and even after he became Emperor he treated her almost as a lawful wife.[85]

In the 30s CE, Caenis was Vespasian's "chosen woman (*dilectam*)," a special relationship but certainly not an official one, particularly given the label of their liaison as *contubernium*. This term, according to Treggiari, normally described an informal relationship between a slave and another person.[86] This may also suggest that Caenis was a slave and not yet freed during the pair's initial romance. After the production of legitimate heirs and the death of his wife Flavia, however, Caenis, now a freedwoman, had a much loftier position with Vespasian and stood in the place of a wife. The "almost" (*paene*)"is a crucial insertion here; Caenis cannot quite conquer the barriers of her lowly position as a freedwoman.

From Flavia's death forward, Caenis served as Vespasian's acknowledged concubine and, as noted at the beginning of this chapter, part of his family. Caenis must have been nearly sixty when Vespasian became Emperor; it is a tribute to the long affection between the pair that she remained Vespasian's mistress for so many years. We do not know the date of her death, although Vespasian took other mistresses after her, so she must have preceded him into the grave.

Lysistrate, the official concubine of the Emperor Antoninus Pius during the mid-second century CE, also exercised direct political power through her relationship with her lover and received a relatively favorable treatment from ancient writers.[87] After his wife Faustina the Elder died in 141 CE, twenty years before the Emperor's own death, Antoninus may have preferred a lengthy relationship with a companion who bore no risk of producing legitimate heirs. Any new children would have complicated the succession of his adopted sons Marcus Aurelius and Lucius Verus. This choice also avoided the dangers of remarriage to an elite woman from a powerful family who would advance her own sons' interests.

The unreliable *Historia Augusta* claims that Lysistrate arranged jobs for her political allies: "[The prefect of the praetorian guard]'s place, upon his death, he [Antoninus] filled with two prefects, Furius Victorinus and Cornelius Repentinus. But Repentinus came under fire through a rumor that he had reached the prefecture through the agency of the Emperor's concubine."[88] In this case, unusually for the Imperial period, Repentinus was hurt by the taint of his connection with a concubine, although the negative reaction may be more due to Repentinus' other lack of qualifications for his lofty post rather than an association with a woman who possessed *infamia*. However, we may see here indications of a mild backlash against powerful concubines within the imperial court.

Marcus Aurelius also took a concubine after the death of his wife Faustina in 175 CE, five years before his own death. We do not know the name or origin of this woman, although she was of low enough status that she was not a reasonable marriage possibility: "He took for himself as a concubine the daughter of his wife's procurator, so as not to place a stepmother over all his children."[89] While the procurator could have been a slave, he is much more likely to have been a freedman or free, and thus his daughter would also have been free although of comparatively low social status. McGinn notes the controversy over this woman's status, which generally otherwise supports his theory that imperial concubines came from imperial matrons' households, theoretically guaranteeing their morality and good upbringing.[90] McGinn's theory attempts to rehabilitate concubines and represent them as virtuous women rather than *meretrices*, but both strands of opinion are present in the ancient discourse – Acte is both a loyal servant and a symbol of Nero's lowly taste in women.

In this case, Marcus' stated reason for not remarrying was explicitly to protect the political and emotional interests of his children. The stereotype of the "wicked stepmother" was apparently more fearsome than that of the evil concubine. Domitian's rudeness to Caenis suggests that tensions between legitimate children and concubines may have existed regardless of the legality of the bond.[91]

Like other imperial concubines, Marcia was an imperial freedwoman and probably originally belonged to the household of Lucius Ceionius Commodus, later known as Lucius Verus, the co-ruler of the more famous Marcus Aurelius.[92] She was likely born in the late 150s or early 160s CE, although we have no direct evidence on this point. According to a dedicatory inscription from the Italian town of Anagnia, she was the daughter of an imperial freedman.[93] She may have been raised in Rome by a wealthy eunuch named Hyacinthus, who was also the Christian presbyter of Pope Victor I.[94] While a child, she may have known or at least observed the Emperor Verus' prominent and beloved concubine, Panthea, who was eulogized by various poets of the period and praised by Marcus Aurelius himself.[95] Panthea's success might have inspired Marcia's own ambitions towards a prominent role in the imperial household.

According to Cassius Dio, Marcia began her career as the mistress of the consul Marcus Ummidius Quadratus, who was executed on charges of attempted assassination in 182 CE. After Quadratus' death, she became Commodus' concubine from 182 until his death at the end of 192. At some point during this time period, she married Commodus' *cubicularius*, or chamberlain, a man named Eclectus. However, this did not affect her ongoing sexual liaison with Commodus.[96]

Unlike other imperial examples, Marcia was neither originally a slave in an imperial woman's household nor sexually faithful and loyal to her emperor. Since she is called Commodus' concubine on multiple occasions, we must assume that she maintained a sexual relationship with Commodus while also married to his chamberlain, a relatively lofty position within the imperial court. McGinn theorizes that Imperial freedwomen concubines were carefully chosen for their relative respectability and moral purity, but Marcia appears to be a major exception to this paradigm.[97] Presumably, her husband tacitly or explicitly permitted her sexual relationship with Commodus.[98] The *Historia Augusta* notes with questionable veracity that Commodus was infamous for having both "matrons and harlots" as his concubines, rather than simply slaves or unmarried freedwomen. Even if this is an accurate allegation, it is unclear whether "matron" here means a noble married woman or a freedwoman like Marcia.[99]

Relationships with Commodus' concubines may have been another means of rising in the convoluted hierarchies of the imperial court. By marrying a concubine, bureaucrats gained indirect access to the emperor himself. Commodus' other concubines also apparently made prestigious marriages, as in the case of Damostratia, who married Cleander, another *cubicularius* or chamberlain of Commodus.[100] Marcia's relationships with Quadratus and Eclectus may have been a pragmatic method for the men to gain power and the favor of Commodus himself.

On the other hand, Marcia might have gained her opportunity to be a concubine through her role as Eclectus' wife. The *cubicularii* controlled imperial access through their roles as guardians of the bedchamber; they participated in daily work and leisure activities with the emperor, much like early modern European royal companions or a twenty-first century American president's "body man."[101] Thus, being the wife of a *cubicularius* would have itself offered opportunity for frequent contact with the emperor. While neither *cubicularii* nor concubines had direct political power, their daily contact with the emperor and control over access to him caused courtiers and senators to perceive them as powerful influences within the world of the imperial court. Such a position therefore transcended the lowly origins that we can presume for both Marcia and her husband.

The *cubicularius* Cleander gave large sums of money "to Commodus and his concubines," which suggests that these women were seen as valuable agents for those interested in influencing the Emperor.[102] Marcia's loyalty, at least initially, seems to have been to Commodus himself rather than to any other patrons. Certainly, Cleander's generosity did not stop Marcia from turning on him when politically expedient in the year 190 CE. When a rioting mob, angry about high grain prices during a famine, approached Commodus, Marcia, here described as "the notorious wife of Eclectus," warned the Emperor of his danger. Commodus responded by immediately ordering Cleander and his son to be killed in order to placate the crowd.[103]

Olivier Hekster suggests that Marcia's role in this story was invented by later chroniclers in order to increase the narrative drama of the situation, rather than simply describing Commodus' unprovoked execution of Cleander.[104] This incident is similar in nature to Acte's warning of Nero about his reputation among the soldiers in Tacitus' *Annales*; this may imply that only one version, at most, is true. However, there is no particular reason to think that this story is invented except for its suspicious similarity to the earlier story of Nero and Acte. There is further controversy raised by the problem that Cassius Dio describes Commodus' informant as Marcia, whereas Herodian names another woman, Fadilla. Cassius Dio is a more reliable source in this case, and Marcia therefore a more likely candidate than the more obscure Fadilla.[105] Among other reasons, Herodian might have omitted Marcia so that her appearance at Commodus' death was more dramatic and more hostile; the role of a "messenger" may have been purely a historical trope, since large riots in the Forum rarely required a concubine to overhear and announce them to an emperor on the Palatine Hill above.[106]

In both the Neronian and Commodean stories, a concubine allied to a political rival undermines the position of a powerful figure by warning the emperor about threats to his popularity. However, Marcia and Eclectus also secured their own safety through this move, as well as rising personally higher in the imperial power structure by arranging for Cleander's execution. While Marcia's influence might have been exaggerated in this case, she certainly possessed both the motive and means to protect Commodus and simultaneously overthrow Cleander.

It is impossible to determine, however, whether Marcia was merely a pawn used by more powerful male politicians or whether she was also advancing her own personal ambitions. Certainly, there is a long tradition in Roman rhetoric of attacking men by representing them as being under the domination of women, especially low-status women.[107] We must therefore be careful to treat critically any depictions of Marcia as a powerful, influential figure in her own right. Most of the surviving histories are highly hostile to Commodus. These sources thus adopted the traditional anti-imperial criticism that Commodus was controlled or influenced by freedmen, concubines, and slaves, rather than by senators of the same elite aristocratic status as the histories' authors.[108]

Nevertheless, Marcia's high level of influence over Commodus' policies is detailed in several specific instances by multiple authors. If nothing else, this suggests that she was a plausible target for misogynistic accusations. The *Historia Augusta* offers a few tantalizing although unreliable anecdotes, such as the claim that Marcia encouraged Commodus' desire to name the rebuilt city of Rome "Colonia Commodiana" after himself, a purely symbolic if impolitic move likely inserted to link Commodus with earlier "bad" emperors like Nero.[109] The late fourth-century CE *Epitome de Caesaribus* describes Marcia as "gaining control over Commodus' mind (*cum animum eius penitus devinxisset*)."[110] Herodian describes her as his "favorite mistress (*pallake*)" and notes that "she was treated just like a legal wife with all the honors due to the Empress except the sacred fire [carried before empresses in processions]."[111]

Marcia may also have supported her lover in his gladiatorial ambitions: Commodus "was called Amazonius because of his passion for his concubine Marcia, whom he loved to have depicted as an Amazon, and for whose sake he even wished to enter the Roman arena in Amazon's dress."[112] Marcia's alleged Amazon costume invokes the motif of the mythical female warrior, which may have been a common one for female gladiators. One of our only surviving visual depictions of female gladiators, the famous relief from Halicarnassus, identifies one of the bare-breasted combatants as "Amazon" or "Amazonia."[113] While the visual record portrays female gladiators as sexualized but praiseworthy athletes, such an association is also strongly linked with literary discourse about unconventional or immodest elite women who defy normal Roman social mores.[114] Furthermore, this anecdote also associates Commodus with earlier canonically "bad" emperors: Nero supposedly dressed up his own concubines as gladiators.[115]

Marcia is best known for her supposed support of Christianity and for being the instigator of Commodus' amnesty for Christians.[116] The sources on this matter are somewhat mixed: Cassius Dio, perhaps our most reliable chronicler for the period, mentions Marcia's support of Christianity. However, Dio gives us no details about such support; the *Historia Augusta* and the *Epitome de Caesaribus* authors do not mention any such connection; Herodian and the Christian writer Hippolytus both provide specific accounts.[117]

Hippolytus reports a specific incident in which Victor, the Bishop of Rome in the 190s CE, appealed to Marcia to gain mercy for convicted Christians in the mines in Sardinia:

> Marcia, a concubine of Commodus, who was a God-loving woman, and desirous of performing some good work, invited into her presence the blessed Victor, who was at that time a bishop of the Church, and inquired of him what martyrs were in Sardinia ... Marcia, obtaining her request from Commodus, handed the letter of emancipation to Hyacinthus. (Hippolytus, *Philosophumena* 9.2.12)

The salvation of Christians through the intercession of a concubine and a notoriously evil emperor somewhat devalues the status of the rescued martyrs. Hippolytus' account is highly influenced by internal Church politics, and he may have deliberately shaded his account to denigrate one particular martyr, the future Bishop of Rome, Callistus. Callistus was a personal enemy of Hippolytus, who accused him of corruption and heresy. In this account, Callistus is accidentally saved not through Victor's compassion but through his own cowardly pleas and the intercession of a eunuch and a concubine. While Callistus himself would presumably have been highly grateful to Marcia, we have no surviving texts from his perspective or that of his supporters.[118] However, there is little reason to doubt the actual facts of the incident: Marcia succeeded in procuring amnesty for a number of Christian "martyrs." She also demonstrated her own sympathy for their religion, or at least her personal affection for Bishop Victor.

We should not overestimate Marcia's impact on preserving Christianity during this period, given the scattered comments of historians suggesting a single intervention in a specific case. However, there is a notable lack of recorded Christian martyrdoms during Commodus' reign.[119] Certainly, her liberation of the Sardinian martyrs does not necessarily imply that Marcia herself was Christian; Cassius Dio's statement that she "greatly favored the Christians" is the most accurate assessment of her behavior available.[120] While Christians were not actively prosecuted during Commodus' reign, it would still have been dangerous for such a highly placed figure to practice Christianity openly.

Notably, the early Church did not respond to Marcia's generosity by beatifying her or otherwise honoring her, further suggesting that while she may have protected the Christians, she was not a member of their faith. The incident demonstrates Marcia's power and ability to influence imperial policy in this regard, although there is little way of knowing what priority Commodus himself placed on persecuting Christians. L. Tomassini suggests that Marcia favored Christians as a means of bolstering her own support and gaining a loyal faction, but this seems an unlikely motive, given the precarious position of the Christian religious leaders at the time.[121]

Marcia may also have been given a high degree of public recognition and status because of her relationship with the Emperor. She may be represented on some of Commodus' official medallions and on treasure pieces from Britannia. Michael Rostovtseff and Harold Mattingly argued that the handle of a silver skillet or *patera* from 192 CE, which depicts Commodus as Hercules, shows a Roman empress who bears the features not of Commodus' wife Crispina but those of Marcia (Figure 2).[122] Unfortunately, as we have no definite portraits of Marcia, this identification is largely a case of elimination of other likely possibilities. The silver handle depicts a middle-aged woman with an elaborate Antonine hairstyle and an idealized, if determined face; her clothing appears fairly modest although she does have a sash crossing her chest diagonally between her breasts, which might suggest the Amazon style of clothing associated with her.

It would be a rare honor for an imperial concubine to be depicted in such a way and would indicate her lofty status as Commodus' partner. While Republican prostitutes and concubines may have frequently been used as the visual models for official art, as in the case of Flora's portrait in the Temple of Castor and Pollux, official imperial numismatic imagery was generally reserved for the legitimate members of the imperial family, especially wives and sisters.[123] Thus, there are reasons to be skeptical about the appearance of Marcia on this piece, particularly given the plethora of other women in the Commodan household, although the possibility is highly intriguing.

While Marcia may have had a gladiatorial costume, she also supposedly spoke out against Commodus' own gladiatorial ambitions. According to Herodian, on December 31, 192 CE, Commodus told her his plan to appear at the New Year's festival dressed not as an emperor but as a gladiator, accompanied by the imperial gladiatorial troop. Marcia threw herself on her knees and, weeping, begged Commodus not to disgrace himself

2. A silver patera handle with the bust of a woman who may be Marcia, Commodus' concubine. Capheaton, Northumberland, late third century CE. British Museum.

in such a fashion "and not to endanger his life by trusting gladiators and desperate men."[124] While we have no other evidence for this particular anecdote, its representation of Marcia as a pragmatic, nervous politician is consistent with other evidence. Marcia might have been perfectly willing to indulge Commodus' gladiatorial fantasies when he was a popular emperor, but she correctly saw them as dangerous and risky when he was at the nadir of his popular and aristocratic support. Unfortunately for all involved, Commodus was unconvinced by this advice. Indeed, he reacted by putting Marcia's name on a list for immediate execution at the end of 192 CE.

After discovering this "death list," Marcia and a few co-conspirators, the praetorian prefect Q. Aemilius Laetus and Marcia's husband, the *cubicularius* Eclectus, allegedly murdered the Emperor Commodus in a desperate attempt to preserve their own power and perhaps to prevent further acts of insanity by the increasingly deranged ruler. This was an elaborate and well-planned plot: they had already selected Pertinax, the urban prefect, as the new emperor.[125] The sources differ on whether Marcia was a pawn of Laetus and Eclectus in this matter or an equal partner. According to the *Historia Augusta*, Marcia initially maintained a position of power in Pertinax's reign as one of his principal advisors, suggesting that she had indeed played a key role in the conspiracy, but this version is not well supported by Dio or Herodian.[126]

The power of Marcia, Laetus, and Eclectus' had fundamentally depended on their close personal ties to Commodus. While they may have saved themselves from immediate execution, they were not able to maintain their power or strengthen Pertinax' claim on the throne.[127] Unfortunately for Marcia, Pertinax reigned for only three months before being killed by the praetorian guard and replaced by Didius Julianus, who bought the affection of the praetorians through outrageous bribes. In an effort to associate himself with the last "legitimate" emperor and restore justice, Didius Julianus ordered both Marcia and Laetus to be executed for Commodus' murder.[128] While she may have survived being killed by Commodus, Marcia was unable to parlay her influence into a lasting role in a new imperial court.

Marcia may be remembered as the most powerful of imperial concubines, since multiple sources record not only her influence on politics but also her participation in the successful assassination of an emperor and the choice of his replacement. In many ways, she appears indistinguishable from a Roman empress: she had a political faction, exercised influence, and enabled her chosen heir to succeed. However, Marcia still fell into the role of the concubine due to her lack of a powerful family or official status, as well as, in particular, her lack of children. The only logical motive for Marcia's assassination of Commodus was fear; it would have been difficult for her to gain more power under Pertinax than she already possessed. In any case, the discourse about her is ultimately ambiguous and confusing; she protects Commodus and supports the Empire, yet also brings about the end of his dynasty and overthrows the social order entirely. Marcia does not fit into any of the prescriptive molds offered by our elite male ancient historians, which may be one major reason for her comparative neglect in both ancient and modern scholarship.

Conclusion

The elite courtesans and concubines of the Roman Republic and high Empire were fundamentally threatening to the stability of the Roman

social order. The discourse about them is largely designed to erase their
liminality and ambiguity by neatly labeling them either as fitting the
wicked whore stereotype or as the virtuous almost-wife figure, even
though the latter status raises its own problems. In no known cases did
these freedwomen from lowly backgrounds actually marry their imperial
or senatorial lovers. The first example known of an emperor pursuing
such a risky path is that of the Emperor Justinian and his wife Theodora,
allegedly a former exotic dancer, in the sixth century CE Byzantine
Empire, who will be discussed in Chapter 8.[129]

Elite authors also used the conventional accusation of greed and avarice, frequently levied at *meretrices* as a class, in order to denigrate specific
influential concubines. While, as discussed in Chapter 1, normal Roman
prostitutes in literary texts sought new bracelets or baubles, women like
Verres' lover Chelidon and Vespasian's concubine Caenis received large
tracts of land from their lovers or significant financial incentives from
men who sought to curry political favor with them.[130]

We have few specifics on how much money these women received or
what they chose to do with it. However, the discourse about these elite
concubines focuses not only on their political influence but on their
independent and substantial wealth. Even if this accusation is merely
part of a standard package of invective, it suggests a continued elite
male fear of female economic independence as well as of governmental
corruption.

Just as Roman freedmen achieved power and wealth through their connections to their patrons during the Republic and to the imperial household during the Empire, Roman freedwomen also had opportunities for
influence and profit. However, the major route of access to such power
for women was through their sexual relationships with powerful men.
While Caenis may have had access to secret knowledge as Antonia's secretary, it was not until she became the Emperor's mistress that she could
sell imperial favors to the highest bidder. During the Republic, such influential concubines were generally popular freedwoman prostitutes who
then became the exclusive mistresses of powerful politicians. During the
Empire, these concubines were generally drawn from within the imperial household itself, as the power structure became more tightly central-
ized and compact. The ancient commentary about these women suggests
profound ambivalence about not only the idea of women in power in
general, but about the social flexibility of the elite Roman world and
the ability of lower status women to achieve power through their sexual
attractiveness and availability.

Unlike respectable matrons, Roman freedwomen could not gain influence through fathers, brothers, or sons; they were marked, as all Roman *meretrices* were, by their lack of a natural social or familial network. For Republican-era concubines, this independence only created more fear and outrage in the eyes of male authors like Cicero, who saw them usurping the privileges of respectable matrons or seizing the power of Roman male officials. In a time of chaos and civil war, women like Cytheris and Chelidon threatened even the most basic notions of the elite family and female social hierarchies.

In the Imperial household, however, their lack of ties served as an asset; freedwomen concubines were viewed as harmless antidotes to the swirl of intrigue surrounding official Imperial marriages to women from powerful families, whose loyalties might not be first to their husbands. Republican concubines were thought to disgrace their noble lovers; Imperial mistresses become "almost-wives" and served as trusted personal companions.

The positive or negative reaction of the sources towards these women depends not on the particularity of their actions but on whether their role in society was viewed as appropriate or necessary. For Cicero, freedwomen concubines were transgressive, ambitious prostitutes; for Suetonius, women following the same path in life were loyal and necessary servants. Political interference that was labeled as corruption by Republican authors seeking to denigrate their opponents was praised as benign mercy by Imperial authors terrified of the absolute power and abusive caprices of the Imperial family.

This evolution in attitudes towards elite mistresses also fits into established models of the change in elite access to power. In the Republic, political power was theoretically tightly restricted to a limited group of senatorial men. Any attempt to infiltrate this network, whether by Italian landowners like Marius and Cicero, or Greek freedwomen prostitutes, like Chelidon and Cytheris, was met with contempt and outrage by the established elites of Roman society. Under the Empire, power centered not on birth but on access to the emperor himself; thus, both the elite and lowborn members of his household could gain immense status and power.

As empresses became powerful public symbols of authority and controlled vast resources of their own, concubines like Vespasian's Caenis sometimes assumed the role of the traditional domestic wife in the private sphere, the *univira* who was solely dedicated to her male partner's interests. Therefore, the change over time in the discourse about "second-class" women is not actually a story of increasing female and non-elite power and influence in the Roman world. It is more accurately a reflection of continued misogyny and an attempt to maintain the power of an elite patriarchy; only the specific types of targeted women have switched. If anything, the praise for imperial concubines suggests the deep concern about the power wielded by the public empresses.

Rather than gifting a respectable woman with the power and influence which became associated with the role of a Roman empress, various emperors chose to deliberately minimize female influence by choosing an unofficial concubine as their primary relationship, usually after the death of an heir-producing empress or between legitimate wives. Since this woman did not have ties to an external family, there was less chance of a new political faction forming around her; she would also not place her children's interests above those of her partner.[131] Both freedmen and freedwomen formed a class of people who were loyal only to their former masters and unable to easily seek independent power.[132]

However, the evidence that even these private mistresses wielded political influence and made themselves financially secure suggests that, as always, some women blurred and crossed the lines of the official male discourse. Any theory that freedwomen concubines would always be submissive, apolitical sex objects is proved incorrect by the historical facts. Women like Caenis, Marcia, and Lysistrate wielded a great deal of political power despite their unorthodox status. These women from slave backgrounds, during both the Republic and the Empire, managed to obtain and to use power over Roman politics and government in ways that were anathema to the traditions and mores of Roman society. While some of them were used and abused by their male lovers to curry favor with other powerful men, others managed to influence political policies in their own right, whether through hiring specific men for important jobs or saving prisoners from execution. These women also profited financially and benefited themselves through their sexual relationships with their powerful lovers.

Some of these women, like Caenis or Cytheris, almost transcended their social status, but the strict barriers in Roman society between *matrona* and *concubina*, noble and notorious, remained an important technicality. Caenis' life was radically different than that of a lowly *scortum* in a brothel, but, legally and socially, they were still linked in their lack of matronhood. A freedwoman concubine under the Republic or Empire could have the power of a praetor, the wealth of an imperial chamberlain, or the public recognition of an empress, but she could never, in the end, be a wife.

4

Matrona as *meretrix*

"Woe unto the man who falls into the meshes of such an unsatiable Messalina."

Krafft-Ebing, Psychopathia Sexualis, *1886*[1]

The Empress Messalina, the wife of the first-century CE Roman Emperor Claudius, was reduced into a caricature of the predatory, consuming, desirous woman shortly after her death; this reputation has continued to pursue her for the last two millennia. While historical evidence does suggest that Messalina had at least one extramarital affair, the literary construction of her as the paradigmatic nymphomaniac elides her identity as an influential empress who nearly orchestrated a successful palace coup, after co-reigning with her husband for ten years and producing two children acknowledged as his legitimate heirs. Such a discourse both in ancient and modern times also weaves together the trope of the prostitute and that of the desirous woman. This blending contrasts with other Roman representations, discussed in the next chapter, which praise women who desire their husbands. This traditional version of Messalina is largely useless as a record of historical reality. Rather, it serves as a male-authored warning to all women of the dangers of an excessively public and prominent role in society and the consequences of attempting to overturn the patriarchal social order.[2]

This chapter explores the labeling of certain historical elite, wealthy wives as *meretrices*, as well as examining the ancient discourse about working women of lower social status who may or may not have moonlighted as actual prostitutes. It focuses on the relationship between a Roman matron's political or economic activities and accusations of her prostitute-like behavior, as well as the question of whether the woman's activities threatened the stability of the Roman social system overall. This rhetorical trope of the negative *meretrix* label illuminates how elite Roman males shaped and attempted to define the ideological representation of women.[3] At the same time, the prominence of historical figures who deliberately rejected the confines of the "good *matrona*" label suggests that such a division of Roman women by both social status and morality inaccurately modeled the behaviors of historical Roman matrons.

Elite Roman male authors like Cicero and Tacitus labeled politically prominent women like Clodia, Cleopatra, and Messalina as not only "wicked whores" but as nymphomaniacs who slept with particularly humble and shameful men like actors and slaves, simultaneously attacking both their fidelity and their respect for social hierarchies. The defining characteristic of these accusations of symbolic prostitutehood, which employ the same techniques of invective discussed in Chapter 1, is that they differentiate threateningly independent, sexually active women from mere adulteresses like Augustus' daughter Julia or manipulative but family-oriented women like Agrippina the Younger. An *adultera* was still fundamentally part of a *familia*, albeit one disgraced by her behavior and distinguished by a specific act of sexual betrayal of her spouse. A *meretrix*, in Roman discourse, was an independent woman sexually available to an infinite variety of men outside her family. The label of prostitute refers not to the actual sexual activities of these women but to their refusal to be *univirae*, to be defined by their relationships with one man alone.

The applicability of the honor–shame model

There has been much debate about whether or not Roman Republican or Imperial society can be understood through the "honor–shame" model popular among historians and anthropologists of later Mediterranean history. One part of this model suggests, at its most simplistic level, that Mediterranean attitudes towards women were shaped by how women's sexual behaviors reflected upon their male kin; female promiscuity incurred shame upon the woman's entire family.[4]

Thomas McGinn and Susan Treggiari have raised serious concerns about the applicability of this theory to the Roman metropolis.[5] The original model largely relied on studies of the social dynamics of small, rural Mediterranean villages, which possessed much more stable and permanent communities than Augustan Rome did, as well as featuring a relative lack of social mobility.[6] In a system with available divorce and little social stigma connected to remarriage, the notion of preventing women from being permanently sexually shamed was, at a minimum, more complex than in early modern Mediterranean times.

Any attempt to understand the honor or shame of Roman women, even as viewed by Roman men rather than by women themselves, must thus take into consideration the relatively lax social framework and permissive sexual mores of elite Roman society. Were there any real women who behaved like Lucretia, or for that matter Messalina, or were these purely abstract paradigms serving as warnings for Roman women not otherwise restricted by rigid spatial or economic segregation?

However, the honor–shame model may still assist us in analyzing the nature of Roman invective towards married women. In many cases, accusations of sexual misconduct were directed at women in an effort to lower the overall honor of their *familia*, rather than out of personal hatred.[7] This does not address the more difficult issue, as raised by Vistilia in the Introduction, of how elite Roman women in the first centuries BCE and CE themselves valued their *pudicitia* in relationship to their own social status. Vistilia's example suggests that some Roman women may have prized sexual freedom above public reputation, or, at least, considered the label of *meretrix* preferable to exile.[8]

In any case, the predominant problem with the honor–shame model in this case is the widely different types of women and situations under investigation. The behavioral choices made by Clodia Metelli, a widowed matron in the war-torn, chaotic late Roman Republic, were motivated by different social factors than those driving the early Imperial Empress Messalina, wife of the most powerful man in the Western world. Similarly, the attitudes of male commentators to each of these women depended dramatically on context and on the social roles of the authors themselves.

The frequent claims that certain *matronae* behaved like *meretrices* during the late Republic and Empire may also indicate that the range of possible sexual behaviors and general freedom for elite women had increased.[9] This general impression may well be tainted by the far greater availability of sources from the late Republican and Imperial era. However, neither the elite matrons of Plautus and Terence's comedies, as discussed in Chapter 1, nor the women of Livy's early histories are frequently accused of engaging in indiscriminate promiscuous sex.[10] In any case, the commonality of the specific accusation of prostitute-like behavior against elite women during this period enables us to contrast the various rhetorical treatments of these women and assess the causes for such attacks.

Meretrices reginae

Certain extremely prominent *matronae* from this period, such as Clodia Metelli and Messalina, received the harshly critical label of *meretrix*, although it is improbable that any of them ever received payment for sex. Arlene Saxonhouse has established a general paradigm in which women who undermine patriarchal power structures are accused of seeking power as part of their physical or sexual proclivities or in order to advance personal relationships.[11] Elite male authors and orators like Cicero and Tacitus interpreted Roman women's political manipulations and other unorthodox behaviors as either directed towards an inevitable goal of promiscuity or as actions which themselves resulted from previous promiscuous behavior. A common ancient assumption was that women became involved in court cases, rebellions, or politics not because of their actual interest in the public sphere, but out of an extension of their private immoral behavior into the public sphere.

At the same time, such a narrow viewpoint erases all of the legitimate methods by which Roman women engaged in public activity – from Terentia's management of her properties, approved and supported by her husband Cicero, to Hortensia's public speech in the marketplace denouncing taxes on elite women. Indeed, most Roman women who acted in the public sphere seem to have done so out of desire for money rather than sex. As demonstrated in previous chapters, the notion of a woman with economic agency was perhaps even more threatening to the Roman social order than a woman with sexual freedom. Prostitution is threatening not just because it involves a lack of male control over women's bodies, but because it can potentially involve female financial independence. Women's financial activities are elided in the elite male discourse by their sexual activities, which, even when inappropriate, are more acceptably part of the bodily, private, dependent female realm.

The infamous Clodia Metelli, a Roman matron of the late Republic, is perhaps the most vivid representation of the trope linking public political and economic action with personal sexual misconduct. While the outlines of her story are generally well known, I will focus particularly on Cicero's characterization of her not only specifically as a *meretrix* but also as a woman who had abandoned all of the standard duties and responsibilities of matronhood. Furthermore, Clodia's wealth enables her to behave in the promiscuous ways that she prefers and to resist any attempt at male control over her activities. Cicero responds to her unorthodox single lifestyle by portraying her in the *Pro Caelio* as a fallen woman, "not only a prostitute but a shameless and insolent prostitute."[12]

Clodia Metelli, a patrician woman of the consular Claudii family, was the sister of the Roman tribune of the plebs, Publius Clodius Pulcher, and the wife of the Roman consul Quintus Caecilius Metellus Celer. She was particularly notorious because of the court case in 56 BCE against her former lover Caelius Rufus, a young Roman politician and lawyer of the time. Cicero's speech in Caelius' defense against the charges of poisoning and extortion, the *Pro Caelio*, attacks Clodia as the *meretrix* seducer of an innocent young man.[13]

Clodia supposedly engaged in numerous affairs with many other men, both during her marriage and after her husband's untimely death. She is generally identified with the Lesbia of Catullus' poetry, whose lengthy and tumultuous affair with the poet was immortalized in Catullus' writings.[14] In both private letters and public speeches, Cicero also accused Clodia of committing incest with her brother Publius Clodius, his political enemy. While this piece of data is tainted by Cicero's political vendetta against Clodius, the accuracy or at least commonality of this insult is tentatively supported by the poetry of Catullus.[15] Clodia's two sisters, who also made lofty marriages to Roman consuls, were similarly accused of promiscuity.[16]

Clodia's only known marriage, to Metellus Celer, was around 80 BCE, at the age of fifteen or sixteen; the couple had one child, a daughter called Metella.[17] Metellus died in his early forties, after two decades of marriage; Cicero implies that Clodia poisoned him.[18] There is no factual evidence for this charge, but Clodia did subsequently set herself up as a wealthy widow, and, somewhat unusually, never remarried. Given her prestigious lineage, she would have been a desirable marriage candidate no matter what her age; it is odd that her family did not use her to make more political alliances after Metellus' death. Rumors of murder, even if unproven, could also naturally have hurt her marital prospects. Clodia may simply have preferred the independence which widowhood potentially offered a Roman woman.

In the *Pro Caelio*, Cicero directly accuses Clodia of sexual profligacy, incest, and murder. Cicero's portrayal of Clodia in his letters is somewhat less hostile than the rhetorical version; these letters also offer evidence for Clodia's political talents and public economic activities.[19] Clodia is the only woman whom Cicero refers to as *nobilis* and the only woman in all of Latin literature described as *illa consularis*, a woman of consular descent.[20] These epithets are highly public labels for a woman. Whether for good or bad, Clodia is a well-known woman.[21]

The historical reality of such public activity is bolstered by Cicero's references to her power of potentially obtaining extra seats at the theater for her brother's clients and of interceding on Cicero's behalf with her brother-in-law Metellus Nepos.[22] M. B. Skinner's representation of Cicero and Clodia's relationship as frequently positive and productive is intriguing. However, this portrayal may also fall victim to confusion between the three Clodia sisters, all of whom were prominent in Roman society of the time. The modern persona of Clodia Metelli may have stolen both her sisters' influence and their scandals.

Regardless of Cicero's earlier or later attitudes towards Clodia Metelli, in the *Pro Caelio* he specifically savages her not as a political figure but as a nymphomaniacal man-eater and, indeed, a *meretrix*. According to the prosecution, Caelius Rufus both accepted money from Clodia and then tried to poison her. Cicero does not address the facts of this charge; rather, he takes the position that the best defense is a good offense and spends most of his speech attacking the reputation, credibility, and morals of Clodia, the supposed victim in the case. A major dynamic of this problematic relationship is that Clodia is financially in control, whereas Caelius Rufus is a dependent boy-toy. Since she cannot be represented as a shrewish *femina dotata*, Cicero chooses another model of financially independent female, the greedy prostitute. He utilizes this prostitute persona even though Clodia is more notorious for generosity than avarice, in part because it allows him to muddle the economic realities of the Caelius–Clodia affair.

From the very beginning of the speech, Cicero portrays Clodia as a wicked whore, in direct contrast to Caelius Rufus, whom he characterizes as a virtuous young Roman man.[23] As previously noted, prostitutes were not competent witnesses in Roman courts; Cicero thus casts simultaneous doubt on both Clodia's virtue and her reliability and veracity as a witness.[24]

McGinn suggests that the entire purpose of this line of insult is to prejudice Clodia's testimony, rather than serving as a general indictment of her character.[25] He references a later case under the Emperor Claudius where an *eques* was shamed when common prostitutes (*scorta*) were allowed to testify against him.[26] Clodia, however, remains far from the lowly legal status of a *scortum*, and her testimony is perfectly valid under law, despite the mud Cicero slings at it. Cicero's goal, then, is not actually to discard Clodia's testimony as invalid but to caricature her as an untrustworthy witness due to her promiscuous, prostitute-like behavior. When a woman's overall character is defined by her fidelity to one man, sexual independence implies the general unreliability of her word. Disloyalty to a husband – or even a single lover – is also a symptom of possible disloyalty to the Roman state and justice system itself. Cicero is not only condemning Clodia as a bad woman, but as a bad Roman citizen, an especially relevant and dangerous charge in the contemporaneous political turmoil.

Cicero partially bases his case on the grounds that Clodia has forfeited her right to be treated as a Roman matron, with the corresponding respect, belief in her testimony, and privileges that such a status entailed:[27]

If a widow were living loosely, a frisky widow living frivolously, a rich widow living ruinously, an amorous widow living like a whore (*libidinosa meretricio more viveret*), should I think any man an adulterer, if he had been a little free in greeting her? (Cicero, *Pro Caelio* 15.38)

In this case, Cicero claims Clodia's licentious behavior has deprived her of the status that she would normally have as a widow, status that would also have included implicit protection from being mocked in a public trial:

If an unmarried woman opens her house to all men's desires, and leads the life of a prostitute (*palamque sese in meretricia vita collocant*); if she is in the habit of dining with completely strange men ... if in fact she behaves so that not only her way of walking (*incessu*), but her dress (*ornatu*) and her companions, not only the boldness of her gaze, not only the freedom of her speech, but also her hugs, her kisses, her beach-parties, her sailing-parties, her dinner-parties, so that she is not only a prostitute, but is seen to be a shameless and insolent prostitute ... (*ut non solum meretrix, sed etiam proterva meretrix procaxque videatur*) (Cicero, *Pro Caelio* 20.49)

Cicero stresses that the most important aspect of Clodia's immorality is not Clodia's actual behavior but her reputation: she appears, publicly, as a prostitute, in open male-dominated spaces like the Forum. She is *palam*, open and public about her sexuality, not merely an adulteress but one who is open to all comers, who "is seen" to be a *meretrix*. She conducts her own affairs and parties, acting as an independent woman without a strong family connection. Cicero describes her as *amicam omnium*, punning not on her friendliness but on her availability, and emphasizes, "far from seeking privacy and shadows (*tenebras*) and the usual coverings (*integumenta*) for vices, she revels in her degraded lusts amid the most open publicity and in the broadest daylight (*sed in turpissimis rebus*

frequentissima celebritate et clarissima luce laetetur).[28] Cicero does not
label Clodia as a brothel girl concealed in shadows behind a curtain,
or as a courtesan who might choose her patron carefully, but rather as
the coarsest of daytime *fornatrices.* Despite the wealth necessary to host
these sailing-parties and dinner-parties and own her valuable real estate,
Clodia must be degraded to the status of an impoverished whore. Just as
Ovid and Martial criticized their lovers for behavior unbecoming even
of semi-respectable courtesans (see Chapter 1), Cicero condemns Clodia
for being less virtuous than a lowly *scortum,* the nadir of Roman female
morality.[29]

Quintilian is quite accurate in claiming that this passage is an example
of rhetorical amplification, but Cicero's exaggeration would be worthless
if it were not possible to extend the *infamia* of the *meretrix* to the shameless *matrona.*[30] In the same way that elite adulteresses were forced to don
a prostitute's toga, symbolically becoming streetwalkers as punishment
for their act, Clodia is rhetorically assimilated to the status of a prostitute, while retaining her technical legal social status and privileges.[31] It is
not that the adulteress actually is a prostitute, but rather that she deserves
to be treated like one and thus to be exiled from the Roman elite.

Cicero himself associates Clodia with the foreign men's baths and suggests that she might have traded sex with the bath attendant in return
for entry, while Quintilian quotes Caelius Rufus in describing her as a
quadrantaria, a quarter-*as* girl.[32] Clodia's public prominence and association with extremely cheap, visible sex places her behavior in direct contrast with the respectable public life of a *vir clarissimus.*[33] Cicero further
claims that, due to her licentious behavior, Clodia was unable to keep a
proper order and hierarchy in her household, unlike a good *matrona:*

> Is anyone ignorant that in a house of that kind, in which the mother of the
> family (*materfamilias*) lives according to the customs of a prostitute (*more mer-
> etricio*) ... that in such a house their slaves are slaves no longer? When such con-
> fidence is placed in them and everything is done by their agency ... (Cicero, *Pro
> Caelio* 23.58)

Clodia has violated not only the conjugal relationship but also the normal relationship between mistress and slave, blurring the lines of distinction so important in Roman society. She is no longer a *matrona,* but a
meretrix. Cicero explicitly rejects the label of *materfamilias* for Clodia,
arguing that that name is reserved for those who also have the *sanctitas*
of a matron, which Clodia has forfeited through her behavior, and the
domina of a *domus.*[34] He plays with the moral associations of these labels

and denies the possibility of any middle ground for a Roman woman: she must be either wife or whore.

Cicero's rhetorical *evocatio* of her male and female virtuous ancestors rebukes Clodia for acting in a way inappropriate for a matron. Her behavior is particularly outrageous in her capacity as a patrician woman and a member of a larger, extended family:

> If the images of the men of our family did not touch your heart, did not even the famous Quinta Claudia, a daughter of our own race, rouse you to show yourself a rival of those virtuous women who have brought glory upon our house?[35] (Cicero, *Pro Caelio* 34)

Cicero does not say that Roman women should never be publicly known or that Clodia invites disgrace by her mere presence in the masculine sphere. By citing these examples of her female ancestors, he demonstrates that Roman women could and did gain fame for explicitly public and political events, even participating in a triumph and preventing a riot. Indeed, as Skinner emphasizes, Cicero is perfectly willing to profit from Clodia's own political activities under other circumstances.[36]

In this case, however, Cicero chose to pursue his argument by shifting the focus of the jury away from the young spendthrift Caelius towards Clodia, whom he labeled as a *meretrix* in order to serve the needs of his legal case. Despite her lofty lineage, Clodia was also a vulnerable figure, because she had neither father nor husband nor son to protect her. Cicero rebukes her for her symbolic disloyalty to the memory and example of her ancestors.[37] She is not just a bad woman but a bad descendant of her female as well as male ancestors and a bad member of the Roman aristocracy. Symbolically, she is disloyal to the Roman social system and the Roman state. Clodia's economic and social independence makes her traitorous by implication, even though she has no reason or means of actually betraying Rome or *Romanitas*.

Catullus portrays a Clodia/Lesbia both similar to and more developed in character than Cicero's Clodia. As is true for Cicero, Catullus categorizes Lesbia both as a prostitute and as the lowest of all possible prostitutes: a streetwalker who performs oral sex.[38] It is not sufficient for Lesbia/Clodia to step barely across the matrona/*meretrix* divide; she must be placed firmly in the category of irredeemable *infamia*, forever *famosa* rather than *nobilis*.

Sempronia, an alleged Catilinarian conspirator of the same era as Clodia, is said by Sallust to have previously "met her enormous expenses

through prostitution (*stupro corporis*)," although at the time of the conspiracy she had abandoned the trade due to age, and instead incurred
large debts.[39] She is a *meretrix* through necessity and greed; Sallust labels
her as part of a general portrait of dissolute, spendthrift, desperate con-
spirators. He also associates Sempronia with many typically meretricious
skills such as dancing, writing, and reading, as well as with sexually promiscuous behavior and economic independence.[40] Still, while she was
both unorthodox and politically active, Sallust describes Sempronia as
masculine (*virilis audaciae*) rather than explicitly as a *meretrix*; her husband and children are mentioned. Sempronia is not independent, merely
financially desperate, and thus she poses less of a threat to Roman elite
gender norms.

Sallust's refusal to use a term like *meretrix* may stem from his desire to
portray the Catilinarians as fallen elites. However, it may also be related
to Sempronia's continued harmonious relationship with her family. While
she was a conspirator against Rome and was outrageous in her personal
life, Sempronia also filled traditional feminine social roles. The focus in
this attack is not to remove one particular woman from the protected,
privileged status of *matrona*, but generally to characterize a despised
group of traitors to the Republic. At the same time, prostitution is again
associated with disloyalty – here to Rome itself rather than to a particular
man. Like their legendary ancestress Tarpeia, Sempronia and her friends
are condemned for choosing personal avarice over their duty to the state.

Cleopatra VII of Egypt was the first woman to be labeled with the ultimate paradoxical juxtaposition of *meretrix regina* or prostitute-queen.
She is arguably the original target and source for this particular form of
invective, although her portrait borrows a variety of details from Sallust's
representation of Sempronia as both intellectual and depraved.[41] While
women like Cornelia the Mother of the Gracchi could be praised for their
brilliance, intellectual accomplishment was also clearly another potential
symptom of dangerous female agency.

During the civil wars between Octavian and Marcus Antonius in the
30s BCE, Octavian and his supporters denounced Cleopatra's supposed
sexual proclivities. This propaganda was a central part of Octavian's
campaign to depict his war as a Roman defense against the machinations
of a debauched foreign queen, rather than as a civil conflict between two
elite Roman male generals.[42] In the portrait painted by Augustus' clients and their descendants, Cleopatra's political power was intertwined
with and inseparable from her sexually profligate persona. However, even
these sources only name two specific lovers, Julius Caesar and Marcus

Antonius. Cleopatra maintained apparently serious relationships of some duration and semi-official status with both these men.

Augustan poetry defines Cleopatra in opposition to the figure of a legitimate Roman wife – specifically Octavia, Octavian's sister, who was married to Antonius. Cleopatra was mockingly called *Aegyptia coniunx*, the Egyptian wife, and she is described as desiring the Eastern Empire as an *obsceni coniugis pretium*, a reward for a scandalous marriage.[43] Again, Cleopatra is slotted into the greedy girl stereotype, despite being the richest woman in the Mediterranean. Propertius accuses her of having sex with her own slaves, thus reducing her, like Clodia, to the status not only of a prostitute but of a cheap *scortum* for slaves. Horace claims that she emasculated the courtiers in Alexandria.[44]

In order radically to demonize Cleopatra and also to place her into a familiar group of unorthodox women, she must be represented not only as a woman who is hedonistic and sexually active but as one indiscriminate in her pleasures. Cleopatra was especially dangerous as the mother of Julius Caesar's only surviving child, Caesarion, who represented a potential threat to Octavian's own claim as Caesar's heir. In order simultaneously to smear her as villainous and lessen her apparent power, Octavian and his poet clients shaped Cleopatra as a *meretrix*, a designated female victim for any man able to conquer her. By reducing her social status, Octavian both achieved symbolic power over Cleopatra and shamed her lover, Marcus Antonius, who had abandoned a loyal, virtuous *matrona* for a debauched *meretrix*. He also symbolically elevated Rome above Alexandria and Egypt. Cleopatra's influence over Antonius is represented as a dire and existential threat for Roman society. Only by defeating her can Octavian restore stability, with himself as the newly enshrined ruler and father of the country in a renewed patriarchal order.

The aforementioned Messalina, wife of the Emperor Claudius, was one of the most infamous of the *meretrices reginae*. Juvenal accused her of being not only a *meretrix augusta* who behaved like a prostitute, as Clodia and Cleopatra did, but of actually making nightly trips to a low-class public brothel.[45] She is depicted not only as a metaphorical *meretrix* but an actual *scortum*, despite the extremely implausible nature of this accusation. For Juvenal, Messalina was the ultimate example of the wealthy, corrupt, selfish woman controlled and driven by her desires and immoral nature. She was not a prostitute out of financial necessity, like the other residents of the brothel, but out of her longing for immoral sex and her desire to flaunt her disloyalty to her husband. Tacitus, while not explicitly calling Messalina a prostitute, also painted a portrait of a

woman constantly seeking new and unusual vices.[46] Tacitus accused her
of an affair with a "ballet-dancing actor," Mnester, which also again links
her not just to adulterous liaisons but also to sex with the most shameful
possible partner.[47] The extreme aspect of her corruption is a necessary
element of the story, as it demonstrates the depths of perversion of imperial power at a more general level. Messalina's "marriage" to Silius was
revealed to Claudius by two of his *paelices*, or concubines, who were
themselves recruited by Claudius' freedmen. In this discourse, the entire
story serves to further reinforce Tacitus' portrayal of an emperor surrounded by freedpersons and corrupt officials.[48] When her conspiracy
was discovered, Messalina tried to reconcile with her husband, but in
order to reach him, she was forced to walk across the city of Rome and
then take a cart loaded down with garbage.[49] This imagery only further
reinforces the connection between Messalina and a lowly streetwalking
prostitute. She is simultaneously morally and economically degraded. Just
as Volumnia Cytheris broke social boundaries by riding in a matron's
litter, Messalina is reduced to *meretrix* status by riding in a garbage cart.
Tacitus here rhetorically defines a binary categorization for women –
either wife or whore.

Cassius Dio also explicitly refers to Messalina as a prostitute, accusing
her of practicing her trade in the palace itself. Dio here appears to con-
flate adultery and prostitution, linking them together – *emoicheueto kai
eporneuto*.[50] Yet Dio chooses to use both words – to prostitute oneself
and also to commit adultery. These are separate if related crimes and it is
surely notable that some women, like Messalina, are accused of both while
Augustus' daughter Julia is tainted with only one.[51] Dio's reference to
Messalina practicing prostitution in the palace perhaps alludes to earlier
stories about Caligula's brothel on the Palatine, and it probably has relatively little basis in fact.[52] Pliny the Elder, meanwhile, accused Messalina
of entering a contest with a slave prostitute for the maximum number of
acts of intercourse each was capable of enduring; Messalina supposedly
won after twenty-five rounds.[53] Again, the emphasis is on Messalina's
extreme sexual desire and low tastes; she wishes to show herself superior
to a slave prostitute not through her lofty status or wealth but through
her sexual fervor. She becomes the paradigmatic wicked wife, one who in
every way chooses to adopt the behavior of a common whore.

The stories of Messalina's sexual escapades are highly exaggerated,
and it is difficult to see past the biases of our sources and gain any sense
either of the level of Messalina's political power or of her actual sexual behavior. Her "marriage" to Silius may have been intended as an

elaborate political coup rather than as a flagrant display of personal desire.[54] However, it is impossible to separate the historical Messalina from the carefully painted portraits of her by highly hostile male authors like Tacitus and Juvenal, and, in this case, any such dissection is largely irrelevant for current purposes. Whether or not Messalina actually controlled the Empire through Claudius and his freedmen, she was certainly perceived by elite male authors and represented by them as exercising undue influence. This unorthodox political activity was then connected with the lowest form of public prostitution. Tacitus deliberately associates a woman with the forces of social chaos and confusion; Messalina's acts collapse both social and epistemic categories.[55] In her characterization as a woman who desires common partners and competes openly with a slave prostitute, Messalina herself is lowered to the status of a streetwalker, the very opposite of an empress.

In all our surviving sources, the image of Messalina is an oxymoron, more stylized rhetoric than any attempt at realistic character portrait. Her realistic threats to Claudius' rule and the established elite political order of the imperial court are replaced by fantastic allegations of uncontrolled, unorthodox promiscuity that invert the social and sexual hierarchy. Messalina the canny politician is transformed in the discourse into Messalina the nymphomaniac, a simultaneously more titillating and less intimidating figure. In Juvenal and Dio's representation, every male reader can imagine himself having sex with Messalina and thus empowering himself at her expense. She becomes far less threatening than the figure of the controlling empress; she is simply a brothel girl whom any man can temporarily possess. If part of the purpose of the discourse about Messalina is to emasculate her husband Claudius, it also serves to disempower Messalina herself. By making her a nymphomaniac, she loses control of her own body, the Empire, and the narrative.

Adulterae and other women with extramarital partners

Sulpicia, the late-first-century BCE elegiac poet in the literary circle of Tibullus, presents our only Roman female perspective on the matrona–meretrix divide.[56] The narrator of the poems, presumably although not certainly Sulpicia, describes herself as an unmarried *puella*.[57] In one of the surviving six poems, she purports to be angry at her lover, Cerinthus, for abandoning her in favor of a prostitute:

A toga-flaunting streetwalker, weighed down by her wool basket, may be more important to you than Sulpicia the daughter of Servius, but there are those who

care for me, and their greatest worry is that I might lose out to the bed of a
nobody. (Sulpicia 4.10 [3.16], Book 3 *Corpus Tibullanorum*)[58]

Sulpicia makes a direct comparison between her own status as an elite
woman – Sulpicia the daughter of Servius (notably not the wife or sister
of anyone) versus a *scortum togata*, who both carries wool, rather than
weaving it as a proper *matrona lanefica* would, and, presumably, sells
herself for sex. This female-authored perspective does not address the
issue of whether or not an elite woman should be judged for her sexual
behavior, but rather condemns the male object for choosing to sleep with
a lowly prostitute rather than a lofty *puella*. The narrator's own sexual
behavior is not a determinant of her morality. However, her male lover's
promiscuity is, unusually, seen as a crime. Sulpicia, despite presumably
engaging in a pre-marital romance, is faithful to Cerinthus; he has committed the offense by preferring a woman of lower social status.

Unlike the typical *scortum*, however, Sulpicia does have influential and
powerful connections, in this case almost certainly her guardian Valerius
Messala, if the poem is to be taken autobiographically. Sulpicia relies on
the network of male protectors available to the elite woman in order to
protect her from her lover's supposed poor taste. She herself is highly
conscious of her own elite social status. Despite her expressed sexual
desires, the narrator is *digna*, and she represents the Roman woman who
is sexually and publicly active without being universally promiscuous.[59]
Indeed, Sulpicia presents herself here as a firm supporter of Roman social
hierarchy. It is her lover who seems to be eliding status distinctions, while
Sulpicia proudly relies on the privileges granted an elite Roman freeborn
woman. While not a *matrona*, she remains a symbolically "good woman."

The Emperor Augustus' daughter Julia, who was notoriously accused
of multiple adulteries and exiled by her father in 2 BCE, possessed a
more mixed and ambiguous reputation. She brought scandal to the imperial family and mocked her father's own laws punishing adultery.[60] She
is certainly not a "good wife," but at the same time, ancient sources do
not condemn her to the social or moral status of a common whore. She
is never specifically referred to as a *meretrix*, although she is said to have
practiced her debaucheries in the Forum and by the statue of Marsyas,
highly public locations.[61]

One reason for this avoidance by ancient historians and poets is that
Julia's story is told largely in terms of the disgrace to her *familia*, especially her father Augustus. Pliny and Suetonius cast Julia as a bad daughter, but she remains viewed as a member of the imperial family even

after her exile. She did not have an independent political or economic role of her own which made it necessary for historical sources to attack her as an autonomous sexual agent.[62] Notably, Julia is not condemned by the sources for committing crimes against either of her later husbands, Agrippa or Tiberius, but instead for betraying the policies of her father. One of her most famous jokes asserted, "I never take on a passenger unless the ship is full," implying that she did not cheat on Agrippa except while pregnant with one of her five children.[63] Although sexually promiscuous, she still fulfilled a traditional familial role of the fecund mother and wife, unlike, for instance, Clodia Metelli, who in decades of marriage produced only one daughter. Julia was a disappointment and a "cancer" to her father, but not dangerous as an individual.[64]

Although the other two dominant Julio-Claudian imperial ladies, Livia and Agrippina the Younger, were noted for their political influence and power, and both were accused of various sexual scandals during their lives, they also escaped the label of *meretrix*. Tacitus characterizes Livia and Agrippina as ambitious poisoners and murderers rather than as prostitutes; he criticizes them for being unemotional and cold-hearted rather than nymphomaniacal and hysterical – too unfeminine rather than excessively driven by female lusts.[65] Similarly, Julia Domna, wife of Septimius Severus, was accused of multiple adulteries, as well as unorthodox political and intellectual influence, but even the *Historia Augusta* never calls her a *meretrix*.[66] Both of the Empress Faustinas receive similar treatment to Julia Domna, although Faustina the Younger is accused of sleeping with a gladiator, a familiar attempt to smear an empress with the most shameful possible sexual partner.[67]

The amnesty granted these women might relate to their roles as mothers of imperial male heirs. While characterized as manipulative and scheming, their energies were directed towards advancing their family members in more appropriately feminine fashions, rather than their own personal interests. Although Livia, Agrippina, and their imperial successors are accused of many negative character traits, they are not represented as independent women and cannot be accused of disloyalty towards their entire family.

Women workers and prostitutes

Roman legal sources such as the *Digest* show that Roman women who held public jobs, especially actresses, tavernkeepers, waitresses, and unmarried marketplace vendors, were sometimes labeled as possible *meretrices* even if prostitution was not the primary or even any source of their income. Thomas McGinn and Catherine Edwards have treated the legal concept of female *infamia* extensively and thoroughly.[68] While publicly working women were not assumed all to be part-time prostitutes, their jobs left them open to accusations and insinuations of promiscuity in a way that was not true for wives who worked in their homes. Such public workers failed to fit into the more rigid categories of wife or whore, demonstrating the practical inadequacy of those categories. Elite authors tended to try to force them into the closest approximation of their social status rather than recognizing a possible alternative category for such figures.

The most relevant ancient source regarding Roman legal assumptions about ordinary working women is Ulpian's definition of a prostitute, in the early third century CE: "not only does the woman who prostitutes herself in a brothel (*lupanario*) make a living openly (*palam quaestum facere*) but also any woman in a tavern or inn (*taberna cauponia*), a common practice (*ut adsolet*), or any other woman who does not spare her sense of shame."[69] Such a statement does not imply that all tavern women were considered to be prostitutes, but rather that there was a common association between the two trades.[70] A modern equivalent example would be the reasonable but potentially incorrect assumptions about the sexual availability of exotic dancers in a strip club, who make their bodies publicly available for viewing but do not necessarily have sex with clients. The sense of shame, *pudor*, is perhaps here particularly relevant; Ulpian is trying to draw a distinction between women who possess *pudicitia* and those who lack it, not between women who enter public spaces and those who reside solely in the domestic realm. What defines a *meretrix* is both her independence and her lack of adherence to norms of submissive deference and proactive avoidance of the male gaze.

Any woman working and earning money in public is a potential *meretrix*; her person is available for open viewing by men, if not necessarily for sexual use.[71] On the other hand, Ulpian distinguishes carefully between *adulterae*, women unfaithful to their husbands with a solitary lover, and *meretrices* who practice their trade openly and without choice of client (*passim, hoc est sine dilectu*).[72] These are presumably the lower-class streetwalkers rather than the freelance courtesans discussed in previous chapters. Freedwomen courtesans' right to choose clients seems to have been a key mark of differentiation for them, as seen earlier in the case of Manilia. Payment for sex may be less crucial as part of the legal definition than the woman's general availability and immodest behavior.[73] Thus someone like Clodia can be called a prostitute, whereas a discreet tavern waitress receiving money once for sex might not be.

John DeFelice has analyzed the connection between taverns and prostitutes in the case of Pompeii, exposing the dubious archaeological evidence that had led to an identification of nearly every tavern waitress as a prostitute.[74] As one example, he cites the tavern of Asellina, located at IX.9.2 on Via dell'Abbondanza in Pompeii, which was identified as a *thermopolium-caupona-lupanar* on the basis of an ithyphallic lamp and graffiti promoting a candidate from election written by the *Asellinas*, the women of Asellina's tavern, "not without Zmyrina."[75] This building may have simply been a female-owned and staffed *thermopolium* which employed no prostitutes. Modern assumptions about the sort of women who write their names on tavern walls may exaggerate the ancient connection between *cauponae* and *meretrices*.

The interest of these barmaids in their local election process offers another glimpse into the lives and voices of marginal Roman women. These women considered themselves to be active members of the political community – citizens, in effect – even if the prescriptive laws labeled their legal citizenship as ambiguous and tentative. Zmyrina could not vote, and her testimony in a legal case might be invalid, but she believed that her opinion about a political candidate was both valuable to herself and potentially persuasive to men who could vote.[76]

A total of fifty-two electoral public graffiti in Pompeii were made by fifty-four different women.[77] Of these women, 25 percent had only Greek *cognomina*, suggesting that they were of a lower social status and likely freedwomen;[78] 43 percent belonged to politically active families and may have been related to the candidates whom they were endorsing.[79] While the specific social status of the vast majority of these women as *matronae*, *meretrices*, or neither is unknown, that very lack of differentiation indicates that these Pompeian women did not consider their profession or social status to be a key aspect of their identity or a determination of their right to participate in the political process. Women in the electoral *programmata* rarely identify themselves by their connection to a male relative; only thirteen of the fifty-four are listed next to a male name, and almost never with a clear familial link.[80]

These graffiti also offer limited but compelling evidence that non-elite Roman women did not necessarily define themselves by their male relationships; their names alone are considered to be sufficient and meaningful support for these male candidates. Furthermore, the implicit

3. A kissing scene on the wall of the tavern of Salvius in Pompeii, Regio VI, Insula XIV, 35 and 36. First century CE, 50 x 205 cm. Museo Archeologico Nazionale, Naples, Italy. Photo: © Scala/ Art Resource, NY.

assumption of these inscriptions is that literate passers by would recognize the names of the women involved, further confirming the relatively public and unproblematic nature of women's interactions with their local community.

Ancient sources do suggest that many, if not all, barmaids were also part-time sex workers, as were other women involved in public economic activities. A set of four tavern vignettes from the outside wall of the Pompeian tavern of Salvius portrays a man and woman standing and kissing in the farthest left image (Figure 3).[81] As the other scenes depict typical tavern activities like drinking, gaming, and fighting, it seems likely that this first image is intended to suggest that prostitute-waitresses are available inside the tavern.[82] The woman wears a yellow garment, a color loosely associated with professional prostitutes, as discussed in Chapter 1.[83] The inscription above the couple's heads reads, *NOLO CUM MYRTALE*, "I don't want to with Myrtale(is)."[84] Whether the girl in question is supposed to be Myrtale, or the young man is supposedly rejecting a second girl, Myrtale, in favor of an alternate companion, is unclear. This graffito could also have been written by someone who was insulting a particular waitress named Myrtale or Myrtalis. In any case, there appears to be a strong connection between this tavern and sexual activity, although not necessarily prostitution. (For more on this vignette, see Chapter 6.)

However, it is still dangerous to assume any general correlation between the two professions of waitress and prostitute, particularly given Ulpian's admission of non-prostitute tavern workers. There is even less evidence for actual associations between prostitution and any other type of public work performed by Roman women. These non-elite working Roman women existed in a liminal, ambiguous state between the clearly defined social roles of the professional streetwalkers and brothel workers and the elite matrons whose economic interests, if any, were focused on real estate and private, domestic sources of income.

For example, Amemone of Tibur, a cook and innkeeper, was praised in her epitaph by her husband for being a *sancta coniunx*, a virtuous wife. However, she was also described as *nota* and possessing *fama ultra fines patriae*, a reputation beyond the borders of her homeland.[85] Like the earlier inscription of Allia Potestas, such an inscription mixes an emphasis on a very public reputation for a woman, one somewhat unusual for a matron, with the moral terminology commonly associated with good wives. In this case, however, Amemone's sexual activities are not described; her husband focuses only on her culinary talents. Even her status as freeborn, freed, or slave is left ambiguous, although her name suggests a Greek origin. Amemone's husband's desire to memorialize her as both wife and chef suggests that he saw no shame in her occupation, despite its frequent association with sex work and the problematic nature of female public employment in general. This evidence further suggests a contrast between elite male proscriptive attitudes towards public women and everyday reality. On the other hand, Amemone may have been safe from reproach precisely because of her husband's existence and affection.

Certainly, Romans at all levels were aware of and in frequent contact with economically active, often independent women. As early as the third century BCE, Ennius titled one of his lost comedies the *Caupuncula*, or "The Tavernkeeper Wench;" we do not know whether the character in question also sold sex.[86] Other inscriptions that reference female inn-keepers do not necessarily imply sex work, although they also do not rule it out.[87]

Meanwhile, Roman women also practiced a wide variety of other occupations, including nurse, grocer, hairdresser, and midwife. The social stigma of such public work appears to have been largely dependent on whether they performed their profession within the context of a familial unit. Female doctors who were members of medical families, like the midwife Scribonia Attike, wife of the surgeon M. Ulpius Amerinus, were proud to memorialize their occupations on their familial tombstones.[88] Their husbands might also commemorate them, like Julia Saturnina of Emerita in Hispania, whose husband described her as both the best of physicians and an incomparable wife.[89] Single independent women seem to have received less recognition overall and perhaps to have been more typically castigated as *meretrices*. The freeborn Asyllia Pollia of North Africa is a rare example of a *medica* who was memorialized only by her freedman when she died at the age of sixty-five, presumably without biological heirs.[90]

The most common kind of working woman praised in funerary inscription is the *nutrix*, or nurse; such women were perhaps often slaves freed by owners grateful for their care as children.[91] Among urban Romans, Sandra Joshel estimates that 41.3 percent of working women mentioned in inscriptions performed domestic service; another 23.6 percent were involved in manufacture.[92] These figures do not suggest that prostitutes were an extreme minority among Roman working women, but rather that they were less frequently, if ever, commemorated in funerary inscriptions by their survivors. Such a conclusion does not even necessarily imply that such exclusion was due to social stigma or shame, for which the only evidence is the somewhat defensive epitaph of Vibia Calybenis discussed in Chapter 2. More pragmatically, freelance courtesans, however prosperous during the height of their careers, were far less likely to leave behind wealthy survivors who desired to memorialize them and their professions for all eternity.[93] The vast majority of prostitutes who were slaves, on the other hand, would rarely have left any documentary record of their existence at all. The absence of memorialization of actual sex workers among other working women does not imply either a lack of prostitutes or a necessary lack of pride, but rather a common lack of either resources or pride by the heirs of such women.

Conclusion

The literary record of accusations of meretricious behavior against elite women suggests that this form of invective was concerned with issues of class and economic agency as well as those of morality. The common thread in all of these insults is not merely that the woman acted as a prostitute, but that she was publicly available and slept with men of low status, even slaves. She is disloyal not just to her family but to the social order itself. The women designated as *meretrices* are placed in a different category than the *adulterae*, although there is obvious overlap in their behavior. They have abandoned their right to belong to an elite, aristocratic *familia* and fallen to the bottom rung of the social ladder. The Vistilia episode from the Introduction is focused, for instance, on Augustus' requirement that her husband divorce the self-proclaimed *meretrix*, rather than on Vistilia's own crimes. It is fundamentally unacceptable for Vistilia both to remain part of the senatorial order and continue in her social role as an elite man's wife while simultaneously labeling herself as a public prostitute.

The application of the label of *meretrix* to elite married women demonstrates that it was not only a term used to describe a specific profession but rather a characterization of a variety of negative attributes, centering on the issue of disloyalty. As Chapters 2 and 3 demonstrated, freedwomen concubines are sometimes depicted as displaying all the virtues of *matronae*. This chapter has shown that patrician women of the noblest blood in Rome could be characterized as lowly, streetwalking *scorta* as a result of their perceived or imputed immoral behavior. Meanwhile, plebeian women who worked publicly as part of a larger familial group were often praised for their work and industry by their families. Although the legal record suggests a strong connection between women's public employment and accusations of prostitution, such an argument is not fully supported by the epigraphic evidence. At the same time, grave inscriptions for *meretrices* are almost entirely lacking, as is any reference to them as part of larger familial groups. *Meretrix* was a label that elite male authors could throw at both elite and ordinary Roman women to smear them with *infamia*; it is not clear, however, that anyone outside the elite male community took such accusations particularly seriously or used them as a means of organizing and defining social relationships.

5

Can you know a *meretrix* when you see one?

Every day, tourists crowd into the famed Pompeii *lupanar* or brothel, considered one of the must-see highlights of any visit. The tour guides point to the images of lovemaking beside each doorway, describing them as advertisements for individual prostitutes and particular sexual positions. An examination of the paintings themselves, however, only confuses the viewer. The women in the pictures have elaborate hairstyles and lounge on expensive couches. The rooms that they "advertise" are small, dark, and cheap. The dichotomy between image and reality is stark, yet the story remains consistent: these are the paintings that inspired the term "pornography," pictures of whores. When the same types of images appear on the walls of isolated rooms in wealthy villas, the common explanation is that, somehow, prostitutes must have crept into the domestic domain to practice their trade in full view of the matron's loom. Public eroticized images of women must be whores, in this view, but there is little space left by many scholars for nude women in the private sphere. This labeling of all erotic art as images of prostitutes further confuses the question of how the label of whore was defined with regard to Roman women in different social settings.

This chapter focuses on Roman visual scenes of lovemaking and the difficulties involved in categorizing either the women depicted in them or the audience of these paintings as definite wives or whores. In considering paintings designed to arouse desire, we must also naturally consider what sort of sexual desire was considered appropriate for different types of Roman women. Modern analysis and assessment of ancient Roman erotic art has been hindered by twentieth-century sexual prejudices and biases. Roman art historians and museum curators have frequently taken the simple approach of labeling fully clothed images of mortal Roman women as wives and erotic, semi-nude mortal women as whores, regardless of other factors such as setting or the context of the image. This dogma is a particular vice of modern scholarship that relates more to current ideas about pornography and its presumed young, male audience than to ancient Roman conceptions of appropriate art for different social contexts.[1]

The Romans themselves failed to make any sharp visual distinction between *meretrix* and *matrona*; indeed, the difference between these categories lay more in the eyes of the beholder or author than in the woman herself. Owing to the nature of the surviving evidence, this chapter will concentrate mainly on the Pompeian frescoes from the first century BCE, as the detail provided in these paintings and the evidence of their physical context is necessary to make any analysis about the identity of the women in these images or their expected audience.

Roman wives, as the Pompeian art and relevant texts will demonstrate, were expected to enjoy and actively participate in sex, although only with their husbands in their own homes. In examining the discourse about Roman female virtues and Roman women's place in society, it is crucial to distinguish between modern (or late antique) and classical attitudes towards pornographic images and married women's sexual desires. The last few chapters have focused largely on what both good and bad women did in Roman public spaces; this chapter interrogates the visual discourse about women in Roman private or semi-private spaces.

A large variety of Roman depictions of lovemaking scenes exist, ranging from relatively crude scenes on Arretine red-figure oil lamps to the exquisite fresco paintings of the Villa under the Farnesina in Rome.[2] At the time of their first excavation in the late eighteenth and nineteenth centuries, nearly all the women in these images were assumed to be prostitutes, given the disarray of their clothing and their active participation in sex. This narrow view has persisted among many scholars today.[3]

In classical Greek art, a woman's status as a *hetaira* rather than a respectable wife might be indicated by a depiction of her either nude or scantily dressed in the setting of a mixed-gender symposium. The lack of a hair veil, often replaced by the presence of elaborate jewelry or a loose hair net, may also be a symbol of a Greek woman's status as a courtesan.[4] In contrast, there are no surviving definite representations of Roman prostitutes, rather than matrons, in Roman art. In determining the social status of women in these images, it is necessary to look at the physical context of the art, the activities depicted in the image, and the portrayal of the female figures.

Erotic art in private homes in Pompeii and Rome

The major scholarly controversy about the intended audience of these images was raised by the location of many of the erotic frescoes in small, isolated rooms (*cubicula*) in elite villas in Pompeii and Rome. These elaborate, elegant dwellings were presumably not the homes of brothel girls and streetwalkers. However, these erotic paintings are stylistically highly similar to those found in the definite Pompeii brothels as well as to the explicit depictions on cheap oil lamps which might have been used by Romans of low social status as well as wealthier individuals. This suggests a commonality of representation in a number of different social settings with distinct expected audiences. The paintings in private elite settings presumably had an intended audience of wealthy married couples. They may also potentially be intended as metaphorical or even literal portraits of their audience, respectable men and women having sex with each other.

On this path, I follow in the footsteps of Molly Myerowitz, who claims, "erotic tabellae from the Augustan Age may have filled needs quite different from our own, which makes it difficult to apply contemporary feminist theories of pornography without risking anachronism."[5] Relatively few of these erotic paintings were found in brothels, where the likely subjects might have been real prostitutes.[6] We find Roman erotic art both in public buildings like baths and inside the rooms of private, elite villas. Within these homes, we find erotic art in the more accessible spaces of the home such as dining rooms, gardens, and atria, as well as in the more secluded, small, private rooms. In other words, depictions of nude women and men engaged in intercourse can be both public and private in the Roman world.

A few general distinctions may be drawn about domestic erotic paintings: mythologically based scenes are more likely to appear in public areas of a house, whereas images of human lovemaking are far more common in the more private areas.[7] Crucially, however, the level of explicit sexual depiction does not appear to vary from space to space. What nymphs and satyrs do to or with each other in the atrium, ordinary men and women do in the *cubiculum*. Modern definitions of erotic imagery also differed from Roman sensibilities. In Pompeii, the smug god Priapus weighs his enormous phallus in a wall painting by the front door of the House of the

Vettii, and other elite homes have wind chimes featuring dangling phalli, intended more as apotropaic symbols than as invitations to arousal. For a modern viewer, the ubiquity of genitalia might be unnerving and scandalous, but for Romans, such representations, when abstracted from scenes of actual lovemaking, were more about male power than about sexual desire.[8]

Recently, Pietro Guzzo and Vincenzo Scarano Ussani have argued that Roman erotic mythological paintings are more allusive than explicit, suggesting a dichotomy between the crude, pornographic "brothel-style" paintings and the more elite, appropriate mythological "romantic" paintings. They distinguish "family quarters" in villas from "slave quarters," suggesting that the respectable elites did not possess explicitly sexual images in their private areas.[9] There are significant potential pitfalls in assigning such rigorous status definitions to spaces in the Roman household.[10] For instance, the secluded private erotic paintings of the imperial Villa della Farnesina are non-mythological but are both elegant and fairly explicit, whereas the public mythological mosaic in the House of the Faun is a crude sexual representation in an elite setting.[11]

For comparison purposes, it is useful to examine briefly public representations of sex in Pompeian painting in commercial buildings, which would probably have been viewed by both genders and by all social groups. We find a number of different types of lovemaking depicted in these images, generally although not exclusively heterosexual. The images from the changing room of the Suburban Baths and from the most well-documented Pompeian brothel (discussed further in Chapter 6) are usually of lower artistic quality than the paintings found in private, elite homes. However, they are quite similar in terms of theme and style, although the Suburban Baths images highlight exotic sexual positions and combinations. Luciana Jacobelli argued originally that this exoticism might result from the images' possible use as mnemonic devices: bathers could remember that they left their clothes "under the threesome."[12] The sheer excess of some of the depictions, featuring not only Rome's sole visual representation of cunnilingus but both a *menage à trois* and a mixed group of four, also provided a certain degree of bawdy humor for the onlookers.[13] The intended purpose may thus be amusing as well as arousing, although it is also possible that the paintings served as indirect advertisements for a brothel located above the baths.[14]

Turning back to the imagery of private rooms, we must first ask whether this is even a meaningful term when discussing the Roman house.[15] Art in Pompeian houses does seem to divide the axes of space among more public and more private areas. However, there are few rooms devoted to a single purpose, and thus the concept of the private "master bedroom" is likely anachronistic.[16] Nonetheless, a distinction can be drawn in elite homes between the areas intended for ostentatious public display, such as the atrium, the garden, and the dining rooms, and the smaller, less accessible private rooms, which would have either been servants' quarters or reserved for the use of the family. It is difficult, however, to firmly designate "slave quarters" as opposed to "family quarters".[17]

This distinction between public and private also suggests a potentially gendered division of space.[18] The erotic paintings in these smaller, more inaccessible rooms tend to feature non-violent encounters between heterosexual couples with individualized faces, although they depict conventional sexual positions similar to those in the Pompeii *lupanar*. In general, these images are painted on the walls of small, interior, windowless rooms known as *cubicula*. While free Romans did generally sleep in *cubicula*, they were not single-purpose rooms. *Cubicula* may have been used by different people at different times of year; they may also have served as small meeting rooms as well as bedrooms.[19] No limited audience can thus be assumed for any domestic erotic image. These paintings would presumably have been viewed by masters, slaves, guests, men, women, and children alike. At the same time, their frequent presence in rooms used for sleeping suggests an intention to arouse or instruct, as small *cubicula* rarely contain other figural scenes and other, larger rooms like *triclinia* (dining rooms) do not often portray human heterosexual scenes of lovemaking.

Paintings of lovemaking are located in a variety of dwellings ranging from the elaborate villas of elite nobility to smaller houses belonging to Pompeian freedmen. They include six panels in the Villa della Farnesina in Rome, located in three adjoining *cubicula*, at least one of which has a separate bed alcove (Figure 4). These paintings are more suggestive than explicit; they display sexually assertive female partners kissing or embracing male partners on luxurious couches and beds. Some panels may be depictions of a wedding night in which the formerly shy bride becomes an enthusiastic lover, serving as a didactic representation of the loyal, passionate wife.[20] Other examples from Pompeii include the House of Caecilius Iucundus, the House of the Cryptoporticus, and the House of the Beautiful Impluvium.

Room 43 of the House of the Centenary, Pompeii, a private, isolated *cubiculum* presumably used as a bedroom, contains two erotic panels of heterosexual lovemaking. One of the images depicts a couple engaged

4. A lovemaking scene on a painted panel from the Villa della Farnesina, Rome. Musei Nationale Romano.

in sex with the woman on top; a small painting in the background may also be erotic, although the details are difficult to discern. This room also has a small interior peephole, originally closed by a wooden shutter, which would have given a view of the room from an exterior dining room (Figure 5).[21] In other words, this is a room designed to allow a voyeur to watch others having sex who are themselves looking at a painting whose subjects are both having sex and looking at a smaller erotic painting. The layers of scopophilia are quite astounding. One imagines that the owners of this house, like Trimalchio and his wife in Petronius' *Satyricon*, might have taken pleasure in viewing guests or friends involved in lovemaking, although it is also possible that the shutter simply served as a way for slaves to check on their masters' needs.[22] In any case, distinguishing this scene as either public or private depends entirely on shifting definitions of these terms – is lovemaking private if viewed by others? The answer for the Romans is unclear.

Not every image of human lovemaking is in even a partially private context; the House of Caecilius Iucundus in Pompeii features a small erotic panel of a reluctant woman and an eager, if non-violent, man,

5. A fresco of an erotic scene from the House of the Centenary, Pompeii. Photo: Fotografica Foglia, Art Resource, NY.

placed on the peristyle between the *triclinium* and an elegant *cubiculum* decorated with mythological romantic scenes of Mars and Venus, Bacchus, and Erato, muse of love poetry. The *cubiculum* would have been a fairly public place for any sexual activity, but the decoration both outside and inside is certainly intended to make the viewer think of physical and romantic love.

The well-known mid-first century CE bronze mirror found near the imperial palaces in Rome probably belonged to a wealthy woman, given its nature and ornamentation; we cannot assume that she was necessarily a wife rather than a concubine. It depicts a lovemaking scene on an elaborately decorated bed.[23] The woman in the image wears jewels and has an elaborate hairdo; various tokens of domesticity, including a puppy and a washbasin, are scattered near the bed, which suggest that this scene is intended to represent a private bedroom rather than an anonymous brothel. On the wall is a miniature *pinax*, or a painting on a wooden panel, and it, too, depicts a scene of lovemaking. However, the couple portrayed on the small *pinax* are engaged in a completely different posture than the larger pair; we cannot take this as simple imitation. In the main image, the man and woman gaze passionately at each other, about to kiss; both male and female bodies are displayed for the gaze and pleasure of the viewer. The lovers within the *pinax* also look at each other; we can see the woman turning her head to gaze at her lover.

The frequent presence of slaves in these representations highlights another striking difference between modern and ancient concepts of privacy. These servants stand idly by, holding chests or waiting for orders, while their master and mistress have sex. In some cases, the slave directly gazes at the viewer, challenging or inviting our intrusive gaze.[24] This further also reinforces the idea that these women are not, as some have suggested, prostitutes; they are presented within the context of an elegant domestic setting as if they were elite matrons or, at a minimum, prosperous freelance courtesans. They are owners of servants and luxury goods, not cheap women hired by the hour or the act.

The erotic paintings in the House of the Vettii

The small *cubiculum* near the presumed servants' atrium in the Pompeian House of the Vettii has generated a substantial degree of scholarly controversy regarding its intended audience and function. This room contains three painted panels, one on each wall, each depicting a scene of heterosexual lovemaking between a mostly nude couple on a relatively ornate bed with striped sheets; a small owl ornaments the fourth wall (Figure 6).[25] J. R. Clarke describes this room as the cook's bedroom, given its location in the servants' quarters, and argues that the paintings were intended as a reward for a good slave, particularly given the Vettii brothers' risqué and unconventional taste in interior decoration.[26] Antonio Varone, as well as Guzzo and Ussani, argue that the room was not for a cook but was rather a private *cella* for the Vettii's household prostitute-slave, Eutychis, where she could practice her trade. Varone bases this theory largely on the existence of a graffito on the outside of the House of the Vettii advertising the services of Eutychis the *verna*, or home-grown slave, for two *asses*.[27] McGinn suggests, meanwhile, that this room was used as a "private sex club" by the Vettii brothers and their guests; he hypothesizes that it was used on special occasions or by privileged friends as a sort of faux-brothel.[28]

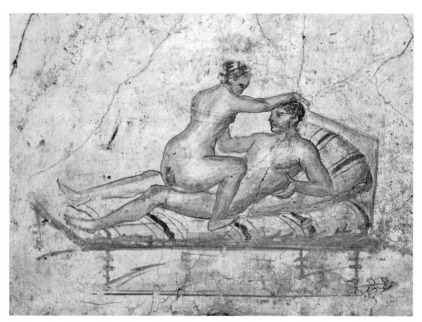

6. A painted panel on the wall of the cook's bedroom in the House of the Vettii, Pompeii, showing an erotic scene. First century CE. Photo: Gianni Dagli Orti/The Art Archive at Art Resource, NY.

Each of these theories attempts to grapple with the perceived incompatibility of brothel-style decorations in a secluded private room in a wealthy *domus*; a room, furthermore, accessible only to a visitor entering through the main door of the building, progressing through the main atrium, turning right into the servants' atrium, and taking another left past a hot oven before entering into a small room on the right (Figure 7). It was not a location that enabled discreet sexual escapades, yet it was also in the presumed servants' quarters.

The graffito on the outside wall is highly suggestive, and arguments later outlined in Chapter 6 about the close proximity of respectable families and brothels lend credence to the idea that the Vettii might have had an active prostitute as part of their household. However, it is still difficult to believe that Eutychis' customers regularly paraded through the atrium of her masters' prosperous villa. Perhaps the "cook" was female and also served as a concubine for one of her masters, rather than as a public prostitute.

In any case, this scholarly controversy illuminates the broader modern debate about distinctions between wives and prostitutes in scenes

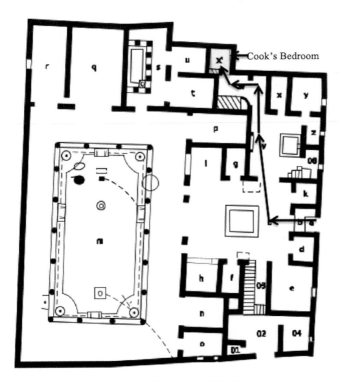

House of the Vettii, Path to Cook's Bedroom, by
author, adapted from Penelope Allison

0   5   10 m

7. The route to the "cook's bedroom," House of the Vettii, Pompeii. Author.

of lovemaking. We assume in this case that these images cannot have
been intended for a matronly audience not because of their content but
because of their location in a small room next to the oven. Yet if they do
not belong to the rooms used directly by the owners of the household, we
must ask why the brothers Vettii chose to spend money having an expensive figural painter ornament this back room. If this household existed
simultaneously as a luxurious villa for a *nouveau riche* family and as a
cheap prostitute's workplace, we must assume regular interaction between
respectable and shameful women, just as seen earlier in Livy's account of
Hispala Faecenia.[29] Alternatively, we must believe that erotic art itself
served as some sort of reward or currency for favored slaves, which at
the least suggests an acknowledgement of slaves' sexual desires by their
masters. Whatever the ideal notion of women's focus on domestic spaces

may have been in the Roman world, any rigid public–private dichotomy breaks down with further study of the material evidence.

Female sexual desire in Roman literature and graffiti

These images of mortal lovemaking from Rome and Pompeii both celebrate consensual lovemaking and looking at erotic art while simultaneously involved in sexual intercourse. Many of the women in these paintings take an active or even dominant role in sex and appear to be passionately focused on their partner. Such obvious desire has led some scholars to argue that these shameless women must be prostitutes.[30] However, Roman texts by both male and female authors provide ample evidence of praiseworthy matronly desire.[31]

The Augustan Age poet Sulpicia, whose condemnation of prostitutes was mentioned in Chapter 4, expresses her physical desire for her pseudonymous lover Cerinthus in her sixth poem. She bemoans the maidenly modesty that made her "desire to hide my passion" (*ardorem cupiens dissimulare meum*). However, the poem itself proudly proclaims her passion, and in context it is clear that she regrets having temporarily refused sexual intercourse with her lover.[32]

The second Sulpicia, a friend of the epigrammist Martial in the late first century AD, is more explicit about her marital pleasure, although only two lines survive, describing "me making love nude with Calenus" (*me ... nudam Caleno concubantem*)."[33] Martial describes the second Sulpicia as an author who taught "chaste and honest loves, the games, the delights, the pleasures of love," who should be read by every girl "who wants to please her husband alone."[34] He also praises her for her devotion to her husband Calenus. In a poem addressed to Calenus after Sulpicia's death, he jokes, "what battles and fights, initiated by both of you, did the lucky little bed and lamp see."[35] Both Martial's statements and other descriptions of her poems suggest that Sulpicia both possessed an active and mutually assertive sex life and proudly celebrated it in her poetry.[36] While both she and her predecessor were highly unusual in their capacity as female authors, their expressions of desire were neither met with surprise nor, until the Christian era, generally criticized as inappropriate.[37]

Male elegiac poets of the Republican and Augustan eras also describe female desire as a natural part of a marital relationship. In his wedding hymn, Catullus describes the bride as *coniugis cupidam novi*, desiring her new husband. He also suggests an equivalence of desire: "in his deepest heart, no less than in yours, the flame burns, but deeper inside."[38] Propertius evokes Arethusa's frustrated longings for her husband Lycotas, who is away at war; she complains of her empty bed and kisses his armor in his absence.[39] In the high Imperial period, the Graeco-Roman author Plutarch tells the story of the passionate widow Ismenodora, who pursued, abducted, and forcibly married a handsome young lad named Bacchon.[40] While Plutarch's tone is wry, he implies that Ismenodora's desire, if not her forcefulness, is entirely natural. Pliny the Younger praises his elderly widowed friend Ummidia Quadratilla for shielding her young grandson from the performances of her private mime troupe, which suggests that the acrobatics were bawdy in nature.[41] While the prudish Pliny is somewhat disapproving of Ummidia's hobby, he does not suggest that her voyeurism is especially scandalous for a woman. Indeed, it seems to be youth rather than gender that is an issue with regard to viewing erotic mimes.

Although Imperial satirists like Juvenal do criticize excessive female desire, they focus their invective on women who stray outside marriage in their pursuit of pleasure, not on women who enjoyed sexual relations with their lawful husbands.[42] Suzanne Dixon argues that authors like Juvenal, Sallust, and Martial criticize female sexual initiative, suggesting that the only appropriate expression of female desire is reactive.[43] Since we have relatively few, mostly male-authored literary texts depicting married female desire, the visual and epigraphic evidence becomes more central to any such discussion and undermines the weight previously given to authors like Juvenal.

The Romans did not have the sort of paranoia about female desire present in Greek literature and scientific texts.[44] Such a social construct of the nymphomaniacal, uncontrolled woman is precisely most threatening in a strongly gender-segregated culture where adult men and respectable women have a minimum of contact. In Rome, women paradigmatically dined with their husbands, as shown in Chapter 1, as well as leaving their homes regularly and interacting with other unrelated men. In such a system, Roman men presumably trusted their wives not to jump into a stranger's arms on the strength of a single convenient unlocked door. At the same time, this made the completely unbounded, unattached woman more of a possibility and therefore more threatening. As established in the previous chapter, it is not Roman women's public presence that threatens their virtue but pursuing public activities openly, without restraint, and without commitment to one man and to the Roman social order. Women's desire, as represented in both literary texts and in the domestic erotic paintings, provides another bond to link women to their husbands.

Since they are socialized to desire sexual relations with their husbands, they are also more likely to remain emotionally and financially loyal.

On the wall in a dark corridor of the Pompeian large theater is scrawled a female-centered declaration of romantic love: *Methe, Cominiaes Atellana amat Chrestum. Corde [si]t utreis que Venus Pompeiana propitia et sem[per] concordes veivan*; "Methe, the Atellan slave of Cominia, loves Chrestus. May Pompeian Venus be favorable to their hearts and may they always live in harmony" (*CIL* 2457).[45] This appears to be the work of a highly literate female slave, although presumably a third party could have written it in their honor, for no clear reason. We have a plausible explanation for Methe's eloquence; the word "Atellan" suggests that she may be an actress and performer of Atellan farces, a career in which literacy would be particularly valuable.[46] She also appears to be the slave of a female owner. The social status of her beloved is unclear, but they seem to be in a long-term relationship.

The theater itself likely served as a temporary home for actresses like Methe, and thus we may read this declaration as a message directly to Chrestus or as a prayer to Pompeian Venus. However, it is also in a paradigmatically public location, where Pompeian citizens attending the performance might easily have viewed and read it. Methe proudly proclaims her love in the same way that Pompeian men declare their passion for various barmaids on the tavern walls across Pompeii. The singular distinction here is that she writes not of her beloved's beauty but of a hope for lasting harmony. This might indicate Roman women's greater emphasis on relationships rather than temporary liaisons, although we lack the data to make any larger statement about female romantic priorities. While such an inscription could, of course, record a purely fictitious relationship, there seems little reason to imagine that Methe or her feelings did not exist.

Erotic art in literature

Both male and female Roman authors suggest that respectable wives could naturally be portrayed as active, enthusiastic sexual partners with their husbands. A woman's presence in an artistic representation of lovemaking, then, does not imply anything about her social or moral status. Meanwhile, erotic paintings were popular enough subjects that Roman authors assumed that women would form a significant part of the intended audience. This also implies that such paintings were assumed to be arousing for women, as well as possibly serving a useful didactic purpose for sheltered young brides.

Ovid claims that Augustus himself possessed erotic paintings, and the Emperor Tiberius is said to have possessed several explicit pieces of statuary and painted panels.[47] Clement of Alexandria, an early Christian writer of the second century CE, preached against: "the pagans who adorn their chambers with painted tablets hung on high ... regarding licentiousness as piety, and while lying on the bed, while still in the midst of their own embraces, ... they fix their gaze upon that naked Aphrodite who lies bound in her adultery ... [They] dedicate these monuments of shamelessness in [their] homes."[48] No gender is specified for Clement's imputed audience; rather the description strongly implies that men and women looked at these paintings together.

Propertius tells us that respectable women were able to view these pictures, even while his narrator condemns them: "It was the artist who first painted lewd panels and set up indecent images in a modest house who corrupted the innocent eyes of girls, refusing to leave them ignorant of his own depravity."[49] While Propertius here is specifically discussing adultery, the indecent images are surely not only those depicting mythical affairs but also simply the more explicit sexual images present in many "modest houses." Propertius assumes both that young girls will have seen these paintings and that they would have been sexually aroused by them. Notably, the problem here is the viewing of such images by unattached girls, who might then desire inappropriate premarital relationships. Propertius does not consider them unsuitable for matrons.

The distinction made here between girls and matrons strongly suggests that desire is a problem only insofar as it threatens female loyalty. *Puellae* – actual rather than metaphorical "girlfriend" *puellae* – ought not to be gazing at erotic art, because they have no appropriate outlet for fulfilling desires caused by such art. An unattached girl looking at such art may seek out an extramarital, promiscuous union. In contrast, they are suitable for the eyes of respectable *matronae* who have learned to look widely but touch only their husbands. This leaves the prostitute, as well as the widow or divorced woman, in an ambiguous position as a viewer. Once again, her agency and self-control is potentially threatening to a patriarchal power structure, requiring proactive rebuke.

Seneca the Younger, also railing against the evils of the modern age, laments, "Women even match their husbands in their passions, although they were born to endure love passively (may the gods and goddesses confound them!). They devise the most exotic acts of shame, and in the company of men they play the part of men."[50] Ironically, Seneca's letter itself implies an active married female sexuality among Romans during the first century CE, the precise date of many of the Pompeian paintings. Seneca may have believed that women were supposed to endure love, but Stoic philosophical theory and social practice appear to have diverged here, given the evidence cited above. Certainly, there would have been little reason for complaint if erotic art was intended only for prostitutes or their customers.

These interior domestic images tend to feature couples that are equally enthusiastic about their sexual activity. Such a display of passion leads to the conclusion that even if men exclusively chose the paintings in these domestic settings, they wished to present women who were taking pleasure in sex.[51] Although certain prescriptive texts from the medical and philosophical traditions advocate sexual restraint for married women, the visual evidence suggests otherwise, as do the comments of Augustan poets and even the complaints of Seneca.[52] Even the prescriptive texts largely advocate moderation and self-control, as they do in other circumstances, rather than suggesting an absence of female desire or that matrons should lie back and think of Rome.

Representations of prostitutes in Roman erotic art

I have established that some erotic images were viewed by respectable matrons and were plausibly created for the use and enjoyment of elite couples. An important question remains concerning the nature of the women in the images themselves: are they wives or whores – good women or bad women? Rather than making blanket generalizations about the moral character of semi-nude women engaged in sex, we must investigate whether there are any telltale symbols in any of these paintings, or in their locations, that indicate that the scene represents a prostitute and client rather than a wife and husband or a man and woman of anonymous social status.

A first obvious step is to examine differences in clothing. Prostitutes, as discussed earlier, were supposed to wear yellow togas, according to legal and literary sources.[53] Kelly Olson has established, however, that the only surviving artistic image of a *femina togata* is a written description of the equestrian statue of the teenage virginal heroine Cloelia from the early Republic.[54] If a toga cannot be a guide to a female prostitute, does a *stola* or mantle at least represent a respectable married woman?

The first pieces of evidence are the images that scholars have most commonly labeled as those of prostitutes. The most obvious candidates are the six erotic panels in the Pompeii main brothel, or *lupanar*, itself,

8. An erotic fresco in the main *lupanar*, Pompeii. Photo: Fotografica Foglia, Art Resource, NY.

which, if not direct advertisements, were presumably intended to make prospective clients think about their forthcoming sex with prostitutes (Figure 8). These images "encode fantasies of upper-class sexual luxuries for viewers who could not afford them," since the rooms in the panels have elaborate draperies and furnishings, rather than being accurate depictions of the tiny cells with masonry beds in the brothel located behind the paintings.[55] At the same time, Levin-Richardson notes that the material objects found in the brothel are fairly similar to those depicted within the images, ranging from glass jars to a small bronze candelabrum, which suggests that the brothel furnishings may have borne more resemblance to the idealized version.[56]

In one of the panels, the woman wears a long green dress and a fashionable hairstyle; Clarke characterizes her as a courtesan or *hetaira* due to the elegance of her costume and her standing position.[57] However, if classification depends on garment quality, the woman might as easily be a respectable *matrona*.[58] Two of the other panels show a short-haired woman wearing only a breast band, two others show a nude woman, and the last is too badly faded to be able to distinguish the clothing well. No slaves are present within these panels.

It seems unlikely that the owners of the *lupanar* would be attempting to portray different types of women within the same set of linked, similar images without more dramatic changes in setting or label. The logical conclusion is that all these figures must be either prostitutes, matrons, or of indeterminate status. Since these images are both similar to those found in private contexts in elite households, and the *lupanar* panels themselves evoke a luxurious environment, these panels are likely intended to represent a fantasy atmosphere of pleasurable, comfortable lovemaking. They refuse to strictly define the social status of the partners involved. While Clarke's idea of the *hetaira* is tempting, Roman culture does not have a sufficiently established representation of an expensive, elegant courtesan to make this an obvious or necessary answer, as was demonstrated textually in Chapter 3.

Another major conclusion to be drawn from this set of panels is that prostitutes cannot be distinguished easily on the basis of clothes, since the panels vary dramatically in how much each woman is wearing. A breast band or *strophium*, for instance, does not appear to be a particular signifier of a prostitute, although we do not see respectable women in non-sexual contexts wearing only breast bands. The so-called "bikini girls," from the late Roman third-century CE Piazza Armerina mosaics in Sicily, also wear breast bands but are clearly represented as athletes rather than as sex workers. The *strophium* may well connote "attractive female" more than "prostitute," much like a modern bikini top. As the *strophium* is largely absent from the literary record, it is difficult to draw any firm conclusions about its use in Roman society.[59]

If we examine other images of lovemaking or seduction commonly labeled as being portraits of Roman prostitutes, the same uncertainty persists. One such representation is a fourth-century CE mosaic medallion in a *cubiculum* in the Villa Romana del Casale in Piazza Armerina, Sicily, which depicts a woman wearing a breast band, a golden necklace, and an elaborate mantle falling to her ankles (Figure 9). The medallion showcases her naked rear to the viewer while she embraces a semi-clad man who is holding some sort of container and a pillow. The couple are apparently in an outdoor setting, perhaps a patio or courtyard, as trees and low columns or walls are evident in the image. Both are standing and embracing each other. This medallion is extremely late in date and differs distinctly in artistic style from the Pompeian works or the Arretine ware, making direct comparison questionable. Notably, however, the image depicts a distinctly different type of scenario from the interior domestic lovemaking scenes so ubiquitous in earlier Roman erotic art.

The rest of the frescoes and mosaics in this *cubiculum* consist of a Dionysiac scene and small medallions depicting women who represent

9. Two lovers: a medallion mosaic from the cubicle of erotic scenes in the Villa Romana del Casale in Sicily. Third–fourth CE. Photo: Erich Lessing, Art Resource, NY.

the four seasons, images highly appropriate for a room used primarily for sex and similar to the mosaics in the purported brothel in Ephesus.[60] On the other hand, Dionysiac imagery is also highly conventional, frequently appearing in Roman *triclinia* and exercise rooms. It seems highly unlikely that a room in an extremely luxurious and enormous villa like the Villa Romana del Casale would be used for professional sex work.

Nevertheless, this particular medallion has been interpreted as a scene not only of lovemaking but of prostitution. The only comparable vertical posture from Pompeian art is a fresco depicting Polyphemus in a passionate embrace with the naked Galatea. The Polyphemus-Galatea painting is explicitly mythological in nature, as established by the sheep at their feet, which implies that the Piazza Armerina medallion is unlikely to be depicting the same characters (Figure 10).

10. An Imperial Roman fresco with an erotic scene depicting the love of Polyphemus and Galatea. *c.* 50–79 CE, from the House of the Capitelli Colorati in Pompeii. Museo Archeologico Nazionale, Naples, Italy. Photo © Vanni Archive/ Art Resource, NY.

Another image that bears even more resemblance to this pose is a mosaic representation of Dido and Aeneas from the house at Low Ham in Britannia, dating from the fifth century CE. While later in time period, this mosaic also portrays a vertical couple, surrounded by trees, with the woman's buttocks bare and exposed to the viewer. This may therefore have been a common image from a pattern book, although at Piazza Armerina the couple are isolated and there is no reference to Dido or Aeneas.[61]

The imagery on Arretine vessels of the Augustan and early Julio-Claudian period ranges widely in its level of explicit depiction. Much variation is also present in the erotic scenes on portable objects of the *instrumentum domesticum* made from more expensive materials like glass and silver. However, most of these images generally retain the structural format of a single couple, either male–female or male–male, upon an elaborately decorated bed.[62] The type of intercourse is no reliable guide to the status of the partners involved, as the woman's coiffure and facial expressions do not significantly vary based on the nature of the act.[63] Like the Pompeian frescoes, these are depictions of sex rather than necessarily of sex for sale.

Only one sexual act, fellatio, might indicate that the woman involved is intended to be a prostitute. Clarke analyzes a variety of similar representations of fellatio on Pompeian oil lamps, one of the fresco panels from the aforementioned Suburban Baths in Pompeii, and ceramic medallions from the Rhone Valley, noting their parallel depictions of a kneeling woman with a reclining man pressing his hand down on her head.[64] One can argue that, since fellatio was shameful according to literary sources, only a prostitute or slave would have been represented as performing this act.[65] However, there is still no way of distinguishing between a professional freelance sex worker and the private *ancilla* or housemaid of a Roman man. While this act might remove the possibility of an encounter between husband and wife as the imagined sexual fantasy, it does not definitely encode a narrative of a prostitute and her customer. We are left without a definitive visual representation of a whore.

The crouching rear-entry, or "lioness," position, as shown in the Suburban Bath frescoes, three Pompeian frescoes of unknown original location, and on various scattered lamps, had a classical Greek association with prostitution.[66] However, the position in Roman art also appears on an elaborate engraved mirror and a cameo-glass vessel, suggesting that wealthy women of unknown social status may have also found the contemplation of this position to be socially acceptable.[67] These owners of these objects might have been courtesans, but we have no positive evidence for such a theory. Thus the symbology of the "lioness" pose becomes unclear. While it may present a less egalitarian mode of sexual activity, it does not necessarily render the woman performing or viewing it impure or infamous, and therefore the married or prostitute status of the woman remains in question.[68]

If clothing is no indication, and the postures of the couple give only indeterminate clues, the last possible signifier of a *meretrix* might be her placement in a setting suggesting solicitation, such as a tavern, or as the character of an actor in a play representing a prostitute. As discussed in Chapter 4, there is a crude painting on the outside of the tavern of Salvius in Pompeii, depicting a woman in a long orange-yellow garment passionately kissing a man in a red tunic (Figure 3).[69] The text above the couple, like a cartoon-style bubble, reads *NOLO CUM MYRTALE...*,

"I don't want to with Myrtale," which happens to be the name of a popular prostitute at the brothel several blocks away. The other three small scenes on this wall appear to depict activities discouraged at the tavern: drunken arguments over service, cheating at dice, and fistfights.[70] It is essentially the equivalent of a "No Shirt, No Shoes, No Service" sign.

The kissing panel may thus indicate that prostitution (or at least on-site foreplay) is not welcome at the tavern. However, the negative of *Nolo* complicates that interpretation, given that the other captions all indicate undesirable activities or statements on the part of customers, with rebukes from the waitstaff and customers. Perhaps the text implies instead that free foreplay or foreplay with prostitutes besides Myrtale, the resident whore, is forbidden. Alternatively, it might specifically ban foreplay with Myrtale herself, perhaps because of a preference for the owner's daughter, Salvia, who may be connected with a graffito, "Daughter of Salvius," which prominently labels the inside of the best room at the nearby Pompeii *lupanar*.[71] In any of these cases, the yellow tunic of the woman, although not a toga, may indicate her prostitute status, but it is hardly definitive evidence.

Alternatively, the Greek style of dress and simple hairstyle of the woman might imply that she is intended to be an elite woman rather than a prostitute.[72] Certainly, the ambiguity of her clothing means that we cannot firmly state that Roman viewers would have looked at this image and assumed that the woman was a whore. However, the color of her dress and her amorous activity are highly suggestive.

In a Pompeian painting currently in the Naples Museum, the artist has depicted a scene from an unknown Roman comedy of three masked actors (Figure 11). As discussed in Chapters 1 and 2, prostitutes were common characters in such comedies. A female figure wearing a plain white mask is dressed in an elaborate yellow and blue stola over a long, brightly colored tunic, with an elegant upswept coiffure. She stands between a male slave figure in a short tunic and a young elite man in a dark long tunic.[73]

The only aspect of her dress that might distinguish her from a respectable matron is the yellow color of her *stola*, but the *stola* itself is a highly respectable garment. She was labeled by the Naples Museum curators as a prostitute because of the comic associations with *meretrices* and her presence in a scene with a slave, a young man, and no other female companion or chaperone. In isolation, however, or without a mask, this woman might very well be interpreted as a highly respectable *matrona*. Her hand is even raised to her mouth in a common gesture of female *pudicitia* or modesty.[74]

11. A fresco scene from a comedy (Atellan farce), Pompeii. Museo Archeologico Nazionale, Naples, Italy. Photo: Erich Lessing, Art Resource, NY.

Meanwhile, women who were definitely elite Roman matrons often depicted themselves in highly erotic fashions on their tombstones or public monuments.⁷⁵ These women used nudity as a costume in order to associate themselves with the Greek goddesses whose statue-types they borrowed. The implication of these nude matron statues was certainly not that respectable middle-aged matrons frequently paraded nude through the Forum – or that they actually possessed the curvaceous bodies depicted in their sculptures. At the same time, such representations invited Roman men to consider these matrons as sexual objects, if only after their death.

One of the best known and most puzzling examples of such a mixture of erotica and respectability is the tomb of Ulpia Epigone, from the late first or early second century CE (Figure 12).⁷⁶ Ulpia Epigone has the hairstyle and accoutrements of an elite matron, although her name suggests that she or her ancestors were former slaves of the imperial family.

DIS MANIBVS
PERMISSV   VLPIAE   EPIGONE   L·N

12. The sepulchral high relief of Ulpia Epigone. Late first or early second century CE. Museo Gregoriano Profano, Vatican Museums. Photo © Vanni Archive/Art Resource, NY.

Her recumbent pose, partial nudity, and prominent breasts, however, invoke the paintings of the Pompeii *lupanar* rather than the modestly draped statues of Livia.[77] Like the woman in the erotic mirror discussed earlier (Figure 4), Epigone is depicted with a dog and a wool basket, but such motifs are also associated with the matronly virtues of fidelity and industry.[78] If a man was present on the couch beside her, this image might be classified as an erotic relief of a prostitute. Instead, Ulpia's relief is categorized as a funerary monument invoking mythological motifs. D'Ambra defines her as "a model of *venustas* and *castitas*," both attractiveness and chastity.[79] Like Allia Potestas, she is a mixture of matron and whore, invoking attributes of both types of women. The visual difference between a Roman *matrona* and a *meretrix* is much smaller than the supposed social gulf that lay between them; we cannot discover any evidence about Ulpia Epigone's sexual freedom or economic agency by gazing at her funerary relief.

Conclusion

Upon examination of the surviving artistic evidence, there is no means of drawing a clear visual division between wives and whores, either in terms of representation or in terms of potential audience for a given image. This suggests that sexual activity was not a means of visual or literary categorization for different types of Roman women. Non-elite men and women in Roman society, who purchased and viewed many such erotic images, may not have considered the distinction between *meretrices* and *matronae* to be particularly important. Visual art is particularly important as a source of evidence here, precisely because it is not limited either in authorship or audience to a tiny class of predominantly male literate elite citizens. Since women of all social backgrounds were expected to have active sexual desires and to be aroused by pornography, the mere presence of a woman in a scene of lovemaking does not indicate that she is a shameless whore. Indeed, such paintings, when displayed in elite domestic contexts, may have been intended as inducements to arouse timid young wives, perhaps in the hope of increasing the odds of pregnancy.

It is an unfortunate legacy of nineteenth-century prudishness, continuing in the discourse of the twentieth and twenty-first centuries, that we often view all representations of lovemaking in Roman art as necessarily representing prostitutes and clients rather than husbands and wives, owners and slaves, or, most likely, imaginary couples of entirely ambiguous social status and relationship to each other. If we do not label these representations as portraits of *meretrices*, however, we are left with no images that definitively portray Roman prostitutes; they remain visual if not literary enigmas. As the various sources discussed have revealed, the most reliable indicator of a whore is not that she has sex, nor even that she has sex for money, an aspect never represented directly in Roman art. Rather, a whore is defined by her behavior and character, which is almost impossible to depict visually. In the Roman imagination, the physical acts of a woman were much less important than the partner or partners who shared those acts, as well as the mental and emotional commitment of the woman to her partner.

6

Prostitutes and matrons in the urban landscape

> Often serious-browed matrons see nude girls positioned for every kind of sex act. Vestal eyes gaze on prostitutes' bodies, nor is that any cause to punish the owner.
>
> *Ovid, Tristia 2.309–12*[1]

In this verse, Ovid attempts to defend his *Ars Amatoria* against the charge that it incited promiscuity and vice in respectable matrons. He argues that both Roman matrons and even the sacred Vestal Virgins regularly encountered prostitutes, even though the Vestals lived in the Forum Romanum itself and presumably traveled only through elite and public neighborhoods. Neither the matron, the owner of the gaze, nor the objectified *meretix*, putative owner of her nude body, ought to be held responsible for such an encounter.

While such a claim fits earlier evidence that Ovid frequently deliberately blended the social spheres of *meretrix* and *matrona* in his work, this poem also contradicts any idea of a separate illicit red-light district.[2] The popularity among modern scholars of the idea of Roman moral zoning may stem from a general contemporary view that public sex work and solicitation is inherently shameful. In particular, streetwalking and sordid brothels, which generally have a lower-class clientele, are ghettoized in the modern imagination, even while high-class escorts advertise openly for "girlfriend-type experiences" in respectable newspapers, magazines and on the Internet.[3] Both the literary and the archaeological evidence in this chapter, however, demonstrate the visibility of prostitutes and the acceptable nature of their activities in the ancient Roman world. Not only men but *matronae* view and are viewed by *meretrices*; this gaze is not morally corrupting for the matron, nor does it humiliate the prostitute.

While Roman prescriptive texts clearly distinguish distinct types of women, any such separation was neither geographical nor temporal in nature. Roman *matronae, meretrices,* and all the women discussed in earlier chapters who transcended or transgressed these labels would have necessarily and frequently encountered each other in the Roman urban landscape. In order to construct any plausible model of such interactions, however, we need first to establish briefly how to locate these women within their physical setting.

The archaeological and literary record cannot give us any statistical sense of how many prostitutes were in a given city or where and how often they practiced their trade. While McGinn has attempted to generate a comparative set of statistics through modern brothel studies, these can give us only wide ranges of possible numbers of customers and prices.[4] Furthermore, McGinn focuses narrowly on evidence from Pompeii. By also examining cities outside southern Italy and considering new criteria for identifying possible locations of sex work, we can gain a more general sense of how Roman prostitutes functioned in the urban landscape of the Empire.

Modern scholarship on the location of sex work in the Roman city has focused almost exclusively on an attempt to label and count brothels, largely within the small city of Pompeii.[5] This is a search concerned, naturally, with definitions and vocabulary: what makes a building a brothel? This hunt for brothels also seeks to locate and segregate Roman prostitutes themselves: both Ray Laurence and Andrew Wallace-Hadrill have suggested "red-light districts" for prostitutes in Pompeii, separating the shameful women from the eyes of respectable matrons and maidens.[6]

While McGinn has recently used archaeological evidence to disprove this theory of "zoning shame" for Pompeii, this chapter establishes that prostitutes worked in highly public locations in urban areas throughout the Roman Empire.[7] While *meretrices* certainly did not share the same social status or respect as married women, they formed a ubiquitous part of the urban landscape. Just as prostitutes formed an essential part of the community during the yearly cycle of Roman religious festivals, as shown in Chapter 7, they also played a public and visible role in the daily lives of urban citizens from Ephesus to North Africa.

Through a set of case studies of possible brothel sites in Pompeii, Ephesus, Ostia, Dougga, and Scythopolis, as well as a review of the surviving literary descriptions, we can further illuminate Roman attitudes towards prostitutes and how they functioned in Roman society. As brothels are the best archaeological proofs of sex work in areas where graffiti have not survived, this chapter will primarily concentrate on using brothels as a means of establishing the prominence of prostitutes in the urban environment and their relationship to their communities.

Limitations of archaeology: prostitution outside brothels

While our existing literary evidence does repeatedly mention and describe brothels, it also strongly suggests that Roman prostitutes were limited neither by neighborhoods nor buildings.[8] As discussed in the Introduction, none of the common words for prostitutes define them with regards to a spatial context.[9] The most common term used for brothel, *lupanar*, merely refers to a wolf-den; it does not convey any specific restrictions for location, structure, or size.

Furthermore, literary texts and the epigraphic evidence of graffiti tell us that sex work took place in a wide variety of locations including baths, graveyards, the back rooms of *tabernae*, and alleyways. In Roman Egypt, one of our best sources of documentary evidence for the Roman Empire, there are indications of major centres of prostitution in the larger Delta towns, as well as at Alexandria, Antioch, and Constantinople, but we have found no clear archaeological record of such activity at these sites.[10] Similarly, no likely brothels have been found in Roman Britain or Gaul, despite the assumption that sex work must have taken place in these provinces.

The late Roman jurist Ulpian distinguishes pimps, or *lenones*, into two categories: those for whom selling prostitutes is a primary business and those who do it as a sideline of related businesses such as managing taverns or baths. Such a distinction suggests that sex work frequently took place in both those locales.[11] Pompeian graffiti, as Clarke and Varone have shown, offer sex for sale outside the doors of relatively respectable houses like the House of the Vettii; we also find advertisements or accusations of promiscuity on apparently random walls and gates.[12] Furthermore, the more prosperous freelance courtesans discussed in earlier chapters may not have had any obvious permanent signifiers of their profession at their workplace or home at all. We must assume that sex was sold in a wide variety of locations where it left no surviving archaeological evidence: by its very nature, sex work is a transitory act. In order to learn what we can about the presence of prostitutes in the urban landscape, then, we must turn reluctantly to the minority of sites which do offer relevant data: possible brothels.

Wallace-Hadrill's brothel-identification model

Most current scholars of Roman brothels extrapolate all their conclusions from the structure, size, and decoration of the most obvious *lupanares* of Pompeii. This method of data collection remains constant even though these studies cannot agree about the definition of a brothel in this one town. While their conclusions are generally accurate with regard to Pompeii, they have the weakness of sifting through the same overused evidence in an effort to establish new theories.[13]

Wallace-Hadrill has developed a model based on his research in Pompeii and Herculaneum, which suggests that the most reliable indicators of a brothel are "a masonry bed set in a small cell of ready access to the public, the presence of paintings of explicit sexual scenes," and a "cluster of graffiti of the *hic bene futui*' type."[14] If at least two of these markers are present, he declares that the archaeologist may be justified in identifying a location as an ancient brothel. Like other scholars, Wallace-Hadrill admits that such buildings may have had multiple uses as taverns or hotels in addition to their sexual purposes.

These signifiers have obvious disadvantages and serious limitations as means of evaluating possible brothel sites. Sexualized graffiti may simply indicate that the author was contemplating sex at the time of its composition. However, a concentration of such inscriptions is certainly suggestive of nearby sexual activity if not prostitution (unless prices are advertised). Graffiti demonstrates thought, not action, and it may well be exaggeration rather than reality. We do not assume that modern public bathrooms with obscene graffiti are probable locations for sex work, rather than surfaces for explicit commentary about sex by both men and women.

Erotic art, as discussed in Chapter 5, indicates more about the artistic tastes of the owners of the room than the owners' professions.[15] For instance, the high-quality paintings of lovemaking in the Villa della Farnesina in Rome are almost certainly unconnected with the payment of money for sex acts.[16] Depictions of sex in art, whether wall paintings or suggestively shaped drinking vessels, were commonly displayed in the atria and gardens of wealthy Roman households, rather than being limited to the *cubicula* where sexual activity presumably actually took place. Furthermore, simple images of genitalia, like the ceramic or plaster phalli frequently found on street corners in Roman towns, probably represent not advertisements for sex but good luck tokens or religious imagery. We may be simultaneously overestimating and underestimating the presence of prostitutes in the urban landscape.

Wallace-Hadrill's reliance on visual motifs is only possible in unusually well-preserved sites such as Pompeii; it fails to be useful in sites like Ephesus that have long been exposed to the elements. As for masonry beds, the presence of these is likely to have been dependent on local building materials and styles, as there is nothing intrinsically related to prostitution about such a bed. Wooden beds may have been common and not survived the eruption in Pompeii; prostitutes may also have used straw pallets or no bed at all.[17]

Non-Pompeian methods of brothel identification

If we cannot rely on art and graffiti, and masonry beds may not have survived or been common in other areas of the Empire, how do we find a Roman brothel? Without knowing where the sex workers were, how can we know if they encountered respectable wives? Until now, the process has been circular: a building is defined as a brothel on its similarity to the "purpose-built brothel," the notorious Pompeii *lupanar*, which in turn was identified partially based on its similarity to descriptions in Juvenal and Petronius, as discussed later in this chapter. The greatest strength of the literary texts is their implication that, while not all sex work took place in brothels, brothels were a common feature of the Roman city and a standard location for sex work.[18]

In order to expand our data set and produce a more useful model, I offer some additional new criteria by which to evaluate potential brothels outside of Pompeii. Locating brothels elsewhere in the Empire helps establish the prominence of Roman prostitutes in general in the urban landscape, rather than relying on the evidence of one possibly atypical town.[19] Many sites previously identified as brothels, like the Ephesus Via Curetes building, have been subsequently dismissed because they did not adhere to the Pompeian canon. By comparing a variety of these other sites and supplementing the archaeological records with literary evidence, it is my hope to establish a new set of possible brothel signifiers for the Roman Empire, which can help to define sites that are not as well-preserved as Pompeii. The location and prominence of these other sites can then inform us about the spatial history of Roman prostitution more broadly.

I propose three major new criteria which, when taken together with the existing signifiers, may enable us to positively identify more brothels: a central urban location, the presence of multiple entrances, and the availability of a private or nearby public water supply. None of these criteria will produce infallible results individually, but as a whole they produce more information both about brothels and, more importantly, how prostitutes functioned in society.

All of the purported brothels discussed in this chapter contain at least one of the generally accepted brothel signifiers, such as *cellae* or erotic art or sexual graffiti, but their definition as brothels has remained contentious due to the lack of sufficient indicators according to the Wallace-Hadrill model.[20] Besides the famous Pompeii *lupanar*, I will primarily be referencing four other far-flung late Imperial brothels, chosen to demonstrate the wide range of common forms: a possible brothel on the Via Curetes in Ephesus, in use during the third–fourth centuries CE, which contains erotic art and a suggestive inscription; the House of the Trifolium in the North African city of Dougga, dating from the second–fourth centuries CE, which possesses erotic art and prophylactic mosaics; the Domus delle Gorgoni from the Italian port of Ostia, from a similar time period, which has a masonry bed; and the sixth-century CE Byzantine potential brothel of Scythopolis, located in modern Israel, which preserves several erotic graffiti.

All these sites remain in relatively good states of preservation due to their abandonment in the later stages of the Roman Empire; this is the cause of the unavoidable if unfortunate focus on a later time period than the evidence presented in earlier chapters. I will briefly describe each site before moving onto the larger conclusions drawn by comparing them as a group.

Pompeii

In Pompeii, over thirty of the various purported brothels, by whichever scholarly standard used, are located to the east and north of the Forum, within a five-block radius of the Stabian Baths (Figure 13).[21] Wallace-Hadrill claims that "impure activities" were displaced into a hidden area of back alleys near the Forum, preserving anonymity while maintaining proximity to the Forum.[22] However, this argument unnecessarily focuses on the physical brothels themselves rather than the presence of prostitutes near and around these brothels, which would certainly have intruded upon the view of any elite residents passing from, for instance, Regio VI through Regio VII to the Forum. The most famous of these sites, the main Pompeii *lupanar*, is located a few blocks from the Forum, near the Stabian Baths. This building has one main entrance on a side street

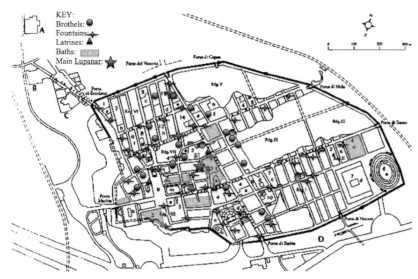

13. Pompeii: map of brothels, public fountains, latrines, and baths, adapted by the author from T. A. J. McGinn, *Economy*, map 5.

and another, smaller entrance onto a side street. It is situated within a block of two of the local street fountains, giving it ready access to water for washing.[23]

The architectural plan of the *lupanar* in Pompeii's Region VII is a narrow hallway, with five *cellae* on the ground floor and a wooden staircase going up to a second floor (Figure 14). Each *cella* contained a raised masonry bed, fairly hard and rough, with a rounded masonry pillow at one end. [Figure 15] There was a bell by the stairs, perhaps to summon the pimp, or *leno*, and a small latrine or washing area located under the stairs themselves.[24]

This floor plan supports the literary notion that brothels were places of work rather than primary residences for the prostitutes themselves (Figures 15, 16). The rooms are narrow and designed for sex rather than sleep, judging by the length of the beds, which averages about 5 feet (1.5 meters), significantly shorter than many of the stone or cement dining couches which have been excavated in Pompeii. There is no atrium or other public space; the building also lacks any *triclinium* or facility for cooking food.[25] The entrances to the *cellae* are narrow, and there is no evidence of doorpost holes that might suggest that wooden doors formally separate the rooms from the hallway. However, hanging cloth partitions may have provided a modicum of privacy for the *meretrices*

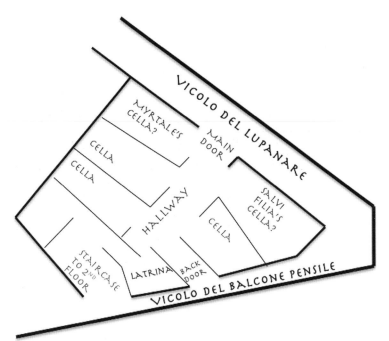

PLAN OF POMPEII'S MAIN LUPANAR, VII-12-18,
Author's Drawing, After Guzzo and Ussani, (2000), 10

14. Map of the main *lupanar* in Pompeii (Author).

and their clients. It is possible that the upper floor was used for residential purposes, but site plans have not yet been fully published, and the second floor is not currently accessible to the public.[26] The *lupanar* also has several erotic panels as discussed in Chapter 5, located in the upper wall zone above the doorways to the *cellae*; the north wall contains an image of a biphallic Priapus. One hundred and thirty-four graffiti decorate the inside and outside walls of the building, mostly sexual in nature or directly referring to prostitution through an association of a woman's name and a price. They are written in both Latin and Greek and appear to be the work of both prostitutes and their customers.[27]

Ephesus

As you walk down the Via Curetes of Ephesus, away from the amphitheater towards the Library of Celsus, you come across a crude drawing of a foot, a heart, and a portrait of Tyche etched on a cobblestone (Figure 17). This image has historically been interpreted as an advertisement for the

15. The interior of the main brothel, Casa di Lupanare, Pompeii. Photo: Fotografica Foglia, Scala/Art Resource, NY.

building on the lower left corner of the approaching crossroads, which has been controversially labeled as a brothel since its excavation.[28]

This major purported brothel of Ephesus lies at an intersection of the Marble Road, one of the principal streets of Ephesus, and the large Via Curetes, one of the other major roads; it adjoins the Scholastikia Baths and the city's largest public men's latrine and is located across the street from the Library of Celsus. The purported brothel was constructed at the same time and as part of the same complex as the latrine and the baths, although it later underwent substantial renovation.[29] The more elite domestic residences are located higher on the hills and away from leisure complexes. Jobst argues that the building was a wealthy residential villa rather than a brothel, largely due to the high quality of the mosaics in the Curetes section of the house.[30] However, this theory does not explain its unorthodox location or other brothel-like features.

This building has two definite entrances and a possible third one: a secluded, turning passageway next to a small corner tavern on the precise

16. The main hallway of the Casa di Lupanare. Photo: Fotografica Foglia, Scala / Art Resource, NY

corner of the Marble Road and Via Curetes; a relatively large doorway about 6 meters from the corner on the Via Curetes itself; and a possible second-story access, now collapsed, from the neighboring large public latrine, which had an inscription in the corner closest to the brothel reading *paidiskeia*, or "brothels." Unfortunately, we have lost the second floor of the Via Curetes building, so we cannot confirm direct access between the latrine and the brothel. However, this seems highly likely given the overall building structure and the graffito.[31] The structure of the building is divided into two main sections: the section abutting the Via Curetes is a residential area with multiple large rooms and elegant mosaics, while the corner section of the building has two main rooms and a number of small *cellae* adjoining them, as well as an occluded entrance.

While the space could have been utilized as an inn, the lack of any hearth, cooking area, or *thermopolium* makes this option less likely than that of a brothel. For comparison purposes, John DeFelice defines *hospitia*, or inns, in Pompeii by the criteria of both potential sleeping areas and

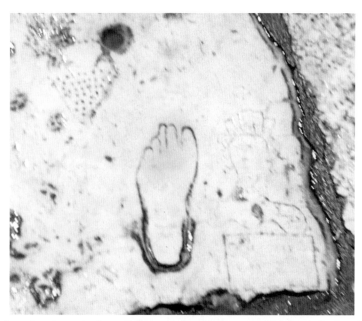

17. An advertisement from Ephesus, possibly for a nearby brothel, showing a heart, foot, and Tyche. Via Curetes, Ephesus. Photo: Art Resource, NY.

hearths for cooking facilities.[32] Furthermore, Jan Bakker distinguishes between hotels and potential brothels in Ostia by studying thresholds with pivot-holes, since hotels tended to have doors that could be locked individually, whereas prostitutes' *cellae* did not.[33]

The exterior doorway onto the Via Curetes possesses such pivot-holes, as does the doorway separating the two sections of the building. The four small rooms off the two main rooms of the corner section do not have them, however, implying that they were likely only shielded by curtains, which would be consistent with the identification of this building as a brothel. As Apuleius and other Roman writers frequently describe the dangers of theft in inns, it seems likely that urban hotels would have placed a high priority on lockable doors, particularly in high-profile locations like the Via Curetes.[34] Other findings include a large statue of Priapus, a hip-bath, a water-spigot, and a graffito instructing visitors to "Enter and enjoy," all highly suggestive if not conclusive evidence of part of this building's use primarily as a brothel at certain points in its long history (Figure 18).[35]

Dougga

The House of the Trifolium, a purported brothel in the North African city of Dougga, is also on a major road next to a public bath and a large

18. A stone statuette of Priapus, 10 cm high, found in a brothel hip-bath. Via Curetes brothel. Second century CE. Ephesus Archaeological Museum. Photo © Vanni Archive/Art Resource, NY.

public latrine (Figure 19). While it is not close to the Forum or Agora as in Pompeii and Ephesus, the Trifolium House is still surrounded by other large centers of public entertainment. Furthermore, it is nowhere near any other residential buildings and is therefore not part of any typical neighborhood.

The architecture of the Dougga House of the Trifolium, which is currently being re-excavated, appears similar to that of the other purported brothels. According to its current excavators, the building was renovated on multiple occasions. Given its portico and elaborate *triclinium*, this edifice was probably originally an elite villa which may have been later repurposed as a brothel. The House of the Trifolium possesses the unusually occluded entrance common among other brothels; the later renovations added more small *cellae*, which also support the theory that this building may have been used for sex work.[36]

Golfetto records various "prophylactic mosaics" but unfortunately does not detail their imagery; the more recent excavations have not

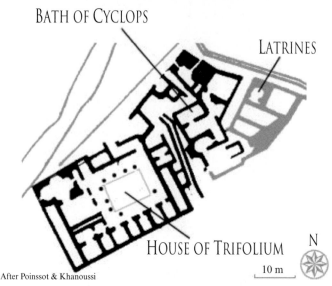

19. Plan of the House of the Trifolium, Dougga, North Africa. Based on Mustapha Khanoussi, *Dougga Collection: Sites and Monuments of Tunisia* (2002).

reached that area of the building yet.[37] A prominent phallus and breasts are inscribed on the wall outside (Figure 20). While there is less evidence for this building's use for sex work than at several of the other locations, the various architectural and locational anomalies and the presence of a variety of brothel signifiers make its identification highly plausible. The House of the Trifolium features a hip-bath and a flowing drain or shallow fountain constructed during the later renovations at Dougga, suggesting a new emphasis on water accessibility during the repurposing of the building.

Scythopolis

The alleged Scythopolis brothel is located on the main Street of Palladius across the street from a bath complex and another latrine, in the ancient province of Judaea, now the site of Beth Shean in modern Israel. The building, also known as the Sigma Plaza or Portico, dates from the beginning of the sixth century CE, when Scythopolis was a city of 40,000 people stretching over 375 acres.[38] The structure is a semicircular exedra

20. A stone relief of phallus and breasts from the House of the Trifolium, Dougga, North Africa. Photo: Manuel Cohen/Art Resource, NY.

measuring 13 by 15 meters; each half possesses six narrow trapezoidal *cellae* with front doors, and another row of small *cellae*, possibly built at a different date, stretch horizontally across the end of the exedra that faces directly onto the Street of Palladius.[39] Some of the ground floor *cellae* also feature multiple exits, which open onto a corridor or alley at the back of the building as well as onto the courtyard.

The courtyard itself measures 21 by 30 meters. Traces remain both of an interior staircase leading to a lost second floor from one of the exedra *cellae* and an exterior staircase with a balcony and perhaps five more *cellae* on the upper floor, a pattern similar to that of Pompeii's brothel. Three out of these five extra exits open directly onto doors leading into the neighboring baths, suggesting easy transit between the two buildings, just as in Ephesus. Two of these particular rooms, both located towards the back of the western side of the semicircle, third and fourth from the left side, contain rough remains of benches, which further supports the theory that they were used for sex work. The floors of the rooms were covered with mosaics depicting poems in Greek, animals and plants, and a Tyche crowned by the walls of Scythopolis.

This building may have had other purposes before possible conversion of some sections into a brothel, given the elegance of its furnishings. It may also have served a loftier clientele than the Pompeii Regio VII *lupanar*, or it may have been a larger marketplace in which only a few rooms were used as prostitutes' *cellae*.[40] Other suggested uses are as a marketplace or guildhall, but the lack of any trace of tools or material deposits of food makes this hypothesis difficult to substantiate positively. At the same time, its general layout is more suggestive of an open forum or market than the brothels discussed elsewhere in this chapter; it seems unlikely that it was a single-purpose structure for sex work. Unlike other such structures, it was also a more public and official building, dedicated by Silvinus, son of Marinus, the first citizen of the town, in 506/7 CE.[41] Its lengthy history and later use as a Muslim cemetery may also have contributed to a lack of artifacts that might conclusively establish its usage patterns.[42]

While no erotic art has survived in the Sigma Portico, sexual graffiti are the primary set of evidence supporting the theory that certain rooms in this building were likely used as regular locations for sex work. In the *cella* featuring the Tyche mosaic, there are two graffiti: "The room of the most beautiful woman" and "I pour passion, like lightning in the eyes." These certainly imply a romantic or sexual purpose for the rooms. An inscription in another *cella* further bolsters this hypothesis: "To the friends of Magus who decorated the room and amused themselves the night long with young women."[43] While this message could refer simply to a sympotic gathering, the highly public nature of the building argues against any private residential purpose for the site. The main entrance also bears an inscription, "Enter and enjoy," which is also a prominent graffito on the Ephesus brothel. However, this particular phrase is often associated simply with inns or other places of public entertainment. It does not necessarily have a specific connotation with sex work, although it does add further evidence for the public nature of the building.

The most plausible explanation of these graffiti is that the Sigma Portico was used as a multipurpose entertainment and shopping complex, located in a central and prominent location, much like the other brothel/bath/latrine complexes discussed in this chapter. The portico's front entrance was on the main Street of Palladius, a Roman odeon was nearby, and a bath complex was across the street. The prostitutes might have paraded on the front portico or across the street at the baths.[44] At

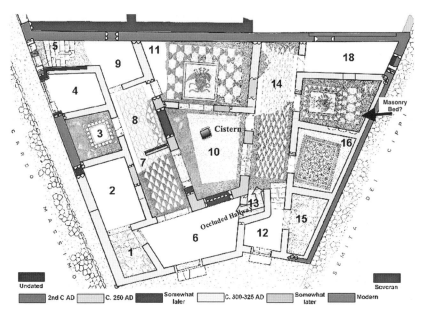

Domus Delle Gorgoni, Ostia, after J.T. Bakker (work in progress)

21. Plan of Domus delle Gorgoni, Ostia. Adapted from J. Th. Bakker; see www
.ostia-antica.org/regio1/13/13–6.htm.

the same time, the Sigma Portico had several rooms with back doors to
a narrow alley, which would enable prostitutes' clients to enter or leave
unobtrusively if desired. If indeed prostitutes worked regularly out of the
Sigma Portico as late as the sixth century CE, it is further evidence that
sex work remained a prominent and socially accepted part of the urban
landscape even into the Christian period.

Ostia

The Domus delle Gorgoni in the Roman port city of Ostia is located on
the corner of two main streets, the Cardo and Semita di Cippi, in Regio
I opposite the Porta Laurentina (Figure 21). According to T. J. Bakker,
"No other large ground floor building in Ostia is at such a busy spot."[45]
The Domus delle Gorgoni also bears the signs of a residential villa that
might have been later repurposed as a brothel.[46] Multiple occluded
entrances to the building are present, although not to the *cellae* themselves. There are also indications of a permanent bed in one of the *cellae*
where the mosaic was not continued, leaving a blank spot, although the
bed itself has not survived. Nevertheless, the evidence suggests that this
was one of Wallace-Hadrill's aforementioned masonry beds. Unlike other

purported brothels, both elaborate dining and kitchen facilities appear to be present in the Domus delle Gorgoni, further confusing its purpose. The building also has a large basin for water in the main courtyard, as well as several small *cellae* and multiple *triclinia*. Bakker currently argues that this structure may have served as an undertakers' guildhall rather than as a site for sex work; his argument is plausible but not conclusive and further work remains to be done.[47]

In a major port city such as Ostia, the presence of prostitutes can be assumed; the architecture of the Domus delle Gorgoni suggests that they may not only have been present but plying their trade by the city gate at the intersection of two major streets. At the same time, the positive arguments for this building as an exclusive location for sex work are relatively weak compared to the other structures discussed in this chapter.

Given the nature of prostitution, any such identification of any structure less obvious than the Pompeii main *lupanar* will necessarily be disputed and controversial. The more useful and pragmatic approach is therefore to draw conclusions from larger commonalities and patterns among these buildings. Trying to establish conclusively all the usages of any one particular structure is likely to be unproductive. However, this does not diminish the value of examining these purported brothels as a set in comparison with the Pompeii *lupanar* and evidence from literary texts. Such a study helps illuminate the likely prominence of sex work in urban settings across the Empire.

Location

One common factor of all of these purported brothels is their location relative to the rest of the city, which would be highly unusual for elite residential villas. In every case, the building is located near the center of town, usually within a few blocks of the Forum or Agora. According to literary references in Catullus, Plautus, and Propertius, the prostitutes of the city of Rome frequently practiced their trade in the most public area of the city, the Forum Romanum, especially near the Temple of Castor and Pollux.[48] Other popular Roman locations for prostitutes, such as Pompeius' portico and the temple of Venus Erycina by the Colline Gate, were all highly public locales.[49]

These locations offer evidence for constant interaction between prostitutes and the elite classes, since senators, *equites*, and other Roman elites regularly traveled through the Forum and other areas of public business. Laurence's theory that Roman elite women and children could regularly avoid contact with prostitutes of either gender is highly implausible; they were as much a part of the center of Roman life as merchants, priests, or watchmen.[50] Rather than any idea of moral zoning, Roman forums and major streets would have necessitated visual contact between all types of women and men.

Of course, while women like the Empress Livia and the Vestal Virgins may have seen prostitutes, this does not mean that they interacted with them publicly or had contact with them. Matrons could demonstrate their own *pudicitia* precisely by ignoring the sight of disrespectable women. In Plautus' *Cistellaria*, a madam complains that the upper-class matrons speak flatteringly to prostitutes in public but mock them behind closed doors, as well as restricting their access to the female social network. In this case matrons do interact with prostitutes but in socially constrained and discriminatory contexts.[51] Furthermore, the privilege of elite matrons to travel in litters in cities may have meant that there was little chance that a matron and a prostitute would actually physically contact each other, even if they traveled on the same street.

Respectable women would generally be accompanied by slaves or husbands; such figures might also have provided a physical barrier between these different classes of women.[52] Elite women, however, would have had to take affirmative steps to prevent themselves from seeing prostitutes, rather than prostitutes being pre-emptively exiled from respectable portions of the city. At the same time, Roman men of all social ranks had the readily available opportunity to gaze at prostitutes and purchase their favors if they desired. Furthermore, prostitutes might easily have seen the clothed bodies if not the veiled faces of matrons.

The centrality of brothels' locations is borne out by the archaeological evidence from towns and cities across the Roman Empire, as shown in the cases of Ostia, Dougga, Ephesus, and Scythopolis, sites which seem to be plausible brothels for non-location reasons. The consistency between these locales establishes the commonality of a prominent location, usually although not necessarily near a bath and a public latrine, for brothels of the Roman Empire. This conclusion is supported by literary evidence from Rome itself, a city in which we sadly lack archaeological data about brothels. Cato the Censor famously admonished a young senatorial son about seeking prostitutes:

Some men are found only with the kind of woman who would live in a stinking brothel. When Cato [the Elder] met a man he knew coming forth from such a place, his divine *sententia* was, "Well done, for when shameful lust has swollen the veins, it is suitable that young men should come down here (*descendere*), rather than fool around with other men's wives." But when Cato later ran into the same young man again at the brothel, he remarked, "Young man, I praised you for going there, not for living there." (Horace, *Sermones* 1.2.31–2; Pseudo-Acro, *Commentary on Horace*)

According to this passage, the exceedingly respectable Cato was able casually to encounter someone multiple times near a brothel, suggesting that, wherever this brothel was, it was not far from Cato's normal haunts of the Forum and the elite residences of Rome. On the other hand, the passage does imply a contrast between the areas in which Cato and other elites live and the general location of brothels, at least in Cato's time in the late second century BCE: the brothel is a "stinking" place to which one descends. *Descendere* may mean that the brothels were not located on the more elite hills of Rome but in the lower-status valleys. However, the late Republican poet Catullus implies that at least some brothels in Rome are situated close to the Forum:

> You companions at the lusty tavern,
> nine doors down from the Capped Brothers,
> do you think that you alone have cocks,
> that you alone can screw all the girls,
> and that the rest of us are some goats? (Catullus 37)[53]

The Capped Brothers are Castor and Pollux, whose temple was a prominent fixture of the Roman Forum. If this literary brothel-tavern was located nine doors away, even metaphorically, it might be on the outskirts of the Subura, the Roman slums, but it certainly intruded upon the notice and gaze of the Roman elite. While this may not be a neighborhood that Roman senators dwell in, they clearly pass by it en route to the Senate each day. Catullus' reference to "scribbling obscenities on the wall" also provides support for a link between taverns used for sexual work and obscene graffiti. Although Catullus may well be speaking metaphorically about the specific tavern, his poem does not suggest that such a location would be surprising. Plautus warned against the same neighborhood centuries earlier: "Behind the temple of Castor are those whom you should not trust too soon. On the Vicus Tuscus are people (*homines*) who sell themselves."[54]

The Vicus Tuscus is a major street near the Forum, dominated by a statue of the Etruscan god Vertumnus. It was a center of Roman male prostitution, while the Argiletum, at the boundary between the Forum and the Subura, was a prime location for female prostitution.[55] It is unclear whether the prostitutes near the Roman Forum were simply advertising their brothels deeper in the Subura or whether they actively practiced their trade against the walls of the Temple of Castor and Pollux.

Horace, addressing his own manuscript contemptuously, comments that, "Book, you seem to look towards Vertumnus and Janus, doubtless so that, scrubbed smooth by the pumice of the Sosii, you may sell yourself."[56] Such a comment potentially locates both popular bookselling and whore-selling markets in Rome between the statue of Vertumnus on the Vicus Tuscus and the Temple of Janus, at the bottom of the Forum, on the Argiletum, near the notorious Subura district.[57]

Prostitutes in Rome, while undoubtedly available throughout the city, thus likely centered their trade in and around the highly public area of the Forum Romanum. Prostitutes were also readily available in other places of entertainment such as the circus, the theater, especially Pompeius' portico, and baths, as well as near the Temple of Venus Erycina at the Colline Gate.[58] The consequence of the location of prostitutes' places of business in Rome would have been high public visibility in the areas frequented by elite and wealthy men, as well as women.

This conclusion also follows simple logic. In a society where visiting a brothel, as Cato proclaims, was a deed without shame, there was no need to exile brothels outside the city walls as would occur later in medieval Europe.[59] We see here a very Roman efficiency in locating brothels near other sources of public entertainment and leisure in order to allow for easy access. Neither brothels nor prostitutes, as argued in earlier chapters, were seen as being fundamentally different than bath attendants, actresses, or gladiators: all possessed the negative reputation of *infamia*, but all were also tolerated within society and provided opportunities for pleasure to a large section of the populace.[60]

McGinn's maps show that there are no fewer than eleven brothels or *cellae meretricia*, including the notorious large *lupanar*, within a block of the Stabian Baths in Pompeii.[61] The obvious difficulty with these maps, as with all the more optimistic assessments of brothels in Pompeii, is why a relatively small city needed such a plethora of locations for sex work within such a small radius, particularly given that graffiti indicate that prostitutes practiced their trade throughout the city. One likely possibility is that many of these proposed sites may have had multiple uses – small stands or shops by day, for instance, and *cellae* for sex work by night.

Furthermore, Wallace-Hadrill's aforementioned criteria may overstate the likelihood that prostitution took place in all these locations. However, if even some of them were used for sex work, it would still represent a publicly prominent social role for Pompeian prostitutes. Women like the famous philanthropist Eumachia or the denizens of the conservative and wealthy House of the Faun could not have avoided passing multiple prostitutes en route to their own respectable daily activities like visiting the baths or temples.

Comparative evidence from the ancient world also supports the public location of these brothels. The most fully excavated likely classical Greek brothel to date is Building Z of the Kerameikos excavations in the Athenian Agora.[62] This building would have been the first encountered by Athenians entering the Sacred Gate along the Sacred Way, a prominent path for both merchants and tourists. Its proximity to water, location, and multiple entrances are all consistent with the criteria used for Roman-era brothels. Furthermore, classical Athenian literary evidence depicts brothels as present near the Agora, the law courts, the Piraeus, and in residential areas.[63] Other Greek brothel-possibilities at Delos, Thessaloniki, and Mytilene, while less well preserved, also possess features consistent with these new brothel-identifiers.[64] Later comparative evidence from modern legalized brothels in Nevada and New Zealand also suggest that public locations, access to water and the presence of multiple entrances are consistently desirable features for brothels, regardless of culture or era.[65]

Multiple entrances and brothel furnishings

Besides a number of small *cellae*, another ubiquitous feature of brothel architecture across the Empire was the existence of multiple entrances, usually one on a main street and one on a side street, to allow for both public and private access. Frequently, at least one entrance will be marked by twisting corridors which block the view of the interior space beyond, directly in contravention of the principles of Vitruvius' atrium house design. The brothel incident in Petronius' late first-century CE *Satyricon*, in which the narrator enters a brothel through one door and flees through another into a "crooked, narrow alley" also supports the popularity of multiple entrances for brothels:

> I took her for a prophetess until, when presently we came to a more obscure quarter, the affable old lady pushed aside a patchwork rag (*centonem*) and remarked, "Here's where you ought to live," and when I denied that I recognized the house, I saw some men prowling stealthily between the rows of placards and naked prostitutes (*inter titulos nudas meretrices*). Too late I realized that I had been led into a sex-house (*fornicem*). After cursing the wiles of the little old hag, I covered my head and commenced to run through the middle of the brothel (*lupanar*) to the exit opposite … . He led me through some very dark and crooked alleys, to this place, pulled out his cash, and commenced to beg me for sex (*stuprum*). (Petronius, *Satyricon* 7.4)

Petronius' account presents a relatively clear picture of the literary idea of a brothel: it is a narrow hallway lined with nude prostitutes labeled by *tituli*, or placards indicating name and possibly price, offering little privacy for either prostitute or client. There are multiple entrances, one at least through "dark and crooked alleys," and the furnishings are generally poor and dirty; the entrance is covered not by a door but by a *cento* or patchwork curtain. The existing purported brothels in the Roman world match this literary picture quite closely, although archaeologists may have deliberately sought out buildings that matched their memories of Petronius.

Juvenal's sixth Satire also offers a variety of tantalizing details about the stereotypical literary representation of a brothel. In particular, it supports the hypothesis of professional, non-residential brothels. In his indictment of Claudius' adulterous Empress, not only Messalina but all the other prostitutes leave at the end of their nightly duties to go home.[66] McGinn argues that this may be a literary device necessitated by the presence of the Empress, rather than reflecting a reality in which prostitutes frequently lived outside brothels.[67]

However, most of the existing probable full-time brothels discussed earlier in this chapter do not contain hearths or other facilities conducive to residential life. The prostitutes may have used braziers rather than hearths or eaten outside the building, however. A dish of green beans and onions was found on the second floor of the Pompeii *lupanar*, but no cooking facilities, suggesting that, at most, the inhabitants brought in food from nearby taverns.[68]

It is unclear where these women might have slept if not at the brothel; the lost second floor of many of these buildings is one possibility, while cheap multi-person rooms in *insulae* are another, particularly given that prostitutes may have kept unusual work hours. While prostitutes may frequently have had sex in taverns or other residential buildings, the literary evidence at least leads us towards a plausible identification of some buildings as brothels precisely because of their lack of residential facilities.

Juvenal provides a wealth of other details about the furnishings, smell, and general poverty of Messalina's supposed brothel:

The whore-empress, covering herself with a hood, dared to leave the Palatine and prefer a mat to a couch, accompanied by not more than a single maid. But hiding her black hair under a yellow cap she entered into a hot brothel behind an old rag and took her empty cell; then nude she exposed her golden nipples under a lying name-board of "Wolf-Girl" and displayed your womb, noble Britannicus ... although exhausted by the men nevertheless she left unsatisfied, with shameful cheeks dirtied by the soot of lamps and took to the divine couch the filth of the brothel. (Juvenal, *Satires* 6. 118–32[69]

It is unlikely that Juvenal's accusation of Messalina is at all accurate, particularly in the precise details, but he presumably drew his vivid imagery from the accoutrements of actual brothels, just as with his descriptions of gladiatorial games or circus races. Thus, we can note from this passage again an emphasis on the *titulus* or name-board, the old patchwork rag or *cento* which may have served as curtain, blanket, or both, the sparse furniture in the brothel, and the presence of dirt and soot. Juvenal contrasts Messalina's own lofty social status with the degradation and crude accommodations of a brothel that closely resembles the existing archaeological remains of purported brothels.

Our other major Roman literary source for the architecture of brothels comes from a hypothetical *Controversia* of Seneca. In this speech, a young Roman maiden was kidnapped in a plot similar to those of the Greek novels and sold to a brothel, where she later killed her one attempted seducer. The question under debate is whether or not she could still qualify to be a public priestess despite the stain on her reputation. As part of the evidence for her shame, Seneca goes into some detail about the dynamics of her brothel:

By Hercules, you did not kill your pimp. You were led into the brothel, accepted a place, a price was fixed, the name-board was written: enquiry can go so far against you – the rest is obscure. Why do you summon me into your closet and to your lecherous little bed? (Seneca, *Controversiae* 1.2.4)

While this is obviously a general fantasy about brothel architecture and life, it can give us a glimpse at a typical pattern. The prostitute has a place in the brothel, possibly in the common area, but she also has a specific room, with her *titulus*, detailing a name, price, or both written above it. She is described as sleeping on a *lectula* in a *cellula*, which may reflect the small and dingy quarters present in most actual brothels. Seneca the Younger mentions curtains or coverings across *cellae* entrances as being a standard feature of brothels; these would obviously not have survived the millennia but may explain the lack of doorposts in places like Pompeii and Ephesus.[70] Turning to the material evidence, we can see that the literary evidence for small quarters and multiple entrances is borne out by the layout of surviving brothels across the Empire.

Water and brothels

Another possible signifier of a Roman brothel is the existence of a private well or hip-bath within the building or nearby, as in the case of the hip-baths and small wells or water-troughs described in the sites above. This association of brothels with private water supplies is supported by not only archaeological but also literary evidence. Frontinus and Cicero both complain about brothels pirating the public water supply for their own usage.[71] Frontinus, possibly directly quoting M. Caelius Rufus, exclaims, "we find farms being irrigated, taverns, even garrets, and finally all the brothels are equipped with constantly flowing taps!"[72] Although this evidence comes from a later period and a different region, a sixth-century CE Egyptian lease from Hermopolis describes a brothel as containing both an external courtyard and a well.[73] Thus we can use archaeological indications of private fountains or baths in unusual settings, such as in or near small buildings with multiple small *cellae* and multiple entrances, as yet another potential sign of sex work.

The association of brothels with baths and bathing appears to be true across many cultures and time periods; in medieval England the words for "brothel" and "bathhouse" were virtually synonymous.[74] Why brothels would particularly desire access to private water supplies is somewhat unclear, although the combination of post-intercourse washing and a frequent literary description of Roman brothels as full of soot from lamps suggests the potential advantages of private baths. Ovid's lover, after unsuccessful intercourse, "takes water to conceal her shame (*hoc dissimulavit*)."[75] Martial tells Lesbia that she does not sin in "*fellas et aquam potas*," fellating a lover and then drinking water afterwards.[76] While neither of these examples are situated within a brothel, there is logical connection between sex that needed to be quickly cleaned up or concealed and the availability of nearby, private water supplies. In any case, the presence of such private fountains is yet another potential indicator of a brothel in towns less well preserved than Pompeii, although one to be used with care and only in the presence of other signifiers.

Separation by time

Even if matrons and *meretrices* walked the same streets of Ephesus and Pompeii, they may have done so at different times of day. Both literary and archaeological evidence indicate that lighting was necessary in Roman brothels.[77] Three terracotta oil lamps were found in the Pompeii *lupanar*.[78] A "very large concentration" of glass oil lamps from the Byzantine period was found in one of the rooms of the purported Scythopolis brothel, although the room could also possibly have been a lamp shop at some point.[79] The presence of lamps in both textual and archaeological sources suggests at least some brothels operated at night.

However, the lack of interior windows in some of the *cellae* in Pompeii or the other purported brothels also means that lamps might have been necessary even during the day, at least for financial transactions if not the sex work itself.

The early third-century Christian writer Tertullian repeatedly describes lanterns and the decking of porticos with leafy wreaths as a means of identifying brothels: "She will have to go forth [from her house] by a gate wreathed with laurel, and hung with lanterns, as if from some new den of public lusts."[80] Neither exterior lanterns nor wreaths would have generally survived in the archaeological record of purported brothels, rendering them largely useless as tools of identification.[81] However, lamps are also problematic as a means of firm brothel identification. Terracotta and bronze oil lamps are sufficiently common in all shops that they are not specific to the profession, even in the case of oil lamps with erotic art on them, which might be more suggestive. Nonetheless, Tertullian, who lived in both Rome and Carthage, may here be providing us with an image of typical brothel advertising, along with the other literary representations of the *centones* or rag curtains, which have also not survived. The ornamentation of wreaths around the door or on the portico also suggests a prominent and decorative main entrance, which is consistent with both the archaeological and literary evidence.

If we accept that lamps are strongly associated with brothels and thus may indicate frequent nocturnal work hours, new questions are also raised about the effect of timing on clientele and on the public prominence of *meretrices*. While elite men might have had their work finished by midday and then proceeded to the baths and other entertainment centers like brothels, common craftsmen and slaves would have worked longer hours and might have needed to postpone brothel trips until the evening or night.[82]

Fikret Yegül argues that by the mid-afternoon and early evening, the baths became a socially mixed zone where "the wise man and fool, rich and poor, privileged and underdog, could rub shoulders and enjoy the benefits afforded by the Roman imperial system."[83] If this is true for the baths, it might well also have been true for the brothels, which would thus have offered a social mixing of clientele from varied social backgrounds, if not direct encounters between matrons and *meretrices*. Such a hypothesis does not restrict the possible duration of daily sex work for prostitutes; indeed, given that at the low end prostitution was not very profitable, Roman streetwalkers and brothel girls may have needed to work long hours, perhaps from mid-afternoon until dawn.

Married women, particularly elite and wealthy women, would presumably have largely remained indoors during the evening, unless trav-
eling by litter to a dinner party. They are unlikely to have encountered
prostitutes who plied their trade only by night. Juvenal seems to express
disapproval of Messalina's nocturnal wanderings as well as her destina-
tion, and Suetonius, as noted in Chapter 4, criticizes Julia for outrageous
debauchery in the Forum Romanum at night.[84] The case of Hostilius
Mancinus and the prostitute Manilia, who drove him away from her
window at night by throwing stones, as discussed in the Introduction,
also took place at night.[85] Manilia appears to have been a more elite and
well-connected courtesan, who could refuse unwanted nocturnal clients,
but presumably the aedile, however drunk, thought that a night-time
solicitation was plausible.

Neither literary nor archaeological evidence, therefore, tightly restricts
the probable hours for prostitution. Morning, a time when nearly all men
would have been at work, was probably the least busy time or possibly
even the rest time for most prostitutes. If prostitutes were active in the
afternoon and early evening, however, they might well have encountered
matrons returning from the baths or, in the case of non-elite women, the
marketplace. Again, no clear moral segregation can be established.

Shame

The occluded multiple entrances of both these archaeological sites and
the literary brothels raise questions about how much shame potentially
attached to prostitutes' clients, if not to prostitutes themselves. The
archaeological evidence and previous chapters have established that prostitutes formed a ubiquitous and valued part of Roman society despite
their *infamia*. Yet, if visiting a prostitute was an ordinary and socially
acceptable act, why would the men of Ephesus feel the need to sneak in
through the back door of a public latrine, or the men of Pompeii exit their
brothel into a back alley? The young man in the Cato anecdote is clearly
somewhat embarrassed to encounter Cato the Censor, but Cato was notorious for being far more prudish than the average Roman senator of his
time. Clients clearly felt comfortable boasting about their encounters with
prostitutes in graffiti all over the Roman world.

This mixture of social acceptability and shame raises the questions
both of the identity of these clients and whom they might have feared
to encounter as they entered or left a brothel. As established by previous
chapters, adult prosperous Roman men might expect to have a reasonably

satisfying sexual relationship with their wives as well as sexual access to the female and male slaves under their control. The most likely frequent clients of brothels, then, are either young unmarried men, men too poor to support families or own slaves whom they could use as sexual objects, or men unhappy with their marital relationships. Such a hypothesis certainly fits the literary evidence of poets like Catullus and authors like Apuleius.

Whom, then, would these men be ashamed to encounter if they left a brothel openly? The most logical presumption is their mother, wife, or other female family members. In a world of legal, regularly taxed prostitution, there is no particular general social stigma or *infamia* associated with visiting a prostitute. However, that does not erase the possibility of unpleasant familial drama or tension resulting from an encounter between a young man and his mother outside a brothel. Given the established location of these brothels, such an accidental meeting, at least during daylight hours, might be very plausible, unless these brothels had a discrete exit.

Conclusion

Neither archaeological nor literary evidence allows us to reconstruct fully the spatial presence of prostitutes in the Roman world. By combining these modes of inquiry and opening the discourse to the possibilities of new identification criteria, however, we may at least identify some plausible brothels located throughout the Roman Empire. These new data points, in turn, can allow more definite conclusions about the location and prominence of brothel workers within the urban landscape.

Necessarily, this study is blind to the vast majority of Roman prostitutes and their locations for sex work; it is limited to the most likely and public brothels throughout the Empire, and some of these sites may not have been used regularly for sex work at all. Furthermore, brothel architecture almost certainly varied with both time and location, given the long history of the Roman Empire and its vast geographical spread. I have examined potential brothels ranging from first-century CE Italy to sixth century-CE Israel; undoubtedly factors ranging from divergent architectural styles to the spread of Christianity affected their design.

It is perhaps even more surprising, then, that these possible brothels have so many features in common. While they differ in many aspects, the commonalities of multiple small *cellae*, prominent public location, multiple entrances, and a private water supply are all remarkably consistent, as are the presences of erotic art and graffiti in locations where these have survived. Through a careful comparison of different literary sources, we can further establish a picture of dark, sooty *cellae*, lit by oil lamps and separated from a common area by thin curtains. We cannot ever firmly declare that a specific building was used exclusively as a brothel, but such narrow identifications are largely irrelevant for the purposes of reconstructing a broader picture of Roman prostitutes' spatial histories. The women themselves may be gone, but their places of work remain to tell their stories.

As the archaeological evidence suggests, prostitutes plied their trade from brothels in highly public locations in cities across the Empire, as well as in many other non-brothel locations. They were neither invisible to the eyes of elite women and men nor excluded from the public areas of civic life. Rather, prostitutes formed a ubiquitous part of the urban landscape. The material record can now support an image always implied by the works of the Roman poets. When we imagine the ancient world, whether in the form of pristine, white-marbled models or in blockbuster Hollywood films and television series, the regular, visible presences of prostitutes in and around urban public spaces ought to be a part of that picture. At the same time, the regular passage of respectable women, whether on their way to the market, escorting their children to school, or coming back from a lavish dinner party, should also be understood as an essential part of that social landscape.

By combining these two sets of gendered movements, we remove Roman women firmly from the purely domestic sphere and visualize a world in which Roman matrons and *meretrices* of all social strata saw and were seen by each other. Their friendly waves or shudders of disdain, conversations or glares, are only present in the very rare mentions in the elite literary record, which was rarely concerned with what Roman women said to each other. However, the archaeological evidence simply does not allow for gender, class, or moral segregation.

Furthermore, the very nature of Roman matronly *pudicitia* depends not only on regular encounters with strange men but on a contrast with women who do not possess *pudicitia*. A virtuous Roman woman regularly demonstrates her shame and modesty through ignoring naked or inappropriately behaving men, some of whom may be directly harassing her. The implication is that there are, necessarily, immodest women out there who are ogling and openly desiring such males.[86] Such women, if not actual sex workers, are certainly metaphorical *meretrices* in the sense of Chapter 4. The Roman urban landscape becomes both a place of constant transgression and a setting where respectable women can repeatedly declare and defend their subjugation to a particular male. While the *meretrices* – the unowned women – do not control the streets and forums in the way that men do, they nevertheless possess the freedom to walk, to gaze, and to engage in dialogue with other citizens around them. In no way are they relegated to the hidden corners of the Roman city.

7

Pious prostitutes

Are there two Venuses, the one a maiden (*virgo*), the other a woman (*mulier*)? Or rather, are there three, one the goddess of maidens (*virginum*), who is also called Vesta, another the goddess of wives (*coniugaturum*), and another of prostitutes (*meretricum*)? To her also the Phoenicians offered a gift by prostituting their daughters before they united them to husbands. Which of these is the wife (*matrona*) of Vulcan? Certainly not the virgin, since she has a husband. Let us not say it is the prostitute (*meretrix*), since we should seem to wrong the son of Juno and fellow-worker of Minerva. Therefore it is to be understood that Venus belongs to the married people; but we would not wish them to imitate her in what she did with Mars.

St. Augustine, early fifth century CE, City of God, *4.10*

According to Roman historical legend, in the year 204 BCE a noble Roman woman, Claudia Quinta, was the subject of unfavorable gossip among elite matrons and "stubborn old men." Specifically, she was accused of changing her hairstyle too frequently and having a witty and sharp tongue, both of which gave her a dubious reputation.[1] This notorious Claudia Quinta attended the public entry into Rome of the new eastern goddess, Magna Mater, imported to promote fertility among Roman women during a time of massive military losses. When the ship carrying the goddess's statue up the Tiber was grounded, Claudia prayed that Magna Mater would defend her questionable chastity and *pudicitia* by enabling the Roman matron to pull the ship with her bare hands. Claudia Quinta duly performed the miracle, towed the barge up the Tiber, and became a role model of chastity and virtue for future generations of Roman women. She even earned the honor of multiple public statues, monumental reliefs, coins, and probably regular re-enactments in plays of her story. As Livy phrases it, she transforms her *fama* from *dubia* to *clara*, or shining.[2]

Beyond its cultural importance for Roman women, this story illustrates the complex relationship between Roman female religious cults and concepts of female virtue and vice. Claudia Quinta, along with the "distinguished matrons" of Rome, is allowed to attend this religious ceremony despite the speculation about her chastity. She then seizes control of the ritual in order to redeem her *pudicitia* in the most public and memorable way imaginable.[3] Indeed, she is able to assume a man's role of performing strenuous manual labor through the power of this maternal goddess. Through an act of public religious devotion, Claudia goes from "bad girl" to "role model." For Roman women, as this tale exemplifies, female virtues and their relationships to social status were intimately connected with religious participation in varied festivals and ceremonies honoring female deities.

For Roman women, religious cultic practice was the most important expression of female membership in a larger public community, especially since they were banned from direct political participation.[4] The strict calendar of annual rituals and religious festivals offered women a chance to play a visible public role as priestesses and worshipers for various Roman goddesses such as Venus and Bona Dea. In several of these festivals, the social and moral status of the women involved became a defining feature of the ritual, revealing a broader cultural anxiety about the need to categorize women both morally and economically. In this chapter, I will demonstrate that while the official divisions of women into good wife or wicked whore established in Chapter 1 also affected the religious participation of distinct Roman social groups, some of these festivals also offered another chance to blend and undermine social and moral distinctions between these groups. In the end, Roman women were more unified by their gender, which strongly affected which gods they worshiped and in what contexts, than they were divided by their social and moral categories. In particular, the participation of prostitutes in these festivals suggests that they were less marginalized and socially ostracized than we might believe from legal or historical texts.

Despite the many legal sanctions against professional Roman prostitutes, they played a surprisingly important role in the religious life of the city of Rome and the Empire itself. Roman prostitutes were central to the major spring festival of the Floralia and in the worship of Venus Erycina. However, these rituals and religious obligations were sometimes kept separate from those of respectable matrons, forming a separate but equal component in the religious worship of women, with certain notable exceptions such as the festivals on the Kalends of April.[5]

Both this noted prominence of *meretrices* in certain rites and their complex interactions with the religious rites of *matronae* may descend in part from Phoenician and Magna Graecian cults like that of Venus Erycina. As discussed later in this chapter, there is little definitive evidence of "sacred prostitution" involving prostitute–client transactions viewed by participants as religious dedications. However, there is a substantial amount of archaeological and literary data suggesting a connection between temples of Venus and prostitutes, who may have been temple slaves or simply had a particular devotion to the goddess.

While we lack strong evidence connecting these earlier practices with later Roman cult rituals, the unusual prominence of prostitute-dominated festivals in the Roman calendar may have been borrowed from the traditions of Italian and Sicilian cities that the Romans subjugated and assimilated. A character in Plautus' *Cistellaria* sternly admonishes a *meretrix* that "this is not a place where after the Etrurian fashion you disgracefully earn a dowry for yourself by prostitution of your person," suggesting that the Romans certainly disparaged rather than imitated certain alleged sexual practices of their neighbors.[6]

However, the prominent presence of *meretrices* in religious rites, both in earlier Italian and Magna Graecian cities and as part of the later Roman festivals, suggests an inheritance or adoption of this pattern in the same way that Roman religion took on many other foreign practices.[7] I do not mean to suggest that practices like temple prostitution itself or free maidens temporarily prostituting themselves for religious purposes ever took place in the Roman Republic or Empire. However, the legacy of such earlier rituals and myths had a significant impact on later Roman cult. As an example, I begin this chapter by analyzing the Ludovisi throne, one of the principal early Italian artistic representations of this religious relationship between *meretrix* and *matrona*.

I then establish the literary evidence for the presence and participation of prostitutes in Roman religious festivals, primarily through a close study of Ovid's *Fasti*, which contains the great majority of our surviving information about such practices, as well as through examination of other related texts such as the *Fasti Praenestini*. I focus particularly here on the worship of Venus Erycina, a deity imported from an earlier, prostitute-associated cult in Sicily. Archaeological and literary evidence also sheds light on the evolution of prostitutes' and matrons' religious roles in the Italian city-states and the Roman world of the sixth–first century BCE. I will not extensively discuss the role of prostitutes in cult during the high and late Roman Empire.[8] However, I do deal briefly with the worship of Isis, a particularly popular cult that openly welcomed prostitutes during the high Empire.

The debate on "sacred prostitution"

Scholars have argued both sides of the ancient "sacred prostitution" controversy for many decades, with some arguing that temples of Aphrodite or Venus in both Greece and Italy ran a formalized business of ritual prostitution, while other authors are diametrically opposed to this theory. The advocates use Pindar's poems and inscriptions to claim that the slave prostitutes of Corinth's temple of Aphrodite may have numbered in the thousands and that links can be traced between the Near Eastern cultic practice related to the goddess Astarte/Mylitta, as described by Herodotus and others, the worship of Aphrodite in Cyprus and Corinth, and religious practices in southern Italian and Sicilian Greek colony cities.[9] Current ancient Near Eastern specialists are highly skeptical about any connection whatsoever between Astarte and sacred prostitution.[10]

On the other side of the argument, which has dominated the scholarly record during the last decade, many scholars of early Italy and Greece seek to separate entirely the sordid business of sex work from the worship of Venus or Aphrodite, generally arguing that literary references to sacred prostitution are either attempts to defame foreign cultures as immoral "Others" or that they explain urban aetiologies through a symbolic reversal of societal norms. Beard, Budin, and other scholars believe that the archaeological evidence has been misinterpreted by archaeologists who were overly inclined to trust the literal truth of textual sources.[11]

As the rest of this chapter will show, we have virtually no evidence of any sort that men paid religious duties to the goddess by sleeping with her prostitutes in the Roman world or in pre-Roman Italy. However, some temples of Venus or other female fertility deities might have had a side market for pilgrims involving the sale of sex. There is little evidence that male clients felt that their acts were ones of religious devotion, but the temple may either have owned the prostitutes themselves or the prostitutes might have contributed a certain percentage of their income to the temple. The story of Phryne, the famous fourth-century BCE prostitute who offered to rebuild the walls of Corinth if and only if her name was inscribed as the donor, suggests that such public contribution by prostitutes was not without precedent.[12] Nevertheless, there remains a difference between the civic duties of prominent courtesans and direct, possibly mandated religious tithes from prostitutes.

This practice of religious tithes may well have faded by the Hellenistic era or been absorbed into less obvious rituals like the Roman Floralia and the cult of Venus Erycina. However, some financial or spiritual connection between prostitutes and certain cults is more probable than the theory that the entire set of literary texts concerning them originated from ancient myths expressing themes of alterity and abstract symbology.

The Ludovisi throne: *meretrix* and *matrona* juxtaposed

A central image of any discussion of the ancient religious roles of both wives and whores is the Ludovisi throne, a large marble relief sculpture found in Rome but probably originally from the southern Italian city of Locri Epizefiri.[13] It is dated to approximately 460 BCE, during the time of the early Roman Republic.[14] The Ludovisi throne, a marble structure of three panels, was likely used as an altar rather than a throne. Each panel portrays a different type of woman. On the front, two female figures help a third rise out of the ground; this image has been interpreted as representing either the birth of Aphrodite or the return of Persephone from the underworld (Figure 22).[15] The Aphrodite hypothesis is the most plausible, given the clinging draperies of the central figure and the apparent dampness of her costume (which suggests Aphrodite's marine birth from foam), as well as the lack of any clear Demeter/Ceres figure who one might normally expect to be present in an image of Persephone's return.

The left panel depicts a young woman, naked except for her headscarf, reclining with her knees crossed while playing a flute (Figure 23). This relief is the earliest known female monumental nude in Greek art (Locri was a Greek colony in the Magna Graecia region of Italy). The juxtaposition of the flute and her nudity suggest that this is meant to represent a *hetaira*, or Greek prostitute, as these are both common visual symbols of the profession. On the right panel, a woman of uncertain age, fully covered from head to toe, sits upon a cushion and places incense in an incense-burner; she is presumably a respectable matron (Figure 24). In other words, both women are participating in religious devotion in different ways, as it seems implausible that one woman would be engaged in a secular activity and the other a religious one. Given the setting, both musical and incense offerings are reasonable and appropriate acts.[16]

On the Ludovisi throne, the flute-girl and the incense-burning woman are linked together in their worship of Aphrodite. These two potential

22. The marble central panel of the Ludovisi throne, showing a goddess. *c.*460 BCE. Museo Nationale Romano. Panel height 0.87 m, length 0.69 m.

primary roles of women in ancient society, prostitute and wife, are explicitly unified in this altar. The two images may be intended to refer to the ideas of Aphrodite Pandemos – the common, vulgar Aphrodite of prostitutes, and Aphrodite Urania – the more heavenly, respectable figure.

Furthermore, the presence of the flute-girl suggests that prostitutes may have played a role in the rites of the temple, as musicians, at least, if not as sex workers. Various locations have been suggested for the Ludovisi throne, which was found in Rome; it has also been linked with another monument, the Boston Throne, which echoes it in various artistic aspects, although the Boston Throne has a mixture of male and female figures, including an elderly female spinner.[17] The authenticity of the Boston Throne is also currently in dispute; in any case, its imagery is largely irrelevant for this particular discussion.[18] Schilling argues that the Ludovisi throne, wherever it was sculpted, ultimately resided in the temple of Venus Erycina by the Colline Gate in Rome, although we have limited evidence for this theory.[19] If true, this would provide a direct link between an earlier Italian prostitute-cult connection and a later Roman cult, the worship of Venus Erycina, in which prostitutes played a prominent role. Even if the Romans imported the monument as booty from the conquest of Locri in 181 BCE, its location near the temple of Venus Erycina by the Colline Gate suggests a continued cultic use of an altar that prominently featured a lowly flute-girl worshiping separately but equally with a respectable matron.[20] In other words, a simultaneous

23. The left panel of the Ludovisi throne, showing a flute-girl. *c.*460 BCE. Museo Nationale Romano. Panel height 0.87 m, length 0.69 m.

segregation and unity of religious worship by both prostitutes and matrons formed a part of urban Roman religious practice from early times.

Eryx

One of the most famous temples of Venus-Astarte is the temple of Venus on Mount Eryx in northwestern Sicily, which also has a strong textual association with prostitution. This temple dates back at least to the Phoenician colonization of Sicily in the fifth century BCE, and possibly earlier.[21] Unfortunately, because a Norman castle was built over the remains of the temple, very little of the ancient site remains. Eryx has not been thoroughly excavated since the work of Marconi and Cultrera in the 1930s. There is some archaeological evidence of female residents, including a perfume bottle and a loom weight.[22]

Despite the paucity of the material remains, we possess a wealth of other information about this temple. A silver denarius of C. Considius

24. The right panel of the Ludovisi throne, showing a matron. *c.*460 BCE. Museo Nationale Romano. Panel height 0.87 m, length 0.69 m.

Nonianus from 56 BCE depicts a diademed, laureate Venus Erycina on the obverse and the temple of Eryx itself on the reverse (Figure 25).[23] Various ancient sources refer to the prominence of the temple of Venus at Eryx and its beautiful temple slaves:

> [Eryx] has a temple of Aphrodite that is held in exceptional honor, and in early times was full of female temple slaves (*hierodules*), who had been dedicated in fulfillment of vows not only by the people of Sicily but also by many people from far away. At the present time, just as the settlement itself, so the temple is in want of men, and the multitude of temple slaves has disappeared. In Rome also, there is a copy of this particular cult – I mean the temple of Venus Erycina before the Colline Gate, which is remarkable for its shrine and surrounding colonnade. (Strabo, *Geography* 6.2.1)

Strabo does not specifically state that the temple's female slaves serve as prostitutes, and it is somewhat surprising that the chronicler of marvels and unusual sights would not mention such a practice, if it existed. However, the fact that their number has decreased due to a lack of men

25. A silver denarius coin, C. Considius Nonianus, 57 BCE, showing a laureate, diademed bust of Venus Erycina. The obverse shows her temple on the summit of Mount Eryx (Sicily), surrounded by city walls with a gate. Classical Numismatic Group, Inc., www.cngcoins.com.

suggests that the hierodules may have had functions beyond merely tending the temple precincts. Cicero also mentions female slaves of the temple of Venus Erycina in Sicily.[24] According to Diodorus Siculus, who had a local interest in promoting the temple, the temple women were notable for their charm and wit, at least in the first century BCE:

> The consuls and praetors ... whenever they come to Eryx ... they enter into games and have conversation with women with much gaiety, believing that only in this way will they make their presence there pleasing to the goddess. (Diodorus Siculus 4.83.1–7)

Siculus' description does not link the temple of Venus on Eryx directly to either sacred or secular prostitution, but the emphasis on female temple slaves, mixed-gender conversations, and the presence of wealthy temple freedwomen strongly suggests that prostitutes were somehow associated with the temple. The foundation of the temple during Phoenician times with a possible link to Astarte also suggests a connection to prostitution, as the earlier goddess was allegedly connected with such worshipers. However, there is no reason to believe that sexual acts were viewed as any kind of religious duty to the goddess.

Venus Erycina in Rome

From literary sources, we know of two separate temples of Venus Erycina in Rome itself, as well as a celebration of her on April 23 and other religious rites specifically associated with prostitutes. The duality of these temples expresses the complexity of the Roman relationship to this sex-associated goddess. The prominence of her festival also demonstrates the general social acceptance of prostitution by official authorities.

The Romans conquered Eryx during the First Punic War in 249 BCE and seized the temple of Venus and its riches. In later traditions, this temple was associated by Romans with Aeneas, who was said to have built it in honor of his mother. It is unclear when this connection was first promulgated, and it may date to the Julio-Augustan emphasis on the cult of Venus Genetrix. In 217 BCE, after the Romans' disastrous defeat by Hannibal at Trasimene, the decemviral priests read the Sibylline Books and announced that, in order to achieve victory, "the Great Games must be vowed to Jupiter, a temple to Venus Erycina and one to Mens."[25] Jupiter, the chief god of the Romans, was a logical deity here; Venus Erycina and Mens, the female deity of good counsel, are more unusual choices.

We know relatively little about Mens, and there is no particular reason to suspect any sexual connotation to this deity.[26] More likely, the Romans felt they needed good advice after the failure of their disastrous tactics earlier in the war. Why, then, choose Venus Erycina as a deity to achieve victory in war? The best explanation is that the Romans indeed viewed Venus Erycina as originally a Phoenician deity, a form of Astarte, and that by placating and honoring her with a temple they strove to carry out their customary tactic of *evocatio*, religiously seducing the enemy's gods to the Roman side by bribes of offerings and temples. *Evocatio* was normally a ritual carried out during the siege of a particular enemy city and focused on its chief god. As a representative of the Carthaginian gods, who had already been assimilated to Venus in Roman-dominated Sicily, Venus Erycina served as a useful tool for this purpose. While Rome was not at war with Eryx, the co-optation of Venus Erycina would be a sign that western Sicily was now in the hands of Rome, not its mortal enemy Carthage.[27] However, Eryx remained a major cultic site itself, and so the deity cannot be said in this case to have "left" Sicily; rather, she was honored with a new, related cult at Rome itself.

Eva Stehle theorizes that Venus Erycina was given a temple inside the *pomerium*, on the Capitoline Hill itself next to the temples of Ceres and Jupiter, precisely as a means of assimilating a foreign "bride" into Rome where she would support domestic institutions inside Rome and honor Sicily.[28] Venus Erycina was associated with a number of peculiarly Phoenician religious traits; for instance, pigs could not be sacrificed to her, in accordance with Phoenician religious customs.[29]

This first temple to Venus Erycina in Rome was built on the Capitoline Hill by Quintus Fabius Maximus in his role as dictator in 215 BCE.[30] April 23, when the festival of its foundation was celebrated, was also the date of the Vinalia Priora, the festival of new wine, a celebration closely connected with Jupiter. The conjunction of cults likely simply reflects the later entrance of a foreign deity onto a calendar already laden with agricultural festivals.

While Venus Erycina's new temple in Rome may have been contemporaneously related to a need to maintain a good relationship with western Sicily during the Second Punic War, the foundation of her temple may also have been part of a larger Roman religious phenomenon of the period, namely, the importation of a multiplicity of foreign fertility cults. The Roman Senate may have desired to attract prominent goddesses of fertility to aid Rome in reproducing the citizen body, particularly necessary at the time due to the recent massive losses of soldiers in the Punic Wars. In 238 BCE, just after the First Punic War, the Roman Senate, in answer to an oracle from the Sibylline Books, built a temple to Flora, goddess of flowers and fertility, and instituted the festival of the Floralia on April 28 to honor her.

In 205 or 204 BCE, the Romans brought Cybele, the Phrygian mother-goddess of fertility, and her famous black stone to Rome, again in response to an oracle from the Sibylline Books regarding the war. Cybele, or Magna Mater, was also associated with Aeneas and the Trojan legend, as she was the patron of Mount Ida, near Troy.[31] A statue to Venus Verticordia, Venus Changer-of-Hearts, was dedicated in the late third or early second century BCE in Rome by the "most chaste (*pudicitissima*) matron in Rome," Sulpicia, wife of Fulvius Flaccus.[32] This cult, at least in its later form as established in 114 BCE, was intended to turn women's minds away from adultery and towards their husbands. In contrast with the general fertility-promoting foreign cults, Venus Verticordia was specifically designed to prevent wives from becoming whores and to promote the birth of legitimate citizen children.

In general, a religious preoccupation with women's marital fertility and fidelity appears to have mirrored the military uncertainty and confusion during this period. In 213 BCE, according to Livy, the senators repressed "a crowd of women sacrificing and praying to the gods, not in the traditional way, publicly in the Forum and on the Capitoline."[33] It is unclear to whom these women were praying or in what ways their rituals were unorthodox, but certainly a female-oriented cult is suggested. There may have been a general rise in the importation of foreign deities worshiped predominantly by women during this period, possibly ones connected particularly to sex and fertility. While some of these cults were founded by elite men and given official approval, other new religions were accused of undermining established social orders and structures.

The second temple to Venus Erycina in Rome, built in 181 BCE outside the Colline Gate, is the subject of much more controversy among scholars. The central question is obviously why the Romans felt such a temple was necessary: there was only one main temple to Cybele, for instance, and while Jupiter's various aspects may have each received a temple, these versions of the god (Capitolinus, Stator, Tonans, etc.) were carefully differentiated. Indeed, Venus herself possessed various temples in her various roles as Verticordia, Obsequens, and later Genetrix; the unusual aspect here is the precise duplication of her aspect as Venus Erycina.

Various explanations have been proffered for the creation of the second temple, some of which argue for a strong differentiation in social status among the worshipers at the two different sites. If one Venus Erycina was for matrons and another for prostitutes, it would strongly suggest that, even in the worship of the same deity, Romans felt a need to segregate based on the marital and moral status of the female worshipers. However, such status differentiation may not have been the dominant reason for the two temples.

Eric Orlin asserts that the second temple was built to attract non-elite worshipers to an approved cult of sexuality and fertility. He notes that the dedication followed several religious crises in Rome, including the Bacchanalian Conspiracy of 186 BCE, the public burning of forged religious and philosophical books of Numa in 181 BCE, and the censorship of Cato the Elder, which attempted to reimpose traditional morality upon the elite. The new temple of Venus Erycina may have represented a move by the Senate to reassert traditional authority over religion and to present an authorized, official type of sexuality cult as opposed to the politically dangerous Bacchanalian rites.[34] Venus Erycina thus represented a tame, controlled outlet for lower-class Roman women and slaves to exercise their more salacious religious impulses.

On the other hand, the temple by the Colline Gate may have been first constructed in 212 BCE, to celebrate the capture of Syracuse, and then merely rebuilt, possibly after destruction or decay, in 181 BCE, since Livy describes it as existing in 202 BCE.[35] In either case, there were eventually two separate temples, and a temple was indeed authorized by the Senate in 181 BCE and duly constructed by the young Lucius Porcius Licinus in honor of his father's vow to Venus during the otherwise unknown Ligurian war.

However, it is still unclear why Porcius Licinus should have chosen to duplicate an existing temple rather than seizing upon another suitable deity for this purpose. Galinsky associates the second temple with a temple of Venus in the Gardens of Sallust, which was round and similar in style to the ancient Temple of Vesta, goddess of the hearth; such a design would link Venus Erycina with a paradigmatically modest and moral goddess.[36] These gardens are also a possible location for the Ludovisi and Boston thrones, as mentioned earlier, which would then directly tie together the Locrian and Erycian cults.

The identification of the precise location of the temple by the Colline Gate in Rome is highly uncertain and relies on later descriptions from the sixteenth century CE, as no trace of the structure remains today.[37] However, Strabo describes the temple as possessing a "remarkable shrine (*neos kai stoa*) and surrounding colonnade."[38] He also refers to the temple as a reproduction of the temple in Sicily; it is unclear whether this means that the temple was a physical copy of the temple on Mount Eryx or whether it merely echoed its rites and customs, possibly including a relationship to prostitutes.[39]

The most notable feature of the temple by the Colline Gate was not architectural but spatial. Unlike the Capitoline shrine, this second temple to Venus Erycina was outside the *pomerium* and indeed, nearly outside the city itself; such a placement implies a marginal and questionable status for the goddess and her worshipers.[40] However, while the temple was located at the edges of the city, the location by one of Rome's major gates was also very prominent. Tens of thousands of ordinary Romans would have passed by it each day.

In the *Fasti*, his calendrical poem of religious festivals, Ovid marks April 23 with the following verse:

> You common girls, celebrate the divine powers of Venus:
> Venus suits those who earn much profit through your work.
> Offer incense that you may be given beauty and the favor of the crowd,
> Pray for sweet talk, and to be blessed with lively jests …
> Now one ought to crowd her temple near the Colline Gate,
> One that takes its name from a Sicilian hill. (Ovid, *Fasti* 4. 865–74)[41]

Here Venus Erycina appears to be particularly associated with prostitutes, although Ovid uses the somewhat nebulous term *volgares*, which might simply refer to non-elite women.[42] Ovid makes no mention of the

Capitoline temple in the *Fasti*, although he specifically describes Rome as the city of Venus' offspring, a reference to Aeneas. According to Ovid, this festival on April 23 was a celebration by prostitutes of their particular patron goddess, Venus Erycina. Martina Kötzle argues that this celebration is a direct descendant of earlier Sicilian rituals of temple prostitution and was deliberately kept separate from the more respectable worship on the Capitoline Hill.[43] Given the lack of any supporting literary evidence, I highly doubt that any sort of actual temple prostitution took place at the Colline Gate temple, as opposed to simply worship of Venus by prostitutes and the temple's use as a popular location for solicitation.

In the *Remedia Amoris*, Ovid describes the Colline temple as a place to cure love, which seems odd for a temple of Venus that generally promoted romance.[44] This passage makes no direct reference to prostitution, unless we assume that both the youths and the *puella* are seeking solace in the arms of a streetwalker or that the *puella* herself is a prostitute. Indeed, Ovid here portrays the temple of Venus Erycina as a fairly traditional shrine to the goddess where the lovelorn could ask for solace in the form of sex or love. Therefore, even if Venus Erycina was a particular patroness of prostitutes, this was not the only item in her portfolio.

Venus Erycina's cult in Rome continued its popularity, especially with prostitutes, during the later Roman Empire, according to various inscriptions and references in poetry.[45] The temple by the Colline Gate kept its unique identity and its association with the Sicilian temple, although it was also referred to as the temple of Venus Horti Sallustiani, suggesting a general assimilation to its location in the Gardens of Sallust.[46] The temple on the Capitoline Hill, however, appears to have largely been assimilated to the cult of Venus Genetrix, and it is referred to in later texts as Venus Capitolina.[47]

The Kalends of April

On the Kalends of April each year, Roman women participated in multiple religious rituals honoring two different goddesses connected with sex, Venus Verticordia (Changer-of-Hearts) and Fortuna Virilis (Masculine Fortune). The social status of the participants in these festivals is somewhat ambiguous: they may have been segregated or they may have included all women worshiping together. However, it is certain that prostitutes played a role in at least some of the rituals. I begin with a general discussion of the relevant passage from Ovid's *Fasti* and its equivalent in Verrius Flaccus' *Fasti Praenestini*, before addressing the current scholarly debate on the nature of these goddesses' worshipers. In his description of the religious worship on the Kalends of April, Ovid instructs Roman women about the details of cultic practice:

> Perform the rites of the goddess, Roman mothers and brides,
> And also you women who shouldn't wear headbands and long robes…
> Learn now why you offer incense to Fortuna Virilis,
> In that place that steams with heated water.
> Women together remove their clothes on entering,
> And every flaw on their naked body is seen:
> Virile Fortune undertakes to hide those from the men,
> And she does this at the offering of a little incense. (Ovid, *Fasti* 4.133–34, 145–50)[48]

This may be a description of the festival of Venus Verticordia, of Fortuna Virilis, both festivals occurring separately with different participants, or, as Staples argues, the same goddess worshiped in one rite under two different names.[49] According to Ovid, these rites were celebrated not only by the respectable women of the community, the *matres nurusque*, but also by the women who were not allowed to wear the characteristic garments of matronhood – whores and adulteresses. These women without headbands may also include married women of lower social status, who were also perhaps denied the elite symbol of the headband. However, there is little archaeological or literary evidence of such a status separation by headdress. In any case, the emphasis here is placed on inclusion rather than division according to wealth, birth, or perceived morality. The different categories of women may perhaps bathe and drink together; they definitely all worship on the same day.[50]

Any mingling of the rituals is particularly noteworthy given that Venus Verticordia is supposed to turn women's hearts away from licentiousness and towards chastity and proper religious behavior. In other words, she ensures that wives remain wives rather than whores.[51] She is herself a goddess of moral categories. Her Roman cult was founded during the Second Punic War around 215 BCE, together with the various other aforementioned female-oriented cults of fertility and fidelity, such as Venus Erycina and Cybele. The celebration of Venus Verticordia's festival on the same day as the festival of Fortuna Virilia, which focused more narrowly on women making themselves sexually attractive to men, may thus have been intended as a means of redirecting Roman women's sexuality exclusively towards their husbands. Only the power of Venus, apparently, was capable of keeping women loyal during a time of such tumult and uncertainty for the Roman state, perhaps in part due to the very lack of young adult freeborn Roman males.[52] The focus of this religious festival is not in repressing female desire but channeling it in appropriately subordinate and loyal fashion.

While Ovid describes women united together in worship of these goddesses, the first-century CE *Fasti Praenestini* of Valerius Flaccus, a large inscribed religious calendar in the Forum of Praeneste, tells a somewhat different story about the Kalends of April.

The women make offerings to Fortuna Virilis; the lower-class women even in the baths, because there that part of the man's body is bared which desires the charm of women. (CIL I, 2.235)[53]

Mommsen amended this inscription to add *honestiores Ven. Verticordiae* after *supplicant*, but there is no trace of these words in the inscription.[54] Ovid suggests three separate rituals on this day: washing and ornamenting the goddess (*Fasti* 4.135–8), women washing themselves in the baths (4.139–50), and the drinking of honeyed milk with poppies (4.151–3); the question remains as to which type of women performed the rite in the baths. While Ovid and Flaccus do not directly contradict each other, the *Fasti Praenestini* do seem to suggest a stronger contrast between the rites of Fortuna and those of Venus Verticordia than the version presented by the inclusive Ovid.[55]

While the rites of Venus Verticordia may have indeed been a festival intended to purify the hearts of licentious *matronae*, none of the descriptions of the worship of Fortuna Virilis suggest that it was entirely reserved for lower-status women, although elite women may not have frolicked in the public baths. Fortuna Virilis, Masculine Fortune, had a small temple still standing in the Forum Boarium in Rome, nowhere near a bath or any other source of water besides the Tiber. She was associated with sexual good fortune, but we know little about this aspect of Fortuna except for this mention in the *Fasti*.

Pomeroy assumes that the two rituals were kept socially distinct out of a Roman desire to dramatize "the dichotomy between respectable women and whores;" this argument neglects Ovid's implication that the women all bathe together (*Fasti* 4.148) and that this group of women explicitly includes both *matronae* and *meretrices*.[56] The idea of separation on the basis of class or moral status for the worship of Fortuna Virilis directly contradicts some of our only existing evidence, Ovid's *Fasti*, and thus it seems more likely than not that all women joined together in this rite.[57]

This conflict between sources might be resolved by arguing that this conglomeration is part of Ovid's general reaction against class distinctions and his particular fondness for courtesans, as discussed in Chapter 1. Fantham argues that the three separate rituals of bathing, washing, and decorating the image are conglomerated in order to confuse women's social and religious roles.[58] The question of whether elite women bathed simultaneously with men in men's baths during this period is also highly disputed, which muddies the waters further.[59] This section of the *Fasti* may reflect Ovid's peculiar egalitarian prejudices rather than normal Roman societal practice. Archaic communal bathing rituals may also have evolved over time to more socially segregated systems, although we have little external evidence of such a possibility.[60]

If wives and whores commingled in this religious bath, it would have been difficult for an onlooker to tell the moral or social status of one nude woman from another. The scholarly debate over Ovid's passage may reflect more about our desire to segregate social classes neatly than an accurate depiction of the rituals. Regardless of prescriptive social category, on this day all women may have worshiped Venus Verticordia, goddess of female loyalty, and Fortuna Virilis, goddess of female sexual attractiveness. Conveniently, such inclusiveness promoted the female virtues most desirable and acceptable to men.

The Kalends of April was not a festival for prostitutes *per se*, but it welcomed their presence and participation in at least some of the rituals. While *humiliores* and references to women who cannot wear matronly garments may refer to a larger social group than *meretrices* alone, it certainly includes them.[61] The Kalends thus represents one of the clearest examples that, unlike the literary and philosophical texts discussed in earlier chapters, religious cults did not always mandate a strict division between virtuous wives and corrupt whores. They are identified separately but join together as Roman women in communal worship for at least part of the day.

In all probability, the rituals of adornment and purification of the goddess were performed by all Roman women acting together as a social unit. This suggests in turn a larger religious community of Roman women, although the precise nature of their interactions during such festivals has not survived in the historical or literary record. As so often in Roman sources, we have almost no knowledge of what women said to other women when alone together.

The Floralia

Ovid also particularly evokes the role of prostitutes in the Floralia from April 28 through the first days of May, a festival which honored the goddess Flora, patron of flowers. Flora was later strongly associated with prostitutes and emblems of fertility such as rabbits; the Floralia was marked by nude female performances on stage, at least during the Augustan Age and the Empire.[62]

Ovid describes *meretrices* as particular celebrants of the *Floralia*. The nude comedic performances of prostitutes were extremely popular among the Roman crowds, although they did provoke outrage among the more conservative moralists of the age. The crowd and *mimae* supposedly taunted and harassed Cato the Censor when he tried to rebuke the obscene ribaldry of the Floralia.[63] In contrast, later medieval prostitute races, presumed echoes of this festival, were designed to elicit shame and castigate outcast members of society, rather than celebrating them. In northern medieval Italy, prostitutes sometimes raced against Jews while respectable Christian crowds mocked and assaulted both groups.[64]

The *Fasti Praenestini* do not mention the presence of *meretrices* as part of the Floralia, focusing instead on the fertility of the grain and flowers.[65] Lactantius, a late Christian writer, does strongly connect the ritual with the presence of prostitutes. He even ascribes the festival to the generous donation of a wealthy and successful *meretrix* named Flora, who established a foundation in her will to support a festival of plays and *ludi* on her birthday.[66] This is almost certainly false etymology designed to denigrate the popular pagan festival as irreligious, as it is not mentioned by the earlier sources.[67] While Flora's relationship to the other deities and her ethnic origin is unclear, she was fundamentally a minor nature goddess of pollination, both horticulturally and with regard to human reproduction.[68]

The Floralia was a festival whose precise date varied from year to year. Ovid emphasizes that it bridges the gap between April and May, the month of Venus and the month of Vesta.[69] The festival thus transitions between a set of festivals that featured the worship of a paradigmatic goddess of prostitutes, the licentious goddess of love and sexuality, and festivals honoring Vesta, the proper protector of hearth and home, who was more associated with *matronae* and virginal maidens. While focusing on wild eroticized entertainment and the less respectable elements of society in a carnivalesque celebration of springtime, the Floralia looks forward towards the more traditional and domestic goddesses of summer, Vesta and Juno. After the gods of war and sex have had their day, the gods of home and marriage arrive. As a transitional ritual, the Floralia marks both the separation and unity of different social groups of women and their distinct forms of worship.

Ovid's account of Flora may derive from one of the mimes performed during the festival, a standard, ritualistic play depicting the myths of Chloris and her scantily clad nymphs, patrons of spring.[70] The actresses in the Floralia plays also may have been available for sex work after the show, which would certainly be good business tactics if nothing else.[71] Not all Roman actors and actresses were necessarily also prostitutes, however. It was not sexual availability but the public display of their bodies that gave performers the legally dubious status of *infamia*.[72] However, while this may have been true for actors in tragedies and at the more respectable Roman *ludi*, the Floralia performances are explicitly connected with sex. A equivalence between actress and whore is likely in this case, especially given the emphasis on the actresses' nudity.

While the Floralia showcased Roman prostitutes as sex objects, it also honored their popularity and provided a public role for them. The specific religiosity of the festival, however, appears to have often been lost in the pageantry of new wine and naked women; Lactantius may have had some reason to denigrate the day as merely a decadent celebration of pleasure.

Nonae Caprotinae

The Nonae Caprotinae or "Nones of the Wild Fig" was a minor festival in honor of the goddess Juno, patron of wives and marriage. It supposedly commemorated the exploits of slave maids who masqueraded as respectable hostages and helped the city of Rome win a victory over the Latins, while preserving the *pudicitia* of their mistresses.[73] According to Plutarch, the festival itself re-enacted the ancient legend by having the *ancillae*, or slave-girls, dress up in their mistress's garments and parade out of the city, where they mocked male passers-by and then engaged in a mock battle with each other.[74] Macrobius claims that the matrons also served the handmaids for this day and were the principal victims of jokes, thus making the Nonae Caprotinae a summer female equivalent of the December Saturnalia rites.[75] Although this particular carnivalesque ritual follows Bakhtinian principles of inversion and humor, it focuses more on a generalized mistress–slave anxiety than on any need for whores to temporarily dominate wives.[76] The masquerade of the maids as wives does not have a particularly sexual aspect, even though the original subterfuge was designed to protect the virginity of elite Roman girls, demanded as brides by the Latins, by substituting slave women whose chastity was not deemed as valuable. There were many distinct borders of tension in the Roman world: male–female, citizen–non-citizen, elite–non-elite, adult–child. The Nonae Caprotinae served as a means of defusing such tension between mistresses and their housemaids, rather than uniting the larger female community or dividing women according to moral status. The deeper irony of the origin myth, in which slave women were valuable to the Roman community precisely because of their ubiquitous sexual objectification and abuse, seems to have vanished from this relatively modest and desexualized festival.

Anna Perenna

Anna Perenna was another minor fertility goddess who was generally represented as either a river nymph or an elderly female baker; her festival was celebrated on the Ides of March long before Julius Caesar's assassination on that day. According to Ovid, the celebration involved a riotous picnic by the banks of the Tiber where *accumbit cum pare quisque sua*, each man lies with his woman.[77] The celebrants drank copiously, sang theatrical songs, and danced, before staggering home in the evening to the city. The *puellae* or girls specifically sang obscene songs with shameful lyrics (*certaque probra*), in memory of a trick that the elderly Anna played on the lustful Mars, who believed that he was marrying Minerva but found himself instead in a bed with the undesirable Anna.[78] Such a myth may allude to the figure of Iambe, Demeter's obscenely joking female friend who had a role in the Greek Thesmophoria festivals. This link suggests that Anna Perenna is indeed a fertility goddess, although her rites are less formal and elite than those of goddesses like the Bona Dea or Magna Mater. The story of Anna Perenna and Mars' "marriage" is also another tale of inversion, like the festival of the Nonae Caprotinae. Instead of a beautiful, elite maiden goddess, the virile male god weds an elderly nature spirit; hilarity ensues.[79]

The status of the female celebrants of this festival is ambiguous, although this certainly appears to be a non-elite festival. *Puellae* might suggest prostitutes, particularly given their knowledge of obscene theatrical songs and their willingness to dance in public. Since each woman is paired off with a specific man, this may simply be a celebration for ordinary Roman married couples. A fountain dedicated to Anna Perenna was excavated in Rome in 2000; various fertility symbols as well as a multitude of curse tablets were found in its basin.[80] There was no particular indication of prostitution or typical prostitute names on the curse

tablets. Without any definite evidence, Anna Perenna's female worshipers fall into an ambiguous category, neither clearly respectable wife nor
shameful whore. While social-status distinctions may work to separate
elite matrons from prostitutes, festivals aimed at common urban Romans
may have largely ignored such moral distinctions. Augustus' moral legislation, as discussed in the Introduction, was relatively unconcerned with
the marriages or romantic entanglements of the impoverished masses.
Public cults may similarly have ignored licentious behavior by non-elite
citizens.

Larentalia

The December 23 Larentalia festival honoring Acca Larentia,
foster-mother of Romulus and Remus and, according to some versions
of the legend, a *lupa* or prostitute, may also have featured prostitutes in
a significant role as worshipers.[81] The *Fasti Praenestini* offer an origin
for Acca Larentina as a prostitute and mistress of Hercules.[82] Verrius
Flaccus claims that her festival was a result of the enormous fortune she
left the Roman people in her will, much like the story that Lactantius
later ascribed to Flora.[83] This is therefore a festival in honor not only of a
prostitute but also of her morally dubious earnings: it uniquely celebrates
a woman as both benefactor and wage-earner. However, we do not have
any particular evidence about the participation of prostitutes in this festival, although it seems plausible that they also honored their professional
foremother in some fashion.

The worship of Isis by prostitutes

The Egyptian goddess Isis, whose cult became very popular throughout
the Roman Empire and Mediterranean world, was also known for having a cult that was both tolerant of prostitution and welcomed female
prostitutes as worshipers. Worship of Isis first spread throughout Italy
in the late second century BCE. Despite various attempts at repression,
it continued to be a popular religion, particularly for women, Easterners,
and people of lower social status.[84] According to the late anti-pagan dia-
tribe of Epiphanus of Salamis, Isis herself was said to have worked as a
prostitute in the city of Tyre for ten years.[85] While this hostile accusation is intended to denigrate Isis as a debauched pagan demon-goddess,
it does offer a potential clue into the attraction of Isis for prostitutes.
The Isis cult theoretically treated all men and women equally; it also

emphasized issues of sex and fertility, making it potentially attractive for sex workers.[86]

Connections between Isis and prostitution also appeared in the Roman literary record. Ovid warns a jealous lover, "Don't ask what happens in the temple of linen-clad Isis, and don't be worried by the theater's arch (*fornix*)!" The innuendo of *fornix* was presumably intentional. This suggests that the temple of Isis, like the theater, was a locale for romantic assignations and possibly encounters with whores.[87] Juvenal satirically comments that women go to meet their lovers "at the temple of the madam (*lena*) Isis."[88] While both Juvenal and Epiphanus intended to criticize and mock the worship of Isis, their writings still suggest a strong connection between her cult and prostitutes.

Pompeii may also offer archaeological evidence for a prostitute-Isis connection. The temple of Isis in Pompeii was located near the theater and numerous graffiti about prostitutes were written on nearby walls.[89] However, there is no conclusive evidence linking specific prostitutes to this temple. While inconclusive, there is enough evidence to establish that *meretrices* were part of the Isian religious community in the Roman world, if not particularly singled out for a special religious role. Isis was a goddess popular among women of all backgrounds. Since her worship emphasized an erasure of external social divisions, the cult may also have offered an opportunity for wives and whores to interact and transgress conventional boundaries, just as on the Kalends of April.

Matrons only

While certain Roman religious rites prominently featured prostitutes, others deliberately excluded them, establishing a special, elite status for Roman matrons, especially *univirae*.[90] Such rituals reinforced the social value placed on marriage and childbirth, as well as enabling matrons to form temporary, exclusive castes similar to the cults reserved for patricians or other subdivisions within Roman society.[91] The exclusion was often both explicit and itself part of the religious ritual, sometimes taking the form of symbolic punishment of women who fell outside the approved category.

For instance, *paelices*, a word of Greek derivation generally referring to concubines but probably here including prostitutes, were explicitly forbidden from the worship of Juno Lucina, a goddess of childbirth.[92] Her festival, the Matronalia, was celebrated on the Kalends of March;

husbands gave presents to wives, daughters gave presents to their mothers, and barren women prayed for fertility. Women also feasted their female slaves on this day, perhaps as part of the general social inversion featured in other early March festivals. In other words, this was a particularly family-centered festival. While married women worshiped communally together in Juno Lucina's grove, the other rites were all designed to reinforce ties within the *familia*. There was no place for unattached women in such a rite, and so they were deliberately excluded. The Kalends also marks the beginning of spring and thus of a symbolically fertile time, as Ovid emphasizes in his description of the day. As discussed in Chapters 1 and 2, whores were paradigmatically infertile and thus unsuited for the worship of Juno Lucina.

Ovid also describes the Matralia, the feast of Mater Matuta in mid-June, as reserved for *matronae*; this presumably excluded *meretrices* as well as *virgines* and slave women.[93] The rites of Mater Matuta involved a symbolic beating and exile of a slave-girl. This implies that this festival, in contrast to the Matronalia or the celebration of the Nonae Capronaria, sought to emphasize the distinction between free mothers and slaves. Just as the Matronalia and Capronaria perhaps defused the resentment of female slaves towards their mistresses by enabling them to play "queen for a day," the Mater Matuta may have been designed to purge the fear and bitterness that some matrons felt towards the slave women who slept with their husbands and raised their children.

The Bona Dea, another goddess strongly connected with fertility, also had her rites reserved for married women. The New Year's festival of Bona Dea was held in the home of a leading aristocratic matron for that year, which presumably excluded non-elite women from the official celebration.[94] Juvenal claims that the debauched matrons of his time corrupted the rites of Bona Dea by competing with prostitutes in sexual endurance contests, but this is almost certainly satirical exaggeration.[95] Still, it betrays a general male fear of such exclusive, secret female mystery cults. The Bona Dea festival, with its rites hidden inside an elite villa and reserved for a tiny minority of the population, stands in sharp contrast to the public nude performances of whores that adorned the Floralia and served as entertainment for male and female audiences.

There are no formal Roman rites except that of Juno Lucina which explicitly exclude prostitutes, as opposed to reserving ceremonies for married women or the elite class. The religious exclusion of prostitutes is not a general part of Roman cults, whereas their inclusion in certain ceremonies is emphasized. However, there are certain cases, mentioned almost exclusively in hypothetical legal speeches of the early Empire, which indicate that prostitutes were viewed as being religiously impure or polluted in some way. One text of Seneca the Elder's features an abducted maiden who was briefly sold into a brothel. She managed to remain chaste, was eventually freed, and subsequently sought a role as a priestess. The opposing lawyer argues against the maiden's ability to assume such a lofty role in society after her colorful past:

> I should call you unfit for a priesthood if you had merely walked through a brothel. Will any prostitute who is working have to flee you? It would not be appropriate for a priestess to have a maid who was like you; shall it be proper for you to be a priestess yourself? As for the drawing of lots [for the Vestals], this woman has been kept apart lest the remaining maidens be contaminated! (Seneca, *Controversiae* 1.2.3)

In this case, the woman's reputation as a *meretrix*, regardless of her physical condition, is sufficient to disbar her from entry, but this is only one side of a case whose entire goal is to prove her unfit for religious service. The fact that Seneca proposes this as a point of contention at all suggests that the question was disputed (as well as of sensational interest to young male students).[96] It is not clear that this woman must be disbarred from respectable religious service, although a legitimate argument can be made for her exclusion. Other sources also suggest that Vestals were physically separated from prostitutes by their attendants.[97] *Meretrices* may also have possessed a certain degree of *nefas*, or religious pollution, by virtue of their unorthodox profession, as well as their legal status of *infamia*. However, this is not consistent and their participation in a variety of other religious festivals certainly argues that, while they may have been segregated from *virgines*, especially religiously pure maidens like the Vestals, they remained a part of the general religious community. As with erotic paintings, they might corrupt the innocent, but not threaten the *pudicitia* of an experienced and virtuous wife. *Meretrices* were not religiously separated from *matronae* except in a few rituals which were reserved explicitly for married women.

Conclusion

Roman prostitutes had a special role in the religious rituals of their city, taking starring roles in some cases such as the Floralia and participating with other women in offerings to a variety of goddesses. This religious prominence of prostitutes is associated particularly with the imported cult of Venus Erycina, and it may well also have borrowed rites from cultic practices at Locri Epizefiri or other places in Italy. We do not know what the attitude of the average Roman man or woman was towards the cult of Venus Erycina or towards the religious participation of prostitutes in public rituals. However, Ovid, a poet particularly concerned with issues of sexuality and desire, chooses to emphasize *meretrices*' religious roles and prominence in cult in his *Fasti*. Every indication is that the Floralia were highly popular festivals, at least as displays of public erotic entertainment, although they may not have focused on more traditional demonstrations of pious devotion.

Such a communal role for these supposed "bad women" strongly implies that their presence and their voices were not kept hidden or separated from cloistered "good matrons." For all that Quinta Claudia, rather than her descendant Clodia Metelli, was upheld as a role model, the actress who portrayed the chaste Quinta Claudia in annual pageants at the festival of Magna Mater might well have been available for sex work immediately after the show. Roman religious rituals demonstrate both the moral segregation of Roman women and its repeated blurring within daily life. Both wives and whores are public in their devotions; how, then, could one tell the difference between them at prayer or in a sacred bath?

Many of the practices and rites of earlier foreign cults relating to the presence of prostitutes, which had perhaps originally been associated with the eastern goddess Astarte, were inherited or adopted to some degree by the later Roman cults of Venus Erycina, Fortuna Virilis, and Flora. I do not claim that the Republican or Imperial Romans practiced sacred prostitution or even temple prostitution. The temple of Venus Erycina by the Colline Gate was a meeting place and popular solicitation zone for Roman prostitutes, just as earlier temples of Venus may have been and later temples of Isis. We have no evidence of a brothel directly connected to either temple of Venus Erycina. However, the Roman toleration for and acceptance of prostitutes into both secular and religious life, as seen in the inclusive Fortuna Virilis ceremonies, may stem from these earlier traditions of prostitution associated with temples like the temple of Eryx in Sicily.

McGinn emphasizes the separation of women of different types of status in certain religious rituals, focusing on the evidence of the *Fasti Praenestini* and childbirth-oriented cults like that of Juno Lucina.[98] However, it is equally important to stress that *meretrices* and *matronae* were merely one of these divisions, along with other rituals that divided cult along the lines of married–unmarried, old–young, and patrician–plebeian. Furthermore, and importantly, the Romans themselves were aware of the distinction between *matrons* and *meretrices* and chose on certain occasions to unify all women in cultic worship together. In other rites, like the Floralia and the worship of Venus Erycina, prostitutes played a prominent and highly public religious role, acting as acknowledged worshipers of significant deities.

Roman society used religion as a means of moral segregation, but religious worship also offered an opportunity for women to escape moral and social stigmas and to join in a larger female community. The diverse treatment of prostitutes in these different festivals betrays the ambiguity and anxiety about the moral categorization of women. It may also suggest that elite Roman men did not have complete control over the structure and celebration of certain female-oriented religious rites. While the Senate could establish cults like Venus Verticordia and Venus Obsequens (Obedient Venus), which propagandized the virtues of fidelity and subservience, Roman women themselves may have escaped normal social constraints by participating in the debauched picnics of Anna Perenna or communally dressing the statue of Fortuna Virilis.

Furthermore, while prostitutes may have been characterized as morally notorious, they were not religiously invisible. Their participation in annual rituals reveals demonstrates their membership in the larger Roman community and as women who were expected to have religious loyalties and devotions. "Sacred prostitution" may be a myth, but the concept of a debauched, atheistic *meretrix* without larger ties to her community is an equal fiction. For Romans, the idea of holy, or at least pious whores was not a contradiction in terms; morality was defined in terms of spousal fidelity and loyalty to the state, not fervent piety. Contrary to St. Augustine, Venus was a goddess of whores as well as wives.

8

The "whore" label in Western culture

Now Theodora became a courtesan (*hetaira*), and such as the ancient Greeks used to call a "foot soldier's woman," at that: for she was not a flute or harp player, nor was she even trained to dance, but only gave her youth to anyone she met, in utter abandonment ... Thus was this woman born and raised, and her name was a byword beyond that of other common girls on the tongues of all men ... But when she came back to Constantinople, Justinian fell violently in love with her. At first he kept her only as a mistress, though he raised her to patrician rank. Through him Theodora was able to acquire immediately an unholy power and exceedingly great riches ... It was then that he undertook to complete his marriage with Theodora. But as it was impossible for a man of senatorial rank to make a courtesan (*hetaira*) his wife, this being forbidden by ancient law, he made the Emperor nullify this ordinance by creating a new one, permitting him to wed Theodora, and consequently making it possible for anyone else to marry a courtesan.

(Procopius, Secret History *9)*

The idea of "whore" as a label applicable to all immoral women remained a major theme in later Western attitudes towards the role of women in society.[1] Prostitutes have continued to be a symbol for class divisions, gender divisions, and generalized anxiety about social mobility and interactions between different groups. Gail Hershatter, in her study of twentieth-century Shanghai prostitutes, notes, "Prostitution was variously understood as a source of urbanized pleasures, a profession full of greedy and unscrupulous schemers, a site of moral danger and physical disease, and a marker of national decay ... The categories through which prostitution was understood were not fixed."[2] Many of these same labels

can be attached to Roman attitudes towards prostitution and *meretrices*.
Cicero's denunciation of Cytheris' assumption of matronly privilege and
Clodia's lack of control over her slaves are both interpreted as signs of the
degradation of the Roman Republic. Prostitution became a larger metaphor for the dangers of change and social mobility, even if most prostitutes, in any society, never rose above a miserable, impoverished social
and economic state. Roman and later European prostitution conceptually
represented a transgression of social boundaries both in terms of class
and gender, especially through concern over women's abandonment of
traditional familial ties.

The nature and tone of invective and anxiety about the intrusion of
prostitutes into the elite sphere, as well as accusations that elite women
were behaving like prostitutes, were profoundly affected by the evolution of Christian attitudes towards sexuality and gender relations. Illicit
extramarital sexual behavior, regardless of the social status of the parties
involved, became generally viewed as immoral in the Christian world.[3]
This makes it difficult to analyze directly the evolution of the Western
conceptualization of the prostitute, as it was filtered through a general
criticism of all sexual behavior as sinful. However, the emphasis on the
prostitute as a symbol of disloyalty, above and beyond her role as sexual
temptress, continued to play a significant role in Western discourse about
women's social roles.

By examining some sample cases and analyses of prostitution
from later Western history, we can explore the evolving definition of
"whore" and its application as a more general pejorative term. The
issue of subcategories and hierarchies within the general category of
"prostitute" also continued to problematize the discourse about this
social label.

Theodora of Constantinople

The Empress Theodora, consort of the Byzantine Emperor Justinian from
527 to 548 CE, is one of the most famous historical women who might
have been an actual prostitute; she was certainly accused of behaving like
one.[4] Her story, as described in the epigraph of this chapter, evokes many
of the contradictions and complexities evidenced in earlier stereotypes of
Roman *meretrices*. Theodora's chronicler Procopius represents her, like
earlier notable women accused of prostitution, as not only adulterous but
sexually indiscriminate. Procopius also accuses her of exotic and impure
sex with slaves and men of the lowest possible social status. Theodora's

story resembles accounts of powerful concubines like Commodus' Marcia, who were also characterized as politically ambitious and personally avaricious.[5]

Theodora shares another characteristic with most of the literary and historical *meretrices* previously discussed: our main source for her is an extremely hostile, vituperative account by an elite male author who despised her political influence nearly as much as her purported sexual behavior. Procopius goes so far as to accuse Theodora and her husband of being demons or vampires in human form, an extreme version of Horace's accusations against *lenae*.[6] In Theodora's case, we are lucky enough to have multiple other sources, including earlier accounts by Procopius himself that are far more favorable to her.[7] Unlike most of the *meretrices* in earlier Roman history, it is therefore possible to form a more nuanced picture of her representation. John of Ephesus's generally favorable portrait describes her as coming "from the brothel (*porneiou*)," and Justinian's own law code includes Procopius' alleged law allowing marriage between a former actress and a patrician.[8] These references support at least some of Procopius' allegations about Theodora's original social status, although the excessive prurience is almost certainly the fruit of Procopius' imagination and his desire to follow in a tradition of Roman and Greek invective.[9]

Regardless of the truth of the claims that Theodora was a former public prostitute, her story illuminates the larger themes of this book, as well as suggesting a general continuity in historical discourse about powerful, unorthodox women. Procopius' use of invective about Theodora's sexual behavior and her open availability reflects earlier diatribes like Juvenal's condemnation of Messalina. Theodora is not just an adulterous empress but one who sleeps with slaves – a familiar charge. Procopius directly invokes Pliny's version of Messalina in his story of Theodora's "duels" with forty or more sexual partners in an evening, which surpasses Messalina's infamous alleged victory of twenty-five rounds.[10] The root of her problematic behavior seems to be not so much Theodora's sexual desire or activities but her transgressive social mobility, both in terms of changing her own social status and in her alleged liaisons with lower-class men.

Medieval and early modern "whores"

The pattern of expanding the narrow definition of professional prostitute to describe a wide variety of unorthodox, politically influential women continued throughout later European history. Theodora and Marozia, a mother and daughter pair of Roman women during the late ninth and tenth centuries CE, were also labeled as *meretrices* by their contemporaries.[11] The women allegedly assisted several of their illegitimate descendants to the papal throne in Rome. As in similar ancient cases, there is little evidence that they ever traded sexual favors for money, but the label was attached to them in part because of their active political lives.

In medieval England, "whore" was used as a term both for professional prostitutes and for other women who engaged in extramarital sex.[12] Later medieval society was also highly concerned with the question of prostitutes' dubious loyalty. In part, this was connected with the general belief, inherited from earlier Roman prejudices, that service professions were more dishonorable than agriculture or the production of commodities.[13] Prostitution itself may have served as a metaphor for a more general societal concern about fleeting economic transactions and an abandonment of traditional bonds of fealty and friendship.[14]

While a more prurient focus on female sexuality dominated, prostitution's specific danger in later European society was still also represented as the absence of familial bonds between men and women. Parent-Duchatelet, an early anthropologist who studied prostitution in the 1830s, wrote a composite personality sketch of the thousands of prostitutes he identified, describing "the prostitute" as a woman with "lightness and mobility of spirit" who could not be "held still" or "pinned down."[15] Prostitutes are identified as "free spirits"; that label carries a highly negative connotation for the women to whom it applies. Freedom and independence for a woman was not an indication of respectability but of immorality: female virtue continued to be associated with dependence upon and loyalty to a husband.

The autobiography of Mrs. Leeson, a Dublin professional prostitute and madam from the late eighteenth century, offers a rare female perspective into the ability of later prostitutes to shift social roles and move among various layers of society during their careers. This memoir illuminates precisely the aspects of social hierarchy and mobility among prostitutes that are difficult to definitively establish in Roman times. Mrs. Leeson, a *nom de plume* adopted from one of Margaret Leeson's early long-term lovers, herself claimed to have been born into a wealthy agricultural family of eight children in rural Ireland.[16] She also profiled a number of her fellow Dublin and London prostitutes who came from lowlier backgrounds: a single wool-spinner's daughter, who eventually married a church rector; a dairy farmer's daughter; a chimney-sweeper's daughter; and several apprentice milliners. These various women had wealthy and aristocratic lovers as well as clients who were butlers or impoverished scoundrels.[17]

Mrs. Leeson herself adopted a more respectable life on several occasions, including a brief marriage to the son of a famous attorney that was shortly thereafter dissolved by the indignant father.[18] This easy mobility among different social classes offers further comparative evidence that the thriving ancient Roman *demi-monde* was not purely a creation of the Augustan poets. Mrs. Leeson's memoirs navigate the complex world of a courtesan who is neither respectable wife nor lowly streetwalker. The idea of the fluidly defined *meretrix* persisted, both in literary texts and historical reality, and it continued to shape ideas about appropriate and inappropriate roles for women in European society.

Parent-Duchalet also established that many French nineteenth-century prostitutes moved from factory jobs to prostitution to respectable work or marriage, a flexibility which Roman female innkeepers and barmaids may also have utilized in the course of their lives.[19] While the complexity of prostitutes' social status is certainly present in the modern scholarly record, it is also an essential part of how prostitutes and wives may have actually functioned in Roman society, despite the elite discourse of rigid segregation. This paradoxical relationship of assimilation and separation persisted through millennia of European and Mediterranean history. Any woman can become a prostitute, yet equally, any prostitute has the potential of repenting and becoming a wife, or of hiding her past from her new husband.

The modern courtesan and whore

While no one denies the presence of prostitutes in the United States in the twenty-first century, the official narrative of elite American culture generally portrays actual prostitution as an illegal institution practiced largely by desperate, young, drug-addicted female streetwalkers controlled by abusive pimps.[20] This ignores any possible hierarchy of prostitutes or any role for the modern *meretrix* except that of a cheap whore. In contrast, the sizable American escort or call girl industry, which is a much closer parallel to the *hetaira* or courtesan model of the ancient world, is rarely seriously analyzed or discussed by scholars. The clients are more likely themselves to belong to an elite class that wishes to divorce itself mentally from the sordid discourse of prostitution, while at the same time the prostitutes have the resources to conceal their profession and evade

arrest more easily. The first-person account of the escort "Barbara," in a
1993 *Social Text* article, echoes many aspects of Roman courtesan–client
relationships, including the political and economic advice given by the
escort to her customers.[21]

Many modern prostitutes, at least in developed nations, explicitly
demand the right to choose and reject clients, placing themselves in a
higher position in the sex work hierarchy, just as some Roman courtesans
did.[22] This right, and detailed regulations spelling out its enforcement
for each client and act, is also spelled out in the recent New Zealand
Occupational Guide to Health and Safety for the legalized sex industry.[23]
Government regulation has further divided both different types of prostitutes in general as well as areas with legalized prostitution from those
lacking such regulation.

A study of legalized prostitutes, especially escorts, in Windsor, Ontario,
includes the revealing comment from one young escort attempting to differentiate herself from streetwalkers: "I'm not like them; I'd never be a
whore."[24] Estimates of current incomes for high-level escorts in Europe,
New York, and the Middle East range from US $1,000 to $5,000 per day,
a level high enough to guarantee a middle- or upper-class lifestyle, at least
if a significant percentage of that sum goes to the woman herself.[25] For
streetwalking prostitutes in Los Angeles in 1995, in contrast, the average
annual salary was $23,845, higher than the wage of an average American
female employee yet not extremely remunerative.[26] This ambiguous social
status of the high-class escort or call girl echoes the complex social hierarchies of Rome and the confusing social roles of women like Chelidon
and Cytheris.

Both ancient and modern audiences find stories about prostitutes compelling and entertaining, especially those which feature elegant courtesans. The dangerous glamor of the *meretrix* both excites and repels the
viewer because of her identity as a socially transgressive figure that defies
accepted moral norms. While she is "not the sort of girl you'd marry,"
the courtesan fascinates us as a symbol of alterity and of unorthodox
constructions of gender identity, even while the "good wife" is often represented as a figure of dullness and repression. The glamor may be misleading and hide the real oppression and degradation that exists for most
prostitutes, both in Rome and modern America. Nevertheless, the allure
and mystery remain in our imagination.

Attitudes towards women, sex and prostitution have of course
changed in the last two millennia. However, there remains a consistent tendency to stereotype and exaggerate women's sexual behavior to

create false labels that are then applied to large segments of the female population. The association between female sexual promiscuity and unorthodox political or economic activity has also remained a strong legacy from the Roman period, although it has been joined by a newer stereotype of cold-hearted, single, career women who, like prostitutes, are represented as estranged from the bonds of a traditional family. Even in 2012, an educated, single, elite woman such as Sandra Fluke who wishes to speak publicly at a political forum may be shamed by male elites as a "slut," while other female politicians are called by similar offensive and misogynistic terms referring to their sexuality and promiscuity.[27]

Conclusion

Liminal women

The stories and images in this book depict how Roman men sought to control Roman women. At the same time, they suggest how many Roman women defied, evaded, or ignored the labels and restrictions placed upon their sexual and economic behavior by elite men. The Roman discourse about *matronae* and *meretrices* shaped the lives of real women through its prescriptive message of virtuous and problematic behavior. At the same time, the actual experiences of those women undermined or directly challenged any attempt at rigid categorization. I would have preferred to write a book revealing how the independence and economic agency of ancient Roman women from a variety of social classes enabled them to achieve control over their own sexual activities and romantic lives. Instead, I have focused necessarily on the historical reality of the patriarchal misogyny that sought to define and circumscribe the lives of Roman women, despite or perhaps because of their comparatively extensive privileges.

While Roman women of all social ranks engaged with the traditionally male public sphere in a variety of ways, powerful male elites were also successful at rebuking them through their control of both actual law and the social discourse. Although Vistilia achieved a few years of sexual freedom, she was still eventually banished to a remote island. While Roman women received public honors and recognition and participated meaningfully in the religious and economic lives of their communities, they were still constrained by a mythic ideal that located them firmly in private domestic spaces. Freedwomen like Hispala Faecenia or Caenis who achieved social mobility, financial stability, and lasting praise did so by promoting the interests and agenda of their male lovers and, even more importantly, the Roman social order. Furthermore, due to the nature of our elite male-authored sources, we have no way of accurately measuring just how many Roman women achieved actual economic or sexual agency. At the end of the day, men are still the centers of all these stories, and women, whether matrons or prostitutes, remain either their loyal supporters or despised traitors.

The ancient evidence categorized Roman women as immoral if they lacked familial ties and acted in their own economic self-interest, largely regardless of the women's sexual behavior or actual economic activities. The negative Roman label of *meretrix* highlights the importance of loyalty and generosity as primary components of Roman female virtue; these are contrasted with promiscuity and greed. While Roman men won glory through their personal deeds, their wives were praised for being supporters of their male kin and placing the interests of the family above their own. Even though women were allowed to own property, both matrons and prostitutes earned the greatest praise through giving their money to their male partners.

Meretrices were the necessary wicked counterpart to the ideal of the good matron. Whores were not only sexually promiscuous, but figures of chaos and disorder – women who were both part of the social structure and fundamentally disruptive to it – unless, of course, they transcended their stereotype to function in "wife-like" ways. In this fashion, the discourse about *meretrices* resembles that about *cinaedi*, Roman males who preferred passive roles in sex and thus overturned the sexual power structure to an even greater degree.[1] The development of *meretrices* as this threatening, queer alternative to the normative Roman female stereotype largely served to reify and support the ideal role model of the loyal *bona matrona*.

Roman women for centuries were instructed in the exempla of the women they should imitate, like Quinta Claudia, Cornelia, and Livia, while also hearing the cautionary tales of Tarpeia and Messalina, figures duly punished for their disloyalty and greed. Even if few women actually followed either extreme of behavior, the approved path for Roman female activity was clear. In order to earn the good public reputation that would cause her descendants to honor her and strangers to admire her epitaph, a Roman woman needed to fit neatly into a prescribed pattern of virtue. Nevertheless, the most prosperous and successful courtesans and concubines possessed some control over their own lives and potentially wielded influence over powerful elite men. The glamour of their image carried powerful weight in the Roman imagination, even if it rarely reflected the historical reality of most Roman prostitutes' miserable lives.

For elite Roman women accused of prostitute-like behavior, condemnations of promiscuous and immoral behavior were a frequent side effect of increased personal power in the political and economic spheres of Roman life. Such slanders may have borne little relationship to the actual sexual activities of these women. Even though Cicero publicly mocked Clodia Metelli as a *meretrix* in 56 BCE, by 45 BCE he found it necessary to conduct business negotiations with her about her extensive real estate holdings.[2] The Empress Messalina tried to demonstrate that she had more power than her husband Claudius, the ruler of the Mediterranean world, through her alleged coup attempt. While she failed in her ambition, and her name became a byword for female debauchery and corrupt scheming, Messalina's story still suggests the potential power available to well-connected Roman women. Even in the highly conventional genre of epigraphy, the epitaph of Allia Potestas displays a striking individuality and rejection of conventional labels, as her description shifts fluidly between wife and whore.

The generalized label of *meretrix* also conceals the complexity of the variable hierarchy and social structures within the shadowy world of unmarried, sexually active women, including both professional sex workers and elite widows. Attitudes towards such women also shifted and evolved over time, depending to some extent on elite male authors' personal views. In Chapter 1, *meretrices* were presented as the antithesis of virtuous, respectable *matronae*: the paradigmatic "Other", according to de Beauvoir and Levi-Strauss's conceptions of the term.[3] Professional prostitutes appeared to be explicit contrasts to elite wives and to be defined by an absence of the positive traits associated with respectable women. Both types of women, however, were *nota*, well known. Elite Roman male social anxiety about defining women by social and moral categories emerges from the ambiguity of what, precisely, a specific Roman woman was well known for.

Before more thoroughly discussing the deconstruction of any possible simple definition for the *meretrix* or the *bona matrona*, it is necessary to re-examine the theoretical structure underlying such analysis. Gender scholars of the ancient world have traditionally drawn very bright lines between *meretrix* and *matron*, utilizing several traditional structuralist pairs to sharply divide public and private space and domestic and public social roles.[4] In some cases, such divisions are easy to locate in the discourse about Roman prostitutes. *Meretrices*, in the limited sense of cheap prostitutes or women who behave like them, are indeed represented in most elite Roman texts as public streetwalkers, openly available for all men's gaze and usage. *Matronae* are private women, who dwell and work primarily inside a house and often travel inside an enclosed litter or carriage as a symbol of their elite status. At the same time, *matronae* may be associated with the private, domestic sphere, but they are not restricted to it, whereas, within the elite discourse, *meretrices* often lack a home of their own entirely. Even archaeological evidence indicates that *meretrices* likely did not live in their brothels; their actual homes remain anonymous.

With regard to sexual activities, *matronae* pursue a natural path, generally engaging, at least according to male-authored sources, in potentially procreative heterosexual intercourse. *Meretrices* indulge their lovers by offering non-procreative, urbane forms of sexual intercourse such as fellatio, and they are almost never represented as maternal figures. Roman texts present a variety of other deceptively simple dichotomies between these two extremes. *Matronae* guard and maintain the household resources of the *familia*; *meretrices* are greedy spendthrifts who bankrupt their lovers. *Matronae* are loyal to their husbands and their *familia*, and they are defined both in name and in purpose as a part of that family, e.g. Julia, daughter of Julius. *Meretrices*, while often slaves or under the economic control of a *leno* or *lena*, are not part of any permanent or structured *familia*; the elite women labeled as *meretrices* are often widows or divorced women.

Roman *meretrices* and *matronae* do appear initially to fall firmly into divisions based on the domestic–public, natural–cultural pairs first established by Rosaldo, Ortner, and others.[5] However, these pairs divided society along male–female lines, with men representing the public, cultured, professional half of society while women were categorized as private, domestic, and more in tune with nature rather than civilization. *Meretrices*, in the Roman imagination, lie in the traditionally masculine half of this paradigm. As discussed in Chapter 1, Roman prostitutes supposedly wore the public, official, male garment of the toga, so perhaps this cross-gender identification should come as no surprise. By abandoning traditional definitions of femininity and social expectations, *meretrices* were thrust into the male spectrum. Like Vestal Virgins, who also lacked many of the conventional accoutrements of a *matrona*, *meretrices* took on aspects of the public male social role by default.[6] The focus on individual success as opposed to familial support, which we have seen associated with *meretrices*, is another aspect of their behavior that echoes male social norms. Virtuous Roman women exist conceptually to nurture and assist their husbands and sons; *meretrices*, who lack such family members, have no option but to intrude conceptually into the masculine sphere, to the extent it exists as a clearly defined space within Roman culture.

However, any cultural history of these two labels of *meretrix* and *matrona* must recognize that the existing sets of representations cannot be boiled down to two separate paradigms of good wife and bad prostitute. To begin with, Roman writers apply the label of *meretrix* to a wide range of women from an enormous variety of social backgrounds, of which the greedy, common street prostitute is only one. A binary structure, as suggested by the more prescriptive ancient texts and many modern scholars, ignores the important distinctions and differentiations between streetwalkers, courtesans, imperial concubines, and sexually adventurous elite wives like Vistilia. At the same time, women who were professional prostitutes, as seen in Chapter 2, can be categorized in Roman discourse as virtuous, loyal, "almost-wives," depending on their behavior and relationship with their male lovers.

The texts and images cited in previous chapters have reflected the ambiguity and complexity in the literary, artistic, and archaeological record concerning the sexual activity of women and the role of prostitutes in Roman society. The epitaph of Allia Potestas, discussed in Chapter 2, itself forms an ironic commentary on any attempt to divide women into only two categories, as it describes at length a woman who is not only industrious and loyal but also expensive, notorious, and polyandrous.

The other texts analyzed in Chapter 2 disassociate feminine virtues from the social status of the women involved. These anecdotes establish that it was possible in Roman discourse to be a generous, loyal *meretrix*; moral qualities are separated, at least in some cases, from economic realities. Meanwhile, the freelance courtesans and concubines of Chapter 3 further refine definitions of good and bad female behavior, depending on the woman's threat or support of the elite male social order. Concubines like Cytheris and Marcia functioned almost as wives, receiving many of the social marks of elite status like litters and official recognition, but they received very different treatment from contemporaneous authors. The distinction between a normal, virtuous elite matron and a woman like the Emperor Vespasian's concubine Caenis, who was his devoted mistress for many decades and had significant political influence over appointments, is largely in the label applied to each. These women played important and influential roles in their lovers' lives, perhaps more so than many respectable wives did.

Chapter 4 similarly establishes that promiscuous behavior on the part of *matronae* was not sufficient to earn the label of *meretrix*. Roman authors labeled elite wives as *meretrices* not just for their notorious adulteries but for undermining the social order through both familial and political disloyalty. Clodia, Cleopatra, and Messalina were in all probability no more promiscuous than their contemporaries. However, they all chose to play prominent public roles in the political and legal life of their times, while simultaneously refusing to be defined by a single male partner. This combination of traits, as well as external political and legal motivations such as Octavian's propaganda war against Antonius, caused elite male authors to condemn them as *meretrices*. All these women are also particularly accused of sexual relations with slaves and other non-elite men; their crime lies not so much in their adultery as in their disruption of the social hierarchy.

The evidence of prostitutes' roles in Roman religious rituals, as analyzed in Chapter 7, suggests both a separation and a complex intertwining of the roles of *meretrix* and *matrona*. The various festivals set aside for specific subsets of Roman women emphasize this constant and formal acknowledgement of difference and connection. Prostitutes and wives did not have the same religious status or practices, but neither did patrician and plebeian women, and all women were joined together in general worship of the gods at certain festivals like the Kalends of April. By taking an active role in the annual rites of Roman religion, *meretrices* demonstrated that they were a vital and socially accepted part of Roman society rather than shunned marginal outsiders. At the same time, Roman religion in general served as an acceptable and safe space for Roman women of all social levels to act in public and engage with each other socially.

Any attempt to strongly marginalize *meretrices* and establish them as social or legal outcasts finds little or no corroboration in the visual and archaeological record. The analysis of Roman images of lovemaking in Chapter 5 reveals that there is no definite visual differentiation between *meretrices* and *matronae* in Roman art. Meanwhile, the archaeological evidence of brothel locations and architecture in Chapter 6 suggests that the urban landscape was not defined by any sort of moral or social segregation.

This book has sought to fill in the void between the two theorized poles of *meretrix* and *matrona* in the world of Roman women and to deconstruct any supposed structuralist dichotomy. The Roman concept of female sexuality was not a binary choice between good, chaste matrons and evil, profligate streetwalkers. Such absolute ideals did not exist in the real world, while the literary and artistic discourse also presented a more complex picture of options for Roman women. While Roman authors certainly spoke of lowly *scorta* and virtuous *univirae matronae*, they also recognized the existence of virtuous, generous *meretrices* and matrons who behaved like greedy whores. This wide variety of tales about both good and bad women offered opportunities for all Roman women, regardless of their social class, to uphold the social order and behave virtuously. Every Roman woman could loyally support a Roman man.

The literary and artistic evidence depicting matrons as actively desirous participants in sexual activities also emphasizes the crucial point that the Roman paradigm was not the Christian dichotomy of virgin–whore, but rather of a fertile, responsible, loyal female partner, who was contrasted with a non-procreative, selfish, faithless woman who made herself sexually available to all men.[7] *Pudicitia* and *castitas*, modesty and purity, do not in the Roman context mean an absence of sexual desire, but rather a restriction of that desire towards one man within an appropriate context.[8]

Attitudes towards *meretrices* and their position in Roman society also undoubtedly changed over the lengthy history of the Roman Empire.[9] This is particularly visible in the case of elite courtesans. As shown in Chapter 3, Republican authors condemned them for usurping the role of the *matrona* and disrupting natural family ties, while later writers like Tacitus praised the emperors' mistresses as uncomplicated sexual objects who removed the threat of a powerful empress from the court. While this may reflect specific authors' prejudices rather than general societal attitudes, all the Imperial historians exhibit a similar, generally positive reaction towards emperors' concubines.

While this might indicate a general trend towards more toleration of *meretrices*, a different progression of social attitudes is present within the genre of poetry, as discussed in Chapter 1. Augustan elegiac poets criticized their greedy *amicae* on the grounds that their valuation of money over poetry marked a personal betrayal. However, the later Imperial epigrammists and satirical poets of the high Empire, like Martial and Juvenal, harshly attacked gold-digging prostitutes as the most visible symbol of the corruption and immorality of all women. Furthermore, the Augustan poets were largely concerned with the relationship between the narrator and his lover, whereas the later authors frequently condemned prostitutes for cutting the ties between a man and his other friends and family.

While the Imperial-era sources treat powerful courtesans more favorably and gold-digging brothel girls more critically, both patterns can be explained by larger social developments in Roman history. Indeed, they may serve as microcosmic symptoms of those changes, which are often hard to comprehend outside the ranks of the elite men of Rome or the surviving literary authors. In both cases, these changing attitudes towards *meretrices* can be explained by shifting perspectives concerning the importance of the elite *familia* and the relative social roles of the authors in question. They are unified by an overall emphasis on Roman social stability and the maintenance of the privileges of elite men.

For elite senators like Cicero, maintaining rigid social boundaries between *meretrices* and *matronae* further emphasized the importance of elite families and their interconnections through marriage.[10] Women like Chelidon and Cytheris represented a threat to that community and ideal. By assuming the privileges and respect due a matron during her tenure as Antonius' mistress, Cytheris devalued the status of less alluring but nobly born women like Terentia, Cicero's own wife. The structure of the Roman Republican oligarchy depended on restrictive standards for admission; prostitutes masquerading as equals to respectable wives endangered the ideology of exclusive elite families.

For wealthy, elite patron-supported poets like Propertius or Ovid in the Augustan Age, romances with *amicae* of ambiguous but probable freedwoman status allowed authors to surreptitiously challenge the unpopular government-enforced promotion of the family and of traditional moral values. These *amicae* were only criticized and attacked when they preferred wealthy freedmen or crass soldiers to the poetic charms of the narrator. While poets express concern about the rapid social mobility of freedmen in these texts, they are only angry at their *amicae* for general disloyalty, not for inappropriate social climbing or, conversely, slumming.

Under the high Empire, the Senate lost much of its tradition of a semi-static elite community of intermarried families, and elite authors like Tacitus and Suetonius distrusted the influence of powerful aristocratic women with access to the emperor's ear. The antipathy towards elite women like Agrippina the Younger led to more generous treatment by historians of inconsequential concubines. Meanwhile, many Imperial-era poets, like Juvenal and Martial, were far less wealthy or influential than many concubines, courtesans, or promiscuous elite wives, at least according to the complaints of their poetic personae.[11] This comic resentment at the unorthodox reversal of traditional dichotomies of power and social status led to generally misogynistic statements.[12] Juvenal and Martial's criticisms of women in general are especially directed at wealthy prostitutes who had risen above their station. While the elite men of Roman imperial society, like Tacitus, found nothing to fear from imperial concubines, men who possessed neither money nor significant influence unleashed their invective upon women who had used their sexual charms to advance above them within the ranks of Roman society.

Roman women were far more than wives or whores, regardless of social status. Many wives and even whores possessed meaningful choices about their partners, their form of religious worship, and their daily activities. If we blindly accept the elite male discourse labeling and defining Roman women as good or bad, we miss much of the nuance and complexity of their lives. However, in all these cases, the underlying message of these authors echoed that of Cicero's comment about the courtesan Volumnia Cytheris. Her presence was acceptable while *habeo non habeor* – as long as the man remained fully in possession and control of the woman. All of these stories and images remind Roman women that their virtue and their good reputation lies in subordination. This narrow line between notability and notoriety intertwines itself with women's sexual and economic behavior, precisely because men seek to demonstrate their possession of their particular women by regulating their sexual and economic activity.

Such elite male anxiety about what it means for a woman to act in the public sphere has persisted and echoed throughout later Western society, as demonstrated in Chapter 8. In the 2008 United States presidential campaign, Senator Hillary Clinton felt the need to promise the voters of Iowa that she did not want a one-night stand, but a long-term relationship with them.[13] In such a statement, one of the most globally prominent female public figures in the early twenty-first century chose to define her political commitment by analogizing it to her sexual loyalty. Iowans could trust that Hillary Clinton would be a loyal representative of their state's interests precisely because she was a faithful and monogamous romantic partner, the most important indicator of virtue for a woman.

The only definite *perpetua virgo*, or permanent maiden, from the Roman era, excepting the Vestals, was the female professional painter Iaia of Cyzicus.[14] All other adult Roman women might be categorized either by their current or previous marriage or by their open sexual availability – either as wives or whores. Until the advent of holy virgins among the early Christian communities, all women's familial and sexual relationships shaped and controlled their identities. Blanket condemnations of female sexual promiscuity have faded somewhat from the modern discourse, although they have by no means vanished, even in the most egalitarian nations. However, the Roman focus on the moral importance of female familial loyalty and its relationship to a woman's public activities and reputation will remain a major social issue until the concept of the family itself has changed.

Appendix I

Text and translation of the Allia Potestas epitaph

Latin Text: CIL VI, 37965 = CLE 1988 Lines 4–5 are disputed due to poor condition, but accepted by Horsfall and Saltelli. Spelling and grammatical errors on the stone have not been edited.	English Translation: Adapted from N. M. Horsfall, "CIL VI, 37965 = CLE 1988 (Epitaph of Allia Potestas): A Commentary," ZPE, 61. (1985) 251–72, and M. Lefkowitz and M. Fant, Women's Life in Greece and Rome (Toronto, 1992). #47.
A (Heading of monument)	**A**
Dis Manib(us) Alliae A(uli) l(ibertae) Potestatis	To the gods of the dead: Aulus's freedwoman, Allia Potestas.
B	**B**
Hic Perusina sita est, qua non pretiosior ulla. Femina de multis uix una aut altera uisasedula. Seriola parua tam magna teneris. «Crudelis fati rector duraque Persiphone, quid bona diripitis exuperantque mala» Quaeritur a cunctis, iam respondere fatigor, dant lachrimas, animi signa benigna sui.	Here lies a woman from Perugia, dearer than any other. One woman so diligent as she has rarely been seen. Great as you were you are now held in a small urn. <<Cruel arbiter of fate, and harsh Persephone, why do you deprive us of good, and why does evil triumph?>> everyone asks, but I am tired of answering. They give me their tears, tokens of their good will.

Fortis, sancta, tenax, insons, fidissima
custos, munda domi, sat munda
foras, notissima uolgo, sola erat
ut posset factis occurrere cunctis;
exiguo sermone, inreprehensa
manebat. Prima toro delapsa fuit,
eadem ultima lecto se tulit ad
quietem positis ex ordine rebus.
lana cui e manibus nuncquam sine
caussa recessit, opsequioque prior
nulla moresque salubres. Haec sibi
non placuit, numquam sibi libera
uisa. Candida, luminibus pulchris,
aurata capillis, et nitor in facie
permansit eburneus illae qualem
mortalem nullam habuisse ferunt,
pectore et in niueo breuis illi forma
papillae. Quid crura? Atalantes
status illi comicus ipse. Anxia
non mansit, sed corpore pulchra
benigno. Leuia membra tulit, pilus
illi quaesitus ubique; Quod manibus
duris fuerit culpabere forsan: nil illi
placuit nisi quod per se sibi fecerat
ipsa. Nosse fuit nullum studium,
sibi se satis esse putabat, mansit
et infamis, quia nil admiserat
umquam. Haec duo dum uixit
iuuenes ita rexit amantes, exemplo
ut fierent similes Pyladisque et
Orestae: una domus capiebat eos
unusque et spiritus illis. Post hanc
nunc idem diuersi sibi quisq(ue)
senescunt; femina quod struxit talis,
nunc puncta lacessunt. Aspicite ad
Troiam, quid femina fecerit olim!
Sit precor hoc iustum exemplis in
paruo grandibus uti. Hos tibi dat
uersus lacrimans sine fine patronus
muneris amissae, cui nuncquam es
pectore adempta, quae putat amissis
munera grata dari, nulla cui post te
femina uisa proba est. Qui sine te
uiuit, cernit sua funera uiuos.

She was courageous, pure, tenacious, honest, the most loyal of guardians. Elegant at home, also elegant in the forums, and very well known to the crowd. She alone could confront whatever happened. With brief speech, she remained blameless. She was first to rise from the couch, and last to return to the bed to rest after she had put each thing in its place. Her wool never left her hands without good reason. Out of respect she yielded place to all; her morals were healthy. She was never too pleased with herself, and never thought of herself as a free woman. White-skinned, with beautiful eyes, golden-haired, and an ivory glow always shone from her face – no mortal, they say, ever possessed a face like it. The curve of her breasts was dainty across her snow-white bosom. What about her legs? Such is the appearance of Atalanta as a comic actress. In her anxiety she never stayed still, but beautiful, with her generous body, moved her smooth limbs, and she sought out every hair. Perhaps one may find fault with her rough hands. She was content with nothing but what she did for herself. There was never any knowledge about which she thought she knew enough. and she remained free of gossip because she did nothing bad.

While she lived she so ruled over her two young lovers that they followed the example of Pylades and Orestes: one house would have held them both and one spirit. But after this, they will separate, and each grow old alone.

Auro tuum nomen fert ille refertque
lacerto, qua retinere potest auro
collata Potestas.

Quantumcumq(ue) tamen praeconia
nostra ualebunt, uersiculis uiues
quandiucumque meis.
Effigiem pro te teneo solacia nostri,
quam colimus sancte sertaque multa
datur, cumque at te ueniam, mecum
comitata sequetur. Sed tamen
infelix cui tam sollemnia mandem?
Si tamen extiterit, cui tantum
credere possim, hoc unum felix
amissa te mihi forsan ero. Ei mihi!
Vicisti: sors mea facta tua est.

Now moments destroy what such a
woman built up; look at Troy, to
see what a woman once did! I pray
that it be right to use such grand
comparisons for this lesser event.
Your patron, whose tears never end,
gives these words to you.

You are lost to gifts, but never will be
taken from his heart.
These are the gifts he believes will be
pleasing to the lost:
After you, no woman can seem
virtuous.
He who has lived without you has
seen his own death while alive.
He wears your name written
backwards and forwards in gold
letters on his arm, where he can
keep it, possessing Potestas. As long
as these published words of ours
survive, so long will you live in
these little verses of mine.
In your place I have only your image
as solace.
We cherish this with reverence and
lavish it with flowers.
When I come to you, it follows in
attendance.
But to whom can I, unfortunate man,
trust such sacred objects?
If there ever is anyone to whom I can
entrust it, I shall be fortunate in this
alone now that I have lost you. Woe
is me! You have triumphed; your
fate and mine are the same.

C (Bottom inscription)

C

Laedere qui hoc poterit, ausus quoque
  laedere diuos: haec titulo insignis,
  credite, numen habet.

The man who tries to harm this
  tomb dares to harm the gods:
Believe me, this woman, made
  famous by this label, has divinity.

Appendix II

Women in the Hebrew Bible

The Hebrew Bible (or Christian Old Testament) served as one of the major sources for Western concepts of morality and provides a useful comparison with regard to the legacy of Roman female stereotypes. While biblical texts largely focus on the lives and deeds of men, a number of prominent moral and immoral women do appear. One frequent biblical motif is the figure of the wicked wife turned prostitute, who serves as a metaphor for Israel's abandonment of God and worship of false idols. For instance, Proverbs 7 describes this metaphorical wicked woman in terms remarkably similar to the Roman stereotype.[1] This harlot, a married adulteress, is not only notable for her sexual promiscuity but for other demonstrations of unorthodox and transgressive behavior: she goes outside publicly, dresses scandalously, talks loudly and rebelliously, and takes the sexual initiative. This portrait is very similar to the standard Roman representation explored in Chapter 1; it stands in opposition to the good and prudent wife (e.g. Proverbs 19.14.) She represents the stereotype of the wicked woman as disloyal, an image frequently used as metaphor for the religious disloyalty of Israel.

The prophet Hosea provides another lengthy representation of the prostitute/adulteress as immoral Israel. God tells Hosea to take "a woman of promiscuity (*zenunim*)" and "children of promiscuity" "because the land is utterly promiscuous (*ki-zanoh*), turning away from the LORD."[2] This woman, Gomer daughter of Diblaim (or "Finish-er daughter of Fig-cakes," a name notable for sexual innuendo), is less a real character than a stand-in for the land of Israel. Indeed, after she has been duly punished for her adulteries as well as "her gaiety, her feasts, her new

moons, her sabbaths, and all her festal assemblies," she returns to her
first husband.[3]

Notably, the major problematic behavior of Gomer is not sexual promiscuity but unorthodox religious celebrations and worship of the Baals.
Being unfaithful to God may be interpreted metaphorically as adultery,
but in practice such unfaithfulness is demonstrated through polytheistic
worship. Once her loyalty has been restored, Gomer is back in the favor
of both God and her husband, who is both Hosea and, metonymically,
God Himself. The stereotype of the wicked, immoral prostitute-wife is
certainly in play here, although it plays a less central role than that of
Roman prostitute-matrons.

The references to actual prostitutes in the Bible are much more mixed
in their attitude, perhaps reflecting a difference between the dogmatic
structuralism of the moralistic texts like Hosea and Proverbs and the
more historical tales of Kings and Judges. We find here another instance
of the good and moral prostitute with a heart-of-gold, as was discussed
in the Roman context in Chapter 2. Rahab, the most notable prostitute
of the Hebrew Bible, is honored for giving aid to Joshua's spies in return
for the protection of her family. Her sex work is largely irrelevant to the
story.[4] However, she is able to help the Israelites precisely because she is a
marginal figure who lives on the outside wall of the city.[5] Her protection
of the spies represents a surprising reversal of expectations; in return for
her act of faith, she is protected and her descendants become an Israelite
clan.[6] The good prostitute ceases to be a prostitute; indeed, in rabbinical
tradition she subsequently marries Joshua himself.[7] Her demonstrated
loyalty to Israel and to Israel's God allows her to escape the social and
moral status of the wicked woman.

Tamar's story, in Genesis 38.1–26, offers another glimpse at possible
slippage or blurring between the roles of good wife and wicked prostitute.[8] In order to fulfill her familial obligations, the widow Tamar veils
herself and sits by the road where her father-in-law Judah sees her and
assumes she is a prostitute (*zona*). He sleeps with her and impregnates her.
When he later discovers that his daughter-in-law has "whored herself out
(*zaneta*)" and is pregnant through whoring (*hara liznunim*), he initially
plans to burn her alive, later relenting when she proves that she was only
fulfilling her religious duty of providing him with an heir.[9] Judah clearly
believes in the stereotypical idea of the fallen woman, the wife-turned
prostitute. Meanwhile, Tamar is willing to use the role of the prostitute
and the sexual freedom it allows in order to fulfill the paramount duty of
a Hebrew wife – providing heirs.

These examples show that all four of the female moral categories discussed in this book – good wife, wicked prostitute, wicked wife, and
good prostitute – existed as part of the rhetoric and representation of
women in early Israelite culture. Indeed, the motif of the wicked prostitute became one of the primary metaphors for a faithless Israel who
had turned away from her husband, the Jewish God. However, one crucial element that is present in the later Roman texts is largely missing.
"Prostitute" is not generally used as an accusation or label against other
prominent or transgressive female characters. Indeed, many particularly
unorthodox women in the biblical narrative are praised. Jael and Judith
both murder military enemies and receive somewhat ambiguous praise
and commendation.[10] Ruth makes herself sexually available to her master
Boaz in order to secure a place for herself and her mother-in-law Naomi;
she earns honor and respect as a convert and a faithful daughter-in-law.
Deborah leads the people of Israel in war against Sisera and receives the
honor of being named a prophetess.

With regard to individual wicked women in the biblical narrative,
their promiscuity or prostitute-like status is generally minimized. Delilah,
although she may have been a concubine, has greed as a weakness rather
than promiscuity. She betrays Samson in return for money rather than
out of sexual profligacy and is never referred to as a *zona*. Eve falls victim
to temptation and the sin of disobedience, but she is necessarily faithful
to Adam.

Jezebel is perhaps the only instance of a "prostitute label" applied
to a transgressive figure, but the main criticism of Jezebel is her worship of foreign gods and her abuse of power. There is no suggestion that
she is unfaithful to her husband or that her son is not legitimate. The
only possible connection between Jezebel and prostitution comes from
Jehu's final denunciation of her: "What peace, so long as the whoring of
your mother Jezebel and her witchcrafts are so many?" (2 Kings 9.22).
However, it is unclear whether this "whoring" or "promiscuity" refer
to literal sexual acts or to Jezebel's worship of foreign gods. Given that
the crime is paired with witchcraft, which has also not been previously
associated with Jezebel, the religious connotation seems much stronger
here than a general association with prostitutes. As in the repeated biblical motif, Jezebel is unfaithful religiously and thus symbolically associated with unfaithful sexuality, but she is not primarily characterized as a
promiscuous woman.

While biblical sources also viewed whores as "useful to think with,"
the application of this label as a general insult in later Western history

comes primarily from the Roman tradition. Certainly, however, both biblical and classical traditions are interwoven in the complex modern American attitudes towards concepts of female virtue, particularly in the sexual realm. The biblical anxiety about the faithlessness of the wicked woman further emphasizes the ancient Mediterranean paranoia about the independent woman, and the need to create official categories to define and attach virtuous women to specific men.

Notes

Introduction

1   Tacitus, *Annales* 2.84–5.

2   S. B. Pomeroy, *Goddesses, Whores, Wives, and Slaves: Women in Classical Antiquity* (New York: Schocken, 1975), 193–201, and 1994 edition, p. ix: "The categorization by class and social status, which points to differences between wives on the one hand and whores and slaves on the other … are in common use."

3   Julia Augusti will be discussed in more detail in Chapter 4.

4   Suetonius, *Tiberius* 35.1 ff.: "Notorious women (*feminae famosae*) had begun to make an open profession of prostitution (*lenocinium profiteri coeperant*), in order to avoid the punishment of the laws by giving up the privileges and respect of matrons (*iure ac dignitate matronali*), while the most decadent young men of both orders [senatorial and equestrian] voluntarily lowered their social rank, so as not to be prevented by the Senate's decree from appearing on the stage and in the arena. All such men and women he [Tiberius] punished with exile, in order to prevent anyone from shielding himself by such a device." These notorious women were made equivalent to male actors in terms of their public display and willing degradation: C. Edwards, "Unspeakable professions: public performance and prostitution in Ancient Rome," in J. Hallett and M. B. Skinner (eds.), *Roman Sexualities* (Princeton University Press, 1997), 81.

5   Tacitus, *Ann.* 2.84–5.

6   Ronald Syme notes that her sister (or possibly aunt) had six husbands and seven children: R. Syme, "Domitius Corbulo," *JRS* 60 (1970), 27; Pliny, *Naturalis Historia* 7.7.39.

7   *Lex Iulia de Maritandis Ordinibus*, 18 BCE.

8   W. Riess, "Rari exempli femina: female virtues on Roman funerary inscriptions" in S. L. James and S. Dillon (eds.), *A Companion to Women in the Ancient World* (Malden, Mass., Oxford, and Chichester: Wiley-Blackwell, 2012), 492; B. Von Hesberg-Tonn, "Coniunx carissima," in *Untersuchungen zum*

Nonncharakter im Erscheinungsbild der römischen Frau, Diss. (Stuttgart, 1983), 103 f.

9   B. E. Stumpp, *Prostitution in der römischen Antike* (Berlin: Akademie Verlag, 1998), 365–7. When dealing with the possible audience of any Roman text, we must always remember the comparatively tiny number of literate individuals: see W. Harris, *Ancient Literacy* (Cambridge: Harvard University Press, 1989). However, the presentations of prostitute characters in comedies, as discussed in Chapters 1 and 2, and the performances of *meretrices* themselves in religious festivals like the Floralia, as noted in Chapter 5, would have been accessible to a much larger potential audience. See also T. A. McGinn, *The Economy of Prostitution in the Roman World: A Study of Social History and the Brothel* (Ann Arbor: University of Michigan Press, 2004), 47.

10 Cicero, *Pro Caelio* 34. Clodia is discussed in more detail in Chapter 4; the story of her ancestress Quinta Claudia is analyzed in Chapter 7.

11 Riess, "Rari exempli femina," 500; K. Milnor, *Gender, Domesticity, and the Age of Augustus: Inventing Private Life* (Oxford University Press, 2005), 14–16, 44–5. This program of family values and social stability continued under many of Augustus' successors.

12 R. Flemming, "Quae corpore quaestum facit: the sexual economy of female prostitution in the Roman Empire," *JRS* 89 (1999), 45–7; McGinn, *Economy*, 71–2. Flemming explicitly claims that "hierarchies … [of prostitutes] are a thing of the past" (47). McGinn is less skeptical than Flemming about the possibility of economically successful prostitutes, but he is largely uninterested in them as a category.

13 M. Wyke, *The Roman Mistress: Ancient and Modern Representations* (Oxford University Press, 2002), 12–17; S. James, *Learned Girls and Male Persuasion: Gender and Reading in Roman Love Elegy* (Berkeley: University of California Press, 2003), 39–41. Wyke presents the most compelling recent argument for the individual fictionality of elegiac women, but she does not address the question of whether the concept of the Roman courtesan itself might be purely literary. See also Sir Ronald Syme, who suggests that the calamities of the Roman first-century BCE civil wars might have forced a large number of well-educated women into a socially marginal existence: R. Syme, *History in Ovid* (Oxford: Clarendon Press, 1978), 200–3. It would be dangerous to view elegiac poetry as evidence for the sexual "female emancipation" of elite freeborn women, given the lack of evidence outside poetry for unmarried elite women. Instead, I use poetry as the more plausible proof of the existence of sophisticated freedwoman courtesans, *contra* G. Fau, *L'Emancipation féminine à Rome* (Paris: Les Belles Lettres, 1978), 103. The evidence for concubines, particularly concubines who served not as unofficial wives of soldiers or other low-status Roman men but rather as long-term mistresses for elite members of society, will be discussed later in this Introduction and in Chapter 3.

14 Ovid, *AA* 1.31–4, *Tristia* 2.303–8.

15 Plautus, *Asinaria* 4.1.9; Petronius, *Satyricon* 1.7.

16 V. L. Bullough and B. Bullough, *Women and Prostitution: A Social History* (Buffalo: Prometheus Books, 1987), p. xv; M. Nussbaum, *Sex and Social Justice* (Oxford University Press, 1998), 285–7.

17 T. A. McGinn, *Prostitution, Sexuality, and the Law in Ancient Rome* (New York: Oxford University Press, 1998),14–16.

18 T. J. Gilfoyle, "Review essay: prostitutes in history: from parables of pornography to metaphors of modernity," *The American Historical Review*, 104.1 (February 1999), 137–8.

19 Ulpian (1 *ad legem Iuliam et Papiam*), *Digest* 23.2.43; Cato, in Aulus Gellius, *Noctes Atticae* 9.12.7; Cicero, *Post Redditum in Senatu* 11, *Cael.* 38, 49; McGinn, *Prostitution*, 102, 127–8.

20 R. Langlands, *Sexual Morality in Ancient Rome* (Cambridge University Press, 2006), 39. For typical uses of *pudicitia*, see Cicero, *In Catilinam* 2.11.25, or Plautus, *Amphitruo* 2.2.210: "That which is called a dowry, I do not consider the same my dowry; but modesty (*pudicitiam*), and shame (*pudorem*), and subdued desires (*sedatum cupidinem*), fear of the Gods, and love of my parents, and concord with my kindred; to be obedient to yourself and bounteous to the good, ready to aid the upright." Here *pudicitia* is expressly not a lack of sexual desire, but controlled and restrained desire. Alcmena is Plautus' ideal wife, passionate but loyal, if somewhat confused about the identity of her husband. For uses of *castitas*, see Cicero, *De Legibus* 2.212.29, who suggests that the purpose of the Vestal Virgins is *ut sentiant mulieres naturam feminarum omnem castitatem pati*, "so that wives might recognize that the nature of women permits complete purity." This might refer either to their physical virginity or to their moral behavior; in either case it does not suggest that total purity is normal to women, but rather an unlikely possibility.

21 R. M. Karras, *Common Women: Prostitution and Sexuality in Medieval England* (New York: Oxford University Press, 1996), 29–30.

22 E. L. Will, "Women in Pompeii," *Archaeology*, 34 (1979), 34–43.

23 This material is discussed further in Chapter 5: E. D'Ambra, "The calculus of Venus: nude portraits of Roman matrons," in Kampen and Bergmann (eds.), *Sexuality in Ancient Art*, 219–32; G. Davies, "Portrait statues as models for gender roles in Roman society," *MAAR* (2008), 208–10.

24 T. A. McGinn does not address the conceptualization of prostitutes by non-prescriptive sources: McGinn, *Prostitution*, 348. For other key recent works in the study of Roman prostitution, see Flemming, "Quae corpore," 38–61, and McGinn, *Economy*.

25 See M. Beard, "Re-reading (Vestal) Virginity," in R. Hawley and B. Levick (eds.), *Women in Antiquity: New Assessments* (London and New York: Routlege, 1995), 176, with regard to the construction of Roman gender identity.

26 Discussion of such marginalization rests significantly on a foundation of modern queer theory. I do not here conceptualize queer theory as pertaining only to same-sex relationships and issues of gay and lesbian identity. Instead, I follow the broader agenda, promulgated by Gayle Rubin and others, of using theoretical tools to deconstruct normative sexualities through a close study of marginalized sexualities in particular places and times: G. Rubin, "Thinking sex," in H. Abelove, M. A. Barale, and D. M. Halperin (eds.), *The Gay and Lesbian Studies Reader* (New York and London: Routledge, 1993), 3–44.

27 A. Saxonhouse, "Introduction – public and private: the paradigm's power," in P. Allen, S. Dixon, and B. Garlick (eds.), *Stereotypes of Women in Power:*

Historical Perspectives and Revisionist Views (Westport, Conn.: Greenwood Press, 1992), 5–8; Nussbaum, *Sex and Social Justice*, 276–98. I have also more indirectly drawn upon B. J. Carpenter, *Re-thinking Prostitution: Feminism, Sex, and the Self* (New York: P. Lang, 2000) and L. Edlund and E. Korn, "A theory of prostitution," *Journal of Political Economy*, 110 (February 2002), 181–214.

28 M. N. Lance and A. Tanesini, "Identity judgements, queer politics," in I. Morland and A. Wilcox (eds.), *Queer Theory* (New York: Palgrave, 2005), 172.

29 R. MacMullen, *Roman Social Relations: 50 BC to AD 284* (New Haven: Yale University Press, 1974), 89–93.

30 Saxonhouse, "Public and private," 6.

31 S. Bell, *Reading, Writing, and Rewriting the Prostitute Body* (Bloomington: Indiana University Press, 2004), 113.

32 Plutarch, *Cimon* 14.7.1.

33 Plutarch, *Pericles* 24.2–11.

34 Apollodorus, *Against Neaera* 111; D. Hamel, *Trying Neaira: The True Story of a Courtesan's Scandalous Life in Ancient Greece* (New Haven: Yale University Press, 2003), 88; A. Glazebrook, "The making of a prostitute," *Arethusa*, 38 (2005), 62.

35 *Meretrix* appears 514 times in classical Latin texts, primarily in comedy and declamation but across a variety of genres; it appears in 259 separate locations in these texts. *Concubina* appears 135 times (in 86 locations), primarily in legal texts, comedy and histories. *Lupa* appears 148 times (in 105 locations), predominantly in elegy and comedy. *Scortum* appears 56 times in 48 locations, primarily in comedy and history. *Moecha* appears 38 times in 30 sources, primarily in elegy. This breakdown helps illustrate the reasons for focusing on *meretrix* as my dominant term.

36 J. N. Adams suggests that the original connection between *scortum* as "skin" and "prostitute" might have come from *scortum*'s use as a term for "pudenda," which then led to subsequent synecdoche as a term for the woman selling her private parts: J. N. Adams, "Words for 'prostitute' in Latin," *Rheinisches Museum*, 126 (1983), 322.

37 For a full discussion of these nuances with regard to Roman comedy, see S. Witzke, "Harlots, tarts, and hussies?: A problem of terminology for sex labor in Roman comedy," *Helios*, 42, no. 1 (2015), 8.

38 Adams, "Words for 'prostitute'," 322.

39 T. A. McGinn notes that concubines are explicitly equated with prostitutes in the legal sources, although there are also unmarried women who were legally treated as wives precisely because they did not make money from prostitution: McGinn, *Prostitution*, 197, and "Concubinage and the Lex Iulia on adultery," *TAPA* 121 (1991), 347–54. The most relevant text is Modestinus, *Digest* 23.2.24: *In liberae mulieris consuetudine non concubinatus, sed nuptiae intellegendae sunt, si non corpore quaestum fecerit.* "Living with a free woman is not concubinage, but is understood to be marriage, if she does not sell her body for money." Jane Gardner emphasizes correctly here, *contra* Raimund Friedl, that *liberae* connotes a free woman but not necessarily a freeborn woman and thus could include former slaves: J. Gardner,

"Concubinage," book review of Raimund Friedl, *Der Konkubinat im kaiser-zeitlichen Rom: von Augustus bis Septimius Severus, The Classical Review,* 48.2 (1998), 414. This implies in turn that freeborn women who were concubines frequently did sell their bodies for money to their lover or to multiple lovers. Concubinage was probably generally a relationship between a free man and a slave, and Modestinus' clarification concerned the rare cases involving two free partners. If a relationship between two people who had the legal ability to marry is not described as marriage by the author, it may be assumed that the woman, while perhaps not a streetwalking prostitute, fell into the larger and generally disreputable category of *meretrix*.

40 S. E. Phang, *The Marriage of Roman Soldiers (13 BC–AD 235).* (Columbia University Press, 2002).

41 Ulpian, *Digest* 48.5.14(13)2; J. Gardner, *Being a Roman Citizen* (London: Psychology Press: 2010),150–1.

42 Flemming, "Quae corpore," 38–61; McGinn, *Economy*, 72; see Chapter 3.

43 M. Kajava, *Roman Female Praenomina: Studies in the Nomenclature of Roman Women*, Acta Instituti Romani Finlandiae, 14 (Rome, 1995).

44 McGinn, *Economy*, 296–302. A rare exception is visible in a graffito in the first room on the left in the Pompeii *lupanar* (VII.12.18), where a woman is identified as *SALVI FILIA*, or daughter of Salvius: *CIL* IV, 2173. Salvius is also the owner of the tavern or *caupona* two blocks away (VI.14.36), which features a painting of a man and woman kissing, and the inscription *NOLO CUM MYRTALE*, "I don't want to with Myrtale," a name which also appears twice in the *lupanar*, in the first room on the right: *CIL* IV, 2268 and IV, 2271. This suggests a possible direct connection between Salvius the *caupona*-owner and the brothel, which might explain the unusual invocation of a father, if he was also a *leno* or pimp. The first room on the left is also the largest, well lit, and has the highest percentage of graffiti. This might indicate that the room belonged to a particularly privileged prostitute or the madam of the place. The other women named in the *lupanar* graffiti all have more stereotypical prostitute or slave names: e.g. Nike from Crete (2178a), Panta (2178b), Beronice (2198, 2256), Restituta (2202) Mola (2204), Marca (2235), and Fortuna (2266). Unfortunately, it is futile to speculate more on the potential relationships involved, given the relative sparsity of data. For more details on the *lupanar* graffiti, see S. Levin-Richardson, "Facilis hic futuit," *Helios*, 38.1 (2011), 71–2.

45 Given the nature of the evidence, I necessarily focus on urban society or the society of small towns rather than rural life. This temporal and geographical focus has necessarily limited my source material, in particular requiring a much greater focus on Pompeian and Herculanean visual records than on papyri or archaeological records from Roman Egypt. Similarly, I largely ignore the Christian evidence, particularly of Magdalen-type reformed prostitutes, because the Christian discourse about sexuality and appropriate gender roles is quite distinct from Roman ideology and would unnecessarily complicate the material under consideration. For an excellent recent treatment of late antique Christian attitudes towards prostitution and female vice, see K. Harper, *From Shame to Sin* (Cambridge: Harvard University

Press, 2013), esp. 158–71, 182–8. I have also chosen to exclude the source material on male prostitutes in the Roman world, due to my focus on the moral categories of women in Roman society. The limited Roman discourse about male prostitutes offers many intriguing insights into societal perceptions of male sexuality, particularly the acceptability of male–male relationships in the Roman world. However, it would only have distracted from an attempt to isolate Roman negative stereotypes about women, which drew on very different sensibilities and prejudices than those about men. Though they may have shared a profession, Roman male and female prostitutes occupied fundamentally different places in the Roman imagination. See J. Walters, "Invading the Roman body: manliness and impenetrability in Roman thought," in Hallett and Skinner (eds.), *Roman Sexualities*, 29–43, or A. Richlin, "Not before homosexuality: the materiality of the cinaedus and the Roman law against love between men," *Journal of the History of Sexuality* (1993), 523–73.

46 S. R. Joshel, "Female desire and the discourse of Empire: Tacitus' Messalina," in Hallett and Skinner (eds.), *Roman Sexualities*, 221–54. On Valerius Maximus, see Langlands, *Sexual Morality*, 121–91. On Livy, see T. J. Moore, *Artistry and Ideology: Livy's Vocabulary of Virtue* (Frankfurt: Athenäum, 1989), 222–4. For a general summary of the *HA*'s problems as a historical source, see R. Syme, *Emperors and Biography: Studies in the Historia Augusta* (Oxford: Clarendon Press, 1971), or A. Cameron, *The Last Pagans of Rome* (Oxford University Press, 2010), 743–81 for the most recent exhaustive treatment of the *HA*'s inaccuracy and dating controversy. See also K. Blomqvist, "From Olympias to Aretaphila: women in politics in Plutarch," in J. Mossman (ed.), *Plutarch and His Intellectual World* (Cardiff: Classical Press of Wales, 1997), 73–98; J. McInerney, "Plutarch's manly women," *Mnemosyne-Leiden-Supplementum* (2002), 319–44. Rebecca Langlands provides an excellent analysis of Valerius Maximus' representation of female exemplars of *pudicitia*: Langlands, *Sexual Morality*, 123–91.

47 J. C. B. Lowe, "Aspects of Plautus' originality in the Asinaria," *The Classical Quarterly*, 42.1 (1992), 160–1. See also I. Lana, "Terenzio e il movimento filellenico in Roma," *RFC* 75 (1947), 60, 173; G. E. Duckworth, *The Nature of Roman Comedy* (Princeton University Press, 1952), 258–61. For more general studies of Plautus and Greek influences, see E. Fraenkel, *Elementi plautini in Plauto* (Florence: La Nuova Italia, 1960); E. Fantham, "Sex, status, and survival in Hellenistic Athens," *Phoenix* (1975), 44–74; E. Lefèvre, E. Stärk, and G. Vogt-Spira, *Plautus barbarus* (Tubingen: Gunter Narr Verlag,1991); W. S. Anderson, *Barbarian Play: Plautus' Roman Comedy* (University of Toronto Press, 1993), 21; D. Dutsch, *Feminine Discourse in Roman Comedy: On Echoes and Voices* (Oxford University Press, 2008) 16, 258–60.

48 Wyke, *Mistress*, 12–17.

49 Langlands, *Sexual Morality*, 248; R. A. Kaster "Controlling reason: declamation in rhetorical education," in Y. L. Too (ed.), *Education in Greek and Roman Antiquity* (Leiden: Brill, 2001), 325.

50 Fau, *L'Emanicpation féminine*, 198.

51 S. Treggiari, "Libertine ladies," *Classical World*, 64 (1970/1), 197; McGinn, *Prostitution*, 53–8, 266–7; *Economy*, 55–62. There is no particular controversy on this point except for the particular ratios of freedwomen, freeborn, and slave prostitutes, where theories range widely; precise percentages, even if they were available, are not relevant for this book.

52 Gellius, *NA* 4.14; McGinn, *Prostitution*, 60; L. Peppe, *Posizione giuridica e ruolo sociale della donna romana in età reppublicana* (Milan: A. Giuffrè 1984), 114–17.

53 Cicero, *Ad Atticum* 6.6; J. P. Hallett, *Fathers and Daughters in Roman Society* (Princeton University Press, 1984), 243; R. Syme, "Dynastic marriages in Roman aristocracy," *Diogenes*, 135 (Fall 1986), 1–10; S. Treggiari, *Roman Marriage: Iusti Coniuges from the Time of Cicero to the Time of Ulpian* (New York: Clarendon Press, 1991), 83–4.

54 McGinn, *Prostitution*, 65–9.

55 Livy 1.57–60, 3.44–58, 8.28; Aulus Gellius, *NA* 4.14; S. Joshel, "The body female and the body politic: Livy's Lucretia and Verginia," in A. Richlin (ed.), *Pornography and Representation in Greece and Rome* (Oxford University Press, 1992), 123; A. Richlin, *The Garden of Priapus* (Oxford University Press, 1993), 223–4.

56 McGinn, *Prostitution*, 326–37.

57 Berlin papyrus 1024.6–8, exc. G.

58 For studies of misogyny during the Imperial period, see especially A. Richlin, "Invective against women in Roman satire," *Arethusa*, 17 (1984), 67–80. This issue is further developed in Chapter 1.

59 J. Bamberger, "The myth of matriarchy: why men rule in primitive society," *Woman, Culture and Society* (1974), 263–80.

1 Faithful wives and greedy prostitutes

1 Major background scholarship on female morality and representation in the Roman world includes Pomeroy, *Goddesses*, 149–226; R. MacMullen, "Women in public in the Roman Empire," *Historia*, 29 (1980), 208–18; E. Forbis, "Women's public image in Italian honorary inscriptions," *TAPA* 111:4 (1990), 493–512; N. Purcell, "Livia and the womanhood of Rome," *Proceedings of the Cambridge Philological Society*, 32 (1986), 78–105; Treggiari, *Roman Marriage* ; R. Bauman, *Women and Politics in Ancient Rome* (London: Routledge, 1992); C. Edwards, *The Politics of Immorality in Ancient Rome* (London: Routledge, 1993); S. Fischler, "Social stereotypes and historical analysis," in L. Archer, S. Fischler, and M. Wyke (eds.), *Women in Ancient Societies* (London: Macmillan, 1995); Milnor, *Gender*; Langlands, *Sexual Morality*. For the best summation of recent scholarship, see James and Dillon (eds.), *A Companion to Women in the Ancient World*. While all of these texts contribute to the scholarly discourse, their exclusive focus either on a particular type of evidence, especially legal and proscriptive texts (Treggiari, Edwards, Bauman) or primarily on elite matrons (Fischler, Milnor, Langlands, Forbis, Purcell) leaves two gaps in the scholarship: an examination

of these stereotypes across genre and class background, on the one hand, and a particular focus on immoral women, on the other. Edwards comes closest to answering this need with her focus on the politics of immorality, but looks exclusively at textual evidence, primarily prose, and does not particularly emphasize women. While Pomeroy and MacMullen are foundational background texts, much recent work and theory since their publication have developed and complicated the field of ancient gender and sexuality.

2 Milnor, *Gender*, 15.

3 Cornelia: Nepos, *Frag.* 59; Valerius Maximus 4.4; Plotina: Pliny, *Panegyrica* 83.

4 Riess, "Rari exempli femina," 500. See also J. Hallett, "The role of women in Roman elegy: counter-cultural feminism." *Arethusa* 6, no. 1 (1973): 104–6.

5 Von Hesberg-Tonn, "Coniunx carissima," 103 f.

6 Riess, "Rari exempli femina," 493.

7 R. Van Bremen, "Women and wealth," in A. Cameron and A. Kuhrt (eds.), *Images of Women in Antiquity* (London: Routledge, 1993), 223–42; Forbis, "Women's public image," 493–6. Most of Van Bremen's examples focus on public inscriptions from the period of Roman dominance, especially in Asia Minor, rather than on private female funerary inscriptions, which are much rarer in the East.

8 Langlands, *Sexual Morality*, 39.

9 Milnor, *Gender*, 32.

10 Livy 3.44 f.; N. Kampen, *Images and Status of Roman Working Women* (Berlin: Mann, 1981); D. Kleiner, "Women and family life on Roman imperial funerary altars," *Latomus* (1987), 545–54; E. Hemelrijk, *Matrona Docta*. (London: Psychology Press, 2004), 28–39; R. S. Bagnall and R. Cribiore, *Women's Letters from Ancient Egypt, 300 BC–AD 800* (University of Michigan Press, 2006), 48 f.

11 Purcell, "Livia," 82.

12 Milnor, *Gender*, 57–64; Milnor analyzes how the monuments named after the Julio-Claudian women form an intersection between public and private spaces.

13 Riess, "Rari exempli femina," 493.

14 Hemelrijk, *Matrona Docta*, 39–50.

15 Suetonius, *Galba* 2.3. While Boatwright argues that women's presence in the Roman Forum itself would have been unusual, especially during the Republic, it certainly occurred often enough to be used as a plot device in comedies, histories (e.g. Livy 3.44–49), and rhetorical speeches. The Forum may have been a gendered space, especially during political events, but that does not mean women were banned from it. See M. Boatwright, "Women and gender in the Forum Romanum." In *TAPA* 141.1. The Johns Hopkins University Press (2011): 116–18.

16 Milnor, *Gender*, 30, 108.

17 Ovid, *Fasti* 3.133–4; J.L. Sebesta, "Symbolism in the costume of the Roman woman," *The World of Roman Costume* (1994), 46–53. C. Vout, "The myth of the toga: understanding the history of Roman dress," *Greece & Rome*, 43.2 (October 1996), 211; K. Olson, "Matrona and whore: the clothing of women in Roman antiquity," *Fashion Theory*, 6:4 (2002), 391–2; Kelly Olson, *Dress and the Roman Woman: Self-Presentation and Society*

(Routledge, 2012), 28; Sebesta, "Symbolism," 49. There is substantial scholarly controversy concerning whether *stolae* were actually in common use for Roman women: See McGinn, "Controversies and new approaches," in T. K. Hubbard (ed.), *A Companion to Greek and Roman Sexualities* (Hoboken, NJ: John Wiley & Sons, 2013), 83–101.

18 Ulpian, *Digest* 47.10.10.15.

19 Olson, "Matrona and whore," 391; Martial 35; Ovid, *AA* 1.31–4, 3.57 f.; McGinn, *Prostitution*, 156–71; R. Gibson (ed.), *Ovid: Ars Amatoria Book 3* (Cambridge University Press, 2003), 32–5.

20 Kampen, *Images and Status*, 64.

21 Olson, "Matrona and whore," 391.

22 Olson, "Matrona and whore," 392.

23 Langlands, *Sexual Morality*, 69–70.

24 This does not imply, however, that Roman women did not generally venture out for fear of harassment, any more than modern Western women stay indoors for fear of frequent cat-calling by strange men in urban settings.

25 There is an image in the Naples Archaeological Museum (see Figure 3) of a comic scene in which a woman wears a long yellow dress; she may be intended to be a prostitute, but the problematic preservation of the fresco and the theatrical nature makes such identification unclear. This image will be further analyzed in Chapter 5.

26 Horace, *Satires* 1.2.63, 1.2.82; Martial 6.64.4; Livy 2.13; Cicero, *Philippics* 2.44; Sulpicia 4.10; Olson, "Matrona and whore," 393–5; McGinn, *Prostitution*, 157. The only visual description of a togate woman is that of the legendary Cloelia, the Roman maiden who led a group of girls in a daring swim across the Tiber, escaping from their Etruscan prison camp. According to Livy, Cloelia was honored for her bravery with a unique equestrian statue in which she was depicted wearing a toga: Livy 2.13; see also Pliny, *NH* 34.11. Olson assumes that this indicates that togas were standard garments for both genders, at least when young, in the early Republic. Cloelia's toga, like her somewhat inexplicable horse, may also have been intended as a symbol of the masculine *virtus* that inspired her deeds. The statue has not survived, but in any case it seems highly unlikely that this representation was connected with the association between the toga and Roman prostitutes.

27 Vout, "The myth of the toga," 206.

28 Ioannis Ziogas discusses how Ovid "strips" his audience of their clothes in order to erase status identifications between potential *matrona* and *meretrix* readers: Ziogas, "Stripping the Roman Ladies," *Classical Quarterly*, 64.2 (2014), 735–44.

29 Beard, "(Re)reading Vestal Virginity," 167–8, 174, referring also to arguments in Beard, "The sexual status of Vestal Virgins," *JRS* 70 (1980), 12–27.

30 A. Staples, *From Good Goddess to Vestal Virgins* (New York: Routledge, 1998), 182, among others.

31 Karras, *Common Women*, 132–8. Karras argues that these reasons are common across a wide variety of Western cultures and time periods, to greater or lesser extents depending on circumstances. For medieval England, she claims that a combination of all three factors prejudiced society against prostitutes.

32 See Dioscorides 3.72. For general literature on ancient birth control and abortion, J. M. Riddle, *Contraception and Abortion from the Ancient World to the Renaissance* (Harvard University Press, 1992); N. Demand, *Birth, Death, and Motherhood in Classical Greece* (Baltimore: Johns Hopkins University Press, 1994); K. Kapparis, *Abortion in the Ancient World* (London: Duckworth 2002). Exposure and infanticide was also, of course, a common means of population control and presumably practiced by prostitutes as well as married couples: W. V. Harris, "Child-exposure in the Roman world," *JRS* 84 (1994), 1–22; B. W. Frier, "Natural fertility and family limitation in Roman marriage," *Classical Philology*, 89.4 (1994), 318–33; W. Scheidel (ed.), *Debating Roman Demography. Mnemosyne* Supplement, 211 (Leiden: Brill, 2001), 34. Frier suggests that demographic patterns indicate that married women, at least, did not regularly practice birth control, but his material evidence is extremely limited.

33 Seneca, *Cont.* 2.4.1.

34 Ovid, *Amores* 2.13.

35 For a more detailed study on this point, see A. K. Strong, "Daughter and employee: mother–daughter bonds among prostitutes," in L. Peterson and P. Salzman (eds.), *Mothering and Motherhood in the Ancient World* (Austin: University of Texas, 2012), 121–39.

36 Horace, *Satires* 1.2.31–2: "When he saw a man he knew coming out of [a brothel], Cato [the Censor] offered the revered opinion, 'May your virtue be honored, for when shameful desire has inflamed the veins, it is appropriate for young men to come here rather than fooling around with other men's wives.' " Cato notably later disapproves when he sees the young man making a repeat visit; apparently brothel trips are only acceptable as an occasional pleasure rather than an everyday activity, as least for the austere Cato.

37 Laudatio "Turiae," *ILS* 8393; for Sulpicia and other generous, loyal Roman matrons, see Valerius Maximus 6.7.1–3. See also Milnor, *Gender*, 197–8; Riess, "Rari exempli femina," 497; H. Parker, "Loyal slaves and loyal wives: the crisis of the outsider-within and Roman exemplum literature," in S. R. Joshel and S. Murnaghan (eds.), *Women and Slaves in Greco-Roman Culture: Differential Equations* (New York: Routledge, 2005), 164–8.

38 Appian, *Bella Civilia* 4.39, 4.48; Tacitus, *Ann.* 15.71.3.

39 Parker, "Loyal slaves," 168–9.

40 Plutarch, *Dialogue on Love* 2. While Plutarch is Greek, he writes during the height of Roman power and influence in Greece, in the second century CE, and his ideas about sexuality and gender relations are decidedly not those of classical Athens. See also Apuleius, *Apologia* 69–83, in which Pudentilla expresses her feelings for Apuleius in her own words, and, as will be further discussed in Chapter 4, Sulpicia's poems of the late first century BCE, especially 1.6 (*Corpus Tibullanorum* 4.7), which also express an active female sexual desire. Chapter 6 also analyzes the visual evidence for married women's enjoyment of sexuality and commentary in prescriptive texts like Seneca, *Epistulae* 95.21.

41 Wyke, *Mistress*, 43–4.

42 *Ibid.* 31.

43 R. Syme, *The Roman Revolution* (Oxford University Press, 1939), 149 ff.;
    R. G. Austin argues that Roman invective, at least in the oratorical tradi-
    tion, is largely borrowed from Greek models and was thus recognized as
    artificial and false by Roman audiences: R. G. Austin, *M. Tulli Ciceronis Pro
    M. Caelio Oratio* (Oxford University Press, 1960), 52; T. Jerome, *Aspects of
    the Study of Roman History* (New York: GP Putnam's Sons, 1923), 50–65;
    Richlin,*The Garden of Priapus*, 105–10; R. G. M. Nisbet, *M. Tulli Ciceronis
    In L. Calpurnium Pisonem Oratio* (Oxford: Clarendon Press, 1961), 192–6;
    A. Corbeill, *Controlling Laughter: Political Humor in the Late Roman
    Republic* (Princeton University Press, 1996), 5–7.
44 See A. Richlin, *Arguments with Silence: Writing the History of Roman
    Women* (Ann Arbor: University of Michigan Press, 2014), 64.
45 *Ibid.* 65–6.
46 A. Keith, "Women in Augustan literature," in James and Dillon (eds.), *A
    Companion to Women in the Ancient World*, 387.
47 Nisbet, *M. Tulli Ciceronis*, 194–6.
48 The precise definition of the terms *hetaira*, *porne*, and *pallake*, as well as
    their roles in society, are matters of some controversy. In this case, I follow
    James Davidson's approach, which acknowledges meaningful distinctions
    between the different terms and generally translates *hetaira* as "courtesan,"
    porne as "common whore" and *pallake* as "concubine" or "mistress.": J.
    Davidson, *Courtesans and Fishcakes* (New York: St. Martin's Press, 1998),
    74–7. Regardless of terminology, however, all these women, as well as adul-
    terous wives, were targets of invective by Greek male authors at various
    points and were generally characterized as less reputable than chaste mar-
    ried women. See also J. Roy, "An alternative sexual morality for Classical
    Athenians," *Greece & Rome*, 44.1 (1997), 11–22.
49 E. Fantham, *Comparative Studies in Republican Latin Imagery* (Toronto
    University Press, 1972), 6. See also Fantham, "Sex, status and survival," 63–6;
    A. Traill, *Women and the Comic Plot in Menander* (Cambridge University
    Press, 2008), 123–5.
50 E.g. "Nike from Crete," *CIL* IV, 2178a, in the Pompeii *lupanar*: S.
    Levin-Richardson, "Sex, Sight, and Societas in the Lupanar, Pompeii," *Seeing
    the Past: building knowledge of the past and present through acts of seeing*
    (Stanford University Archaeology Center Conference, February 4–6, 2005,
    unpublished), 16.
51 There is no specific Latin word for a high-class prostitute or courtesan; *mer-
    etrix*, as described in the Introduction, is a more general term.
52 For typical Greek representations of the crafty, witty *hetaira*, see Menander,
    Samia; Xenophon, *Memorabilia* 3.11; and from the Imperial period,
    the second-century CE portraits of courtesans offered by Athenaeus'
    Deipnosophistae, Book 14, and Lucian's *Dialogues of the Courtesans*, which
    may hearken back to earlier oral traditions. For scholarship on represen-
    tations of *hetairai* in ancient Greece, especially in comedy, the most thor-
    ough modern treatments are M. Henry, *Menander's Courtesans and the
    Greek Comic Tradition* (Frankfurt: P. Lang, 1985); D. Wiles, "Marriage and
    prostitution in classical New Comedy," *Themes in Drama* II (1989), 31–48;

P. Brown, "Plots and prostitutes in Greek New Comedy," *Leeds International Latin Seminar* 6 (1990), 241–66; Davidson, *Courtesans*; M. Krieter-Spiro, *Sklaven, Köche und Hetären: Das Dienstpersonal bei Menander: Beiträge zur Altertumskunde* 93 (Stuttgart and Leipzig: B. G. Teubner, 1997); L. Kurke, *Coins, Bodies, Games and Gold* (Princeton University Press, 2000); L. K. McClure, *Courtesans at Table: Gender and Greek Literary Culture in Athenaeus* (Routledge, 2003); Traill, *Women and the Comic Plot*.

53 Demosthenes 48.53–5.

54 Cicero, *Att.* 10.10.5. See Chapter 3 for a full discussion of Cicero's attitude towards Cytheris' place in elite Roman society.

55 Davidson, *Courtesans*, 121.

56 P. López Barja de Quiroga. "Freedmen's social mobility in Roman Italy," *Historia*, 44:3 (1995), 326–7; S. Treggiari, *Roman Freedmen during the Late Republic* (Oxford: Clarendon Press, 1969).

57 Plautus, *Menaechmi* 130.

58 Plautus' *Asinaria* was based on the minor Greek playwright Demophilus' comedy *Onagos*, now lost, according to its prologue: Plautus, *As.* 10; Duckworth, *Nature of Roman Comedy*, 52.

59 D. Elmer, "The Economy of Desire in Plautus' *Asinaria*," conference paper, American Philological Association (Boston, 2004); Dutsch, *Feminine Discourse*, 58–60.

60 H. Parker, "The teratogenic grid," in Hallett and Skinner (eds.), *Roman Sexualities*,52.

61 *Ibid.* 52–3. Within this system penetration of the vagina is praised more than penetration of the anus, which in turn is considered less degrading than penetration of the mouth. Parker fails to deal persuasively with the question of the contradiction between active–passive and pleasuring–pleasured with respect to oral sex, but this is not particularly a matter of concern here. In general, Parker's system, while useful from a structuralist perspective, oversimplifies Roman social attitudes towards sexual behavior; it draws on both Foucault's theoretical strengths and weaknesses in this regard.

62 Plautus, *Bacchides* 174; *Truculentus* 854.

63 J. Hemker, "Commerce, passion, and the self in Plautus' 'Truculentus'," *Pacific Coast Philology* (1991), 35–7.

64 Wyke, *Mistress*, 43. Wyke argues that representations of Roman prostitutes in literary contexts do not so much elaborate "their metaphors in terms of female power but explore, rather, the concept of male dependency."

65 In this context, most translators interpret *lauta* as having the connotation of "elegant" or "well trained;" another possible meaning is a difference in status between a cheaper, "dirty girl" and a more expensive, "clean" one. My choice of "polished" conveys some of these nuances. See Plautus, *Miles Gloriosus* 789, ed. M. Hammond, A. M. Mack and W. Moskalew (Cambridge: Harvard University Press, 1963); *Plautus: Four Comedies*, trans. Erich Segal (Oxford University Press, 1996).

66 While, as Nisbet warns, we must be wary of drawing historical facts from literary stereotypes, Plautus feels no need to explain or justify this detail.

67 Plautus, *Miles Gloriosus* 690.
68 Plautus, *Truculentus* 854.
69 Plautus, *Cistaria* 81.
70 Plautus, *Bacchides* 474.
71 Hippocrates, *Places in Human Anatomy* 47 = V 344–6; Galen, *On the Usefulness of the Parts of the Body* 14.6–7.
72 Plautus, *Truculentus* 70.
73 As Saller notes, such women were quite real figures and their dowries may have given them considerable control and influence over their husbands. Although the *uxor dotata* may be a comic *topos*, it reflects authentic male anxiety about the potential of financial ruin if they did not please their wives: R. Saller, *Patriarchy, Property and Death in the Roman Family* (Cambridge University Press, 1996), 221–4.
74 Plautus, *Casina* 199–202.
75 Plautus, *Stichus* 48–70; Dutsch, *Femine Discourse*, 152.
76 Plauus, *Stichus* 57–8.
77 Cf. Xenophon, *Oeconomius* 7.5–6, where the wife has been "trained to control her appetites," but she must still be taught not to wear makeup or behave inappropriately. Lysias' first oration also represents women as constantly vulnerable to sexual temptation.
78 Ovid, *Heroides* 3 and 7; *Metamorphoses* 12.146–209.
79 Ovid, *AA* 1.31–4; *Amores* 1.4, 1.5, 1.7.
80 The references to *meretrices* are: *Amores* 1.10.21, specifically describing a greedy streetwalking prostitute; 1.15.18, in a list of comic characters made popular by Menander; and 3.14.9, in reference to a brothel girl or a prostitute in her own apartment closing the door before sex. The *Ars Amatoria* reference is 1.435, to the *sacrilegas artes meretricum* or "scandalous tricks of prostitutes," as cited in the epigraph at the beginning of this chapter.
81 Ovid, *Amores* 1.10.11. *Cur sim mutatus, quaeris? quia munera poscis.* *Munera* here is a crucial choice of word: it means both "gifts" and the duties owed by a public official to his town in the form of public entertainments and endowments, and often occurs elsewhere in elegiac poetry. It conveys a sense of obligation and responsibility. *Munera* are not freely offered gifts but a duty, something expected by the recipient. Just as if she were a group of voters, Ovid's mistress will only be appeased if he performs the necessary steps to gain her favor, in this case, the presentation of numerous gifts.
82 *Contra* James, who argues that elegiac prostitutes are based on comedic representations: S. L. James, "The economics of Roman elegy: voluntary poverty, the recusatio, and the greedy girl," *AJP* 122.2 (2001), 225.
83 L. Curran, "Ovid 'Amores' 1.10," *Phoenix*, 18.4 (Winter 1964), 315–16. I disagree with Curran's contention that Ovid proposes an alternate form of economic contract with his final promise of *fidem*.
84 Ovid noticeably disregards the case of male prostitutes or boy lovers in this matter, where, among other issues, the question of whether ancient writers perceived same-sex relationships as ones of mutual pleasure arises.

85 Davidson, *Courtesans*, 110; Frier, *The Rise of the Roman Jurists*, 257; J. A. Crook, *Law and Life of Rome* (New York: Cornell University Press, 1967), 87–92. While the *lex Cincia* of 204 BCE originally forbade advocates from receiving payment for defending their clients, by the time of the Emperor Claudius in the mid-first century CE, payment had become so frequent that it was deemed necessary to set a maximum of 10,000 *sestertii*.

86 Women also served as midwives, occasionally doctors, and witches, i.e. other "service sector" occupations, but, like prostitution, these were largely ignored as respectable crafts from the perspective of elite men. Midwives and female doctors also generally catered to women's needs, lessening their public prominence in Roman society. Other female workers, such as fishmongers and bakers, were generally part of a male-dominated household rather than individual practitioners; see Chapter 4 for more detail: Kampen, *Images and Status*; S. Joshel, *Work, Identity, and Legal Status at Rome: A Study of the Occupational Inscriptions, vol. XI* (Norman: University of Oklahoma Press, 1992).

87 Cassius Dio 54.18.2; Juvenal 7.106 ff.; Cicero, *Pro Cluentio* 57; Crook, *Law and Life*, 90; Frier, *Roman Jurists*, 257.

88 Ovid, *Amores* 1.10.45–6.

89 *Ibid.* 1.10.49; Propertius 4.4; M. Janan, "Beyond good and evil: Tarpeia and philosophy in the feminine," *The Classical World* (1999), 429–43.

90 Propertius also evokes Tarpeia in 4.4, but he changes her motivation from greed to sexual desire for the Sabine general Tatius. She still breaks bonds to her city and family (and her religious vows as a Vestal), but for the much more traditionally feminine reason of her uncontrollable passion.

91 Ovid, *Amores* 1.10.51–2.

92 *Ibid.* 1.10.56.

93 Ovid, *Tristia* 1.2.37, 1.3.17–20. For more on Ovid's wife, see S. Thakur, "The construction and deconstruction of the ideal Roman wife," *Feminism & Classics*, 6 (Brock University, 2012).

94 Ovid, *Tristia* 1.3.63–8: *simul ah! simul ibimus, inquit, | te sequar et coniunx exulis exul ero … | te iubet e patria discedere Caesaris ira, | me pietas. pietas haec mihi Caesar erit.*

95 Plutarch, *Roman Questions* 30; the Romans of Ovid's day were themselves somewhat confused about the precise meaning of this phrase. For one novel interpretation, see G. Forsythe, " 'Ubi tu gaius, ego gaia': new light on an old Roman legal saw," *Historia*, 45.2 (1996), 240–1.

96 Ovid, *Tristia* 1.6.5–8.

97 *Ibid.* 1.6.23–8; see A. Barrett, *Livia: First Lady of Imperial Rome* (New Haven: Yale University Press, 2004), for more on Livia as *exemplum*.

98 Ovid, *Tristia* 5.5.45.

99 Ovid, *Tristia* 4.3.73–84, 5.14.20. H. B. Evans, *Publica Carmina: Ovid's Books from Exile* (Lincoln: University of Nebraska Press, 1983), 79.

100 M. Helzle, "Mr and Mrs Ovid," *Greece and Rome (Second Series)*, 36, no. 02 (1989), 183–193.

101 "Lupus" is a male version of a common term for female prostitutes, *lupa*; the significance is unclear, unless Martial means to imply some insult like "gigolo."

102 Martial 9.3, 9.

103 *Ibid.* 9.10.

104 *Ibid.* 9.2.11; McGinn, "Feminae probrosae and the litter," *Classical Journal* (1998), 241.

105 Juvenal 10.236–9.

106 For Greek legal cases featuring this issue, see Apollodorus, *Against Neaera* 41, 55–9; Antiphon, *Prosecution of a Stepmother* 14; Isaeus 6.19–21, 8.18–20; Hamel, *Trying Neaeira.*

107 See *Marshall* v. *Marshall*, 253 B.R. 550 (Bankr. Ct. D.C. Cal. 2000) for the fullest description of Ms. Smith's case history. Smith died in 2007; lawsuits have continued over her estate.

108 *CIL* IV, 4398. See McGinn, *Economy*, 300. For comparable Greek evidence, see E. Cohen, "An economic analysis of Athenian prostitution," in C. Faraone and L. McClure (eds.), *Prostitutes and Courtesans in the Ancient World* (Madison: University of Wisconsin Press, 2006). 1 *as* has the approximate buying power of 1 US$ (2014), since for 2 *asses* you could purchase bread or cheap wine.

109 McGinn, *Economy*, 42–3; Cicero, *Cael.* 62; Quintilian, *Institutio Oratoria* 8.6.53; Plutarch, *Cicero* 29.4.

110 Flemming, "Quae corpore," 48; Stumpp, *Prostitution*, 216–17; McGinn, *Economy*, 42. A charge of 32 *asses*, from an epigram of Martial's, may either be the price of a particularly glamorous courtesan, simple exaggeration, or an advance payment for multiple sexual acts. We have relatively little evidence outside Italy except for the second-century CE Palmyran tax law, which gives 6, 8, and 16 *asses* (1 *denarius*) as possible sample prices for local prostitutes. This suggests that the Pompeii graffiti prices may be low on average, at least compared to those in the wealthy Eastern Empire. The poor economic conditions in Pompeii after the earthquake of 62 CE may have necessitated such discounts.

111 McGinn, *Prostitution*, 276–9.

112 It is unclear whether this tax is for one woman or multiple prostitutes: *I. Portes* 67 = *OGIS* 2.674; *IGR* 1.1183 (Coptos, 90 CE).

113 McGinn, *Prostitution*, 282.

114 Flemming, "Quae corpore," 49. Flemming, however, does not believe in the existence of prosperous Roman courtesans as a general phenomenon.

115 S. Treggiari, "Divorce Roman style: how easy and how frequent was it?" in B. Rawson (ed.), *Marriage, Divorce, and Children in Ancient Rome* (Oxford University Press, 1996), 45–6.

116 Gaius, *Inst.* 1.190: "For women of full age manage their affairs themselves, and in certain cases the guardian (*tutor*) imposes his will as a matter of form and often is obliged by the praetor to give his authorization even against his will." See also Cic. *Ad. Fam.* 14.1, among many others, on Terentia's control of her own wealth; J. Gardner, *Women in Roman Law and Society* (Indianapolis: Indiana University Press, 1986), 15.

117 *CIL* IV, 3061; Varone, *Erotica Pompeiana*, 162; E. Diehl, J. Moreau and
H. I. Marrou (eds.), *Inscriptiones latinae christianae veteres*, vol. 1 apud
Weidannos (1967), 673.

118 *CIL* IV, 1574; Varone, *Erotica Pompeiana*, 164.

119 Varone, *Erotica Pompeiana*, 160; H. Geist, *Pompeianische Wandinschriften*
(Munich: Ernest Heimeran Verlag, 1960).

120 *ILS* 4372; see M. Lefkowitz, "Wives and husbands," *Greece & Rome*, 30.1
(1983), 44.

121 *ILS* 4154; Lefkowitz, "Wives and husbands," 45–6.

122 The plot of the *Menaechmi*, for instance, centers on the transfer of the
wife's mantle to the *meretrix* Erotium, but Erotium is also given the more
practical gifts of housing and food by her lover: Plautus, *Menaechmi* 200.

2 Good little prostitutes

1 *CIL* IX, 2029: *Vibia L. 1. Chresta mon(umentum) fecit sibi et suis et
C. Rustio C. 1. Thalasso filio e(t) Vibiae G. 1. Calybeni libertae lenae ab asse
quaesitum lucro suo sine fraude aliorum. H. M. H. N. S*; Kampen, *Images
and Status*, 110;

2 S. Treggiari, "Lower class women in the Roman economy," *Florilegium*, 1
(1979), 73.

3 See, for instance, Silenium in Plautus, *Cistellaria* 85, who declares her reluc-
tance to sleep with any man she does not love: D. Konstan, *Roman Comedy*
(Ithaca and London: Cornell University Press, 1983), 111, but cf. N. Zagagi,
*Tradition and Originality in Plautus: Studies of the Amatory Motifs in
Plautine Comedy* (Gottingen: Vandenhoeck & Ruprecht, 1980), 82, 89.

4 However, much of the surviving evidence about these virginal prostitute
characters is based on Roman plays based tightly on Greek models, rather
than on the direct text of Menander's originals: Fantham, "Sex, status and
survival," 56–9.

5 O. Knorr "The Character of Bacchis in Terence's *Heautontimorumenos*,"
The American Journal of Philology, 116.2 (Summer 1995), 221.

6 Terence, *Hecyra* 115; Fantham, "Sex, status, and survival," 68–70;
T. McGarrity, "Reputation vs. reality in Terence's *Hecyra*," *Classical Journal*,
76.2 (1980–81), 149–56; Konstan, *Roman Comedy*, 130–41; N. Slater, "The
fictions of patriarchy in Terence's *Hecyra*," *Classical World*, 81.4 (1988),
249–60. The *Hecyra* was probably based on a comedy by Apollodorus, but
the original has been lost; it is unclear how closely Terence might have hewed
to the original text.

7 D. Gilula, "The concept of the bona meretrix: a study of Terence's courtesans," *RFIC* 108 (1980), 155–6; Dutsch, *Feminine Discourse*, 71–5, 192.

8 The minor character Philotis also argues for an ethical treatment of lovers by
prostitutes: Terence, *Hecyra* 58–72.

9 Terence, *Hecyra* 776.

10 *Ibid.* 799.

11 Langlands, *Sexual Morality*, 93.

12 Traill, *Women and the Comic Plot*, 3–9.
13 Plutarch, *Moralia* 712c; Traill, *Women and the Comic Plot*, 4; Gilula, "Bona meretrix," 512–13.
14 Traill, *Women and the Comic Plot*, 9.
15 Dutsch offers some discussion of the importance of shifting gender boundaries in this passage: *Feminine Discourse*, 169–70.
16 Livy does not tell us whether Aebutius was merely one of Hispala's many customers, but he does identify her as an active *meretrix*: Livy 39.9.9. It is also unclear whether Hispala charged Aebutius for sex at any point during the relationship. Livy may neglect such details out of a wish to portray Hispala positively and in contrast to conventional prostitutes.
17 *ILS* 18; this inscription does not mention Hispala or Aebutius themselves, *contra* Walsh's assertion: P. G. Walsh, "Making a drama out of a crisis: Livy and the Bacchanalia," *Greece and Rome*, 43.2 (October 1996), 196.
18 For discussions of the social context, see J-M. Pailler, *Bacchanalia, la repression de 186 av. J.C. a Rome et en Italie* (Rome: Ecole française de Rome, 1988); E. Gruen, *Studies in Greek Culture and Roman Policy* (Leiden: University of California Press, 1990), ch. 2; P. G. Walsh, "Making a Drama," 188–96.
19 Flemming, "Quae corpore," 52; see *Digest* 23.2.43.
20 Walsh, "Making a drama," 188–203; T. P. Wiseman, *Roman Drama and Roman History* (University of Exeter Press, 1998), ch. 4. J-M. Pailler provides an exhaustive historiographical bibliography of other discussions of this theory, but Walsh and Wiseman are the strongest recent arguments: Pailler, *Bacchanalia*, ch. 2.
21 Walsh, "Making a drama," 199.
22 Wiseman, *Roman Drama*, ch. 4 deals extensively with the Bacchanalian crisis, arguing that Livy's version is based on a comic play circulated throughout Italy in reaction to the discovery and extermination of the conspiracy.
23 Walsh, "Making a drama," 199.
24 Livy 39.9.
25 This detail, while possibly borrowed from comic tradition, may also argue against the shame-segregated zoning theory proposed by Ray Laurence, which suggests that prostitutes and respectable families did not live in the same areas. R. Laurence, *Roman Pompeii: Space and Society* (London: Routledge Press, 1994), 73.
26 Livy 39.10.1.
27 Livy 39.11.
28 Cf. Terence, *Adelphoe* 747, in which the characters are shocked at the notion of a *meretrix* and a *materfamilias* in the same house.
29 Livy 39.13.
30 Livy 39.14: *Calis ferentibus in publicum obseratis, aditu in aedes uerso.*
31 Livy 39.19. During Hispala's lifetime, there were no formal legal restrictions on elite–freedwoman intermarriage; Livy may here be invoking the effects of the Augustan moral legislation during his own era.
32 Langlands, *Sexual Morality*, 247 f.; S. F. Bonner, *Roman Declamation: In the Late Republic and Early Empire* (Berkeley: University of California Press, 1949), 52–3; W. M. Bloomer, "Schooling in persona: imagination and

subordination in Roman education," *Classical Antiquity*, 16.1 (1997), 63–4;
J. Connolly, *The State of Speech* (Princeton University Press, 2009), 217–18.

33 The chronological date for Speeches 14 and 15 is unclear; it is not particularly relevant, as the other texts demonstrate that the stereotype of the
bona meretrix was relatively consistent in its characterization throughout
the Roman Republican and Imperial periods. While none of these characters actually existed, their depiction in didactic literary speeches suggests a
common trope which would have been familiar to an elite, educated male
audience.

34 Ps.-Quintilian, *Decl. Maior.* 14, 15; *The Major Declamations Ascribed
to Quintilian*, trans. L. A. Sussman (Frankfurt: Lang, 1987); D. K. van
Mal-Maeder, "[Quintilian]. The poison of hatred (Declamationes maiores
14–15)" (2012), 549–51.

35 *Timeo, ne, si coepero simplicissimae puellae laudare mores, referre probitatem, amare rursus pauper incipiat. sive enim, iudices, malignitas est persua-
sionis humanae formam vacantem vocare meretricem, seu miserae nomen
istud inposuit aliquis amator, cui cum corporis bonis fortuna non dederat,
unde severi matrimonii castitati sufficeret, laboravit necessitatium suarum
custodire probitatem. nullius umquam per hanc matrimonii turbata concor-
dia est, nemo questus est pro filio pater, nemo exhaustas facultates in avidis-
simos sinus paenitentiae dolore deflevit.*

36 Ps.-Quintilian, *Decl. Maior.* 15.2.25.

37 *Itaque ex vocabulo mulieris quaerit invidiam. "meretricem," inquit,
"accuso ..." rei expecto mehercules ut sit ante omnia minax vultus, feralis
habitus; horreant squalore crines, rigeat super nefandas cogitationes efferata
tristitia vides veneficae non horridos vultus placidamque faciem.*

38 Corbeill, *Controlling Laughter*, 30–5.

39 Seneca, *Cont.* 2.4.3. Notably, this woman is still referred to as a *mulier*,
rather than the more respectable *femina* or *matrona*.

40 *Ibid.* 2.4.5; Riddle, *Contraception and Abortion*, 19.

41 CIL VI, 37965= CLE 1988; G. Mancini, *Roma. Nuove scoperte nella città
e nel suburbia. Notizie degli scavi di antichità*, vol. IX (Rome: Accademia
Nazionale dei Lincei, 1912), 155. The complete text is listed in Appendix I.
The marble slab, which was broken into two pieces at some point, is 0.59
by 0.66 by 0.025 meters; it must have been quite expensive to produce.
The text consists of two columns, each of twenty-five verses, as well as a
separate initial inscription and a final warning to tomb robbers in larger
font sizes. See N. M. Horsfall, "*CIL VI 37965 = CLE 1988* (Epitaph of
Allia Potestas): A Commentary," *ZPE* 61 (1985), 251–72. Horsfall deals
thoroughly with the complexities of the dating issue in pages 252–4, as
well as providing an extensive philological analysis. See also E. Saltelli,
"L'epitafio Di Allia Potestas (*CIL VI 37965; CLE 1988*): un commento,"
Biblioteca Scientifica di Ca' Foscari 1; E. d'Ambra, "The cult of virtues and
the funerary relief of Ulpia Epigone," *Latomus*, 48.2 (1989), 397–400. The
dating is largely irrelevant for my purposes, but I will summarize their arguments briefly. Linguistically, the deliberate use of archaisms by the author
renders a precise dating by style difficult; suggestions have ranged from

the late Augustan or Tiberian period (A. E. and J. S. Gordon, *Illustrated Introduction to Latin Epigraphy* (Berkeley: University of California Press, 1983), 145–8) to the more commonly argued late fourth-century date (Mancini, "Roma", 155–8, and M. L. de Gubernatis, "L'epitafio di Allia Potestas," *RPh* 41 (1913), 385–400.) Both Horsfall and Saltelli argue for a date of the late second–early third century CE on the basis of linguistic terminology.

42 See Modestinus, *Digest* 23.2.24 for legal definitions of Roman prostitutes.

43 Petronius, *Satyricon* 1.7.

44 Horsfall, "*CIL* VI, 37965," 251; N. Terzaghi, "Perché Allia fu infamis? (A proposito dell'iscrizione di Allia Potestas)," *A & R* 17 (1914), 115–19.

45 Saltelli, "L'eptiafio di Allia Potestas," 11. See Petronius, *Satyricon* 70.1; Seneca *Ep.* 87. 4 (in reference to Thais); and Plautus, *Bacchides* 1.1.41, for similar uses of *pretiosior*.

46 Horsfall, "*CIL* VI 37965," 263 suggests that Atalanta's legs had a specifically sexual connotation within the context of Roman mimes. Allius also praises his lover's breasts in a way that makes them far more reminiscent of a prostitute than a respectable matron. They are described as small, rather than as the more typically sizable emblems of fertility and bounty associated with depictions of matrons or married goddesses' breasts. Perhaps the reference to Atalanta is also intended to evoke images of a slender maiden rather than a buxom matron, reflecting either Allia's actual body shape or Aulus' own ideal of female beauty. See also Edwards, *The Politics of Immorality*, 124–33, on actresses and *infamia*.

47 Horsfall, "*CIL* VI 37965," 264; Ovid, *AA* 3.194. *Cinaedi*, or males who prefer sexually passive roles, are often accused of plucking themselves, which associates this behavior with women, but not necessarily with prostitutes: Richlin, *The Garden of Priapus*, 36–8.

48 This is a difficult and complex line without obvious parallel; I disagree with Horsfall's interpretation that *nosse* cannot be meant in either an intellectual or sexual sense (or both). For other interpretations, see Horsfall, "*CIL* VI 37965," 265.

49 Juvenal 6.434–56.

50 Seneca, *Cont.* 2.4.1.

51 Livy 39.9.

52 Plautus, *Aulularia* 478–535, *Asininaria* 97; S. James, "A courtesan's choreography," in Faraone and McClure (eds.) *Prostitutes and Courtesans*, 224-51. 249.

53 S. Dixon, "Polybius on Roman Women and Property," *AJP* 106:2 (1985), 149–50.

54 "Laudatio 'Turiae'," *ILS* 8393, 30–5.

55 *CIL* VI, 1527; E. K. Wistrand, *The So-Called Laudatio Turiae*, Acta Universitatis Gothoburgensis, vol. 34 (1976).

56 W. Fitzgerald, *Slavery and the Roman Literary Imagination* (Cambridge University Press, 2000), 70, 75; Parker, "Loyal slaves," 155–6.

57 Livy 23.14.

58 Appian, *BC* 4.36; Parker, "Loyal slaves," 164.

59 Parker, "Loyal slaves," 156.

60 Appian, *BC* 4.32–4.
61 Parker, "Loyal slaves," 164–5; see Appian, *Civil Wars* 4.36–40; Valerius Maximus 6.7.3.

3 Powerful concubines and influential courtesans

1 Cicero, *Att.* 10.10.5.
2 Cicero, *Ad Familiares* 9.26.
3 Suetonius, *Domitian* 12. We do not know why she traveled to Istria, in modern Croatia. Perhaps she visited Vespasian during one of his military campaigns against Byzantium, or perhaps her own natal family was from there.
4 J. M. Bennett, *History Matters: Patriarchy and the Challenge of Feminism* (Philadelphia: University of Pennsylvania Press, 2011), 54–81.
5 W. Scheidel, "Monogamy and polygyny," in B. Rawson (ed.), *A Companion to Families in the Greek and Roman Worlds* (Hoboken, NJ: John Wiley & Sons, 2011), 108–15.
6 Homer, *Odyssey* 6.181–4.
7 M. Foucault, *The History of Sexuality*, vol. III. *The Care of the Self* (New York: Random House, 2012), 151–2; Musonius Rufus, *Reliquiae* 14; Homer, *Od.* 6.181–2. Marital desire will be further discussed in Chapter 6.
8 P. Allison, *Pompeian Households: An Analysis of the Material Culture*, UCLA Monograph 42 (Los Angeles: Cotsen Institute of Archaeology, 2004), 154–8.
9 Livy 39.42. This lover is referred to by Livy as a *scortum*, a neuter derogatory term for "whore" or low-class prostitute; the figure is alternately identified as male or female by various different sources over time. Livy himself describes the *scortum* as a *puer* in 39.42, but admits that the annalist Valerius Antias describes the prostitute as female (Livy 39.43). Other authors who characterize the prostitute as female are primarily later writers: Seneca, *Cont.* 9.2, and Valerius Maximus 2.9.3. Cicero, the earliest source, uses *scortum*; Plutarch, in the second century CE, describes the prostitute as male. Cicero, *De Senectute* 42; Plutarch, *Flamininus* 18; C. A. Williams, "Greek Love at Rome," *The Classical Quarterly*, 45.2 (1995), 520, and E. Cantarella, *Bisexuality in the Ancient World* (New Haven: Yale University Press, 1994), 101–2. In any case, the gender here is less relevant than the fact that Flamininus incurs shame and public disgrace through abusing his power to gratify a lowly *scortum*.
10 Hippolytus, *Philosophumena* 9.2.12. Marcia's motivations and the question of her religious background will be discussed later in the chapter. The crucial point is that she became a figure worthy of praise even to a group that would otherwise be likely to condemn her behavior.
11 See, for instance, J. McNamara and S. Wemple. "The power of women through the family in medieval Europe: 500–1100," *Feminist Studies* 1, no. 3/4 (1973), 126–41; C. Pateman, *The Disorder of Women: Democracy, Feminism, and Political Theory* (Stanford University Press, 1989), 17–18; T. Hillard, "On the

stage, behind the curtain," in Allen, Dixon, and Garlick (eds.), *Stereotypes of Women in Power*, 40–2; Bauman, *Women and Politics*, 4–7.

12 E.g. Dio 47.8.2–5; Tacitus, *Ann.* 1.3–8, 12.64–69. Roman invective against women is more generally discussed in Chapter 1.

13 Cicero, *Philippics* 2.58–61; Plutarch, *Lucullus* 6.2; Cicero, *In Verrem* 1.136–7.

14 L. Edmunds, "Lucilius 730M: a scale of power," *Harvard Studies in Classical Philology*, 94 (1992), 219.

15 Cicero, *Att.* 15.20.4: S. Dixon, "Family finances: Tullia and Terentia," *Antichthon*, 18 (1984): 78-101.

16 Cicero, *Att.* 10.10.5.

17 Hillard, "On the stage," 41.

18 As Tacitus and Suetonius freely criticize dead Imperial empresses and daughters, it cannot be a simple lack of freedom of speech that causes such restraint and praise with respect to emperors' concubines, e.g. Tacitus, *Ann.* 1.10.

19 As discussed in the Introduction, the difference between a courtesan and a concubine is largely that the courtesan may have multiple simultaneous lovers. Both types of women are at the top of the ambiguous hierarchy of Roman *meretrices*. As the Imperial evidence primarily focuses on emperors' mistresses, who generally did not take other lovers, it is convenient if coincidental to describe the Republican women as courtesans and the Imperial ones as concubines. Most of these women seem to have only been in one sexual relationship at any given time, however, and thus may be best characterized as "mistresses," regardless of time period.

20 On Cicero and women, see Hillard, "On the stage," 48.

21 Flemming, "Quae corpore," 45–7.

22 Martial 9.32.5.

23 Plautus, Poenulus, 265–70, for further distinctions among prostitutes: "You don't want to mingle there [at the temple of Venus] with those girls who advertise themselves outside, do you? The girlfriends of millers, the queens of the groat mills ... The ones who smell of the brothel and standing outside, of chair and seat, whom moreover no free man has ever touched or taken home, the two-obol prostitutes of filthy little slaves (servolorum)?".

24 B. Rawson, "Roman concubinage and other de facto marriages," *TAPA* 104 (1974), 279–305; Treggiari, *Roman Marriage*, 50–1; McGinn, "Concubinage," 335–75.

25 Ulpian, *Digest* 24.2.11.2; Constantinus, C. 5.26.1. McGinn notes that concubines are equated with *meretrices* in the legal sources when they are not assimilated to wives. There were also unmarried women in long-term relationships who were legally treated as wives precisely because they did not make money from prostitution: McGinn, *Prostitution*, 197, "Concubinage," 347–54; Modestinus, *Digest* 23.2.24. It was not possible to be a concubine who was neither a wife nor a *meretrix*, at least in terms of legal social status during the high Empire.

26 Friedl, *Der Konkubinat*, 184. Friedl also notes that epigraphy may better represent the practices of ordinary Romans than prescriptive legal texts,

although even in this case we are missing the records of men and women too poor to commission stone inscriptions.

27 Treggiari, *Roman Marriage*, 51.
28 Modestinus, *Digest* 23.2.24.
29 Suetonius, *Claudius* 21.
30 Plutarch, *Pompeius* 2.8; Plutarch, *Lucullus* 6.2; Tacitus, *Ann.* 13.12.
31 Plutarch, *Pompeius* 2.8. It is uncertain which of the various Gemini of the period this man was; the most plausible possibility is probably a member of the Fufius Geminus family, fairly prominent *equites* who eventually sided with Octavian: Cassius Dio 49.36. It seems unlikely that he was the astronomer and mathematician Geminus, although the date would be reasonable: Proclus 11; O. Neugebauer, *A History of Ancient Mathematical Astronomy* (Berlin: Springer, 2012), vol I, 2.579–80.
32 See Chapter 5 for more information on the Floralia and the goddess Flora.
33 Plutarch, *Pompeius* 2.8.
34 Plutarch, *Cato Minor* 25.1–5. The exchange of women from one family to form alliances with another elite Roman family was common, e.g. Octavian's sister Octavia or Julius Caesar's daughter Julia, married respectively to Marcus Antonius and Pompeius Magnus. However, such women were normally the daughters or sisters of one man, rather than a former wife as in Marcia's case.
35 During the early Empire, the ambitious senator and future brief emperor Otho similarly shared a wife, Poppaea Sabina, with the Emperor Nero; this tie seems to have temporarily damaged rather than strengthened his political career, however: Suetonius, *Otho* 3.
36 A. Keith, "Lycoris Galli/Volumnia Cytheris: a Greek courtesan in Rome," *EuGeStA* no.1 (2011).
37 Plutarch, *Lucullus* 6.2.
38 *Ibid.* 6.3. *Misthos* is the standard Greek term for a prostitute's wage for a specific act, although the amount of the *misthos* obviously ranges widely depending on the status of the *hetaira*: Davidson, *Courtesans and Fishcakes*, 276.
39 Plutarch, *Lucullus* 6.4.
40 Cicero, *Fam.* 9.26. Eutrapelus himself had an unsavory and hedonistic reputation: Horace, *Epistles* 1.18.31–6.
41 Pomeroy, *Goddesses*, 198.
42 S. Treggiari, "The Influence of Roman Women," book review of J. P. Hallett, 'Fathers and Daughters in Roman Society', *The Classical Review* 36.1 (1986), 102.
43 G. Traina, "Lycoris the mime," in A. Fraschetti (ed.), *Roman Women* (Chicago University Press, 2001), 89. Traina argues that Cytheris was freed from slavery precisely so that her former master, Eutrapelus, could offer her sexual services as a favor to his powerful political allies. He claims, "it would have been unseemly for any man to keep company with an actress who was not a free woman." This contention is not well supported by positive evidence, although indeed most of the notorious actors and actresses we know

of appear to be freedpersons, such as Sulla's male lover Metrobius: Plutarch, *Sulla* 2.

44 Cicero, *Att.* 10.10.5.

45 D. R. Shackleton Bailey, "Two studies in Roman nomenclature," *American Classical Studies*, 3 (1976), 77. While Volumnia is not an uncommon Roman female name, Volumnia Cytheris was certainly in a high position of influence and power in early 47 BCE, and the relative lack of response or tact shown by this Volumnia may indicate that she was not a natural ally of the Cicerones. This evidence is therefore consistent with an identification of Volumnia as Volumnia Cytheris, although other explanations are plausible. See also Traina, "Lycoris the mime," 91.

46 Cicero, *Fam.* 14.16.

47 Appian, *BC* 4.32–4. Cicero himself requested a political favor from Clodia Metelli and Mucia, Pompeius' wife, in 63 BCE, however, suggesting that men could contact wives directly, even if women were restricted to negotiations with other women (Cicero, *Fam.* 5.2.6).

48 Cicero, *Fam.* 9.26.

49 *Ibid.* 9.32–3.

50 *Ibid.* 9.26.

51 Cicero, *Att.* 10.16.5.

52 Livy 34.1–7; Polybius 31.23 ff. While the *Lex Oppia* refers specifically to women riding in horse-drawn vehicles, the wealthy women's privilege of riding in vehicles of any sort was a means of displaying wealth and elite status.

53 Cicero, *Att.* 15.22. "Cytherius" also refers to Venus herself, who was born on the island of Cythera according to some accounts, and therefore Cicero may also intend to paint Antonius as a weak lover of the goddess rather than as a courageous follower of Mars.

54 Cicero, *Philippics* 2.44;, L. A. Sussman, "Antony the Meretrix Audax: Cicero's novel invective in Philippic 2.44–46," *Eranos*, 96.1–2 (1998), 114–28. The details of the supposed relationship between Curio and Antonius are irrelevant for these purposes, although an intriguing source for any investigation into Roman attitudes towards same-sex affairs.

55 Eventually, Octavian borrowed this tactic from Cicero to describe Antonius as in thrall to Cleopatra, as discussed in Chapter 4.

56 F. Hartog, *Mirror of Herodotus* (1980), 260.

57 Cicero, *Phil.* 2.68.

58 Cytheris supposedly appeared in Cornelius Gallus' largely lost poetry under the pseudonym of Lycoris: Servius Honoratus, *Ecl.* 6.11.5; *Fragmenta Bobiensia* 543.34; Keith, "Lycoris Galli/Volumnia Cytheris," 23–53. Extrapolating historical information about her from references to these poems is as risky as with any other "elegiac woman," although her representation within them is fascinating as a depiction of ambiguous morality in and of itself. There are no contemporary sources supporting the claim of a relationship between Cytheris and Brutus. Our only reference comes from an early fifth-century CE source: S. Aurelius Victor, *De viris illustribus* 82.2. This casts fairly serious doubt on the entire episode, as it may be a case of trying to associate Cytheris with as many famous contemporary men as possible. Notably, from 47 to 43

BCE, the years in which they might have had an affair, Marcus Brutus was first in Greece on the side of the Pompeians and then newly married to Cato's daughter Porcia; it is unclear when he would even have found the time to indulge in a relationship with Cytheris. Antonius, meanwhile, married Fulvia during this period. See R. D. Anderson, P. J. Parsons, and R. G. M. Nisbet, "Elegiacs by Gallus from Qaṣr Ibrîm," *JRS* 69 (1979), 153.

59 Vergil, *Ecl.* 10; Keith, "Lycoris Galli/Volumnia Cytheris".

60 Cicero, *Phil.* 2.61; Traina, "Lycoris," 93.

61 Cf. Cicero, *Verr.* 1.136–7; M. McCoy, "The politics of prostitution," in Faraone and McClure (eds.), *Prostitutes and Courtesans*, 179–81.

62 Cf. Cicero's representation of Clodia in the *Pro Caelio*, as discussed in Chapter 4.

63 Cicero, *In Verrem*, 1.136–7, trans. adapted from C. D. Yonge. *Statuunt id sibi esse optimum factu, quod cuivis venisset in mentem, petere auxilium a Chelidone, quae ista praetore non modo in iure civili privatorumque omnium controversiis populo Romano praefuit, verum etiam in his sartis tectisque dominata est. Venit ad Chelidonem C. Mustius, eques Romanus, publicanus, homo cum primis honestus; venit M. iunius, patruus pueri, frugalissimus homo et castissimus; venit homo summo pudore, summo officio, spectatissimus ordinis sui, P. Titius tutor … Ut omittam cetera, quo tandem pudore talis viros, quo dolore meretricis domum venisse arbitramini? Qui numquam ulla condicione istam turpitudinem subissent nisi offici necessitudinisque ratio coegisset.*

64 T. Hillard, "Republican women, politics, and the evidence," *Helios*, 16 (1989), 169.

65 Cicero, *Verr.* 1.104.

66 *Ibid.* 4.71.

67 Ovid, *Amores* 1.11.

68 Cicero, *Verr.* 3.78.

69 Treggiari, *Roman Freedmen*, 252–64.

70 Tacitus, *Ann.* 13.12: *Ceterum infracta paulatim potentia matris delapso Nerone in amorem libertae, cui vocabulum Acte fuit … ne senioribus quidem principis amicis adversantibus, muliercula nulla cuiusquam iniuria cupidines principis explente, quando uxore ab Octavia, nobili quidem et probitatis spectatae, fato quodam, an quia praevalent inlicita, abhorrebat, metuebaturque, ne in stupra feminarum inlustrium prorumperet, si illa libidine prohiberetur.*

71 She may also have had these other men as lovers, but Nero does not seem like the type of young man who shared well with others: Tacitus, *Ann.* 13.15–17.

72 Tacitus, *Ann.* 13.13. *Sed Agrippina libertam aemulam, nurum ancillam aliaque eundem in modum muliebriter fremere, neque paenitentiam filii aut satietatem opperiri, quantoque foediora exprobrabat, acrius accendere, donec vi amoris subactus exueret obsequium in matrem seque [Se]necae permitteret, ex cuius familiaribus Annaeus Serenus simulatione amoris adversus eandem libertam primas adulescentis cupidines velaverat praebueratque nomen, ut quae princeps furtim mulierculae tribuebat, ille palam largiretur. Tum Agrippina versis artibus per blandimenta iuvenem adgredi, suum potius cubiculum ac sinum offerre …*

73   Tacitus, *Ann.* 14.2, citing the contemporary consul Cluvius as his source. *Senecam contra muliebris inlecebras subsidium a femina petivisse, immissamque Acten libertam, quae simul suo periculo et infamia Neronis anxia deferret pervulgatum esse incestum gloriante matre, nec toleraturos milites profani principis imperium.*

74   Tacitus, *Ann.* 14.2; CIL X, 7489, 7980, VI, 15027; *P. Berl. Inv.* 7440 (recto);

75   Suetonius, *Nero* 28.2.1.

76   Cassius Dio 61.7.1.

77   *Ibid.*

78   Tacitus, *Ann.* 13.46. *Paelice ancilla et adsuetudine Actes devinctum, nihil e contubernio servili nisi abiectum et sordidum traxisse.*

79   Suetonius, *Nero* 50.

80   *Ibid.*

81   Rawson, " Roman concubinage," 288.

82   Cassius Dio 64.13. Rawson reasonably concludes that she must have been at least twenty by the time she was appointed as Antonia's secretary, which I believe to be a conservative estimate (Rawson,"Roman concubinage," 288). Such an elite position would more likely have gone to a somewhat more experienced slave. Antonia died in 37 CE and Caenis presumably remained a part of the *familia Caesaris* or imperial household after her death.

83   Cassius Dio 64.13.

84   Suetonius, *Vespasian* 3. Vespasian's first son, Titus, was born in December 39 CE and his younger son Domitian in October 51 CE. This allows us to establish a rough chronology for Vespasian and Caenis' relationship, which lasted for many years after the death of Vespasian's wife Flavia, who died sometime before Vespasian's accession in December 69 CE. Presumably, the affair persisted throughout the 30s and then again in the 60s and 70s, when Caenis would have been at least fifty.

85   *Ibid. Post uxoris excessum Caenidem, Antoniae libertam et a manu, dilectam quondam sibi revocavit in contubernium, habuitque etiam imperator paene iustae uxoris loco.*

86   Treggiari, *Roman Marriage*, 52–4.

87   SHA, *Antoninus Pius* 8.9.

88   *Ibid.*

89   SHA, *Marcus* 29.10.

90   McGinn, "Concubinage," 353.

91   Marcus himself, in his *Meditations*, suggests that family life with concubines may have been rather more complex than the legal sources imagine: "I am thankful to the gods that the time I was brought up with my grandfather's concubine did not last any longer, and that I preserved the flower of my youth, and that I did not make proof of my virility before the proper season, but even deferred the time" (Marcus Aurelius, *Meditations* 1.17). Marcus was raised by his grandfather Verus and his mother. Apparently, this otherwise unknown concubine initially assisted in his education and provided a great degree of temptation for the young philosopher. This

dilemma in a real household involving an elderly man, a much younger woman, and his son or grandson highly resembles a Roman comedic plot, suggesting that there may frequently have been domestic disturbances over this sort of issue, given Roman family demographics.

92　Cassius Dio 73.4.6–7; *HA* (*Comm.* 8.6, 11.9, 17.1), *Pert.* 5.2, *Did. Jul.* 6.2. For other non-Christian sources regarding Marcia, see Dio 72.13–22, *Epit. De. Caes.* 17.5, *Herod* 1.16–17. For other scholarly treatments of Marcia, see Friedl, *Der Konkubinat*, 173; E. Wallinger, *Die Frauen in der Historia Augusta* (Vienna: Selbstverl. d. Österr. Ges. für Archäologie,1990), 70 ff; W. Eck, "The emperor and his advisors," in A. Bowman, P. Garnsey and D. Rathbone (eds.), *Cambridge Ancient History* (Cambridge University Press, 2000), vol. XI, 210. Dio is our major source here except for the *HA*, which is less generally reliable on the subject of Commodus: Millar (1964), 126–31; M. Hose, "Cassius Dio: a senator and historian in the age of anxiety," in J. Marincola (ed.), *A Companion to Greek and Roman Historiography* (Wiley, 2009), 161–7; Marincola (2009), 295–6. On the *HA* and Commodus specifically: F. Kolb, *Literarische Beziehungen zwischen Cassius Dio, Herodian und der Historia Augustus* (Bonn: Antiquitas, 1972), 7–53; R. Syme, *Emperors and Biography* (Oxford: Clarendon Press, 1971), 30 ff.; A. Chastagnol, *Les Empereurs des IIe et IIIe siècles* (Paris: Éditions Robert Laffont, 1994), 249–75.

93　*CIL* X, 5918= *ILS* 406.

94　Hippolytus, *Philosophumena* 9.12.

95　Lucian of Samosata; Marcus Aurelius, *Med.* 8.37; Vout, "The myth of the toga," 215–16.

96　Cassius Dio 73.4.6–7.

97　McGinn, "Concubinage," 353.

98　Friedl, *Der Konkubinat*, 173. Friedl argues that after Marcia's rise to power as the "de facto Empress," her relationship with Eclectus was purely symbolic and platonic. However, there is no direct textual evidence to support this theory.

99　*SHA, Commodus* 5.8, 5.4.

100　Cassius Dio 73.12.

101　Philo, *Leg.* 175; J. Paterson, "Friends in high places" in A. J. S. Spawforth (ed.),*The Court and Court Society in Ancient Monarchies* (Cambridge University Press, 2007), 142.

102　Cassius Dio 73.13.

103　Cassius Dio 73.13; C. de Ranieri, "Retroscena politici e lotte dinastiche sullo sfondo della vicenda di Aurelio Cleandro," *RSA* 27 (1997), 149.

104　O. Hekster, *Commodus: An Emperor at the Crossroads* (Amsterdam: Gieben,2002), 74.

105　Hekster, *Commodus* 74; G. Alföldy, "Cleanders Sturz und die antike Überlieferung," *Die Krise des Römischen Reiches. Geschichte, Geschichtsschreibung und Geschichtsbetrachtung. Ausgewählte Beiträge* (1989), 113.

106　Hekster, *Commodus* 74.

107　Cf. Verres' mistress Chelidon: Cicero, *In Verrem* 1.136–7. With regard to issues of Christianization particularly, see K. Cooper, "Insinuations of womanly influence," *JRS* 82 (1992), 151. For depictions of influential women as means of criticizing their male partners, see Hillard, "Republican women," 166–9; S. Dixon *The Roman Family* (London: John Hopkins University Press, 1992), 212; Saxonhouse, "Public and private," 7.

108 Epictetus, *Discourses* 1.19.7; Suetonius, *Claudius* 29; Cassius Dio 50.2.8; Paterson, "Friends in high places," 129.

109 *SHA, Commodus* 8.9.

110 *Epit. De Caes.* 17.5.

111 Herodian 1.16.4. Herodian is a less reliable source than Cassius Dio or even the *Historia Augusta*, so such statements must be viewed with some skepticism: Kolb, *Literarische Beziehungen*, 47–53.

112 *SHA, Commodus* 12.1.

113 K. Coleman, "Missio at Halicarnassus," *Harvard Studies in Classical Philology*, 100 (2000), 487.

114 Juvenal 6.104–5, 1.22.3.

115 Suetonius, *Nero* 44.1; Coleman, "Missio at Halicarnassus," 499.

116 While I do not generally treat Christian attitudes towards prostitution in this book, Christians here serve as an example of an interest group that sought favor with a concubine, rather than as a group with its own particular beliefs about prostitution and female sexuality. The prisoners' status as Christians is largely irrelevant in Marcia's case, except insofar as it led to their persecution.

117 Cassius Dio 73.4; Hippolytus, *Philosophumena* 9.2.12; Herodian 1.16.4.

118 Hippolytus, *Phil.* 9.12.10; Lampe 336. Hippolytus is notably anti-Callistus in his description of this scene; he also claims that the Christian eunuch Hyacinthus was Marcia's foster-father, and used this connection to gain the freedom of Callistus, who was not included in the initial decree releasing the other prisoners: *Phil.* 9.2.12. It is unclear whether Hyacinthus served as a spiritual father to Marcia or actually raised her, and as Hippolytus is our only source for this detail, I am disinclined to speculate as to the resulting implications for Marcia's life and relationship to the Christian movement.

119 G. R. Stanton, 'Marcus Aurelius, Lucius Verus, and Commodus: 1962–1972," *ANRW* II.2 (1975), 532; Hekster, *Commodus*, 185.

120 Cassius Dio 73.22.4.

121 L. Tomassini, "La congiura e l'assassino di Commodo: i retroscena," *Acme*, 47:3 (1994), 81–2. Hekster notes that Marcia was already in a very strong political position, as the Emperor's favorite mistress and confidante; she did not need assistance from a politically dubious religious cult (Hekster, *Commodus* 79).

122 M. Rostovtseff, and H. Mattingly. "Commodus-Hercules in Britain,"*JRS* 13 (1923), 100.

123 Plutarch, *Pompeius* 2.

124 Herodian 1.16.4; B. Levick, *Julia Domna* (New York: Routledge, 2007), 70.

125 *SHA, Commodus* 16.8; Cassius Dio 73.22.4–6; *Epitome de Caesaribus* 17.154.

126 *SHA, Pertinax* 4.3–5; C. de Ranieri, "La gestione politica di età Commodiana e la parabola di Tigidio Perenne," *Athenaeum*, 86 (1998), 398; Friedl, *Der*

Konkubinat, 173; E. Champlin, "Notes on the Heirs of Commodus," *AJP* 100.2 (1979), 296.

127 Hekster, *Commodus* 83.

128 Cassius Dio 74.16.5; *SHA, Didius Iulianus* 7; *SHA, Pertinax* 11.10–11.

129 Procopius, *Secret History* 9.

130 Cicero, *Verr.* 4.71; Cassius Dio 64.13.

131 None of the imperial concubines are said to have borne children. Whether this is due to an omission in the record or careful use of birth control and infanticide remains an open and unanswerable question. Without positive evidence demonstrating deliberate family planning, it is unwise to draw any larger conclusions. However, this lack suggests a conceptualization of the concubine as sexual partner and lover rather than as mother, even of illegitimate offspring.

132 P. R. C. Weaver, *Familia Caesaris: A Social Study of the Emperor's Freedmen and Slaves* (Cambridge University Press, 1972), 5, 224.

4 *Matrona* as *meretrix*

1 R. Krafft-Ebing, *Psychopathia Sexualis: With Especial Reference to the Antipathic Sexual Instinct: a Medico-Forensic Study* (New York: Arcade Publishing, 1965 edn.), 403.

2 Joshel, "Female desire," 56–7.

3 *Ibid.* 58.

4 For specific recent discussions of the honor–shame model in Roman society, see D. Cohen, "The social context of adultery at Athens," in P. Carledge, P. Millett, and S. Todd (eds.), *Nomos: Essays in Athenian Law, Politics, and Society* (Cambridge University Press, 1990), 147–65; R. Saller, "Corporal punishment, authority and obedience in the Roman household," in Rawson (ed.), *Marriage, Divorce and Children in Ancient Rome*,144–65; A. Wallace-Hadrill, "Public honour and private shame: the urban texture of Pompeii," in T. J. Cornell and K. Lomas (eds.), *Urban Society in Roman Italy* (London: Psychology Press, 1995), 51–62. In general, I think that the model is far more applicable to the small city-states of archaic and classical Greece, particularly given their highly restrictive treatment of wives, than to the cosmopolitan, comparatively less misogynistic cities of the Hellenistic and Roman world.

5 McGinn, *Prostitution*, 10–14; Treggiari, *Roman Marriage*, 439–83.

6 Shaw, "Roman Honor," 285. See also R. MacMullen, " 'Roman History' book review: C. Barton's *Roman Honor*," *Yale Review* 90.2 (2002), 154–60, in which Macmullen comments on the importance of context and scenarios for any definition of concepts; and W. V. Harris, "Book review: C. Barton, *Roman Honor*," *American Historical Review*, 108.2 (April 2003), 561, which similarly emphasizes the need for precise examinations of specific periods and areas within the Roman world rather than generalized and static ideas about the nature of Roman attitudes about morality.

7 For a more general discussion of the traditions of Roman invective, see Chapter 1. It is crucial to remember that many of these accusations followed

a standardized pattern and were no more based on truthful accounts than a modern tabloid newspaper.

8 Suetonius, *Tiberius* 35.1 ff.; D. Cohen, "The Augustan law on adultery," in D. Kertzer and Richard Saller (eds.), *The Family in Italy from Antiquity to the Present* (New Haven: Yale University Press, 1991),110.

9 Many of these women, like Clodia and Sempronia, lived during the chaos of lengthy civil war, during which many of their husbands were away from Rome for long periods of time or died prematurely. This likely increased both their personal wealth and their control over their own lives as well as their opportunities for extramarital liaisons.

10 While Livy certainly portrays many immoral women in his chronicles of the early Republic, their vices tend more towards homicide and riot than widespread debauchery. The relevant stories also more typically feature groups of evil women conspiring together, rather than individual prominent *meretrix*-like women, e.g. Livy 8.18, on the poisoning trials of 331 BCE. While the Bacchanalian conspiracy of 181 BCE, as discussed in Chapter 2, did involve supposed sexual orgies, the official fear was directed more at the corruption of youths than at the unorthodox behaviors of specific matrons.

11 Saxonhouse, "Public and private," 7.

12 Cicero, *Cael.* 20.49: *ut non solum meretrix, sed etiam proterva meretrix procaxque videatur.* This passage will be discussed more in depth later in the chapter.

13 Cicero, *Cael.*, *passim*; *Att.* 2.1.5, 9.1, 12.2, 14.1, 22.5; *Ad Familiares* 5.2.6; M. B. Skinner, "Clodia Metelli," *TAPA* 113 (1983), 273–87; A. Leen, "Clodia Oppugnatrix: the domus motif in Cicero's Pro Caelio," *Classical Journal* (2000), 141–62; M. B. Skinner, *Clodia Metelli: The Tribune's Sister* (Oxford University Press, 2011).

14 Skinner, "Clodia Metelli," 273–4; C. Martin, *Catullus* (New Haven: Yale University Press, 1992), 43; T. P. Wiseman, *Catullus and His World: A Reappraisal* (Cambridge University Press, 1985), 15–53. There is little modern disagreement on the basic identification, although we cannot extrapolate legitimate biographical evidence from Catullus' poetry, as he frequently relied on poetic conventions or allusions to Greek poets rather than chronicling a linear history of his relationship with Lesbia.

15 Of course, since the identification between Lesbia and Clodia is primarily based on a similarity of accusations in Cicero's speeches and Catullus' poetry, it is dangerous to use them as corroborative evidence for each other.

16 According to Plutarch, the other two Claudian sisters also committed incest with their little brother: "Lucullus proved, by his women-servants, that he [Clodius] had debauched his youngest sister when she was Lucullus' wife; and there was a general belief that he had done the same with his other two sisters": Plutarch, *Cicero* 29.

17 Skinner, *Clodia Metelli*, 79; Bauman, *Women and Politics*, 69.

18 Cicero, *Cael.* 24.59–60.

19 Skinner, "Clodia Metelli," 278–83; cf. Cicero, *Att.* 2.12.2; Skinner, *Clodia Metelli*, 112.

20 Hillard, "On the stage," 48.

21 Leen, "Clodia Oppugnatrix," 145–6.

22 Cicero, *Att.* 2.1.5; *Fam.* 2.5.6.

23 Cicero, *Cael.* 1.1, 2.3.

24 Ulpian, *Digest* 16.3.1.36; Cicero, *Pro Flacco* 51; Bauman, *Women and Politics*, 69.

25 McGinn, *Prostitution*, 63–4.

26 Suetonius, *Claudius* 15.4.

27 This argument conveniently ignores the detail that even if a *meretrix* could not be prosecuted for adultery, it was still quite illegal to attempt to poison her, as Caelius was charged with doing.

28 *Ibid.* 47. *Integumenta* is a rarely used Latin word meaning covering or "skin of the body," first used in Plautus' *Bacchides* 4.2.19 to describe a parasite character or bodyguard. It may thus have sexual or theatrical associations from the comic usage, as well as possibly being another word with the same meaning as *scortum*, which is also either a skin or a lowly prostitute. *Integumenta* also appears in a late antique context as the suggestive *integumenta carnalia*. (Ambrosius, *De Isaac et Anima* 4.16).

29 Ovid, *Amores* 1.10.21–4; Martial 9.2. See Chapter 1 for a further exploration of this comparison to the simple sale of sex by prostitutes of low status.

30 Flemming, "Quae corpore," 52; Quintilian, *Inst.* 8.4.2.

31 Cf. Martial 2.39: *Coccina famosae donas et ianthina moechae: uis dare quae meruit munera? mitte togam*, "You're giving the notorious adulteress scarlet and violet clothes? Do you wish to give her the gifts she deserves? Send her a toga."

32 Cicero, *Cael.* 62; Quintilian, *Inst.* 8.6.53; Plutarch, *Cicero* 29.3 –5.

33 Hillard, "On the stage," 51.

34 Cicero, *Cael.* 32; Leen, "Clodia Oppugnatrix," 150.

35 Quinta Claudia will be further discussed in Chapter 5.

36 Skinner, "Clodia Metelli," 277.

37 Clodia did, of course, have several brothers, including the powerful Publius Clodius. However, in Roman literature and history, sisters both appear less often and are less frequently figures of unquestioned virtue, and they are rarely defended by their siblings. Examples of Roman women famous for their sibling relationships include Clodia herself and Servilia, the outspoken sister of Marcus Cato, mother of Marcus Brutus, and lover of Julius Caesar, a woman with highly complex loyalties. The most famous mythical Roman sister was Horatia, who was killed by her brother for daring to express sorrow that her brother had killed her fiance; this sets a precedent for Roman sisters as, at the best, morally complex figures, perhaps because women identified historically as sisters would presumably have failed in their responsibilities as mothers and wives.

38 Parker, "The teratogenic grid," 52. Arguably, passive anal sex is represented as equally disreputable in Roman literature.

39 Sallust, *Catiline* 24.

40 *Ibid.* 25.

41 Propertius 3.11.39; H. Volkmann, *Cleopatra: A Study in Politics and Propaganda* (London: Elek Books, 1958); R. Gurval, *Actium and Augustus:*

The Politics and Emotions of Civil War (Ann Arbor: University of Michigan Press, 1998); D. Kleiner, *Cleopatra and Rome* (Cambridge: Harvard University Press, 2009).

42 Wyke, *The Roman Mistress*, 196–7; K. Galinsky, *Augustan Culture: An Interpretive Introduction* (Princeton University Press, 1996), 39–41.

43 Wyke, *Mistress*, 206; Vergil, *Aeneid* 8.688; Propertius 3.11.31.

44 Propertius 3.11.30; Horace, *Ep.* 9.13–14; Wyke, *Mistress*, 207.

45 Juvenal 6.118–32. Juvenal characterizes Messalina as dirty, deceptive, exhibitionist, and sexually voracious: *lassata uiris necdum satiata*, "exhausted by the men yet unsatisfied." See Joshel, "Female desire," 50–82.

46 Tacitus, *Ann.* 11.26.

47 *Ibid.* 11.27.

48 Joshel, "Female desire," 221; Tacitus, *Ann.* 11.29.

49 Tacitus, *Ann.* 11.32.

50 Dio 60.31.1; McGinn, *Prostitution*, 170.

51 Wyke, *Mistress*, 325–6.

52 Suetonius, *Caligula*, 41.

53 Pliny, *NH* 172.

54 Joshel, "Female desire," 56.

55 *Ibid.* 60.

56 M. Santirocco, "Sulpicia reconsidered," *Classical Journal*, 74 (1979), 232; J. R. Bradley, "The Elegies of Sulpicia," *New England Classical Journal*, 22 (1995), 1; K. Milnor, "Sulpicia's (corpo)reality: elegy, authorship, and the body in [Tibullus] 3. 13," *Classical Antiquity*, 21 (2002), 269–74; M. Skoie, *Reading Sulpicia: Commentaries 1475–1990* (Oxford University Press, 2002), 13. *Contra* Skoie's uncertainty regarding Sulpicia's chronology, I date Sulpicia's poetry to the 20s BCE. Her father Servius died in 43 BCE and it seems unlikely that she wrote her poetry later than her early twenties, given her apparently single state and Tibullus' own death in 19 BCE. See Bradley, "Sulpicia," 1, with regard to chronology.

57 Sulpicia, *Corpus Tibullanorum* 4.11.

58 *Sit tibi curae togae potio pressumque quasillo | scortum quam Servi filia Sulpicia: | solliciti sunt pro nobis, quibus illa dolori est | ne cedam ignoto maxima causa, toro.*

59 Sulpicia 4.7. It is unclear, however, whether one can generalize a category of such women based only on Sulpicia's poems, and it is much more likely that she was a largely unique case both in Roman literature and Roman social patterns.

60 Velleius Paterculus 2.100.3; Pliny, *NH* 149; Suetonius, *Augustus* 65.1–4. See also Macrobius, *Saturnalia* 2.5.4–9; A. Richlin, "Julia's jokes, Galla Placidia, and the Roman use of women as political icons," in Allen, Dixon, and Garlick (eds.), *Stereotypes of Women in Power*, 65–91.

61 Seneca the Younger moralistically describes Julia as moving *ex adultera in quaestuariam*, "from adulteress to gold-digger," which certainly has a strong implication of prostitute-like behavior: Seneca the Younger, *Ben.* 6.32.1, and see Ulpian, *Digest* 23. 2. 4 for a reference to a *mulier quaestuaria*, apparently a prostitute. However, this representation is inconsistent with the

multiple other texts that describe Julia, including the near-contemporaneous
Velleius Paterculus, and in any case does not dare to go so far as to label
her a *meretrix*. Rebecca Flemming suggests that Julia's indiscriminate availability allows her to be characterized as a prostitute by Seneca, and this
argument has some merit, although it ignores the repeated characterization
of Julia as a disobedient daughter rather than an independent, adulterous
wife: Flemming, "Quae corpore," 52.

62 Richlin, "Julia's jokes," 68–70. For arguments that Julia was exiled not
because of her adulteries but because of her role in a complex political conspiracy involving Marcus Antonius' son Iullus and the poet Ovid, see Barbara
Levick, "Julians and Claudians," *Greece and Rome*, 22 (1975), 33, and A.
Ferrill, "Augustus and his daughter: a modern myth," in Carl Deroux (ed.),
Studies in Latin Literature and Roman History (Brussels: Latomus, 1980),
vol. II, 332–46. However, I find this suggestion lacking in sufficient evidence,
despite the temptation to recast Julia as a powerful, politically influential
member of the Julio-Claudian dynasty. Given the numerous prominent,
manipulative Imperial women portrayed by Tacitus and Suetonius, it seems
doubtful that they would have ignored or omitted any active political participation by Julia.

63 Macrobius, *Saturnalia* 2.5.9. Julia's role as fertile mother and the sole con-
duit of Augustus' divine blood to future generations also redeems her somewhat from the potential lowly status of *meretrix*.

64 Suetonius, *Augustus* 65.4.

65 Tacitus, *Ann.* 1.4, 12.20. For more on Livia and Agrippina's representation, see S. Fischler, "Social stereotypes and historical analysis," in
L. Archer, S. Fischler and M. Wyke (eds.), *Women in Ancient Societies*
(London: Macmillan, 1995), 115–33; and for an excellent summary of
the most recent scholarship, D. Kleiner, "Livia Drusilla and the remarkable power of elite women in imperial Rome," *International Journal of the
Classical Tradition*, 6.4 (2000), 563–9 Milnor, *Gender*.

66 *SHA, Severus* 18.8; Cassius Dio 78.2.1–6; Levick, *Julia Domna*; J.
Langford, *Maternal Megalomania: Julia Domna and the Imperial Politics of
Motherhood* (Baltimore: Johns Hopkins University Press, 2013).

67 *SHA, Marcus Aurelius* 19.

68 McGinn, *Prostitution*, 127–9; Edwards, "Unspeakable professions," 66–95.

69 Ulpian (1 *ad legem Iuliam et Papia*), *Digest* 23.2.43: *palam quaestum facere
dicemus non tantum eam, quae in lupanario prostituit, verum etiam si qua
(ut adsolet) in taberna cauponia vel qua alia pudori suo non parcit.*

70 McGinn, *Prostitution*, 127.

71 *Ibid.*, 128–9; see also B. Meil. Hobson, *Uneasy Virtue: The Politics of
Prostitution and the American Reform Tradition* (University of Chicago
Press, 1990), 213.

72 Ulpian, *Digest* 23.2.43.1.

73 McGinn, *Prostitution*, 130–1.

74 J. DeFelice, *Roman Hospitality: The Professional Women of Pompeii*, Marco
Polo Monographs 6 (Warren Center, Pa.: Shangri-La Publications, 2001),
115–23.

75 *CIL* IV, 7862–76, 7221, 9096–99; 9351. The particular expression of election support ends with the line "Not without Zmyrina." Zmyrina is a notably foreign or possible slave name, suggesting that the woman in question came from the city of Smyrna, which does imply that she was perhaps of low social status. See also Cantarella, *Bisexuality in the Ancient World*, 75.

76 Ulpian, *Digest* 16.3.1.36; Cicero, *Flacc.* 51; Bauman, *Women and Politics*, 69.

77 L. Savunen, 'Women and elections in Pompeii,' in Hawley and Levick (eds.), *Women in Antiquity*, 195.

78 *Ibid.* 200.

79 *Ibid.* 199.

80 *Ibid.* 195.

81 The tavern of Salvius is located at VI.14.36 in Pompeii, in a prominent location on one of the main streets.

82 Kampen, *Images and Status*, 155.

83 K. Olson, *Dress and the Roman Woman: Self-Presentation and Society* (New York: Routledge, 2012), 77–8;

84 A woman named Myrtale is also mentioned in two other inscriptions in the Pompeii *lupanar*, where it is claimed that she offers fellatio: *CIL* VI, 2268, 2271. While this does not mean it is the same woman, the *lupanar* is only a few blocks from this tavern, as mentioned in the Introduction, so there may be some connection. For more discussion of these paintings, see J. R. Clarke, "Look who's laughing," *MAAR* (1998), 27–48.

85 *CIL* XIV, 3709; *ILS* 7477; Kampen, *Images and Status*, 110–11.

86 Nonius 155.30; T. Kleberg, *Hotels, restaurants et cabarets dans l'antiquite romaine* (Uppsala: Almqvist & Wiksells, 1957); N. K. Rauh, M. J. Dillon, and T. D. McClain, "Ochlos nautikos: leisure culture and underclass discontent in the Roman maritime world," *MAAR* (2008), 228.

87 *IG* 14.24; *CIL* IV, 8442; Rauh, Dillon and McClain, "Ochlos nautikos," 228.

88 *ISIS* 133; Krug (1993), 106; Kampen 69–72.

89 *CIL* II, 497: *uxori incomparabili medicae optimae mulieri sanctissimae.*

90 *CIL* VIII, 24679.

91 Kampen 109; there are over sixty examples in *CIL* VI alone.

92 Joshel, "The body female," 69.

93 Strong, "Daughter and employee," 60–1.

5   Can you know a *meretrix* when you see one?

1 The more conservative positions in the current debate about the audience and characters of Roman erotic art are those of Italian art historians like Antonio Varone, Pietro Guzzo, and Vincenzo Ussani, who locate prostitutes inside otherwise elite residences and assume that all erotic paintings are connected either with prostitutes or slaves. John Clarke is the leading exponent of the alternative theory; he argues that erotic art in the first-century CE Roman world portrayed sex involving both elites and professional prostitutes, without particular concern about morality, shame, or differentials in social status. I have more sympathy generally for Clarke's perspective, but I retain some skepticism

about any visual erasure of significant power dynamics between husband and wife or master and slave: J. R. Clarke, *Looking at Lovemaking : Constructions of Sexuality in Roman Art, 100 BC–AD 250* (Berkeley: University of California Press, 1998), 169–77; A. Varone, *Erotica Pompeiana*, Rome: L'Erma di Bretschneider, 2001 145 and *Eroticism in Pompeii* (Los Angeles: J. Paul Getty Trust 2001); P. Guzzo and V. Ussani, *Veneris Figurae* (Naples: Soprintendenza Archeologica di Napoli e Caserta, 2003), 31.

2 See B. Andreae, "Stuckreliefs und Fresken der Farnesina," in W. Helbig and H. Spier (eds.), *Führer durch den offentlichen Sammlungen Roms* (Tübingen University Press, 1969), vol. III, 430–52; Otto Brendel, "The scope and temperament of erotic art in the Greco-Roman world," in T. Bowie and C. V. Christenson (eds.), *Studies in Erotic Art* (New York: Basic Books, 1970), 40–7; Molly Myerowitz, "The domestication of desire," in A. Richlin (ed.), *Pornography and Representation in Greece and Rome* (Oxford University Press, 1992), 139–42.

3 For this approach, see Andreae, "Stuckreliefs," 440; Guzzo and Ussani, *Veneris figurae*, 25–35; McGinn, *Economy*, 119, 157–66.

4 D. Williams, "Women on Athenian vases: problems of interpretation," in Cameron and Kluhrt (eds.), *Images of Women in Antiquity*, 99; R. F. Sutton, Jr., "Pornography and persuasion on Attic pottery," in Richlin (ed.), *Pornography*, 19. While prostitutes at Greek symposia can readily be identified as to profession, there are some representations in Greek art that offer a more ambiguous woman who might be either a *hetaira* or a *gyne* (wife). One such controversial example is Berlin F 2269, an Attic red-figure kylix, which shows a youth and a girl of uncertain social status kissing: J. D. Beazley, *Attic Red-Figure Vases in American Museums* (Havard University Press, 1918), and *Athenian Red-Figure Vase-Painters* (Oxford: Clarendon Press, 1963), 2.177.1.

5 Myerowitz, "Domestication of desire," 151.

6 This lack is primarily due to the paucity of clearly identified brothels, further discussed in Chapter 6.

7 D. Fredrick, "Beyond the atrium to Ariadne: erotic painting and visual pleasure in the Roman house," *Classical Antiquity*, 14.2 (1995), 268–9.

8 Richlin, *The Garden of Priapus*, 63; Johns (2002), 92; P. P. de Abreu Funari, "Apotropaic symbolism at Pompeii: a reading of the graffiti evidence," *Revista de História*, 132 (1995), 9–17.

9 Guzzo and Ussani, *Veneris figurae*, 25–35.

10 Guzzo and Ussani do not fully follow the work of Andrew Wallace-Hadrill and Bettina Bergmann regarding wall painting as a means of drawing such distinctions: A. Wallace-Hadrill, *Houses and Society in Pompeii and Herculaneum* (Princeton University Press, 1994), 17–37; B. Bergmann and I. Victoria, "The Roman house as memory theater: the House of the Tragic Poet in Pompeii," *Art Bulletin* 76.2 (1994), 225–56.

11 Clarke, *Lovemaking*, 97–101.

12 L. Jacobelli, *Le pitture erotiche delle Terme Suburbane a Pompei* (Rome: L'Erma di Bretschneider, 1995), 99–102.

13 Clarke, *Lovemaking*, 196–240.

14 McGinn, *Economy*, 211.

15 For recent work on this subject beyond Wallace-Hadrill, see P. Allison, "How do we identify the use of space in Roman housing?" in E. Moorman (ed.), *Functional and Spatial Analysis of Wall Painting* (Leiden: Stichting Babesch, 1995), 1–8; E. Leach, "Oecus on Ibycus: investigating the vocabulary of the Roman house," in S. E. Bon and R. Jones (eds.), *Sequence and Space in Pompeii* (Oxford University Press, 1997), 50–72; A. Riggsby, " 'Public' and 'private' in Roman culture: the case of the *cubiculum*," *JRA* 10 (1997), 36–56; P. Allison, "Using the material and written sources: turn of the millennium approaches to Roman domestic space," *AJA* 105 (2001), 181–208.

16 Wallace-Hadrill, *Houses*, 17–38.

17 Guzzo and Ussani, *Veneris figurae*, 29.

18 Fredrick, "Visual pleasure," 267–8. Women were certainly present in these public zones of the house; we find loom weights, for instance, within many atria. See R. Ling, *The Insula of the Menander at Pompeii* (Oxford: Clarendon Press, 1997), 49–51, 268. Any such distinctions are also problematized by a reliance on literary typologies popularized by elite male authors like Vitruvius and Varro: Allison, "Using the material and written sources," 196. For a thorough discussion of the current archaeological evidence used to gender or degender Roman domestic spaces, see P. Allison, "Characterizing Roman artifacts to investigate gendered practices in contexts without sexed bodies," *American Journal of Archaeology*, 119.1 (2015), 103–23.

19 Clarke, *Lovemaking*, 94.

20 *Ibid.* 103–7.

21 J. Pollini, "The Warren Cup: homoerotic love and symposial rhetoric in silver," *The Art Bulletin*, 81.1 (March 1999), 39–40; Clarke, *Lovemaking*, 161 ff.

22 Petronius, *Satyricon* 26.4–5.

23 Myerowitz, "Domestication of desire," 145; C. Johns, *Sex or Symbol* (London: British Museum Publications, 1982), 116; J. Boardman and E. LaRocca, *Eros in Greece* (London: John Murray, 1978), 162–3.

24 Clarke, *Lovemaking*, figs. 29–34.

25 In one panel, the woman wears a breast band; she is completely nude in the other two.

26 Clarke, *Lovemaking*, 169–77.

27 Varone, *Erotica Pompeiana*, 145; Guzzo and Ussani, *Veneris figurae*, 31.

28 McGinn, *Economy*, 162–6.

29 Livy 39.9.

30 E.g. Andreae, "Farnesina," 3:440.

31 Clarke, *Lovemaking*, 103.

32 Sulpicia (1) 6.6; M. Santirocco, "Sulpicia reconsidered," 229–39; Milnor, "Sulpicia's (corpo)reality," 259–82.

33 Sulpicia 2, fragment; C. Merriam, "The other Sulpicia", *The Classical World* (1991), 303–5; A. Richlin, "Sulpicia the satirist," *The Classical World* (1992), 125–40.

34   Martial 10.35.
35   *Ibid.* 38.6–7: *O quae proelia, quas pugnas utrimque pugnas | felix lectulus et lucerna vidit.*
36   Ausonius, *Nuptial Cento.*
37   Sidonius Apollinaris, *Poems* 9.261–2;, Fulgentius, *Mythologies* 1.23. Ideologies of Roman marriage as romantic and sexually fulfilling are still somewhat controversial. I follow primarily Suzanne Dixon here, rather than the harsher verdicts of R. A. M. Lyne, K. R. Bradley, or A. Richlin: S. Dixon, *Reading Roman Women* (London: Duckworth, 2001), 36–44; R. A. M. Lyne, *The Latin Love Poets from Catullus to Horace* (Oxford: Clarendon Press, 1980), 8–13; K. R. Bradley, "Ideals of marriage in Suetonius' *Caesares*," *Rivista storica dell'antichità*, 15 (1985), 86–91,"; Richlin, *The Garden of Priapus*, 69.
38   Catullus 6.169–71.
39   Propertius 4.3.29–32.
40   Plutarch, *Dialogue on Love* 2. While Plutarch is, of course, Greek, he writes during the height of Roman power and influence in Greece, in the second century CE, and his ideas about sexuality and gender relations are decidedly not those of classical Athens.
41   Pliny, *Epistulae* 7.24.
42   Juvenal 6; Catullus 11.17–20.
43   Dixon, *Reading Roman Women*, 38.
44   *Ibid.* 35; *contra* J. P. Sullivan, *Martial, the Unexpected Classic: A Literary and Historical Study* (Cambridge Unversity Press, 1991), 198–200.
45   Varone, *Erotica Pompeiana*, 164.
46   J. Franklin, Jr., 'Pantomimists at Pompeii: Actius Anicetus and his troupe,' *AJP* 108.1 (Spring 1987), 103.
47   Ovid, *Tristia* 2.521–8: see epigraph to Chapter 5. Suetonius claims that Tiberius' palace on Capri "had bedrooms furnished with the most salacious paintings and sculptures, as well as an erotic library, in case a performer should need an illustration of what was required." Suetonius, *Tiberius* 43–4.
48   Clement of Alexandria, *Protreptikos* 4.53P; Myerowitz, "Domestication of desire," 150.
49   Propertius 2.6.27–30.
50   Seneca, *Ep.* 95.21.
51   Myerowitz, "Domestication of desire," 154: "What we see in Roman erotic paintings in the context of domestic interiors is the reflection of a sexual reality that includes two participants and objectifies both."
52   E.g. Musonius Rufus, *On Sexual Indulgence*, arguing that the purpose of sex should only be procreation, and Plutarch, *Advice to the Bride and Groom* 11.104: "A wife is for *dignitas*, not sensuality." See A. Rousselle, *Porneia* (Oxford: Basil Blackwell, 1988). Rousselle notably ignores most non-prescriptive genres of Latin literature and any visual evidence in her argument linking Christian ideas of chastity to earlier Roman values. See also Foucault, *The History of Sexuality* ; S. Goldhill, *Foucault's Virginity: Ancient Erotic Fiction and the History of Sexuality* (Cambridge University Press, 1995), 46–111. Treggiari's chapter on sexual relations

largely deals with adultery, rather than marital sex, although she argues, "a woman who pleases herself in love [like Clodia Metelli] is behaving like the most blatant kind of *meretrix*": Treggiari, *Iusti Coniuges*, 309. At the same time, Treggiari acknowledges that matrons are allowed sensuality, if tightly focused, husband-directed sensuality, although they are supposed to be passive recipients rather than active pursuers (p. 315).

53 Ulpian, *Digest* 47.10.15.5: *Si quis virgines appellasset, si tamen ancillari veste vestitas, minus peccare videtur: multo minus, si meretricia veste feminae, non matrum familiarum vestitae fuissent. si igitur non matronali habitu femina fuerit et quis eam appellavit vel ei comitem abduxit, iniuriarum tenetur.* Although Ulpian thus draws clear distinctions between the garments of a maid, a maiden, and a *materfamilias*, removing blame from someone who accosts a matron or maiden dressed like a prostitute, there is no trace of such easy identifications in the visual record, and this may well represent a legal oversimplification of reality.

54 Olson, "Matrona and whore," 387–420; Livy 2.13. See Chapter 1 for a further discussion of Cloelia.

55 Clarke, *Lovemaking*, 205; S. Levin-Richardson, "Roman provocations: interactions with decorated spaces in early imperial Rome and Pompeii," Diss. (Stanford University, 2009), 137–42.

56 Levin-Richardson, "Roman provocations," 139–40.

57 Clarke, *Lovemaking*, 202. Unfortunately, this particular panel is in too poor a condition to photograph adequately at this point, due to the general degradation of the images in the *lupanar*. Clarke's version, fig. 83, shows little detail, and we must rely on earlier descriptions to get any sense of the painting.

58 Olson, "Matrona and whore," 387–420.

59 For instance, Cicero accuses Publius Clodius Pulcher of wearing a *strophium* when he dressed in drag to infiltrate the rites of the Bona Dea, and Catullus describes Ariadne as abandoning her breast band in her grief for Theseus, but neither of these citations particularly implies that the *strophium* was anything but a normal undergarment for women: Cicero, *Har. Resp.* 21.44; Catullus 64.65. See also K. Olson, "Roman underwear revisited," *The Classical World* (2003), 201–10.

60 S. Akok, *Ephesus and Environs* (Çankaya, Ankara: Ekonomist Yaynevi Tic. Ltd., 2001).

61 Fredrick, "Beyond the atrium," 276–7.

62 Clarke, *Lovemaking*, 108.

63 *Ibid.* 109, 116.

64 For well-known representations and discussions of fellatio in Roman art, see P. Wuilleumier and A. Audin, *Les Médaillons d'applique gallo romains de la vallée du Rhône* (Paris, 1952), 125 no. 217, 128 fig. 217, 127 no. 218, 128 fig. 218, 127 no. 219, 129 fig. 219; G. Vorberg, *Glossarium Eroticum* (Rome: L'Erma, 1965), 184–6; D. M. Bailey, *Roman Lamps Made in Italy* (London: Cambridge University Press, 1980), 64; A. Desbat, *Vases à médaillons d'applique des fouilles récentes de Lyon* (Lyon: Figlina, 1982), 98 E 002, 110 E 026; Johns, *Sex or Symbol*, 150 fig. 122; Clarke, *Lovemaking*, 220.

65 Martial 11.61.

66   Clarke, *Lovemaking*, 230.
67   A. F. Stewart, "Reflections," in Kampen and Bergmann (eds.), *Sexuality in Ancient Art*, 148.
68   *Ibid.*
69   The tavern is located in Regio VI.14.36. For an alternative interpretation, see J. R. Clarke, *Art in the Lives of Ordinary Romans* (Berkeley: University of California Press, 2003), 161–8.
70   The cartoon bubbles above each panel would have been meaningless to the vast illiterate majority of Pompeian citizens. Without the words of criticism and complaint, the images would appear to indicate "Kissing! Drinking! Dicing! No Fighting!" Even for illiterate viewers, however, the tavernkeeper would still communicate the most important message of keeping fistfights out of the tavern.
71   *SALVI FILIA*, the daughter of Salvius, is invoked in a graffito in the first and largest room on the left in the *lupanar*: *CIL* IV, 2173; Myrtale's name appears twice in the first room on the right: *CIL* IV, 2268 and 2271. While the possibility of competition between the two women remains hypothetical, Salvia is the only woman identified as someone's daughter in the *lupanar* or indeed in any Pompeian prostitute graffito. Since the nearby tavern is the tavern of Salvius, a connection seems very plausible.
72   Clarke, *Ordinary Romans* 167.
73   The painting was originally located at Regio I.6.2 in Pompeii and dates to the first century CE. It is now in the Naples Museum.
74   G. S. Aldrete, *Gestures and Acclamations in Ancient Rome* (Baltimore and London: Johns Hopkins University Press, 1999), 65.
75   D'Ambra, "The calculus of Venus," 219–32; Davies, "Portrait statues," 208–10.
76   E. d'Ambra, "The cult of virtues," 392–400.
77   Riess, "Rari exempli femina," 495; D. Kleiner, "Second-century mythological portraiture: Mars and Venus," *Latomus*, 40 (1981), 512–44.
78   D'Ambra, "The cult of virtues," 398.
79   *Ibid.*

6   Prostitutes and matrons in the urban landscape

1   *Saepe supercilii nudas matrona seueri et Veneris stantis ad genus omne uidet. Corpora Vestales oculi meretricia cernunt nec domino poenae res ea causa fuit.*
2   E. Fantham, *Ovid Fasti: Book IV (Commentary)* (Cambridge University Press, 1998), 255–6.
3   J. Lewis and E. Maticka-Tyndale, *Escort services in a border town* (Health Canada CDC, 2000), 13; M. Pruitt, and A. C. Krull. "*Escort advertisements and male patronage of prostitutes,*" *Deviant Behavior*, 32.1 (2010), 38–63.
4   McGinn, *Economy*, 47–9. McGinn suggests that prostitutes' work-patterns in both the ancient and modern world range from a barely living wage corresponding to a large number of sex acts per day to a highly remunerative,

relatively relaxed lifestyle, as indeed one might expect in such a variable, unregulated profession.

5 See Laurence, *Roman Pompeii*, 73–85; Wallace-Hadrill, "Public honour," 51–62; Stumpp, *Prostitution*, 60–77; McGinn, *Economy*, 182–239.

6 Laurence, *Roman Pompeii*, 74; Wallace-Hadrill, "Public honour," 51.

7 McGinn, *Economy*, 182–239; Rauh, Dillon, and McClain, "Ochlos nautikos," 218.

8 Juvenal 6. 7.4; Petronius, *Satyricon* 118–32; Seneca, *Cont.* 1.2.4, etc. These texts and others are discussed in depth later in the chapter.

9 Typical terms for prostitute in Latin are either generally derogatory or descriptive of the life of a professional woman: *meretrix*, a woman who earns; *lupa*, a bitch; *scortum*, a skin or hide. See Adams, "Words for 'prostitute'," 321–58.

10 D. Montserrat, *Sex and Society in Graeco-Roman Egypt* (New York: Columbia University Press, 1996), 117.

11 Ulpian, *Digest* 3.2.4.2.

12 For the Vettii inscription, see *CIL* IV, 4592. Clarke, *Lovemaking*, 169–77; Varone, *Erotica pompeiana*, 133–4.

13 McGinn, *Economy*, 182–239.

14 Wallace-Hadrill, "Public honour," 52.

15 Clarke, *Lovemaking*, 147. This point is more fully discussed in Chapter 4.

16 *Ibid.* 101.

17 McGinn, *Economy*, 201.

18 McGinn, *Economy*, 39.

19 Wallace-Hadrill, *Houses and Society*, 68–9.

20 McGinn, *Economy*, 220–30.

21 McGinn, *Economy*, map 5. McGinn uses a fairly inclusive standard for brothels on this map and collects the data of various other scholars, including Wallace-Hadrill and Laurence.

22 Wallace-Hadrill, "Public honour," 51; McGinn, *Economy*, map 8.

23 Laurence, *Roman Pompeii*, map 3.1.

24 Clarke, *Lovemaking*, 196. 25 The atrium couches may have been designed for three people rather than two, however.

25 A carbonized dish of green beans and onions was found in the upper story of this building, suggesting that food consumption, if not preparation, took place there: M. Borgongino, *Archeobotanica: reperti vegetali da Pompei e dal territorio vesuviano* (Rome: L'Erma di Bretschneider, 2006); P. G. Guzzo and V. S. Ussani, *Ex corpore lucrum facere: la prostituzione nell'antica Pompei* (Rome: L'Erma di Bretschneider, 2009).

26 Clarke, *Lovemaking*, 196; McGinn, *Economy*, 232; the upper floor of the *lupanar* may not have been used for sex work at all: McGinn, "Sex and the city," in P. Erdkamp (ed.), *The Cambridge Companion to Ancient Rome* (Cambridge University Press, 2013) 377; McGinn, "Sorting out prostitution in Pompeii," in Guzzo and Ussani, *Ex corpore lucrum facere*, ch. 3.

27 S. Levin-Richardson, *Roman Provocations*, appendix.

28 The only other building after the graffito on that street is the Library of Celsus. As images of Tyche were frequently associated with places of public

entertainment like taverns and brothels (cf. Scythopolis), the "advertise-ment" certainly renders it more rather than less likely that this message refers to the brothel rather than to the Library. The Via Curetes graffito, given the foot, appears to indicate a forward direction. The foot itself has the elon-gated second and third toes commonly associated with beauty in the Greek world: this is the so-called "Greek foot," which apparently occurs naturally in about 18 percent of the population. J. Park Harrison claimed that, in fact, the elongated toes were much more common among Italians than Greeks, and that the appearance of the elongated toe in ancient statuary may have been an addition of Roman copyists. It would be an unreasonable leap to assume that the model for the Ephesus foot was necessarily an Italian man or woman, however. J. P. Harrison, "On the relative length of the first three toes of the human foot," *The Journal of the Anthropological Institute of Great Britain and Ireland*, 13 (1884), 258–69.) The heart with many dots in it, however, may not necessarily be related to the foot, nor are hearts a standard piece of iconography for love or sex in the ancient world. The representation of Tyche appears to be in a different hand, as it is much lighter, and the head of Tyche is about the same size as the foot. There is a rectangle at the bot-tom of the bust of Tyche that may once have contained a written inscription, but no discernible letters remain. However, the general imagery of head and chest on top of an inscribed rectangle suggest that this may be a drawing of a portrait bust, possibly one of Tyche that was originally located nearby the cobblestone in question, or, for that matter, next to the supposed brothel. The three surviving pieces of the image – heart, foot, and Tyche – may be a case of multiple graffiti on the same cobblestone, created by different writers who wished to communicate distinct messages. We may be misinterpreting the stone as a unified message because of the eventual conglomeration of graffiti. As a graffito on the surface of a major street, it was clearly intended for public display and prominence. At the same time, it does not definitely indicate a particular building, and may have stood in front of a temporary stall that has been lost in the archaeological record.

29 W. Jobst, "Das 'offentliche Freudenhaus' in Ephesos," *Jh.* 51 (1976–77), 63; D. Boulasikis, "Das sogenannte Freudenhaus zu Ephesos," *Jahreshefte of the Austrian Archaeological Institute in Vienna*, 72 (2003), 29–40.

30 Jobst, "Das 'offentliche Freudenhaus,' "63; McGinn, *Economy*, 225. These artworks include a *triclinium* mosaic of the four seasons, thin marble tiling in the hallways and courtyard of that section, and, on the bottom of the small ovoid pool, a mosaic medallion in the centre depicting three women drink-ing, a servant standing, a mouse nibbling crumbs and a cat. However, if this building was a residential villa, some major and difficult questions immedi-ately arise. What elite family would choose to live in such a public and noisy location, far away from the other residential areas of Ephesus? Why would one of the major entrances have such a narrow and twisting passageway? Unfortunately, there are no published images available of the "banqueting" mosaic in the bath, nor is it clear what the social status of the women repre-sented may be. One alternative possibility that might explain the luxury of the mosaics and furnishings is that the Curetes section may have served as

the residential area for the *leno* or *lena*, or these rooms might have been used for entertainments or dinner parties, or rented out to a wealthy customer. It is also possible that the two sections were more clearly separated and formed two separate, largely unrelated buildings.

31 While the Ephesus tour guides unanimously assert that there is an underground tunnel between the Library of Celsus and the brothel, the excavation records offer neither positive nor negative confirmation of this urban legend.

32 DeFelice, *Roman Hospitality*, 34.

33 J.Th. Bakker, "Casa delle Volte Dipinte," in *Living and Working with the Gods* (Amsterdam: Brill, 1994), 1. At least one lock, likely for the outer door onto the alleyway, has also been found in the Pompeii *lupanar*: Levin-Richardson, *Roman Provocations*, 140.

34 E.g. Apuleius, *Metamorphoses* 1.8, in which witches must magically break a variety of locks and bolts in order to attack Lucius inside his hotel room.

35 The statue was found in a 1.2 by 1 meter (4 by 3 feet) circular water basin in one of the two main rooms in the "brothel" section. Such a statue of Priapus is described as the central ornament of a brothel in the anonymous Greek romance novel *Apollonius, King of Tyre* (33).

36 A. Golfetto, *Dougga: Die Geschichte einer Stadt im Schatten Karthagos* (Basle: Raggi Verlag Basel, 1961), 20.

37 The site also possesses the image of a phallus and testicles below two circular discs, generally interpreted as breasts, next to the main door. This image is somewhat more graphic than the usual apotropaic phalli and thus may well be related to the professional purpose of the building: Archäologisches Institut Freiburg, "Das Thugga Projekt: Ausgrabungen des Institut National du Patrimoine in Tunis und des Archäologischen Instituts der Universität Freiburg im Breisgau" (1995–2000). www.archaeologie.uni-freiburg.de/thugga. Although not fully published, this website records the progress of current excavations on the site.

38 R. Bar-Nathan, and G. Mazor, "City center (south) and Tel Iztabba area: excavations of the antiquities Authority Expedition, the Bet She'an Excavation Project (1989–1991), *Excavations and Surveys in Israel*, 11 (1993), 44.

39 C. Dauphin, "Brothels, baths, and babes: prostitution in the Byzantine Holy Land," *Classics Ireland*, 3.1–9 (1996), 3.

40 Dauphin, "Brothels," 3.

41 Y. Tsafrir, and G. Foerster, "Urbanism at Scythopolis-Bet Shean in the fourth to seventh centuries," *Dumbarton Oaks Papers* (1997), 121.

42 *Ibid.*

43 *Ibid.*

44 Dauphin, "Brothels," 3.

45 Bakker, *Living and Working*, 98.

46 As at Dougga, there are signs of later repairs in the third century, creating more small rooms. There is also both an internal and external staircase, suggesting that the space may have been divided among owners or, in any case, that there were reasons for a private exit from the second floor of the building: *ibid.* 98.

47 J. Th. Bakker, work in progress: www.ostia-antica.org/regio1/13/13-6.htm
48 Catullus 37.1 ff.; Plautus, *Curculio* 481; Propertius 4.2.
49 Catullus 55.1 ff.
50 Laurence, *Roman Pompeii*, 74.
51 See Plautus, *Cistellaria*, 23–37: "When you see those highborn ladies, the married women of the upper class (gnatas summatis matronas), how they perform friendship and network with each other socially...these women flatter people of our walk of life (ita nostro ordino palam blandiuntur) to their faces, but in secret, if there's ever an opportunity, they pour cold water over us on the sly. They say that we have affairs with their husbands, they claim that we're their mistresses, and they try to put us down (eunt depressum). Because we're freedwomen, I and your mother, we were both prostitutes." This comic scene certainly does not imply a lack of contract between *matronae* and *meretrices*, even if some tension and disdain were likely involved.
52 Ulpian, *Digest* 47.10.10.15.
53 *Salax taberna vosque contubernales, | a pilleatis nona fratribus pila, | solis putatis esse mentulae vobis, solis licet, | quidquid est puellarum confutuere | et putere ceteros hircos?*
54 Plautus, *Curculio* 481–2. *Pone aedem Castoris, ibi sunt subito quibus credas male. In Tusco vico, ibi sunt homines qui ipsi sese venditant.*
55 V. Vanoyeke, *La Prostitution en Grèce et à Rome* (Paris: Belles Lettres, 1990), 71–2; K. O'Neill, "Propertius 4.2: Slumming with Vertumnus?" *American Journal of Philology*, 121.2 (2000), 264; Persius 5.32; Martial 2.17, 6.66.1–2, 9.61.3, 9.78.11; *Priap.* 40.1; Porphyrio 1.2.94. Violane Vanoyeke adds the nearby Vicus Turarius and the Vicus Jugarius as "rues chaudes": Vanoyeke, *Prostitution*, 71.
56 Horace, *Ep.* 1.20.1–13.
57 O'Neill, "Propertius 4.2," 264.
58 Catullus 55; see Chapter 5 for more detail on the temple of Venus Erycina.
59 Such exclusion was probably largely due to the Christian reaction against open sexual promiscuity. The second-century BCE placement of the temple of Venus Erycina by the Colline Gate outside the *pomerium* is discussed in Chapter 7.
60 For more detailed comparisons between prostitutes, actors, and gladiators, see Edwards, "Unspeakable Professions," in Hallett and Skinner (eds.), *Roman Sexualities* (1997), 81.
61 McGinn, *Economy*, map 5.
62 A. Glazebrook, "Porneion: prostitution in Athenian civic space," in Glazebrook and M. M. Henry (eds.), *Greek Prostitutes in the Ancient Mediterranean 800 BCE–200 CE* (University of Wisconsin Press, 2011), 34–59; B. A. Ault, "Building Z in the Athenian Kerameikos: house, tavern, inn, brothel?", in A. Glazebrook and B. Tsakirgis (eds.), *Houses of Ill Repute* (Philadelphia: University of Pennsylvania Press, 2015).
63 Glazebrook, "Porneion," 47–8; Isaeus 6.19, 20; Xenophon, *Mem.* 2.2.4; Athenaeus 13.569e.
64 Rauh and McClain in Glazebrook, "Porneion," 154–5; *ibid.* 34.
65 K. Hausbeck and B. G. Brents, "McDonaldization of the sex industries: the business of sex," in G. Ritzer (ed.), *McDonaldization: The Reader* (Newbury Park: Pine Forge Press), 102–18; B. G. Brents, C. A. Jackson, and K.

Hausbeck. *The State of Sex: Tourism, Sex and Sin in the New American Heartland* (New York: Routledge, 2010).

66 Juvenal 6.127.

67 McGinn, *Economy*, 236.

68 Borgongino, *Archeobotanica*; Guzzo and Ussani, *Ex corpore lucrum facere*.

69 *sumere nocturnos meretrix Augusta cucullos* | *ausa Palatino et tegetem prae- ferre cubili* | *linquebat comite ancilla non amplius una* | *sed nigrum flauo crinem abscondente galero* | *intrauit calidum ueteri centone lupanar* | *et cel- lam uacuam atque suam; tunc nuda papillis* | *prostitit auratis titulum mentita Lyciscae* | *ostenditque tuum, generose Britannice, uentrem* | *et lassata uiris necdum satiata recessit* | *obscurisque genis turpis fumoque lucernae* | *foeda lupanaris tulit ad puluinar odorem.*

70 Seneca, *Quaestiones Naturales* 1.16.6.4.

71 C. Bruun, "Water for Roman brothels: Cicero *Cael.* 34," *Phoenix*, 51 (1997), 367.

72 Frontinus, *De aquaductu* 76.1–2.

73 P. Lond. V. 1877. Cf. Montserrat, *Sex and Society*, 125. Juvenal, Tertullian, and Paulus, as well as other sources, refer to *aquarioli*, or water-boys, who were attendants upon promiscuous women, usually although not ubiq- uitously professional prostitutes. This particular type of servant is not asso- ciated with residential villas or with any other type of entertainment activity. A specific water-related term for a slave connected with prostitution implies a strong link between prostitutes and ready access to water. Juvenal claims that the *aquariolus* is brought in to service women during rites of the Bona Dea: Juvenal 6.332. Tertullian groups *aquarioli* together with "pimps, and panders, assassins, poisoners, and sorcerers; soothsayers, too, diviners, and astrologers": Tertullian, *Apologeticus* 43. Paulus refers to *aquarioli* as sordid followers of *mulierum impudicarum*: Paulus, 22M; J. Butrica. "Using water 'unchastely': Cicero 'Pro Caelio'" 34 Again–Addendum,' (1 and 2) *Phoenix*, 53. 1/2; 3/4 (Spring/Summer 1999; Fall/Winter 1999), 136–9; 339.

74 Karras, *Common Women*, 35.

75 Ovid, *Amores* 3.7.

76 Martial 2.50.

77 Juvenal 6.131.

78 Levin-Richardson, *Roman Provocations*, 140.

79 Bar-Nathan, "City-center south," 43.

80 Tertullian, *Uxorem*, 2.6.1; cf. *Apologia* 35.4, *Idolatria* 15.

81 McGinn, *Economy*, 203.

82 Laurence, *Roman Pompeii*, 129.

83 F. Yegül, *Baths and Bathing in Classical Antiquity* (Cambridge: MIT Press, 1992), 32.

84 Suetonius, *Augustus* 65.1–4.

85 Gellius, *NA* 4.14.

86 Seneca, *Cont.* 2.7.8: "There wasn't a single *pudica* woman in his birthplace, and in the place where he made his money, because there wasn't a single woman who hadn't prostituted herself there" (*Illic ubi natus est nulla pudica erat, atque illic ubi negotiatus est nulla non prostituta erat*); Langlands, *Sexual Morality*, 278. See also Cassius Dio 58.2.5.

7 Pious prostitutes

1   Livy 29. 14; Ovid, *Fasti* 305–26; M. R. Salzman, "Cicero, the Megalenses and the defense of Caelius," *American Journal of Philology*, 103 (1982), 299–304; E. W. Leach, "Claudia Quinta (Pro Caelio 34) and an altar to Magna Mater," *Dictynna: Revue de poétique latine*, 4 (2007).

2   Livy 29.14.

3   K. Burns, "Cybele and her cult at Rome: national embarrassment or benevolent savior?" *Chronika*, 1 (2011), 33.

4   Staples, *Good Goddess*, 7–8.

5   The controversies surrounding the multitude of rituals on this date and the social status of their worshipers are discussed extensively later in this chapter, particularly with regard to the different accounts of Ovid in the *Fasti* and of Verrius Flaccus in the *Fasti Praenestini*. See Fantham, *Ovid: Fasti Book IV*, 116.

6   Plautus, *Cistellaria* 562.

7   See M. Beard, J. North, and S. Price, *Religions of Rome* (Cambridge: Harvard University Press 1998), vol. I, 79–98; or J. Scheid, "Graeco ritu: a typically Roman way of honoring the Gods," *Harvard Studies in Classical Philology*, 97 (1995), 15–31.

8   What little evidence we have about changing attitudes towards the religious role of prostitutes during the Empire comes mostly from later Christian writers like Augustine and Lactantius, as cited in the epigraph of this chapter. They do not generally distinguish between current practices of their time and earlier rites and are highly hostile in any case towards the perceived debauchery of pagan religious rituals. Apuleius, another major source on later Roman religious practices, does not address the role of prostitutes in religious worship, although the rites of Magna Mater are certainly highly sexualized: Apuleius, *Metamorphoses* 8.23–31.

9   For this approach, in the case of Locri, see H. Prückner, *Die Lokrischen Tonreliefs* (Mainz: Philipp von Zabern, 1968), 14; S. de Franciscis, *Stato e societa in Locri Epizefiri* (Naples: Libreria scientifica editrice, 1972), 152–3; M. Torelli, "Considerazioni sugli aspetti religiosi e cultuali," in D. Musti (ed.), *Le tavole di Locri* (Naples: Edizioni dell'Ateneo & Bizzarri,1977), 93–4; L. Woodbury, "The Gratitude of the Locrian Maiden: Pindar, *Pyth.*, 2.18–20," *TAPA* 108 (1978), 290–1; R. Strong, "*The Most Shameful Practice: Temple Prostitution in the Ancient Greek World*," *Los Angeles: UCLA*, 1997, 148–57. For other sites in Italy and Sicily, see E. Yamauchi, "Cultic prostitution," in H. A. Hoffner, *Orient and Occident* (Oxford University Press, 1973), 213–22; W. Fauth, "Sakrale Prostitution im vorderen Orient und im Mittelmeerraum," *JAC* 31 (1988), 73–82; A. La Regina, "Legge del popolo marrucino," in A. Campanelli and A. Faustoferri (eds.), *I luoghi degli dèi Sacro e natura nell'Abruzzo italic* (Chieti: Pescara, 1997), 62–3.

10 M. Roth, "Marriage, divorce, and the prostitute in ancient Mesopotamia," and S. Budin, "Sacred prostitution in the first person," in Faraone and McClure (eds.), *Prostitutes and Courtesans*, 234 and 813.

11 For skeptics about Greek and Italian sacred or temple prostitution, see S. Pembroke, "Femmes et enfants dans les foundations de Locres et de

Tarente," *Annales: Économies, sociétés, civilizations,* 25.5 (1970), 12–69; C. Sourvinou-Inwood, "The Votum of 477/6 BC and the foundation legend of Locri Epizephyrii," *CQ* 27 (1974), 186–98; M. Beard and J. Henderson, "With this body I thee worship: sacred prostitution in Antiquity," *Gender and History,* 9.3 (1998), 480–503; Stumpp, *Prostitution,* 137–48; J. M. Redfield, *The Locrian Maidens* (Princeton University Press, 2003), 411–16; S. Budin, *The Myth of Sacred Prostitution in Antiquity* (Cambridge University Press, 2008), *passim,* esp. 183–4.

12 Athenaeus, *Deipnosophistae* 13.3.

13 M. Torelli argues that the Ludovisi throne may come from Eryx itself, but this recent theory, although intriguing, is not yet widely accepted among scholars and is necessarily fairly speculative. M. Torelli, "Il 'Trono Ludovisi' da Erice all'Oriente," rep. in ΣΗΜΑΙΝΕΙΝ. *Significare. Scritti vari di ermeneutica archeologica* (2012), 463–70; A. Bottini, "Il Trono Ludovisi: una proposta di ricostruzione", *Eidola,* 6 (2009), 9–32.

14 B. Ashmole, "Locri Epizephyrii and the Ludovisi Throne," *JHS* 42.2 (1922), 248–53; Redfield, *The Locrian Maidens,* 332–4.

15 P. Zancani Montuoro, "Persefone e Afrodite sul mare," in *Essays in Memory of Karl Lehmann* (New York: Institute of Fine Arts, 1964), 395; Redfield, *Locrian Maidens,* 333.

16 Redfield, *Locrian Maidens,* 333–4; C. Sourvinou-Inwood, "The Boston relief and the religion of Locri Epizephyrii," *JHS* 94 (1974), 127.

17 The Ludovisi throne was found in Rome near the Gardens of Sallust, not far distant from the location of the temple of Venus Erycina: R. Schilling, *La Religion romaine de Vénus, depuis les origines jusqu'au temps d'Auguste* (Paris: E. de Boccard, 1955), 260. See also E. M. Steinby (ed.), "Erucina," V.114, *Lexicon Topographicum Urbis Romanae* (Rome: Edizioni Quasar, 1999–2000). Redfield offers an intriguing analysis of the Ludovisi and Boston thrones as two halves of the same monument, viewing the Boston reliefs as a Roman copy of the Locrian original. He interprets them as a general sculptural program linking sex, marriage, gender, and the afterlife but generally agrees with the parallel roles of wife/prostitute as expressed on the Ludovisi portion: Redfield, *Locrian Maidens,* 334–42.

18 W. J. Young, and Bernard Ashmole. 1968. "The Boston Relief and the Ludovisi Throne". *Boston Museum Bulletin* 66 (346). Museum of Fine Arts, Boston: 124–66.

19 Schilling, *Vénus,* 260.

20 K. Galinsky, *Aeneas, Sicily, and Rome* (Princeton University Press, 1969), 245–6.

21 Thucydides 6.2.3; Strabo 13.1.53. Thucydides and Strabo both identify Mount Eryx as originally belonging to the Sicilian tribe known as the Elymes; it is unknown whether a temple to any goddess existed during Elymian rule. Punic inscriptions mentioning Astarte at Mount Eryx, somewhat surprisingly, date from the third-second centuries BCE, even after the Roman conquest: S. Moscati, *The World of the Phoenicians* (London: Weidenfeld and Nicolson, 1968), 93.

22 On the top of the mountain, near the eastern edge of the old temple, there is a large, 6-meter diameter, bell-shaped plastered well or pool dating back

to antiquity, popularly known as "Aphrodite's well." There are remnants of small rooms from the Punic period, but their precise shape or use is unclear. Near the front of the temple, the remnants of a small Roman bath, including a *caldarium*, have been excavated: U. Zanotti-Bianco, "Archaeological discoveries in Magna Graecia and Sicily," *JHS* 59.2 (1939), 213–28.

23 This coin shows a tall mountain, surrounded by a wall and a gate with the letters "ERUC;" on the top of the mountain is a Greek tetrastyle temple with four columns. There is no sign of an associated building or any clear brothel on the mountain, but the coin establishes in any case the firm existence of a temple on the peak. The Emperor Claudius restored the temple of Venus on Eryx during his reign, because it had apparently fallen into disrepair. This suggests that its former fame and wealth may have eroded: Suetonius, *Claudius* 25.5.5.

24 In particular, he describes a wealthy freedwoman and probable prostitute who tried to defend herself in a lawsuit by claiming that she and all her slaves were the property of Venus: Cicero, *Divinatio in Caecilium* 55. In the Verrine orations, Cicero also mentions occasions of people leaving inheritances to the temple of Venus on Eryx, suggesting that it was a wealthy and well-known temple: Cicero, *Verr.* 2.1.27.14. Verres also appears to have had male servants of the temple, or *Venerii*, working for him; it is not clear whether these are male prostitutes or simply financial agents: Cicero, *Verr.* 2.92, 3.50, 3.61, 5.140–2.

25 Livy 22.9.10.

26 The cult was popular among slaves and freedpersons during the Imperial period: Plutarch, *De Fortuna Romanorum* 5.

27 Elaine Fantham suggests that the Romans were trying both to assimilate the Carthaginian population in Sicily and to honor the supposedly "Trojan" community of Segesta in western Sicily, which may have already venerated Venus Erycina as the mother of Aeneas: Fantham, *Ovid Fasti: Book IV*, 255.

28 E. Stehle, "Venus, Cybele, and the Sabine Women: the Roman construction of female sexuality," *Helios*, 16.2 (1989), 150; Steinby (ed.), "Erucina."

29 R. E. A. Palmer, *Rome and Carthage at Peace, Historia Einzelschriften*, 113. (Stuttgart: Franz Steiner, 1997), 67.

30 Livy 23.31.9.

31 Galinsky, *Aeneas*, 53. Galinsky emphasizes the aspect of fertility associated with these various goddesses.

32 Ovid, *Fasti* 4.155–160.

33 Livy 25.1.6–12: *Sed in publico etiam ac foro Capitolioque mulierum turba erat nec sacrificantium nec precantium deos patrio more.*

34 E. Orlin, "Why a second temple for Venus Erycina?" *Latomus*, 10 (2000), 75, 89.

35 Livy 40.34; Appian, *BC* 1.428; Strabo 6.2.5; C. Koch, "Studies on the history of the Roman Venus-worship," *Hermes*, 83.1 (1955), 28, 38. Fantham, "Women's participation in Roman cult," in G. Herbert-Brown (ed.), *Ovid's Fasti: Historial Readings at its Bimillennium* (Oxford University Press, 2002), 255, 272. Livy 30.38: "The Tiber rose so high that the Circus was flooded and arrangements were made to celebrate the Games of Apollo outside the Colline Gate at the temple of Venus Erucina."

36 Galinsky, *Aeneas*, 182–5.

37 *Ibid.*

38 Strabo 6.2.6.

39 Galinsky and Orlin argue the latter hypothesis, and the representation of the temple on Mount Eryx on the Considius coin does not fit the description of a shrine surrounded by a colonnade: Galinsky, *Aeneas*, 182–5; Orlin, "Why a second temple," 89.

40 Many other later temples in Rome were also necessarily outside the *pomerium*, so we should not put too much evidentiary weight upon this detail. However, there is a strong contrast with the central location of the first temple to Venus Erycina on the Capitoline.

41 *numina, volgares, Veneris celebrate, puellae: | multa professarum quaestibus apta Venus | poscite ture dato formam populique favorem, | poscite blanditias dignaque verba ioco … | templa frequentari Collinae proxima portae | nunc decet; a Siculo nomina colle tenent.*

42 Fantham argues that this must here refer to *meretrices*, noting that Ovid here also uses terms associated with prostitutes like *blanditias*, charming words, and the *"favor populi"*: Fantham, *Ovid Fasti Book IV*, 255–6.

43 M. Kötzle, *Das Standesfest der Dirnen ist wohl ein Ersatz fur die auf dem Eryx praktizierte, orientalische Tempelprostitution* (Frankfurt: Peter Lang, 1990), 22.

44 Ovid, *Remedia Amoris* 549–54.

45 Schilling, *Venus*, 262–3.

46 *Ibid.*; see also *IGUR*, V.114.

47 Suetonius, *Galba* 18.5.

48 *Rite deam colitis, Latiae matresque nurusque | et vos, quis vittae longaque vestis abest … | discite nunc, quare Fortunae tura Virili | detis eo, gelida qui locus umet aqua. | accipit ille locus posito velamine cunctas | et vitium nudi corporis omne videt; | ut tegat hoc celetque viros, Fortuna Virilis | praestat et hoc parvo ture rogata facit.*

49 Staples, *Good Goddess*, 65. The other major recent arguments on this topic, after the original statement of S. Pomeroy, *Goddesses*, 208–9, which separated the two cults into Fortuna of the Baths and the elite Venus Verticordia rite, are G. Herbert-Brown, *Ovid and the Fasti: An Historical Study* (Oxford: Clarendon Press. 1994), 93–4; McGinn, *Prostitution*, 25; Fantham, *Ovid: Fasti Book IV*, 115–20; Fantham, "Women's participation," 3–37.

50 Ovid, *Fasti* 4.139–49.

51 Macrobius. *Saturnalia* 1.12.15; Lydus, *De Mensibus* 4.65; C. Schultz, *Women's Religious Activity in the Roman Republic* (Raleigh: UNC Press, 2006), 202–3. Schultz claims that the cult was reserved for matrons, but while it was certainly intended to turn wives faithful, none of the ancient sources explicitly exclude non-matrons.

52 Valerius Maximus 8.15.12; Pliny, *NH* 7.180; Palmer, *Rome and Carthage*, 122–9.

53 *Frequenter mulieres supplicant Fortunae Virili; humiliores etiam in balineis quod in iis ea parte corporis utique viri nudantur qua feminarum gratia desideratur.*

54 Both Fantham and Degrassi are skeptical about the addition, although there may indeed be some missing words: Fantham, *Ovid: Fasti Book IV*, 116; A. Degrassi (ed.), *Inscriptiones Latinae Liberae Rei Publicae* (1963), 126–7.

55 McGinn follows Pomeroy's theory that the rituals of Fortuna Virilis and Venus Verticordia were kept separate, with the rites of Fortuna Virilis reserved for lower status women, especially prostitutes, and Venus Verticordia's worship set aside for matrons. However, Pomeroy's argument relies significantly on references to the festival of Venus Verticordia's creation by a group of elite matrons in the late third century BCE in order to turn women's hearts away from adultery, and on the mention of *humiliores* by Verrius Flaccus: Pliny, *NH* 7.120; Valerius Maximus 8.15.12.

56 Pomeroy, *Goddesses*, 208.

57 R. S. Kraemer, *Her Share of the Blessings* (New York: Oxford University Press, 1992), 212.

58 Fantham suggests that Ovid is reacting against "the bourgeois insistence on distinguishing honest women from elegiac mistresses, ladies of the night, or even simple working women. By addressing all the women together, with the same imperatives for each cult in turn, he can associate all women together in what may well have been practiced only by some of them": Fantham, "Women's participation," 37.

59 *Ibid.* 36, but see the third-century CE Gallic inscription *CIL* XIII, 1983, in which Pompeius Catussa the plasterer commemorates going to the baths with his wife. For further discussion, see Fagan, *Bathing in Public in the Roman World* (Ann Arbor: University of Michigan Press, 1999), 26.

60 Fantham, "Women's participation," 36.

61 *Humiliores* is not generally a term used specifically to distinguish prostitutes, as opposed to non-elite women in general, although non-elite women may generally have been suspected of *meretrix*-like behavior. See Chapter 4 for a further discussion of the relationship between the "whore" label and other Roman women of lower social status.

62 Ovid, *Fasti* 5.347–52; Fantham, *Ovid: Fasti Book IV*, 272.

63 Seneca, *Ep. Mor.* 97.8.

64 L. L. Otis, *Prostitution in Medieval Society: The History of an Urban Institution in Languedoc* (Chicago University Press, 1985), 71; J. Rossiaud, *Medieval Prostitution* (Oxford and New York: Blackwell, 1988), 68.

65 Verrius Flaccus, *Fasti Praenestini*, *CIL* I, 2.24: *Ludi Florae: Feriae ex S. C. quod eo di[e aedes] et Vestae in domu Imp. Caesaris Augu[sti Po]ntif. ma. dedicatast (sic) Quirinio et Valgio Cos. (u. c. 742). Eodem die aedis Florae, quae rebus florescendis praeest, dedicata est propter sterilitatem frucum [sic].* Pliny also focuses on the agricultural aspects of the festival: *NH* 18.286.

66 Lactantius, *Divinae Institutiones*, 1. 20.

67 Fantham, *Ovid: Fasti Book* IV, 273.

68 *Ibid.*

69 *Ibid.* 272.

70 T. P. Wiseman, "*Ovid and the Stage*," in G. Herbert-Brown (ed.), *Ovid's Fasti* (Oxford University Press, 2002), 297; cf. Plautus, *Casina* 1016–18, *Truculentus* 965–6, and Cicero, *De Finibus* 2.23.

71 Plautus, *Casina* 83–4: "She won't be guilty of any illicit sex (stuprum) in this Comedy at least. But by Hercules, just as soon as the play is over, if any one gives her silver, I bet she'll readily enter into matrimony with him, and not wait for good omens (ultro ibit nuptum, non manebit auspices)."

72 Edwards, "Unspeakable Professions," 81.

73 Plutarch, *Camillus* 33.

74 *Ibid.*

75 Macrobius, *Saturnalia* 11. As will be discussed later, the Matronalia also had an element of status inversion, in which mistresses feasted their female slaves.

76 C. Newlands "Transgressive acts: Ovid's treatment of the Ides of March," *Classical Philology*, 91.4 (October 1996), 322.

77 Ovid, *Fasti* 3.526.

78 *Ibid.* 3.676–96.

79 Newlands, "Transgressive Acts," 322.

80 M. Piranomonte, "Religion and magic at Rome: the fountain of Anna Perenna," and J. Blänsdorf, "Texts from the Fons Anna Perennae," in R. Gordon and F. Marco Simon (eds.), *Magical Practice in the Latin West* (2010), 191–214 and 215–44.

81 Staples, *Good Goddesses*, 66.

82 *Ibid.*

83 Valerius Flaccus, *Fasti Praenestini* 1.3.27: *illum Accam Larentiam, nobilissimum per id tempus scortum* ("that Acca Larentina, the most noble whore of the time").

84 Pomeroy, *Goddesses*, 217; R. E. Witt, *Isis in the Ancient World* (Ithaca: Cornell University Press, 1971); Kraemer, *Her Share of the Blessings*, ch. 6.

85 Epiphanius of Salamis, *Ancorata* 104; *FRA* 605, 33;.Witt, *Isis*, 85.

86 Pomeroy, *Goddesses*, 219.

87 Ovid, *Amores* 2.2.25.

88 Juvenal 6. 490.

89 Witt, *Isis*, 85. However, graffiti about prostitutes adorned many public walls throughout Pompeii and cannot be used as conclusive evidence for the location of nearby sex work, as noted in Chapters 5 and 6. To suggest a parallel, it would be ridiculous to assume that all gas-station bathrooms were part-time brothels, even if they contained names, phone numbers, and testimonials to the sexual prowess of certain women.

90 Although some of his theories are unsupported by sufficient evidence, the best analysis to date of Roman religious rituals centered on matrons is J. Gage, *Matronalia: essai sur les dévotions et les organisations cultuelles des femmes dans l'ancienne Rome* (Brussels: Latomus, 1963). *Univirae* were particularly honored in the cults of Patrician and Plebeian Chastity, which did not accept women who had been married multiple times, let alone prostitutes.

91 Schultz, *Women's Religious Activity*, 147.

92 Aulus Gellius, *NA* 4.3.3; Festus 248L.

93 *Fasti* 6.473–568.

94 Kraemer, *Her Share of the Blessings*, 53; McGinn, *Prostitution*, 24–5.

95 Juvenal 6.306–48. Given that Juvenal also claims that the nymphomaniacal worshipers, when they had run out of slaves, would "rape the donkeys," it seems highly questionable to take this accusation of debauchery at all seriously, *contra* Pomeroy, *Goddesses*, 210.

96 Flemming, "Quae corpore," 43.

97 McGinn, *Prostitution*, 24.

98 *Ibid.* 24–5.

8   The "whore" label in Western culture

1   "Because the whore was also a metaphor, commercial sex was transformed into a vehicle by which elites and middle classes articulated their social boundaries, problems, fears, agendas, and visions": Gilfoyle, "Prostitutes in history," 138–9; G. Hershatter, *Dangerous Pleasures: Prostitution and Modernity in Twentieth-Century Shanghai* (Berkeley: University of California Press, 1998), 4.

2   Hershatter, *Dangerous Pleasures* 4.

3   Bullough and Bullough, *Women and Prostitution*, 65–7; Harper, *From Shame to Sin*, 48–50, 220–2.

4   Procopius, *Secret History*, 9. St. Pelagia or Margaret of Antioch, the legendary fourth-century CE actress-prostitute who cross-dressed as a male hermit, is another example, but her biography is more strongly influenced by Christian attitudes towards sexuality than Theodora's, even though both lived during a time of Christian dominance. She is also less well attested, and the hagiographical tradition preserves almost no details about her life as a prostitute. See R. M. Karras, "Holy harlots: prostitute saints in medieval legend," *Journal of the History of Sexuality*, 1.1 (1990), 3–32.

5   Together with her husband Justinian, Theodora is also notable for promoting social works designed to lessen or eliminate prostitution in Constantinople; she sent prostitutes without families to a special Convent of Repentance on the banks of the Bosporus, for instance. This political program suggests that, at the least, she had a particular interest in prostitutes as a social group, even if she was not a former prostitute herself. See R. Browning, *Justinian and Theodora* (London: Thames and Hudson, 1971), 58–62; A. Cameron, *Procopius and the Sixth Century* (Berkeley: University of California Press, 1985), 91–102; Charles Pazdernik, "'Our Most Pious Consort Given Us by God'," *Classical Antiquity*, 13:2 (1994), 256; J. A. S. Evans, *The Empress Theodora: Partner of Justinian* (Austin: University of Texas Press, 2002), 4.

6   Procopius, *Secret History* 12; Horace, *Epode* 12.

7   Procopius, *On Buildings* 1.8–11.

8   John of Ephesus, *Ecclesiastical History* 17.1.188–9; *Codex Justinianus* 5.4.23.

9   Evans, *Theodora*, 3.

10 Procopius, *SH* 9; Pliny, *NH* 172.

11 Bullough and Bullough, *Women and Prostitution*, 120; P. Buc, "Italian hussies and German Matrons: Liutprand of Cremona on Dynastic Legitimacy," *Issues*, 46 (2013).

12 Karras, *Common Women*, 29–30.

13 *Ibid.* 132.

14 R. I. Moore, *The Formation of a Persecuting Society: Power and Deviance in Medieval Europe 950–1250* (Oxford University Press, 1987), 95.

15 A. Parent-Duchatelet, *La Prostitution à Paris au XIXe siècle* (Paris: Editions Du Seuil, 1836), 121; K. Kempadoo, "Prostitution and sex work studies," in P. Essed, D. T. Goldberg, and A. Kobayashi (eds.), *A Companion to Gender Studies* (Hoboken, NJ: John Wiley & Sons, 2009), 255.

16 M. Leeson and M. C. Lyons, *The Memoirs of Mrs Leeson: in Three Volumes* (Dublin: Lilliput Press, 1995), 5; J. Peakman, "Memoirs of women of pleasure: the whore biography," *Women's Writing*, 11.2 (2004), 163–84.

17 Leeson, *Memoirs*, 154–61.

18 *Ibid.* 168–9.

19 Parent-Duchatelet, *Prostitution à Paris*, 586. Shannon Bell argues that his assumptions simultaneously figure the prostitute and wife as same and different, permanently marked and yet socially mobile, and that this ambiguity strongly influences later studies of prostitution: Bell, *Reading, Writing*, 50.

20 While Nevada has legalized brothels, as have countries like the Netherlands, such legalized institutions of prostitution are still largely viewed as aberrational and disreputable by most Americans. Furthermore, women in the Nevada brothels have little choice as to client or type of act, and thus fall firmly in the lower categories of the possible prostitute hierarchy: Bell, *Reading, Writing*, 126–7. This interpretation has been recently disputed by Brents and Hausbeck, who offer evidence of a more independent, profitable, elite brothel industry in Nevada and the frequent mobility of women between the pornographic film industry and Nevada brothels: Brents, Jackson, and Hausbeck, *The State of Sex*.

21 Barbara, "Pleasure doing business," in *Social Text*, 37 (Winter 1993), 11–22.

22 G. Pheterson, *The Whore Stigma: Female Dishonor and Male Unworthiness* (The Hague: Dutch Ministry of Social Affairs and Employment, Emancipation Policy Co-ordination, 1986), 39.

23 New Zealand Occupational Safety and Health Administration, "Sex Industry," Fact Sheet 1 (2005).

24 Lewis and Maticka-Tyndale, "Escort services," 13.

25 Edlund and Korn, "A theory of prostitution," *Journal of Political Economy*, 110 (February 2002), 182.

26 L. Lillard *et al.*, "The market for sex: street prostitution in Los Angeles," unpublished paper (RAND Corporation, 1995).

27 "Limbaugh: "Student denied spot at contraception hearing says 'She must be paid to have sex, so she's a slut and a prostitute'." http://mediamatters.org/video/2012/02/29/limbaugh-student-denied-spot-at-contraception-h/186411 Retrieved 3 March 2012.

Conclusion: Liminal women

1 Richlin, "Not before homosexuality," 530–1.

2 Cicero, *Att.* 12.42.2. Specifically, Cicero sought to buy the very gardens that he had accused Clodia of using for her numerous liasions. He considered the gardens an ideal site for the tomb and shrine of his deceased daughter Tullia; Cicero apparently had no qualms about doing business with such a notorious woman. Marilyn Skinner describes Clodia as "self-sufficient" and notes that she was "a woman in enviable circumstances, blessed with money, living

in attractive surroundings, having the leisure to appreciate the charm of her environment" M. Skinner, "Clodia Metelli," 285. While Skinner's portrait is optimistic, Clodia did not measurably suffer from the invective hurled at her in the *Pro Caelio*, and she may perhaps have lived a more pleasant life than many virtuous *matronae*.

3 De Beauvoir emphasizes the social construction of gender and specifically the construction of the concept of femininity in relationship and opposition to masculinity: Simone de Beauvoir, *The Second Sex* (New York: Vintage, 1949), 4. Levi-Strauss's structuralist theory provides a model for understanding the literature about prostitutes in terms of binary pairs and patterns: C. Levi-Strauss, "The structural study of myth," *Journal of American Folklore*, 68 (1955), 428–44.

4 M. Rosaldo, "The use and abuse of anthropology: reflections on feminism and cross-cultural understanding," *Signs*, 5:3 (1980), 396–9; S. Ortner, "Is female to male as nature to culture?" in M. Rosaldo and L. Lamphere (eds.), *Woman, Culture and Society* (Stanford University Press 1974), 75.

5 All such absolute dichotomies have been further refined and elaborated upon in recent years, as the grey areas between such extremes, as well as the existence of societies which do not fit this pattern, were further explored: S. Ortner, *Making Gender: The Politics and Erotics of Culture* (Boston: Beacon Press, 1996); R. Lancaster and M. di Leonardo (eds.), *The Gender/Sexuality Reader* (New York: Routledge, 1997).

6 In "The sexual status of Vestal Virgins," 13, Mary Beard discusses in depth how Vestal Virgins are accorded various symbols and privileges of masculinity and achieve a permanently interstitial status. Naturally, they were given far more respect and official recognition than prostitutes, but both cases demonstrate the lack of a normal, female-defined place for unmarried women in Roman society. Her reconsideration of Vestal Virgins in 1995 argues that the ambiguous status of Vestals in and of itself assisted in the construction of gender identity for the Romans, rather than simply reflecting it. While considering many of the same questions about labels and social categories raised in this book, Beard reduces the possibilities of Roman female roles to virgin and *matrona*, neglecting the ways in which the *meretrix* similarly constructed and deconstructed the gender identity of women in Roman society: Beard, "Re-reading (Vestal) Virginity," 175.

7 Treggiari, *Roman Marriage*, 12, 262.

8 Langlands, *Sexual Morality*, 39.

9 Attitudes also varied greatly across the provinces of the Roman Empire: the Eastern Empire continued to uphold the tradition of the relatively elite *hetaira*, while prostitutes served as unofficial soldiers' wives at garrison towns ranging from Hadrian's Wall to Egypt. However, the limits of this book do not allow for any extended discussion on this matter. For soldiers' wives, see Phang, *The Marriage of Roman Soldiers*.

10 G. Williams, "Some aspects of Roman marriage ceremonies and ideals," *JRS* 48.1 (1958), 23; Treggiari, *Roman Marriage*, 84–5.

11 G. Highet, "The life of Juvenal," *TAPA* 68 (1937), 485–6.

12 S. Braund, "Juvenal – misogynist or misogamist?" *JRS* 82 (1992), 71–2. While Braund argues that Juvenal undercuts his own misogynist statements in satire 6 by highlighting the hypocrisy of the narrator, the accusations themselves still stem from general anxiety about the power and unorthodox behavior of women in Roman society.

13 Eloise Harper, "Clinton doesn't want a one-night stand," December 2, 2007: http://abcnews.go.com/blogs/politics/2007/12/clinton-doesnt-2/ Senator Clinton's husband's marital fidelity, of course, was a more problematic issue but apparently irrelevant to voters.

14 Treggiari, *Roman Marriage*, 83; Pliny, *NH* 35.147.

Appendix II: Women in the Hebrew Bible

1 Proverbs 7.10–13, 18–19.

2 Hosea 1.2.

3 Hosea 2.11–20. The parallels with Cicero's criticism of Clodia Metelli are striking.

4 Joshua 2.8–22; S. Ackerman, *Warrior, Dancer, Seductress, Queen: Women in Judges and Biblical Israel* (New York: Doubleday, 1998), 227–31.

5 P. Bird, *Missing Persons and Mistaken Identities: Women and Gender in Ancient Israel* (Minneapolis: Augsburg Fortress, 1997), 214.

6 *Ibid.* 216.

7 L. Bronner, *From Eve to Esther: Rabbinic Reconstructions of Biblical Women* (Louisville: Westminster John Knox Press, 1994), 147.

8 Bird, *Missing Persons*, 202–8.

9 Genesis 38.24–6.

10 G. C. Streete, *The Strange Woman: Power and Sex in the Bible* (Louisville: Westminster John Knox Press, 1997), 57–61, 103–6.

Bibliography

Abreu Funari, Pedro Paulo de. "Apotropaic symbolism at Pompeii: a reading of the graffiti evidence." *Revista de História*, 132 (1995): 9–17.

Ackerman, Susan. *Warrior, Dancer, Seductress, Queen: Women in Judges and Biblical Israel.* New York: Doubleday, 1998.

Acquaro, E., A. Filippi, and S. Medas. "La devozione dei naviganti. Il culto di Afrodite Ericina nel Mediterraneo." *Atti del convegno di Erice 27–28 novembre 2009, Lugano (2010).*

Adams, J. N. "Words for 'prostitute' in Latin." *Rheinisches Museum*, 126 (1983): 321–58.

Akok, S. *Ephesus and Environs.* Çankaya, Ankara: Ekonomist Yaynevi Tic. Ltd, 2001.

Aldrete, Gregory S. *Gestures and Acclamations in Ancient Rome.* Baltimore and London: Johns Hopkins University Press, 1999.

Alföldy, G. "Cleanders Sturz und die antike Überlieferung." *Die Krise des Römischen Reiches. Geschichte, Geschichtsschreibung und Geschichtsbetrachtung. Ausgewählte Beiträge* (1989): 81–126.

Allen, Pauline, Suzanne Dixon, and Barbara Garlick (eds.). *Stereotypes of Women in Power: Historical Perspectives and Revisionist Views.* Westport, Conn.: Greenwood Press, 1992.

Allison, Penelope M. "How do we identify the use of space in Roman housing?" in Eric Moormann (ed.), *Functional and Spatial Analysis of Wall Painting*, 1–8. Leiden: Stichting Babesch, 1997.

"Using the material and written sources: turn of the millennium approaches to Roman domestic space," *American Journal of Archaeology*, 105 (2001): 181–208.

Pompeian Households: An Analysis of Material Culture. UCLA Monograph 42. Los Angeles: Cotsen Institute of Archaeology, 2004.

"Characterizing Roman artifacts to investigate gendered practices in contexts without sexed bodies." *American Journal of* Archaeology, 119, no. 1 (2015): 103–23.

Ammerman, Rebecca Miller. "The naked standing goddess: a group of Archaic terracotta figurines from Paestum." *American Journal of Archaeology*, 95, no. 2 (April 1991): 203–30.

Anderson, R. Dean, P. J. Parsons, and R. G. M. Nisbet. "Elegiacs by Gallus from Qaṣr Ibrîm." *Journal of Roman Studies*, 69 (1979): 125–55.

Anderson, William S. *Barbarian Play: Plautus' Roman Comedy.* University of Toronto Press, 1993.

Andreae, Bernard. "Stuckreliefs und Fresken der Farnesina," in Wolfgang Helbig and Hermione Spier (eds.), *Führer durch den offentlichen Sammlungen Roms*, vol. III, 4th edition, 430–52. Tübingen University Press: 1969.

Archäologisches Institut Freiburg. "Das Thugga Projekt: Ausgrabungen des Institut National du Patrimoine in Tunis und des Archäologischen Instituts der Universität Freiburg im Breisgau." 1995–2000: available online: www.archaeologie .uni-freiburg.de/thugga.

Ashmole, Bernard. "Locri Epizephyrii and the Ludovisi Throne," *The Journal of Hellenic Studies*, 42, part 2 (1922): 248–53.

Ault, Bradley A. "Building Z in the Athenian Kerameikos: house, tavern, inn, brothel?" in A. Glazebrook and B. Tsakirgis (eds.), *Houses of Ill Repute*, 75–102. Philadelphia: University of Pennsylvania Press, 2015.

Austin, R. G. M. T. M. *Tulli Ciceronis Pro M. Caelio Oratio.* Oxford University Press, 1960.

Bagnall, Roger S. "The prostitute tax in Roman Egypt," *Bulletin of the American Society of Papyrologists*, 28 (1991): 5–12.

Bagnall, Roger S., and Raffaella Cribiore. *Women's Letters from Ancient Egypt, 300 BC–AD 800.* Ann Arbor: University of Michigan Press, 2006.

Bailey, D. M. *Roman Lamps Made in Italy: A Catalogue of the Lamps in the British Museum*, vol. II. London: Cambridge University Press, 1980.

Baird, Jennifer A. "On reading the material culture of ancient sexual labor," *Helios* 42, no. 1 (2015): 163–75.

Bakker, J. Th. *Living and Working with the Gods: Studies of Evidence for Private Religion and Its Material Environment in the City of Ostia.* Amsterdam: Brill, 1994.

Balsdon, J. P. V. D. *Roman Women: Their History and Habits.* Westport, Conn.: Greenwood Press, 1962.

Bamberger, Joan. "The myth of matriarchy: why men rule in primitive society." *Woman, Culture and Society* (1974): 263–80.

Barbara. "It's a pleasure doing business with you," Social Text 17 (1993): 11–22.

Barra Bagnasco, M., and F. Niutta. *Locri Epizefiri.* Florence: Sansoni, 1977.

Barrett, Anthony. *Livia: Frst Lady of Imperial Rome.* New Haven: Yale University Press, 2004.

Bar-Nathan, R., and G. Mazor. "City center (south) and Tel Iztabba area: excavations of the Antiquities Authority Expedition." The Bet She'an Excavation Project (1989–1991), *Excavations and Surveys in Israel*, 11 (1993).

Bassermann, L. *The Oldest Profession: A History of Prostitution.* New York: Stein and Day, 1968.

Bauman, R. *Women and Politics in Ancient Rome.* London: Routledge, 1992.

Beard, Mary. "The sexual status of Vestal Virgins." *Journal of Roman Studies*, 70 (1980): 12–27.

"Re-reading Vestal Virginity," in Hawley and Levick (eds.), *Women in Antiquity: New Assessments*, 166–77.

Beard, Mary, and John Henderson. "With this body I thee worship: sacred prostitution in antiquity." *Gender & History*, 9, no. 3 (1997): 480–503.

Beard, Mary, John North, and Simon Price. *Religions of Rome*, vols I–II. Cambridge: Harvard University Press, 1998.

Beauvoir, Simone de. *The Second Sex*. Translated by H. M. Parshley. New York: Vintage, 1949.

Beazley, John Davidson. *Attic Red-Figured Vases in American Museums*. Cambridge: Harvard University Press, 1918.

Athenian Red-Figure Vase-Painters. Oxford: Clarendon Press, 1963.

Bell, S. *Reading, Writing, and Rewriting the Prostitute Body*. Bloomington: Indiana University Press, 2004.

Bennett, Judith M. *History Matters: Patriarchy and the Challenge of Feminism*. Philadelphia: University of Pennsylvania Press, 2011.

Benz, Lore, Ekkehard Stärk, Gregor Vogt-Spira, and Eckard Lefèvre. *Plautus und die Tradition des Stegreifspiels: Festgabe fur Eckard Lefevre zum 60. Geburtstag*, vol. 75. Gunter Narr Verlag, 1995.

Bergmann, Bettina, and Victoria I. "The Roman house as memory theater: the House of the Tragic Poet in Pompeii." *Art Bulletin*, 76.2 (1994): 225–56.

Bernheimer, C. *Figures of Ill Repute: Representing Prostitution in Nineteenth-Century France*. Cambridge: Harvard University Press, 1989.

Bird, P. *Missing Persons and Mistaken Identities: Women and Gender in Ancient Israel*. Minneapolis: Augsburg Fortress, 1997.

Blänsdorf, Jürgen. "The Texts from the Fons Annae Perennae," in R. Gordon and F. Marco Simon (eds.), *Magical Practice in the Latin West: Papers from the International Conference held at the University of Zaragoza*, 168 (2010): 215–244.

Blomqvist, Karin. "From Olympias to Aretaphila: women in politics in Plutarch," in J Mossman (ed.), *Plutarch and His Intellectual World*, 73–98. Cardiff: Classical Press of Wales, 1997.

Bloomer, W. Martin. "Schooling in persona: imagination and subordination in Roman education." *Classical Antiquity* 16, no. 1 (1997): 57–78.

Boardman, John, and Eugenio La Rocca. *Eros in Greece*. London: J. Murray, 1978.

Boatwright, Mary T. "Women and gender in the Forum Romanum." *Transactions of the American Philological Association*, 141, no. 1 (2011): 105–41.

Bonner, Stanley Frederick. *Roman Declamation: In the Late Republic and Early Empire*. Berkeley: University of California Press, 1949.

Education in Ancient Rome: From the Elder Cato to the Younger Pliny. Berkeley: University of California Press, 1977.

Bonnet, C. *Astarté: dossier documentaire et perspectives historiques*. Rome: Consiglio nazionale delle ricerche, 1996.

Borgongino, M. *Archeobotanica: reperti vegetali da Pompei e dal territorio vesuviano*. Rome: L'Erma di Bretschneider, 2006.

Bottini, A. "Il Trono Ludovisi: una proposta di ricostruzione," *Eidola* 6 (2009): 9–32.

Boulasikis, D. "Das sogenannte Freudenhaus zu Ephesos." *Jahreshefte of the Austrian Archaeological Institute in Vienna*, 72 (2003): 29–40.

Boyd, Barbara Weiden. "Virtus effeminata and Sallust's Sempronia," *Transactions of the American Philological Association*, 117 (1987): 183–201.

Bradley, J. R. "The Elegies of Sulpicia: An introduction and commentary." *New England Classical Journal* (1995) 22.

Bradley, K. R. "Ideals of marriage in Suetonius' *Caesares*," *Rivista storica dell'antichità*, 15 (1985): 77–95.

Braund, Susanna H. "Juvenal – misogynist or misogamist?" *The Journal of Roman Studies*, 82 (1992): 71–86.

Brendel, Otto. "The scope and temperament of erotic art in the Greco-Roman world," in T. Bowie and C. V. Christenson (eds.), *Studies in Erotic Art, Studies in Sex and Society*. 40–7. New York: Basic Books, 1970.

Brennan, T. Corey. "Perceptions of women's power in the late Republic: Terentia, Fulvia, and the generation of 63 BCE," in James and Dillon (eds.), *A Companion to Women in the Ancient World*, 354–66.

Brents, B. G., C. Jackson, and K. Hausbeck. *The State of Sex: Tourism, Sex, and Sin in the New American Heartland*. New York: Routledge, 2010.

Bronner, L. *From Eve to Esther: Rabbinic Reconstructions of Biblical Women*. Louisville: Westminster John Knox Press, 1994.

Brown, Peter. "Plots and prostitutes in Greek New Comedy." *Leeds International Latin Seminar*, 6 (1990): 241–66.

Browning, Robert. *Justinian and Theodora*. London: Thames and Hudson, Ltd., 1971.

Bruun, Christer. "Water for Roman brothels: Cicero *Cael.* 34," *Phoenix*, 51 (1997): 364–73.

Buc, Philippe. "Itälian hussies and German matrons Liutprand of Cremona on dynastic legitimacy," *Issues*, 46 (2013).

Budin, Stephanie Lynn. "Pallakai, prostitutes, and prophetesses." *Classical Philology*, 98, no. 2 (2003): 148–59.

"Sacred prostitution in the first person," in Faraone and McClure (eds.), *Prostitutes and Courtesans in the Ancient World*, 77–92.

The Myth of Sacred Prostitution in Antiquity. Cambridge University Press, 2008.

Bullough, V. L. and B. Bullough. *Women and Prostitution: A Social History*. Buffalo: Prometheus Books, 1987.

Burford, E. J. and J. Wotton. *Private Vices, Public Virtues: Bawdry in London from Elizabethan Times to the Regency*. London: Robert Hale, 1995.

Burns, Krishni. "Cybele and her cult at Rome: national embarrassment or benevolent savior?" *Chronika*, 1 (2011): 33–7.

Butrica, James. "Using water 'unchastely': Cicero 'Pro Caelio' 34 again." *Phoenix*, 53, no. 1 (1999): 136–9.

"Using water 'unchastely': Cicero 'Pro Caelio' 34 Again–Addendum." *Phoenix*, 53, no. 1 (1999): 336.

Cameron, Alan. *The Last Pagans of Rome*. Oxford University Press, 2010.

Cameron, Averil. *Procopius and the Sixth Century*. Berkeley: University of California Press, 1985.

Cantarella, Eva. *Bisexuality in the Ancient World*. New Haven: Yale University Press, 1994.

Carpenter, B. J. *Re-thinking Prostitution: Feminism, Sex, and the Self*. New York: P. Lang, 2000.

Champlin, Edward. "Notes on the heirs of Commodus." *American Journal of Philology*, 100.2 (1979): 288–306.

Chastagnol, André. *Les Empereurs des IIe et IIIe siècles*. Paris: Éditions Robert Laffont, 1994.

Clark, G. (ed.). "Women in the ancient world," *Greece and Rome: New Surveys in the Classics*, no. 21 (1989).

Clarke, John R. "The décor of the House of Jupiter and Ganymede at Ostia Antica: private residence turned gay hotel?" in Elaine K. Gazda. (ed.), *Roman Art in the Private Sphere* 89–104. Ann Arbor: University of Michigan Press, 1991.

  Looking at Lovemaking: Constructions of Sexuality in Roman Art, 100 BC–AD 250. Berkeley: University of California Press, 1998.

  "Look who's laughing: humor in tavern painting as index of class and acculturation." *Memoirs of the American Academy in Rome* (1998): 27–48.

  Art in the Lives of Ordinary Romans: Visual Representation and Non-elite Viewers in Italy, 100 BC–AD 315. Berkeley: University of California Press, 2003.

  "Representations of the Cinaedus in Roman art: evidence of 'gay' subculture?" *Journal of Homosexuality*, 49, nos. 3–4 (2005): 271–98.

  Looking at Laughter: Humor, Power, and Transgression in Roman Visual Culture, 100 BC–AD 250. Berkeley: University of California Press, 2007.

Clover, Carol J. "Regardless of sex: men, women, and power in early northern Europe." *Representations*, 44 (Autumn 1993): 1–28.

Cohen, David. "The social context of adultery at Athens," in P. Carledge, P. Millett, and S. Todd (eds.), *Nomos: Essays in Athenian Law, Politics, and Society*, 147–65. Cambridge University Press 1990.

  "The Augustan law on adultery," in David Kertzer and Richard Saller (eds.), *The Family in Italy: from Antiquity to the Present*, 110–26. New Haven: Yale University Press, 1991.

Cohen, E. "An economic analysis of Athenian prostitution," in Faraone and McClure (eds.), *Prostitutes and Courtesans in the Ancient World*, 95–124.

Coleman, Kathleen. "Missio at Halicarnassus." *Harvard Studies in Classical Philology*, 100 (2000): 487–500.

Colonna, Giovanni. "Novità sui culti di Pyrgi," *Rendiconti della Pontificia accademia di archeologia* (1984–85): 57–88.

  (ed.). *Santuari d'Etruria*. Milan: 1985.

Comstock, M. B. and C. C. Vermeule. (1976) *Sculpture in Stone: The Greek, Roman, and Etruscan Collections of the Museum of Fine Arts, Boston*. Boston: MF, 1976.

Connolly, Joy. *The State of Speech: Rhetoric and Political Thought in Ancient Rome*. Princeton University Press, 2009.

Cooley, A. *The Epigraphic Landscape of Roman Italy*. London: Institute of Classical Studies School of Advanced Study, University of London, 2000.

Cooper, K. "Insinuations of womanly influence: an aspect of the Christianization of the Roman aristocracy." *The Journal of Roman Studies*, 82 (1992): 150–64.

Corbeill, Anthony. *Controlling Laughter: Political Humor in the Late Roman Republic*. Princeton University Press, 1996.

Corbin, Alain. *Women for Hire: Prostitution and Sexuality in France after 1850*. Translated by Alan Sheridan. Cambridge: Harvard University Press, 1990.

Costamagna, L. and C. Sabbione. *Una città in Magna Grecia: Locri Epizefiri*. Reggio Calabria: Laruffa Editore, 1990.

Courtney, E. *A Commentary on the Satires of Juvenal*. London: Athlone Press, 1980.

Crook, John Anthony. *Law and Life of Rome*. Ithaca: Cornell University Press, 1967.

Culham, Phyllis. "Ten years after Pomeroy: studies of the image and reality of women in antiquity," in Marilyn Skinner (ed.), "Rescuing Creusa: new methodological approaches to women in antiquity." *Helios*, 13, no. 2 (1987): 9–30.

Curran, Leo. "Ovid 'Amores' 1.10," *Phoenix*, 18, no. 4 (Winter 1964): 314–19.

Dalby, A. *Empire of Pleasures: Luxury and Indulgence in the Roman World*. New York: Routledge, 2000.

D'Ambra, Eve. "The cult of virtues and the funerary relief of Ulpia Epigone." *Latomus*, 48, no. 2 (1989): 392–400.

"The calculus of Venus: nude portraits of Roman matrons" in Kampen and Bergmann (eds.), *Sexuality in Ancient Art*, 219–32.

Dauphin, Claudine. "Brothels, baths, and babes: prostitution in the Byzantine Holy Land." *Classics Ireland*, 3 (1996): 1–9.

Davidson, James. *Courtesans and Fishcakes*. New York: St. Martin's Press, 1998.

Davies, Glenys. "Portrait statues as models for gender roles in Roman society." *Memoirs of the American Academy in Rome. Supplementary Volumes*, (2008): 207–220.

DeFelice, John. *Roman Hospitality: The Professional Women of Pompeii*. Marco Polo Monographs 6. Warren Center, PA: Shangri-La Publications, 2001.

Delia, Diana. "Fulvia reconsidered," in Pomeroy (ed.), *Women's History and Ancient History*.

Demand, Nancy. *Birth, Death, and Motherhood in Classical Greece*. Baltimore: Johns Hopkins University Press, 1994.

Desbat A. *Vases à médaillons d'applique des fouilles récentes de Lyon*. Lyon: Figlina, 1982.

Desmed, R. "L'Épitaphe d'Allia Potestas (CIL VI, 37965) et ses problèmes." *Revue belge de philologie et d'histoire*, 47 (1969): 584–85.

Diehl, Ernst, Jacques Moreau, and Henri Irénée Marrou (eds.) *Inscriptiones latinae christianae veteres*. Vol. 1. apud Weidmannos, 1967.

Dixon, Suzanne. "Polybius on Roman women and property." *The American Journal of Philology*, 106, no. 2 (1985): 147–70.

"Family finances: Tullia and Terentia," *Antichthon*, 18 (1984): 78–101.

"The marriage alliance in the Roman elite." *Journal of Family History*, 10: (1985): 353–75.

The Roman Mother. Norman: University of Oklahoma Press, 1988.

The Roman Family. London: John Hopkins University Press, 1992.

Reading Roman Women. London: Duckworth, 2001.

Duckworth, George E. *The Nature of Roman Comedy*. Princeton University Press, 1952.

Dutsch, D. *Feminine Discourse in Roman Comedy: On Echoes and Voices*. Oxford University Press, 2008.

Eck, W. "The emperor and his advisors," in A. Bowman, P. Garnsey and D. Rathbone (eds.), *Cambridge Ancient History*, vol. XI, 195–214. Cambridge University Press, 2000.

Edlund, Lena and Evelyn Korn. "A theory of prostitution." *Journal of Political Economy*, 110 (February 2002): 181–214.

Edmunds, Lowell. "Lucilius 730M: a scale of power." *Harvard Studies in Classical Philology*, 94 (1992): 217–25.

Edwards, Catherine. *The Politics of Immorality in Ancient Rome*. London: Routledge, 1993.

"Unspeakable professions: public performance and prostitution in Ancient Rome," in Hallett and Skinner (eds.), *Roman Sexualities*, 66–95.

Evans, Harry B. *Publica Carmina: Ovid's Books from Exile*. Lincoln: University of Nebraska Press, 1983.

Evans, J. A. S. *The Empress Theodora: Partner of Justinian*. Austin: University of Texas Press, 2002.

Evans, Jane DeRose. "Prostitutes in the Portico of Pompey? A reconsideration," *Transactions of the American Philological Association* 139, no. 1 (2009): 123–45.

Eyben, Emiel. *Restless Youth in Ancient Rome*. London: Routledge Press, 1993.

Fagan, Garret. *Bathing in Public in the Roman World*. Ann Arbor: University of Michigan Press, 1999.

Fantham, Elaine. *Comparative Studies in Republican Latin Imagery*. Toronto: Toronto University Press, 1972.

"Sex, status, and survival in Hellenistic Athens: a study of women in New Comedy." *The Phoenix* (1975): 44–74.

Ovid: Fasti Book IV. Cambridge University Press, 1998.

"Women's participation in Roman cult," in Geraldine Herbert-Brown (ed.), *Ovid's Fasti: Historical Readings at Its Bimillennium*, 197–217. Oxford University Press, 2002.

Fantham, Elaine, Helene P. Foley, Natalie B. Kampen, Sarah B. Pomeroy, and H. Alan Shapiro. *Women in the Classical World*. Oxford University Press, 1994.

Faraone, Christopher A., and Laura K. McClure (eds.), *Prostitutes and Courtesans in the Ancient World*. Madison: University of Wisconsin Press, 2006.

Fau, G. *L'Emancipation féminine à Rome*. Paris: Les Belles Lettres, 1978.

Fauth, W. "Sakrale Prostitution im vorderen Orient und im Mittelmeerraum." *Jahrbuch für Antike und Christentum* 31 (1988): 73–82.

Fear, A. T. "The dancing girls of Cadiz." *Greece & Rome*, 38 (1991): 75–9.

Ferrill, Arthur. "Augustus and his daughter: a modern myth," in Carl Deroux (ed.), *Studies in Latin Literature and Roman History, vol.* II, 332–46. Brussels: Latomus, 1980.

Finley, Moses I. "The silent women of Rome." *Horizon,* 7 (1965): 57–64.

Fischler, Susan. "Social stereotypes and historical analysis: the case of the imperial women at Rome," in L. Archer, S. Fischler, and M. Wyke (eds.), *Women in Ancient Societies: An Illusion of the Night.* London: Macmillan, 1995: 115–33.

Fitzgerald, William. *Slavery and the Roman Literary Imagination.* Cambridge University Press, 2000.

Flemming, Rebecca. "Quae corpore quaestum facit: the sexual economy of female prostitution in the Roman Empire." *The Journal of Roman Studies,* 89 (1999): 38–61.

Flory, Marleen B. "Livia and the history of public honorific statues for women in Rome." *Transactions and Proceedings of the American Philological Association,* 123 (1993): 287–308.

Foley, Helene (ed.). *Reflections of Women in Antiquity.* New York: Gordon and Breach Science Publishers, 1981.

Forbis, Elizabeth P. "Women's public image in Italian honorary inscriptions," *The American Journal of Philology,* 111, no. 4 (Winter 1990): 493–512.

Fornaciari, E. *Donne di piacere dell'antica Roma.* Milano: EDIS, 1995.

Forsythe, Gary. "'Ubi tu gaius, ego gaia': new light on an old Roman legal saw." *Historia: Zeitschrift für Alte Geschichte,* Bd. 45, H. 2 (1996): 240–1

Foucault, Michel. *The History of Sexuality,* vols. 1–3. Random House LLC, 2012.

Fraenkel, Edward. *Elementi plautini in Plauto.* Florence: La Nuova Italia,: 1960.

Franciscis, S. de. *Stato e societa in Locri Epizefiri (L'archivio dell'Olympieion Locrese),* Naples: Libreria scientifica editrice, 1972.

Franklin, J. Jr. "Pantomimists at Pompeii: Actius Anicetus and his troupe." *American Journal of Philology,* 108, no. 1 (Spring 1987): 95–107.

Fredrick, David. "Beyond the atrium to Ariadne: erotic painting and visual pleasure in the Roman house." *Classical Antiquity,* 14, no. 2 (1995): 266–87.

Friedl, Raimund. *Der Konkubinat im kaiserzeitlichen Rom. Von Augustus bis Septimius Severus.* Stuttgart: Historia Einzelschriften, 1996.

Frier, Bruce W. *The Rise of the Roman Jurists: Studies in Cicero's Pro Caecina.* Princeton University Press, 1985.

"Natural fertility and family limitation in Roman marriage," *Classical Philology,* 89.4 (1994): 318–33.

Fuchs, Werner. *Die Skulptur der Griechen.* Munich: Hirmer, 1969.

Gage, Jean. *Matronalia. Essai sur les dévotions et les organisations cultuelles des femmes dans l'ancienne Rome.* Brussels: Latomus, 1963.

Geist, H. *Pompeianische Wandinschriften.* Munich: Ernest Heimeran Verlag, 1960.

Galinsky, K. *Aeneas, Sicily, and Rome.* Princeton University Press, 1969.

Augustan Culture: An Interpretive Introduction. Princeton University Press, 1996.

Gardner, Jane F. *Women in Roman Law and Society.* Indianapolis: Indiana University Press, 1986.

"*Concubinage*," book review of Raimund Friedl, *Der Konkubinat im kaiserzeitlichen Rom: von Augustus bis Septimius Severus*, The Classical Review, New Ser. 48, no. 2 (1998): 413–14.

Being a Roman citizen. London: Psychology Press, 2010.

Gibson, R. *Ovid: Ars Amatoria Book 3. Edited with Introduction and Commentary*. Cambridge University Press, 2003.

Gilfoyle, Timothy J. "Review essay: prostitutes in history: from parables of pornography to metaphors of modernity." *The American Historical Review*, 104, no. 1 (February 1999): 117–41.

Gilmore, D. D. (ed.). *Honor and Shame and the Unity of the Mediterranean*. American Anthropological Association Special Publication 22. Washington, D.C.: American Anthropological Association, 1987.

Gilula, Dwora. "The concept of the Bona Meretrix: a study of Terence's courtesans." *Rivista di Filologia e di Istruzione Classica*, 108 (1980): 142–65.

"Terence's *Hecyra*: a delicate balance of suspense and dramatic irony," *Scripta Classica Israelica*, 5 (1979/80): 137–57.

Glazebrook, Allison. "The making of a prostitute: Apollodoros' portrait of Neaira." *Arethusa*, 38 (2005): 161–87.

"Porneion: prostitution in Athenian civic space," in Glazebrook and M. M. Henry (eds.), *Greek Prostitutes in the Ancient Mediterranean 800 BCE–200 CE*, 34–59. University of Wisconsin Press, 2011.

"Beyond courtesans and whores: sex and labor in the Greco-Roman world," *Helios* 42, no. 1 (2015): 1–5.

Glinister, Fay. "The Rapino bronze, the Touta Marouca, and sacred prostitution in early central Italy," in A. Cooley (ed.), *The Epigraphic Landscape of Roman Italy*, 19–38. London: Institute of Classical Studies Press, 2000.

Goldberg, Christiane. *Carmina Priapea: Einleitung, Übersetzung, Interpretation und Kommentar*. Heidelberg: Carl Winter Universitatsverlag, 1992.

Goldhill, Simon. *Foucault's Virginity: Ancient Erotic Fiction and the History of Sexuality*. Cambridge University Press, 1995.

Golfetto, Arthur. *Dougga: Die Geschichte einer Stadt im Schatten Karthagos*. Basle: Raggi Verlag Basel, 1961.

Gordon, A. E. and J. S. *Illustrated Introduction to Latin Epigraphy*. Berkeley: University of California Press, 1983.

Grewing, F. "Priapic poems," review of Goldberg, *Carmina Priapea. Classical Review*, 45 (1995): 31–3.

Grubbs, J. E. *Women and the law in the Roman Empire: A Sourcebook on Marriage, Divorce and Widowhood*. London: Routledge, 2002.

Gruen, Erich. *Studies in Greek Culture and Roman Policy*. Leiden: University of California Press, 1990.

Gubernatis, M. Lenchantin de. "L'epitafio di Allia Potestas." *Revue de philologie, de littérature et d'histoire anciennes*, 41 (1913): 385–400.

Gullini, G. *La cultura architettonica di Locri Epizefirii. Documenti e interpretazioni*. Taranto: Collana Magna Grecia, 1980.

Gurval, R. *Actium and Augustus: The Politics and Emotions of Civil War*. Ann Arbor: University of Michigan Press, 1998.

Guzzo, Pietro Giovanni, and Vincenzo Scarano Ussani. *Veneris Figurae: Immagini di prostituzione e sfruttamento a Pompei*. Naples: Soprintendenza Archeologica di Napoli e Caserta, 2003.
  Ex corpore lucrum facere: la prostituzione nell'antica Pompei. Rome: L'Erma di Bretschneider, 2009.
Hallett, Judith P. *Fathers and Daughters in Roman Society*. Princeton University Press, 1984.
Hallett, Judith P., and M. B. Skinner (eds.). *Roman Sexualities*. Princeton University Press, 1997.
Hamel, Debra. *Trying Neaira: The True Story of a Courtesan's Scandalous Life in Ancient Greece*. New Haven: Yale University Press, 2003.
Harper, Kyle. *From Shame to Sin*. Cambridge: Harvard University Press, 2013.
Harris, W. *Ancient Literacy*. Cambridge: Harvard University Press, 1989.
Harris, W. V. "Child-exposure in the Roman Empire." *The Journal of Roman Studies*, 84 (1994): 1–22.
  "Book review: C. Barton, *Roman Honor*," *American Historical Review*, 108, no. 2 (April 2003): 561.
Harrison, J. Park. "On the relative length of the first three toes of the human foot." *The Journal of the Anthropological Institute of Great Britain and Ireland*, 13 (1884): 258–69.
Hausbeck, K., and B. G. Brents. "McDonaldization of the sex industries: the business of sex," in G. Ritzer (ed.), *McDonaldization: The Reader*, 102–18. Newbury Park: Pine Forge Press, 2009.
Hawley, R., and B. Levick. *Women in Antiquity: New Assessments*. New York: Routledge, 1995.
Hekster, Olivier. *Commodus: An Emperor at the Crossroads*. Amsterdam: Gieben, 2002.
Hemelrijk, Emily Ann. *Matrona Docta: Educated Women in the Roman Élite from Cornelia to Julia Domna*. London: Psychology Press, 2004.
Hemker, Julie. "Commerce, passion, and the self in Plautus' 'Truculentus'." *Pacific Coast Philology* (1991): 35–40.
Henry, Madeleine. *Menander's Courtesans and the Greek Comic Tradition*. Frankfurt: P. Lang, 1985.
Herbert-Brown, Geraldine. *Ovid and the Fasti. An Historical Study*. Oxford: Clarendon Press, 1994.
Hershatter, Gail. *Dangerous Pleasures: Prostitution and Modernity in Twentieth-Century Shanghai*. Berkeley: University of California Press, 1998.
Herter, Hans. "Dirne," *Rivista di archeologia Cristiana*, 3 (1957): 1149–1213.
  Die Soziologie der Antiken Prostitution im Lichte des heidnischen und christlichen Schrifttums," *Jahrbuch fur Antike & Christentum*. 3 (1960): 70–111.
Highet, Gilbert. "The life of Juvenal," *Transactions and Proceedings of the American Philological Association*, 68 (1937): 480–506.
Hill, M. W. *Their Sisters' Keepers: Prostitution in New York City, 1830–1870*. Berkeley: University of California Press, 1993.
Hillard, Tom. "Republican women, politics, and the evidence." *Helios*, 16 (1989): 165–82.

"On the stage, behind the curtain: images of politically active women in the late Roman Republic," in Allen, Dixon and Garlick (eds.), *Stereotypes of Women in Power*, 37–64.

Hobson, Barbara Meil. *Uneasy Virtue: The Politics of Prostitution and the American Reform Tradition*. University of Chicago Press, 1990.

Horsfall, N. M. "*CIL* VI, 37965 = *CLE* 1988 (epitaph of Allia Potestas): a commentary." *Zeitschrift für Papyrologie und Epigraphik*, 61 (1985): 251–72.

Hose, M. "Cassius Dio: a senator and historian in the age of anxiety," in Marincola (ed.), *A Companion to Greek and Roman Historiography*, 161–7.

Hubbard, Thomas K. (ed.). *A Companion to Greek and Roman Sexualities*. Hoboken, NJ: Wiley-Blackwell, 2013.

Hueber, F. S. Erdemgil, *et al. Ephesos: gebaute Geschichte*. Mainz am Rhein: P. von Zabern, 1997.

Humphreys, S. C. *The Family, Women and Death: Comparative Studies*. Ann Arbor: University of Michigan Press, 1993.

Jacobelli, Luciana. *Le pitture erotiche delle Terme Suburbane a Pompei*. Rome: L'Erma di Bretschneider, 1995.

James, Sharon L. "The economics of Roman elegy: Voluntary Poverty, The Recusatio, and The Greedy Girl," *American Journal of Philology*, 122, no. 2 (2001): 223–53.

Learned Girls and Male Persuasion: Gender and Reading in Roman Love Elegy. Berkeley: University of California Press, 2003.

"A courtesan's choreography: female liberty and male anxiety at the roman dinner party," in Faraone and McClure (eds.), *Prostitutes and courtesans in the Ancient World*, 224–51.

James, Sharon L., and Sheila Dillon (eds.). *A Companion to Women in the Ancient World*, Blackwell Companions to the Ancient World, vol. 95. Malden, Mass., Oxford, and Chichester: Wiley-Blackwell, 2012.

Janan, Micaela. ""Beyond good and evil": Tarpeia and philosophy in the feminine." *The Classical World* (1999): 429–43.

Jerome, Thomas. *Aspects of the Study of Roman History*. New York: GP Putnam's Sons, 1923.

Jaschok, M. *Concubines and Bondservants: A Social History*. London and Atlantic Highlands, NJ: Zed Books, 1988.

Jobst, W. "Das 'offentliche Freudenhaus' in Ephesos.' *Jh.* 51 (1976/7): 61–84.

Johns, C. *Sex or Symbol: Erotic Images of Greece and Rome*. London: British Museum Publications, 1982.

Joshel, Sandra R. S. *Work, Identity, and Legal Status at Rome: A Study of the Occupational Inscriptions, vol. XI*. Norman: University of Oklahoma Press, 1992.

"The body female and the body politic: Livy's Lucretia and Verginia," in Richlin (ed.), *Pornography and Representation in Greece and Rome*, 112–130. Oxford University Press: 1992.

"Female desire and the discourse of Empire: Tacitus' Messalina," in Judith P. Hallett and Marilyn B. Skinner (eds.), *Roman Sexualities*, 221–54. Princeton University Press, 1997.

Joshel, Sandra R., and Sheila Murnaghan (eds.). *Women and Slaves in Greco-Roman Culture: Differential Equations*. New York: Routledge, 2005.

Kajava, M. *Roman Female Praenomina: Studies in the Nomenclature of Roman Women*, Acta Instituti Romani Finlandiae, 14. Rome, 1995.

Kampen, Natalie B. *Image and Status of Roman Working Women: Second and Third Century Reliefs from Ostia*. Berlin: Mann, 1981.

"The muted other." *Art Journal*, 47.1: *The Problem of Classicism: Ideology and Power* (Spring 1988): 15–19.

"Between public and private: women as historical subjects in Roman art," in Sarah B. Pomeroy (ed.), *Women's History and Ancient History*, 218–48. Chapel Hill: University of North Carolina Press, 1991.

Kampen, Natalie B., and B. A. Bergmann (eds.). *Sexuality in Ancient Art: Near East, Egypt, Greece, and Italy*. Cambridge University Press, 1996.

Kampen, Natalie B., E. Marlowe, *et al*. *What Is a Man? Changing Images of Masculinity in Late Antique Art*. Portland, Ore.: Douglas F. Cooley Memorial Art Gallery at Reed College, 2002.

Kapparis, Konstantinos A. *Abortion in the Ancient World*. London: Duckworth, 2002.

Karras, R. M. *Common Women: Prostitution and Sexuality in Medieval England*. New York: Oxford University Press, 1996.

"Holy harlots: prostitute saints in medieval legend." *Journal of the History of Sexuality*, 1, no. 1 (1990): 3–32.

Kaster, Robert. "Controlling reason: declamation in rhetorical education at Rome," in Yun Lee Too (ed.), *Education in Greek and Roman Antiquity*, 317–37. Leiden: Brill, 2001.

Keegan, Peter. "Faint praise in pain(t)ed phrases: a narratological reading of the *Laudatio Murdia*." *Eras Journal*, 4 (2002).

Keith, Alison. "Lycoris Galli/Volumnia Cytheris: a Greek courtesan in Rome," *EuGeStA* no.1 (2011).

"Women in Augustan literature," in James and Dillon (eds.), *A Companion to Women in the Ancient World*, 385–99.

Kempadoo, Kemala. "Prostitution and sex work studies," in Philomena Essed, David Theo Goldberg, and Audrey Kobayashi (eds.), *A companion to gender studies* (Hoboken, NJ: John Wiley & Sons, 2009).

Kertzer, D. I., and R. P. Saller. *The Family in Italy from Antiquity to the Present*. New Haven: Yale University Press, 1991.

Keuls, E. C. *The Reign of the Phallus: Sexual Politics in Ancient Athens*. Berkeley: University of California Press, 1993.

Khanoussi, Mustapha. *Dougga Collection: Sites and Monuments of Tunisia*. Tunis: Ausonius: 2002.

Kleberg, T. *Hotels, restaurants et cabarets dans l'antiquité romaine*. Uppsala: Almqvist & Wiksells, 1957.

Kleiner, Diana E. E. "Second-century mythological portraiture: Mars and Venus." *Latomus*, 40 (1981): 512–44.

"Women and family life on Roman imperial funerary altars." *Latomus* (1987): 545–54.

"Livia Drusilla and the remarkable power of elite women in imperial Rome: a commentary on recent books on Rome's first empress." *International Journal of the Classical Tradition*, 6, no. 4 (2000): 563–69.

Cleopatra and Rome. Cambridge: Harvard University Press, 2009.

Knorr, Ortwin. "The Character of Bacchis in Terence's *Heautontimorumenos*." *The American Journal of Philology* 116, no. 2 (Summer 1995): 221–35.

Knudsen, J. The Lady and the Emperor: A Study of the Domitian Persecution. *Church History*, 14.1 (1945): 17–32.

Koch, C. "Studies on the history of the Roman Venus-worship." *Hermes*, 83, no. 1H (1955): 1–51.

Kolb, Frank. *Literarische Beziehungen zwischen Cassius Dio, Herodian und der Historia Augusta*. Bonn: Antiquitas 1972

Koloski-Ostrow, Ann Olga, and Claire L. Lyons (eds.). *Naked Truths: Women, Sexuality, and Gender in Classical Art and Archaeology*. London: Psychology Press, 1997.

Konstan, David. *Roman Comedy*. Ithaca and London: Cornell University Press, 1983.

"Between courtesan and wife: Menander's 'Perikeiromene'," *Phoenix*, 41.2 (Summer 1987): 122–39.

Koster, Severin. *Die Invective in der griechischen und römischen Literatur*. Meisenheim am Glan: 1980.

Kötzle, Martina. *Weibliche Gottheiten in Ovids Fasten*. Frankfurt: Peter Lang, 1990.

Das Standesfest der Dirnen ist wohl ein Ersatz fur die auf dem Eryx praktizierte, orientalische Tempelprostitution. Frankfurt: Peter Lang, 1990.

Kraemer, R. S. *Her Share of the Blessings: Women's Religions among Pagans, Jews, and Christians in the Greco-Roman World*. New York: Oxford University Press, 1992.

Women's Religions in the Greco-Roman world: A Sourcebook. New York: Oxford University Press, 2004.

Krafft-Ebing, Richard. *Psychopathia Sexualis: with Especial Reference to the Antipathic Sexual Instinct: A Medico-Forensic Study*. New York: Arcade Publishing, 1965.

Krieter-Spiro, Martha. *Sklaven, Köche und Hetären: Das Dienstpersonal bei Menander. Beiträge zur Altertumskunde 93*. Stuttgart and Leipzig: B. G. Teubner, 1997.

Kurke, Leslie. *Coins, Bodies, Games and Gold*. Princeton University Press, 2000.

Lampe, Peter. *From Paul to Valentinus: Christians at Rome in the First Two Centuries*. Philadelphia: Fortress Press, 2003.

Lana, I. "Terenzio e il movimento filellenico in Roma." *Rivista di filologia e di istruzione classica*, 75, N.S. 25 (1947): 44–80, 155–75.

Lancaster, R., and M. di Leonardo (eds.). *The Gender/Sexuality Reader*. New York: Routledge, 1997.

Lance, M. N., and A. Tanesini. "Identity judgements, queer politics," in Iain Morland and Annabelle Wilcox (eds.), *Queer Theory*, 42–51. New York: Palgrave, 2005.

Langford, Julie. *Maternal Megalomania: Julia Domna and the Imperial Politics of Motherhood*. Baltimore: Johns Hopkins University Press, 2013.

Langlands, Rebecca. *Sexual Morality in Ancient Rome*. Cambridge University Press, 2006.

La Regina, A. (1997) "Legge del popolo marrucino per l'istituzione della prostituzione sacra nel santuario di Giove padre nell'arce Tarincra (Rapino)", in A. Campanelli and A. Faustoferri (eds.), *I luoghi degli dèi. Sacro e natura nell'Abruzzo italic*, 62–3. Chieti: Pescara, 1997.

Laurence, Ray. *Roman Pompeii: Space and Society*. London: Routledge Press, 1994.

Leach, Eleanor W. "Ciceronian "Bi-Marcus": correspondence with M. Terentius Varro and L. Papirius Paetus in 46 BCE." *Transactions of the American Philological Association (1974–)*, 129 (1999): 139–79.

"Claudia Quinta (Pro Caelio 34) and an altar to Magna Mater." *Dictynna. Revue de poétique latine*, 4 (2007).

Leach, E. "Oecus on Ibycus: investigating the vocabulary of the Roman house," in S. E. Bon and R. Jones (eds.), *Sequence and Space in Pompeii*. Oxford University Press, 1997, 50–72.

Leen, Anne. "Clodia Oppugnatrix: the domus motif in Cicero's 'Pro Caelio'." *Classical Journal* (2000): 141–62.

Leeson, M., and M. C. Lyons. *The Memoirs of Mrs Leeson: in Three Volumes*. Dublin: Lilliput Press, 1995.

Lefèvre, Eckard, E. Stark, and G. Vogt-Spira. *Plautus barbarus: sechs Kapitel zur Originalität des Plautus*. vol. viii. Tubigen: Gunter Narr Verlag, 1991.

Lefkowitz, Mary R. "Wives and husbands." *Greece and Rome*, 30, no. 1 (April 1983): 31–47.

Lefkowitz, Mary R., and Maureen B. Fant. *Women's Life in Greece and Rome*, 2nd edn. Baltimore: Johns Hopkins University Press, 1992.

Levick, Barbara. "Julians and Claudians." *Greece and Rome*, 22 (1975): 29–38.

Julia Domna: Syrian Empress. New York: Routledge, 2007.

Levin-Richardson, Sarah. "Sex, sight, and societas in the Lupanar, Pompeii." *Seeing the Past: Building knowledge of the past and present through acts of seeing*, Stanford University Archaeology Center conference, February 4–6, 2005. Unpublished.

"Roman provocations: interactions with decorated spaces in early imperial Rome and Pompeii." Diss. Stanford University, 2009.

"Facilis hic futui: graffiti and masculinity in Pompeii's' purpose-built brothel." *Helios*, 38, no. 1 (2011): 59–78.

Levi-Strauss, C. 'The structural study of myth.' *Journal of American Folklore*, 68 (1955): 428–44.

The Raw and the Cooked: Introduction to a Science of Mythology. London: Cape, 1969.

Lewis, Jacqueline, and Eleanor Maticka-Tyndale. *Escort Services in a Border Town: Transmission Dynamics of STDs within and between Communities*. Division of STD Prevention, Health Canada CDC, 2000.

Lietz, Beatrice. *La dea di Erice e la sua diffusione nel Mediterraneo. Un culto tra Fenici, Greci e Romani*. Pisa: Edizioni della Normale, 2012.

Lightman, M., and B. Lightman. *Biographical Dictionary of Ancient Greek and Roman Women: Notable Women from Sappho to Helena*. New York: Facts On File, 2000.

Lillard, Lee, *et al.* "The market for sex: street prostitution in Los Angeles." RAND Corporation, unpublished paper, 1995.

Ling, Roger. *The Insula of the Menander at Pompeii.* 4 vols. Oxford: Clarendon Press, 1997.

Locri epizefirii: atti del sedicesimo Convegno di studi sulla Magna Grecia. Taranto, 3–8 ottobre 1976. Naples: Arte tipografica, 1977.

López Barja de Quiroga, Pedro. "Freedmen social mobility in Roman Italy." *Historia: Zeitschrift für Alte Geschichte,* 44, no. 3 (1995): 326–48.

Lowe, J. C. B. "Aspects of Plautus' originality in the Asinaria." *The Classical Quarterly,* N.S. 42, no. 1 (1992): 152–75.

Lyne, R. A. M. *The Latin Love Poets from Catullus to Horace.* Oxford: Clarendon Press, 1980.

McAuslan, I., and P. Walcot. *Women in Antiquity.* Oxford and New York: Oxford University Press on behalf of the Classical Association, 1996.

McClintock, Anne, guest ed. *Social Text* (Winter 1993): 1–252.

McClure, Laura. *Courtesans at Table: Gender and Greek Literary Culture in Athenaeus.* New York: Routledge, 2003.

McCoy, Marsha. "The politics of prostitution," in Faraone and McClure (eds.), *Prostitutes and Courtesans in the Ancient World,* 179–81.

McGarrity, T. "Reputation vs. reality in Terence's *Hecyra.*" *Classical Journal,* 76, no. 2 (1980–81): 149–56.

McGinn, T. A. "The taxation of Roman prostitutes." *Helios* 16, no. 1 (1989): 79–103.

Concubinage and the Lex Iulia on adultery." *Transactions of the American Philological Association (1974–),* 121 (1991): 335–75.

"Controversies and new approaches," in T. K. Hubbard (ed.), *A Companion to Greek and Roman Sexualities.* Hoboken, NJ: John Wiley & Sons, (2013), 83–101.

Prostitution, Sexuality, and the Law in Ancient Rome. New York: Oxford University Press, 1998.

"Feminae probrosae and the litter." *Classical Journal* (1998): 241–50.

The Economy of Prostitution in the Roman World: A Study of Social History and the Brothel. Ann Arbor: University of Michigan Press, 2004.

"Sorting out prostitution in Pompeii: the material remains, terminology and the legal sources," in Guzzo and Ussani (eds.), *Ex corpore lucrum facere: la prostitutuzione nell'antica Pompeii.*

"Sex and the city," in P. Erdkamp (ed.), *The Cambridge Companion to Ancient Rome,* 369–88. Cambridge University Press, 2013.

(ed.). "Pompeian brothels, Pompeii's ancient history, mirrors and mysteries, art and nature at Oplontis, the Herculaneum 'Basilica'." *Journal of Roman Archaeology,* 47 (2002).

McInerney, Jeremy. "Plutarch's manly women." *Mnemosyne-Leiden-Supplementum* (2002): 319–44.

MacMullen, Ramsay. *Roman Social Relations: 50 BC to AD 284.* New Haven: Yale University Press, 1974.

"Women in public in the Roman Empire," *Historia,* 29 (1980): 208–18.

"'Roman History' book review: C. Barton's *Roman Honor,*" *Yale Review,* 90, no. 2 (2002): 154–60.

McNamara, Jo Ann, and Suzanne Wemple. "The power of women through the family in medieval Europe: 500–1100." *Feminist Studies*, 1, no. 3/4 (1973): 126–41.

Magini, L. *Le feste di Venere: fertilità femminile e configurazioni astrali nel calendario di Roma antica.* Roma: L'Erma di Bretschneider, 1996.

Mancini, G. *Roma. Nuove scoperte nella città e nel suburbia. Notizie degli scavi di antichità*, vol. IX, 155–8. Rome: Accademia Nazionale dei Lincei, 1912.

van Mal-Maeder, Danielle Karin. "[Quintilian]. The poison of hatred (Declamationes maiores 14–15)." (2012): 549–51.

Marcadé, J. *Roma amor: essai sur les représentations érotiques dans l'art etrusque et romain.* Geneva: Les Éditions Nagel, 1961.

Marincola, J. (ed.), *A Companion to Greek and Roman Historiography* Hoboken, NJ: Wiley, 2009.

Martin, C. *Catullus.* New Haven: Yale University Press, 1992.

Meiggs, R. *Roman Ostia.* Oxford University Press, 1973.

Merriam, Carol U. "The other Sulpicia." *The Classical World* (1991): 303–5.

Milnor, Kristina. "Sulpicia's (corpo)reality: elegy, authorship, and the body in [Tibullus] 3. 13." *Classical Antiquity*, 21 (2002): 259–82.

   Gender, Domesticity, and the Age of Augustus: Inventing Private Life. Oxford University Press, 2005.

Montserrat, Dominic. *Sex and Society in Graeco-Roman Egypt.* New York: Columbia University Press, 1996.

Moore, R. I. *The Formation of a Persecuting Society: Power and Deviance in Medieval Europe 950–1250.* Oxford University Press, 1987.

Moore, T. J. *Artistry and Ideology: Livy's Vocabulary of Virtue.* Frankfurt: Athenäum, 1989.

Moscati, Sabbatino. *The World of the Phoenicians.* London: Weidenfeld and Nicolson, 1968.

Myerowitz, Molly. "The domestication of desire: Ovid's *Parva Tabella* and the Theater of Love," in Richlin (ed.), *Pornography and Representation in Greece and Rome*, 131–5.

Myers, K. Sara. "The poet and the procuress: the *Lena* in Latin love elegy," *Journal of Roman Studies*, 86 (1996): 1–21.

Neugebauer, Otto. *A History of Ancient Mathematical Astronomy.* Berlin: Springer Science & Business Media, 2012.

Newlands, Carole. "Transgressive acts: Ovid's treatment of the Ides of March." *Classical Philology*, 91, no. 4 (1996): 320–38.

Nisbet, R. G .M. (ed.), *M. Tulli Ciceronis: In L. Calpurnium Pisonem Oratio.* Oxford: Clarendon Press, 1961.

Nussbaum, M. C. *Sex and Social Justice.* Oxford University Press, 1998.

Ogden, D. *Polygamy, Prostitutes and Death: The Hellenistic Dynasties.* London: Duckworth with the Classical Press of Wales, 1999.

Olson, Kelly. "Matrona and whore: the clothing of women in Roman antiquity."*Fashion Theory: The Journal of Dress, Body and Culture*, 6, no. 4 (2002): 387–420.

   "Roman underwear revisited." *The Classical World* (2003): 201–10.

Dress and the Roman Woman: Self-Presentation and Society. New York: Routledge, 2012.

O'Neill, Kerill. "Propertius 4.2: Slumming with Vertumnus?" *American Journal of Philology*, 121, no. 2 (2000): 259–77.

Orlin, Eric. "Why a second temple for Venus Erycina?" *Latomus*, 10 (2000): 70–90.

Ortner, Sherry. "Is female to male as nature to culture?" in Michelle Rosaldo and Louise Lamphere (eds.), *Woman, Culture and Society*, 67–88. Stanford University Press, 1974.

Making Gender: The Politics and Erotics of Culture. Boston: Beacon Press, 1996.

Otis, Leah Lydia. *Prostitution in Medieval Society: The History of an Urban Institution in Languedoc.* Chicago University Press, 1985.

Pailler, J. M. *Bacchanalia: la répression de 196 av. J.-C. à Rome et en Italie.* Rome: Ecole française de Rome, 1988.

Palmer, R. E. A. *Rome and Carthage at Peace. Historia Einzelschriften* 113. Stuttgart: Franz Steiner, 1997.

Parent-Duchatelet, Alexandre. *La Prostitution à Paris au XIXe siècle.* Translated by Kelly Buttermore. Paris: Editions Du Seuil, 1836.

Parker, Holt. "The teratogenic grid," in Hallett and Skinner (eds.), *Roman Sexualities*, 47–65.

"Loyal slaves and loyal wives: The crisis of the outsider-within and Roman exemplum literature, "in Joshel and Murnaghan (eds.), *Women and Slaves in Greco-Roman Culture: Differential Equations*, 152–73.

Pateman, Carole. *The Disorder of Women: Democracy, Feminism, and Political Theory.* Stanford University Press, 1989.

Paterson, J. "Friends in high places: the creation of the court of the Roman emperor," in A. J. S. Spawforth (ed.), *The Court and Court Society in Ancient Monarchies*, 121–56. Cambridge University Press, 2007.

Pazdernik, Charles. " 'Our most pious consort given us by God': dissident reactions to the partnership of Justinian and Theodora, AD 525–548," *Classical Antiquity*, 13, no. 2 (1994): 256–81.

Peakman, Julie. "Memoirs of women of pleasure: the whore biography." *Women's Writing*, 11, no. 2 (2004): 163–184.

Pembroke, Simon. "Femmes et enfants dans les foundations de Locres et de Tarente." *Annales: Économies, sociétés, civilizations,* 25, no. 5 (1970): 1240–70.

Peppe, Leo. *Posizione giuridica e ruolo sociale della donna romana in età repubblicana.* Milan: A. Giuffrè, 1984.

Peristiany, J. G. (ed.). *Honour and Shame: The Values of Mediterranean Society.* London: Weidenfeld and Nicholson, 1966.

Phang, S. E. *The Marriage of Roman Soldiers (13 BC–AD 235): Law and Family in the Imperial Army.* Columbia Studies in the Classical Tradition, vol. 24. Columbia University Press, 2002.

Pheterson, Gail. *The Whore Stigma: Female Dishonor and Male Unworthiness.* The Hague: Dutch Ministry of Social Affairs and Employment, Emancipation Policy Co-ordination, 1986.

Piranomonte, Marina. "Religion and magic at Rome: the fountain of Anna Perenna." in R. Gordon and F. Marco Simon (eds.), *Magical Practice in the Latin West: Papers from the International Conference held at the University of Zaragoza*, 168 (2010): 191–213

Pollini, John. "The Warren cup: homoerotic love and symposial rhetoric in silver," *The Art Bulletin*, 81, no. 1 (1999): 21–52.

Pomeroy, Sarah B. *Goddesses, Whores, Wives, and Slaves: Women in Classical Antiquity*. New York: Schocken, 1975.

(ed.), *Women's History and Ancient History*. Chapel Hill: University of North Carolina Press, 1991.

Prückner, Helmut. *Die Lokrischen Tonreliefs: Beitrag zur Kultgeschichte von Lokroi Epizephyrioi*. Mainz am Rhein: Philipp von Zabern, 1968.

Pruitt, Matthew V., and Amy C. Krull. "Escort advertisements and male patronage of prostitutes." *Deviant Behavior*, 32, no. 1 (2010): 38–63.

Purcell, Nicholas. "Livia and the womanhood of Rome." *Proceedings of the Cambridge Philological Society*, N.S.32 (1986): 78–105.

Rabinowitz, Nancy and Amy Richlin. *Feminist Theory and the Classics*. New York: Routledge, 1993.

Raepsaet-Charlier, M.-T. "Les activités publiques des femmes sénatoriales et équestres sous le Haut-Empire romain," in W. Eck and M. Heil (eds), *Senatores populi Romani. Realität und mediale Präsentation einer Führungsschicht*, 169–212. Stuttgart, 2005.

Raia, A. "Women's roles in Plautine comedy." The Fourth Conference on Greek, Roman, and Byzantine Studies, 1983.

Ranieri, Christina de. "*Renovatio Temporum* e'rifondazione di Roma' nell'ideologia politica e religiosa di Commodo." *Studii Classice*, 5 (1995): 329–68.

"Retroscena politici e lotte dinastiche sullo sfondo della vicenda di Aurelio Cleandro." *Revue de synthèse*, 27 (1997):139–89.

"La gestione politica di età Commodiana e la parabola di Tigidio Perenne." *Athenaeum*, 86 (1998): 397–417.

Rauh, Nicholas K., Matthew J. Dillon, and T. Davina McClain. "Ochlos nautikos: leisure culture and underclass discontent in the Roman maritime world."*Memoirs of the American Academy in Rome. Supplementary Volumes* (2008): 197–242.

Rawson, B. "Roman concubinage and other de facto marriages." *Transactions of the American Philological Association (1974 –)*, 104 (1974): 279–305.

Rawson , B. (ed.) *Marriage, Divorce, and Children in Ancient Rome*. Oxford University Press, 1996.

Rawson, B. and P. R. C. Weaver (eds.) *The Roman Family in Italy: Status, Sentiment, Space*. Canberra, New York, Oxford: Humanities Research Centre, Clarendon Press, 1997.

Redfield, J. M. *The Locrian Maidens: Love and Death in Greek Italy*. Princeton University Press, 2003.

Richlin, Amy. *The Garden of Priapus: Sexuality and Aggression in Roman Humor*. Oxford University Press, 1983.

"Invective against women in Roman satire." *Arethusa*, 17 (1984): 67–80.

"Julia's jokes, Galla Placidia, and the Roman use of women as political icons," in Allen, Dixon, and Garlick (eds.), *Stereotypes of Women in Power*, 65–91.

"Sulpicia the satirist." *The Classical World* (1992): 125–40.

"Not before homosexuality: the materiality of the cinaedus and the Roman law against love between men." *Journal of the History of Sexuality* (1993): 523–73.

Arguments with Silence: Writing the History of Roman Women. Ann Arbor: University of Michigan Press, 2014.

(ed.). *Pornography and Representation in Greece and Rome.* Oxford University Press, 1992.

Riddle, John M. *Contraception and Abortion from the Ancient World to the Renaissance.* Harvard University Press, 1992.

Riess, Werner. "Rari exempli femina: female virtues on Roman funerary inscriptions,"in James and Dillon (eds.), *A Companion to Women in the Ancient World*, 491–501.

Riggsby, A. "'Public' and 'private' in Roman culture: the case of the *cubiculum*," *JRA* 10 (1997), 36–56.

Ringdal, N. J. *Love for Sale: A World History of Prostitution.* New York: Grove Press, 2004.

Rives, James. "Venus Genetrix outside Rome." *Phoenix*, 48, no. 4 (Winter 1994): 294–306.

Roberts, N. *Whores in History: Prostitution in Western Society.* London: HarperCollins, 1993.

Rogers, Robert Samuel. "Fulvia Paulina C. Sentii Saturnini." *The American Journal of Philology*, 53, no 3. (1932): 252–6.

"Heirs and rivals to Nero." *Transactions and Proceedings of the American Philological Association*, 86 (1955): 190–212.

Roller, Matthew. "Horizontal women: posture and sex in the Roman *Convivium*." *American Journal of Philology*, 124, no. 3 (2003): 377–422.

Rosaldo, Michelle. "The use and abuse of anthropology: reflections on feminism and cross-cultural understanding." *Signs*, 5, no. 3 (1980): 389–417.

Rosivach, Vincent J. "Solon's brothels," *Liverpool Classical Monthly*, 20: nos. 1–2 (1995): 3–4.

Rossiaud, J. *Medieval Prostitution.* Oxford and New York: Blackwell 1988.

Rostovtseff, Michael, and Harold Mattingly. "Commodus-Hercules in Britain." *The Journal of Roman Studies*, 13 (1923): 91–109.

Roth, M. "Marriage, divorce, and the prostitute in ancient Mesopotamia," in Faraone and McClure (eds.), *Prostitutes and Courtesans.*

Rousselle, Aline. *Porneia: On Desire and the Body in Antiquity.* Oxford: Blackwell, 1988.

Roy, J. "An Alternative Sexual Morality for Classical Athenians." *Greece and Rome*, 2nd Ser. 44, no. 1 (April 1997): 11–22.

Rubin, Gayle S. "Thinking sex: notes for a radical theory of the politics of sexuality," in Carole S. Vance (ed.), *Pleasure and Danger: Exploring Female Sexuality.* London: Routledge, 1984.

"Thinking sex," in H. Abelove, M. A. Barale, and D. M. Halperin (eds.), *Gay and Lesbian Studies Reader*, 3–44. New York and London: Routledge, 1993.

Saller, Richard P. "Corporal punishment, authority and obedience in the Roman household," in Rawson (ed.), *Marriage, Divorce and Children in Ancient Rome*, 144–65.

Patriarchy, Property and Death in the Roman Family. Cambridge Studies in Population, Economy and Society in Past Time, vol. 25. Cambridge University Press, 1996.

Saltelli, Elisabetta. "L'epitafio di Allia Potestas (*CIL*, VI, 37965; *CLE* 1988) un commento" *Biblioteca Scientifica di Ca' Foscari* (2004): 1–27. (also online: http://lettere2.unive.it/saltelli/index.htm).

Salzman, M. R. "Cicero, the Megalenses and the defense of Caelius," *American Journal of Philology*, 103 (1982): 299–304.

Santirocco, Matthew. "Sulpicia reconsidered." *Classical Journal*, 74 (1979): 229–39.

Savunen, L. 'Women and elections in Pompeii,' in Hawley and Levick (eds.), *Women in Antiquity: New Assessments*, 94–206.

Saxonhouse, Arlene. "Introduction – public and private: the paradigm's power," in Allen, Dixon, and Garlick (eds.),*Stereotypes of Women in Power*, 1–9.

Scheid, J. "Graeco ritu: a typically Roman way of honoring the gods." *Harvard Studies in Classical Philology*, vol. 97: *Greece in Rome: Influence, Integration, Resistance* (1995): 15–31.

Scheidel, Walter. "The most silent women of Greece and Rome: rural labour and women's life in the ancient world," *Greece and Rome* 42, no. 2 (1995): 202–17.

"Monogamy and polygyny," in B. Rawson, (ed.), *A Companion to Families in the Greek and Roman Worlds*, 108–15. Hoboken, NJ: John Wiley & Sons, 2011.

(ed.), *Debating Roman Demography. Mnemosyne Supplement*, 211. Leiden: Brill, 2001.

Schilling, R. *La religion romaine de Vénus, depuis les origines jusqu'au temps d'Auguste*. Paris: E. de Boccard, 1955.

Schultz, Celia. *Women's Religious Activity in the Roman Republic*. Raleigh: University of North Carolina Press, 2006.

Scott, K. and C. Arscott. *Manifestations of Venus: Art and Sexuality*. Manchester University Press, 2000.

Sebesta, J. L. 1997. "Women's costume and feminine civic morality in Augustan Rome." *Gender and History*, 9.3: 529–41.

Segal, Erich. book review of Netta Zagagi, *Tradition and Originality in Plautus: Studies of the Amatory Motifs in Plautine Comedy*, in *The American Journal of Philology*, 103, no. 2 (Summer 1982): 217–19.

Shackleton Bailey, D. R. "Two studies in Roman nomenclature." *American Classical Studies*, 3 (1976).

Shaw, Brent. "Roman Honor." Book review of Carlin A. Barton, *Roman Honor: The Fire in the Bones*, in *Journal of Interdisciplinary History*, 33 (2002): 284–6.

Shelton, Jo-Ann. *As the Romans Did*. Oxford University Press, 1998.

Sicari, A. *Prostituzione e tutela giuridica della schiava: un problema di politica legislativa nell'impero romano.* Bari: Cacucci, 1991.

Skinner, M. B. "Clodia Metelli." *Transactions of the American Philological Association*, 113 (1983): 273–87.

Clodia Metelli: The Tribune's Sister. Oxford University Press, 2011.

Skoie, Mathilde. *Reading Sulpicia: Commentaries 1475–1990.* Oxford University Press, 2002.

Slater, Niall W. "The fictions of patriarchy in Terence's *Hecyra.*" *Classical World*, 81, no. 4 (1988): 249–60.

Sourvinou-Inwood, Christine. "The Boston relief and the religion of Locri Epizephyrii." *Journal of Hellenic Studies*, 94 (1974): 126–37.

"The votum of 477–6 BC and the foundation legend of Locri Epizephyrii." *Classical Quarterly*, 27 (1974): 186–98.

Stanton, G. R. "Marcus Aurelius, Lucius Verus, and Commodus: 1962–1972." *Aufstieg und Niedergang der römischen Welt*, 2, no. 2 (1975): 478–559.

Staples, A. *From Good Goddess to Vestal Virgins: Sex and Category in Roman Religion.* New York: Routledge, 1998.

Stehle, E. "Venus, Cybele, and the Sabine Women: the Roman construction of female sexuality." *Helios*, 16, no. 2 (1989): 143–64.

Steinby, E. M. (ed.). "Erucina," V.114, *Lexicon Topographicum Urbis Romanae.* Rome: Edizioni Quasar, 1999–2000.

Stewart, Andrew, F. "Reflections." In Kampen and Bergmann (eds.),*Sexuality in Ancient Art*, 136–54.

Streete, Gail Corrington. *The Strange Woman: Power and Sex in the Bible.* Louisville, Ky.: Westminster John Knox Press, 1997.

Strong, Anise K. "Daughter and employee: mother–daughter bonds among prostitutes," in L. Peterson and P. Salzman (eds.), *Mothering and Motherhood in the Ancient World*, 121–39. Austin: University of Texas, 2012.

Strong, R. "The most shameful practice: temple prostitution in the Ancient Greek world." History dissertation. Los Angeles: UCLA, 1997.

Stumpp, B. E. *Prostitution in der römischen Antike.* Berlin: Akademie Verlag, 1998.

Sullivan, J. P. "Lady Chatterley in Rome." *Pacific Coast Philology*, 15 (October 1980): 53–62.

Martial, the Unexpected Classic: A Literary and Historical Study. Cambridge University Press, 1991.

Sussman, Lewis A. "Antony the meretrix audax: Cicero's novel invective in Philippic 2.44–46." *Eranos*, 96, nos. 1–2 (1998):114–28.

Sutton, R. F. Jr. "Pornography and Persuasion on Attic Pottery," in Richlin (ed.), *Pornography and Representation in Greece and Rome*, 3–35

Syme, Ronald. *The Roman Revolution.* Oxford University Press, 1939.

"Domitius Corbulo." *Journal of Roman Studies*, 60 (1970): 27–39.

Emperors and Biography: Studies in the Historia Augusta. Oxford: Clarendon Press, 1971.

History in Ovid. Oxford: Clarendon Press, 1978.

"Dynastic marriages in Roman aristocracy." *Diogenes*, 135 (Fall 1986): 1–10.

Terzaghi, N. "Perché Allia fu infamis? (A proposito dell'iscrizione di Allia Potestas)." *A & R* 17 (1914): 115–19.

Thakur, S. "The construction and deconstruction of the ideal Roman wife." *Feminism and Classics*, 6 (2012).

Thornton, B. S. *Eros: The Myth of Ancient Greek Sexuality*. Boulder, Colo.: WestviewPress, 1997.

Tlatli, S.-e. *Cités antiques de Tunisie pour visiter: Dougga, Thuburbo Majus, Mactar, El Jem, Gightis*. Tunis: Cérès Productions, 1970.

Tomassini, L. "La congiura e l'assassino di Commodo; i retroscena." *Acme*, 47, no. 3 (1994): 79–88.

Torelli, Mario. "Considerazioni sugli aspetti religiosi e cultuali," in Domenico Musti (ed.), *Le tavole di Locri: Atti del colloquio sugli aspetti politici, economici, cultuali e linguistici dei testi, dell'archivio Locrese, Napoli 27–27 Aprile 1977*, 91–112. Naples: Edizioni dell' Ateneo & Bizzarri.

"I culti di Locri". *XVI Convegno di Studi sulla Magna Grecia*, 148–56 Tarento: 1977.

"Gli aromi e il sale. Afrodite et Eracle nell'emporia arcaica dell'Italia." *Ercole in occidente*, 91–117. Trento: 1993.

"Il 'Trono Ludovisi' da Erice all'Oriente," rep. in *Significare: Scritti vari di ermeneutica archeologica*, 463–470. Rome: Fabrizio Serra Editors, 2012.

Traill, A. *Women and the Comic Plot in Menander*. Cambridge University Press, 2008.

Traina, G. "Lycoris the mime," in A. Fraschetti (ed.), *Roman Women*, 82–99. University of Chicago Press, 2001.

Treggiari, Susan. *Roman Freedmen During the Late Republic*. Oxford: Clarendon Press, 1969.

"Libertine Ladies." *Classical World*, 64 (1970/1): 196–8.

"Lower class women in the Roman economy." *Florilegium*, 1 (1979): 65–86.

"The Influence of Roman Women." Review of J. P. Hallett, *Fathers and Daughters in Roman Society: Women and the Elite Family. The Classical Review*, N.S. 36, no. 1 (1986): 102–5.

Roman Marriage: Iusti Coniuges from the Time of Cicero to the Time of Ulpian. New York: Clarendon Press, 1991.

"Divorce Roman style: how easy and how frequent was it?" in Rawson (ed.), *Marriage, Divorce, and Children in Ancient Rome*, 31–46.

Tsafrir, Y, and G. Foerster, "Urbanism at Scythopolis-Bet Shean in the fourth to seventh centuries." *Dumbarton Oaks Papers* (1997): 85–146.

Van Bremen, R. "Women and wealth," in A. Cameron and A. Kuhrt (eds.), *Images of Women in Antiquity*, 223–42. London: Routledge, 1983.

Vanoyeke, V. *La prostitution en Grèce et à Rome*. Paris: Belles Lettres, 1990.

Varone, Antonio. *Erotica Pompeiana. Love Inscriptions on the Walls of Pompeii. (Studia archaeologica 116)*. Rome: L'Erma di Bretschneider, 2001.

Eroticism in Pompeii, Los Angeles: J. Paul Getty Trust Publications, 2001.

Volkmann, Hans. *Cleopatra: A Study in Politics and Propaganda*. London: Elek Books: 1958.

Von Hesberg-Tonn, B. "Coniunx carissima." *Untersuchungen zum Nonncharakter im Erscheinungsbild der römischen Frau*. Diss. Stuttgart, 1983.

Vorberg, Gaston. *Glossarium Eroticum*. Rome: L'Erma, 1965.

Vout, Caroline. "The myth of the toga: understanding the history of Roman dress." *Greece and Rome*, 2nd ser. 43, no. 2 (October 1996): 204–20.

Power and Eroticism in Imperial Rome. Cambridge University Press, 2007.

Wagenvoort, H. "De deae Veneris origine," *Mnemosyne*, ser. IV, 17. 47–77, 1964.

Walcot, P. and I. McAuslan. *Women in Antiquity.* Oxford: Clarendon Press, 1995.

Wallace-Hadrill, Andrew. *Houses and Society in Pompeii and Herculaneum.* Princeton University Press, 1994.

"Public honour and private shame: the urban texture of Pompeii," in T. J. Cornell and Kathryn Lomas (eds.), *Urban Society in Roman Italy*, 39–62. London: Psychology Press, 1995.

Wallinger, E. *Die Frauen in der Historia Augusta.* Vienna: Selbstverl. d. Österr. Ges. für Archäologie,1990.

Walsh, P. G., ed. and trans. *Livy Book XXXIX.* Warminster: Aris & Phillips, 1994.

"Making a drama out of a crisis: Livy on the Bacchanalia." *Greece and Rome*, 43, no. 2 (1996): 188–203.

Walters, J. "Invading the Roman body: anliness and impenetrability in Roman thought," in Hallett and Skinner (eds.), *Roman Sexualities*, 29–43.

Weaver, P. R. C. *Familia Caesaris: A Social Study of the Emperor's Freedmen and Slaves.* Cambridge University Press, 1972.

Wiles, David. "Marriage and prostitution in classical New Comedy." *Themes in Drama*, 11 (1989): 31–48.

Will, E. Lyding. "Women in Pompeii." *Archaeology* 39 (1979): 34–43.

Williams, Craig A. "Greek love at Rome." *The Classical Quarterly*, N.S. 45, no. 2 (1995): 517–39.

"Sex and art in Ancient Rome." *GLQ: A Journal of Lesbian and Gay Studies*, 6, no. 2 (2000): 347–350.

Williams, D. "Women on Athenian Vases: Problems of Interpretation," in A. Cameron and A. Kuhrt (eds.), *Images of Women in Antiquity*, 92–106. New York: Routledge, 1993.

Williams, Gordon. "Some aspects of Roman marriage ceremonies and ideals." *The Journal of Roman Studies*, 48, no. 1 (1958): 16–29.

Winkler, J. J. *The Constraints of Desire: The Anthropology of Sex and Gender in Ancient Greece.* New York: Routledge, 1990.

Wiseman, T. P. *Catullus and His World: A Reappraisal.* Cambridge University Press, 1985.

Roman Drama and Roman History. Exeter Studies in History. University of Exeter Press, 1998.

"Ovid and the stage," in Herbert-Brown (ed.),*Ovid's Fasti: Historical Readings at its Bimillennium*, 275–99. Oxford University Press, 2002.

Wistrand, E. *The So-Called Laudatio Turiae: Introduction, Text, Translation, Commentary.* Acta Universitatis Gothoburgensis, vol. 34 (1976).

Witt, R. E. *Isis in the Ancient World.* Ithaca: Cornell University Press, 1971.

Witzke, Serena S. "Harlots, tarts, and hussies? A problem of terminology for sex labor in Roman comedy," *Helios* 42, no. 1 (2015): 7–27.

Woodbury, Leonard. "The Gratitude of the Locrian Maiden: Pindar, *Pyth.*, 2.18–20." *Transactions of the American Philological Association*, 108 (1978): 259–99.

Wuilleumier, P. and A. Audin. *Les Médaillons d'applique gallo romains de la vallée du Rhône*. Paris: 1952.

Wyke, Maria. *The Roman Mistress: Ancient and Modern Representations*. Oxford University Press, 2002.

Yamauchi, E. M. "Cultic prostitution," in Harry A. Hoffner (ed.), *Orient and Occident. Essays presented to Cyrus H. Gordon on the occasion of his sixty-fifth birthday*, 213–22. Oxford University Press, 1973.

Yegül, Fikret. *Baths and Bathing in Classical Antiquity*. Cambridge: MIT Press, 1992.

Zagagi, Netta. *Tradition and Originality in Plautus: Studies of the Amatory Motifs in Plautine Comedy*. Göttingen: Vandenhoeck & Ruprecht, 1980.

Zancani Montuoro, Paola. "Persefone e Afrodite sul mare," in *Essays in Memory of Karl Lehmann*, 386–95. New York: Institute of Fine Arts, 1964.

Zanotti-Bianco, Umberto. "Archaeological discoveries in Magna Graecia and Sicily." *The Journal of Hellenic Studies*, 59, Part 2 (1939): 213–28.

Zetzel, James E. G. "Servius and triumviral history in the Eclogues." *Classical Philology*, 79, no. 2 (April 1984): 139–42.

Zevi, Fausto. "L'arte 'popolare'," in *La pittura di Pompei*, 267–73. Milan: Jaca Book, 1991.

Ziogas, Ioannis. "Stripping the Roman ladies: Ovid's rites and readers," *Classical Quarterly*, 64, no. 2 (2014): 735–44.

Index